When Souls Transition

30 Cases of Past-Life and Life-Between-Lives Regressions

When Souls Transition

30 Cases of Past-Life and Life-Between-Lives Regressions

Pieter Elsen & Jenna Iantorno

Copyright © 2023 Pieter Elsen & Jenna Iantorno Elsen
ALL RIGHTS RESERVED

****

Title: When Souls Transition - 30 Cases of Past-Life and Life-Between-Lives Regressions

ISBN 13: 978-1-7352856-4-1

Library of Congress Control Number: 2023916949

****

FOR MORE INFORMATION

If you wish to learn in greater detail about our work, please email us at elsenhypnotherapy@gmail.com

For information on our Books, Audio and Video visit:

www.pathoflightcenter.com

****

Printed in the USA

Table of Contents

Dedication		7
Preface		9
Introduction		11
Case 1: Amber	From slavery to enlightenment	15
Case 2: Amelia	The lightworker	38
Case 3: Nicole	A deeper meaning behind loss	74
Case 4: Stephen	Scars from past lives	93
Case 5: Derick	The mason	114
Case 6: Bianca	The sacrifice of self	138
Case 7: Karen	An instrument of light	157
Case 8: Clara	A civil war soldier	180
Case 9: Barry	A conduit of infinity	196
Case 10: Reina	A trail of karma running through lifetimes	218
Case 11: Kelly	Love and loss	237
Case 12: Hank	A royal mystic	253
Case 13: James	The struggle to surrender	271
Case 14: Henry	The guilt of the Father	299
Case 15: Iris	Near the sacred mountain	312
Case 16: Iris	A view of heaven	333
Case 17: Marianne	Permission to be free	357
Case 18: Carry	A Council Incarnate	372
Case 19: Elizabeth	I am what I am	395
Case 20: Minnie	The desert healer	411
Case 21: Devi	Beyond loneliness	428
Case 22: Mike	Surfing the waves of infinity	448
Case 23: Gloria	Surrendering to love	471
Case 24: Jake	Killed too young	489
Case 25: Jake	Rising above duality	506
Case 26: Sue	The executioner	523
Case 27: Tiffany	The fur trader	540
Case 28: Lynn	The little girl in the forest	569
Case 29: Jaimy	The golden bowl from the temple of healing	583
Case 30: Eric	The alchemist	604
About the authors	About the authors	623

Dedication

We dedicate this book to the wise ones that have come before us. Without their knowledge, guidance, and unselfish effort to share their knowledge with us, none of us would be where we are today. It is this sharing and cultivating of knowledge that is so critically important for our human evolution. Not only for ourselves and our personal journey but as a collective. The knowledge of the eternal nature of our soul, when truly understood on a deep collective unconscious level, could help mankind find peace and encourage us to work together, towards a more enlightened world.

Preface

This is a a book about past-life and life-between-lives regression cases. Unlike Pieter's previous book; "When Souls Awaken, Real-life Accounts of Past-Life and Life-between Lives Regressions", which, along with cases, also shared a lot of philosophical information, this book focuses solely on the cases themselves. We received a lot of beautiful feedback from; "When Souls Awaken", which can be summarized into two distinct categories. The first group wanted more philosophy and to go even deeper into the topic, and the second group wanted more cases. To satisfy the first group we created an extensive online course with over 60 instructional videos.

You can visit it here: http://www.whensoulsawaken.com/, and to satisfy the second group we wrote this book.

This book is a collaboration between Pieter and his wife Jenna. They are both Newton-trained regression therapists and do this work for a living. They have their wellness retreat center in Montvale Virginia, 'The Path of Light', where they conduct intimate retreats and receive guests for spiritual counseling and healing programs.

Visit here for more information:
https://pathoflightcenter.com/

Introduction

We present to you a collection of 30 cases of past-life and life-between-lives regressions. Allow these special cases to take you on a spiritual journey where you can vicariously experience the amazing spiritual world and all the wisdom that comes with it. We added a minimum amount of commentary to give the reader space for their own interpretation.

When you meet as many wonderful souls as we do, their souls' unique and radiant luster inevitably spills over into our own lives. Therefore we cannot help but want to share the beauty of the human spirit with you. The diversity of cases presented to you in this book is awe-inspiring. We journey back in time, jump from century to century, and travel to the in-between spheres and incredible realms of higher consciousness.

From early western settlers to medieval royalty, alchemists, and more, these accounts show the eternal journey of the soul through many lifetimes, aspiring to develop ever higher forms of evolution and spiritual unfoldment.

The combination of a past-life regression together with a life-between-lives regression session represents two wings of the same bird. Both are required to fly. To rise high above your current life situation you need perspective. Going back to the past to discover tendencies and situations that help you understand who you are today, with the ability to transcend birth and life itself and ascend into a higher disembodied state of consciousness between lives, provides such a perspective. This helps you quickly understand your current life with its numerous difficulties and challenges. As the well know quote states: 'You cannot solve a problem with the same kind of mindset that caused the problem." You need to rise above it to see things more clearly. That is the power of this work, and this is what we hope to share with you, the reader. An insight into the evolutionary process, through reincarnation, helps you reflect on your day-to-day life and motives, thereby advancing self-awareness. This awareness is key to making any changes in your life. This lack of awareness leaves us subject to the whims of nature and therefore drags us from life to life, unable to get a sense of control over our destiny. When the soul awakens and becomes aware of its final purpose and destination, it starts to initiate the required changes to help the individual evolve more rapidly. Knowledge is power and this power will set us free.

We steer clear of any difficult language, intellectual constructs, or academic lingo during our sessions. This is healing work and the art of regression is to be able to connect to the heart and spirit of our clients and guide them on their inner journey. It's key to get out of the thinking mind and into the feeling heart, where the true presence of Now exists.

You may notice that we transcribed the audio files literally and we avoid editing except for some rare instances where a sentence may be incomprehensible. Accordingly, some of the sentence construction may appear short and crude. We have not changed the sentence constructions of our clients to keep the experience as authentic as possible. Please understand that these people are not only in a deep theta state but are also connected to the mindset of someone living centuries ago. This obviously can affect the way they talk, even though they speak through their current bodies and use their current brains and language capacities. You may further notice that we have removed most of the therapeutic instructions to guide the client to the past life and life-between lives. Not only before the actual past-life regression but also in the transition between the past life and the life-between lives. These are very long instructions and guided imageries, with sessions lasting often over 3.5 hours long.

As therapists who have the honor of conducting these incredible experiences for our clients, we know that it has truly changed our lives for the better. We would love to share this blessing with you as well.

Pieter and Jenna

Case 1: Amber
From slavery to enlightenment

Amber, a 36-year-old Kindergarten Teacher from the East Coast, proclaimed herself to be a staunch atheist before the session and said she only signed up for a session out of curiosity. She described being depressed and anxious and wanted to reconnect with her dad who had just passed away.

Therapist: Now tell me, is it daytime or nighttime?

Amber: It's daytime.

Therapist: Are you inside or outside?

Amber: Outside.

Therapist: When you look down at your feet, what, if anything, are you wearing on your feet?

Amber: Nothing.
Therapist: You're bare feet?
Amber: Yes.
Therapist: What else are you wearing?
Amber: A dress.
Therapist: Is it a one-piece dress or made from multiple pieces?
Amber: I don't know.
Therapist: Is it fancy or is it more simple, poor, or affluent?
Amber: Poor.
Therapist: When you look at the color of your skin, what is the color?
Amber: It's brown.
Therapist: How old are you now?
Amber: 12, maybe.
Therapist: What is the color of your hair?
Amber: Black.
Therapist: Now, as you look straight ahead of you, what are you aware of?
Amber: I see shacks.
Therapist: What kind of shacks?
Amber: Just small shacks.
Therapist: Are they like dwellings?
Amber: Yes.
Therapist: Are there people there?
Amber: Yeah. There are a lot of people.
Therapist: What do they look like, these people?
Amber: They look dirty and tired and scared.
Therapist: Why do you think they're scared?
Amber: Because they're not with their families.

Therapist: Where are their families?
Amber: They don't know.
Therapist: They're separated?
Amber: Yeah.
Therapist: Is your shack also nearby?
Amber: Yes.
Therapist: What does it look like when you go inside?
Amber: There's a lot of wood and holes and rats. It's dirty.
Therapist: Is there anybody living with you, your parents?
Amber: There are a lot of people, but it's not my family.
Therapist: You're separated from your family?
Amber: Yes.
Therapist: All the people that are here, are they all grownups and children, or a mixture? What are their ages?
Amber: It's mainly grownups.
Therapist: You're one of the few young ones around?
Amber: Yeah.
Therapist: How do you feel in this place?
Amber: Isolated.
Therapist: How come it's isolated? Where are you now?
Amber: Just everyone's so busy.
Therapist: Is that why you feel isolated because everybody's busy?
Amber: Yeah.
Therapist: What are they all doing?
Amber: They're having to work. They're getting ready to start their day.
Therapist: Where are you now in the world?
Amber: I'm inside the shack, just...

Therapist: Do you know which country you are in?

Amber: I think America.

Therapist: Where in America?

Amber: I don't know the maps.

Therapist: What time comes to mind? Whatever number pops up in your mind is fine.

Amber: 1860s.

Therapist: So it's a pretty poor area where you are right now, huh?

Amber: Yes.

Therapist: So how do you spend your day?

Amber: I clean.

Therapist: Is it just your house you clean, or do you clean somewhere else as well?

Amber: Another house.

Therapist: Like you're working?

Amber: Yes.

Therapist: Who makes you work?

Amber: A woman, a white woman.

Therapist: You're in her service?

Amber: Yes.

Therapist: Do you get paid or are you not getting paid?

Amber: I don't get paid.

Therapist: You're like slaves?

Amber: Yes.

Therapist: All of you?

Amber: Yes.

Therapist: The whole community is enslaved?

Amber: Yes.

Therapist: Is that why there is so much fear?

Amber: Yes.

Therapist: Now what is your name? Whatever pops up in your mind is fine.

Amber: Mika? I don't know.

Therapist: Mika?

Amber: Maybe, I don't know.

Therapist: Okay. I'm just going to call you Mika, okay? Now, Mika, if you describe to me the most relevant observation about this moment in your life, at this time around the 1860s in the mountains, as this little slave, either within you or around you, what would this most significant observation be?

Amber: Just helping her get ready, seeing how beautiful she is and how spiteful she can be.

Therapist: Towards you?

Amber: Towards everybody.

Therapist: How does it make you feel?

Amber: Bad. Insignificant.

Therapist: Now Mika, I'm going to count from 3 down to 1 and an account of 1, we're going to move forward a few years in your life as Mika till you get a little bit older to another relevant moment in your life. Going from 3, 2, 1. And you're there now. And tell me what is happening now.

Amber: I still work there. There's no hope.

Therapist: How old are you now, Mika?

Amber: 17. Every day I do the same thing.

Therapist: What is it that you're doing now?

Amber: Sweeping.

Therapist: Are you still working for the same lady?

Amber: Yes.

Therapist: Did anything change during the last few years?

Amber: Nothing.

Therapist: What about the people around you? How's the community where you live?

Amber: It's still isolated. It's not... Everyone's just sad and depressed. There is no community.

Therapist: Everybody is just enslaved here in this place?

Amber: Yeah.

Therapist: Do you still live in the same shack, or do you have a different place?

Amber: I think I live in the same place.

Therapist: Are you kind of alone and on your own?

Amber: No, there are a lot of people that live here.

Therapist: In the same shack?

Amber: Yeah.

Therapist: Is there anybody you have some sort of relationship with, somebody close, like family, friends, or another kind of relationship?

Amber: I don't think so.

Therapist: You're then in that way, pretty on your own?

Amber: Yeah.

Therapist: What is your state of mind right now at 17 years old?

Amber: I want to get married.

Therapist: Do you have anybody in mind?

Amber: No.

Therapist: No? Is there any chance you could get out of this place?

Amber: No.

Therapist: Could you get married and still stay in the same place?

Amber: No.

Therapist: They don't allow you to marry?

Amber: I just don't think there's anyone here.

Therapist: How would you describe your mental and spiritual state right now?

Amber: There is none. There's just existence.

Therapist: Now, going to count again from 3 down to 1, Mika, and the count of 1 we're going to, again, move forward to your life, a few years older, to another relevant moment in your life. Something that shapes your mind, your heart, your soul, your destiny. Going from 3, 2, 1, and were there now. And tell me what is happening now.

Amber: I think I'm getting married.

Therapist: Tell me what's going on.

Amber: It's someone older.

Therapist: Where are you now?

Amber: I'm outside.

Therapist: You're away from this place?

Amber: Yeah, but I have to go back. It's my wedding day.

Therapist: How do you feel?

Amber: I feel happy, but it's not the life I want.

Therapist: What can you tell me about that?

Amber: I'm just getting married because he's someone that asked.

Therapist: How come you agreed?

Amber: I don't want to be lonely.

Therapist: He's older than you?

Amber: Yes.

Therapist: How do you feel about him?

Amber: He's a nice guy.

Therapist: How old are you now?

Amber: Maybe 20.

Therapist: How do you look on your wedding day?

Amber: I look how I do every day, but I took a bath.

Therapist: You don't have any fancy clothes, I assume?

Amber: No.

Therapist: Are there others with you here now?

Amber: Yeah. Everyone I live with is there.

Therapist: How does the procedure of this wedding unfold?

Amber: There are older women getting me ready, and they're giving me a speech that we have to find happiness any way we can get it. They're being motherly.

Therapist: Are they nice to you, these women?

Amber: Yes.

Therapist: How are the people, all the slaves among themselves? How are relationships?

Amber: Well, today they seem to be in better moods because there's something to look forward to.

Therapist: Now, I want you to move forward a little bit and tell me how life unfolds as a married woman.

Amber: I have a kid, but it's hard to get work done and take care of the kid.

Therapist: How's the white woman?

Amber: She's getting older and meaner every day.

Therapist: So now you must juggle her household as well as your own?

Amber: Yeah.

Therapist: How do you feel?

Amber: Overwhelmed.

Therapist: How is your relationship with your new husband?

Amber: I don't see him.
Therapist: He's not there?
Amber: No, he works all the time.
Therapist: He never comes home?
Amber: No.
Therapist: How does it make you feel?
Amber: Lonely.
Therapist: Now, what is your most significant observation at this point in your life Mika?
Amber: We're fighting.
Therapist: Who's fighting?
Amber: My husband and me.
Therapist: Why?
Amber: I don't know. I need more help. I need more help.
Therapist: From him?
Amber: Yeah.
Therapist: He can't give it to you?
Amber: No.

I move her forward in her life again.

Amber: My son died.
Therapist: What happened?
Amber: It was a plowing accident.
Therapist: How old was he?
Amber: 17. We're burying him.
Therapist: How do you feel?
Amber: So sad.
Therapist: Was he still living with you?
Amber: Yes.

Therapist: He was also working for the whole white community, I guess, right? Is it one family you're working for or is it several families?

Amber: I don't know. Just one.

Therapist: Can you describe the scene to me? What is going on during this burial?

Amber: There's not a lot of people there. There's the preacher.

Therapist: The preacher, is he one of yours or is he a white guy?

Amber: He's one of mine. I'm sobbing because my husband's gone too.

Therapist: He died too?

Amber: Yeah.

Therapist: When did that happen?

Amber: A few years before. Maybe 10.

Therapist: Do you have more children?

Amber: No.

Therapist: Just this one?

Amber: Yeah.

Therapist: Is this near your shack? Where is this taking place?

Amber: No, somewhere else.

Therapist: You say there are only a few of you there?

Amber: Yeah.

Therapist: Did anything change in your life other than the death that has taken place?

Amber: I don't think I work there anymore.

Therapist: No? What has changed?

Amber: I think I'm living on my own.

Therapist: You live where?

Amber: I think I live on my own somewhere.

Therapist: Have you been freed somehow?
Amber: Maybe.
Therapist: Tell me about where you live right now.
Amber: I live in a small shack. It's cold.
Therapist: If you don't live there anymore, then how do you make ends meet? Do you work or what is it that you do?
Amber: I don't know.
Therapist: Just look around you and see what is going on.
Amber: I think it's like a community. We just help each other.
Therapist: You are not slaves anymore?
Amber: No.
Therapist: How did you get freed from this situation?
Amber: I think they died.
Therapist: And you just kind of left? You just went away?
Amber: Yeah.
Therapist: Is it legal to be free or did you just escape?
Amber: It's legal.

I'm moving her forward to the last day of her life.

Therapist: How old are you on this last day of your life?
Amber: 50s.
Therapist: Is there anything going on around you or within you to suggest that your physical death will come on this day?
Amber: I can't move my body, and I'm in bed.
Therapist: Is there anybody with you?
Amber: Yes.
Therapist: What's going on right now?
Amber: There's a woman holding my hand.
Therapist: How do you feel?

Amber: Relief.

Therapist: What do you think about this life you just lived as Mika?

Amber: It's traumatic. It's unfair.

Therapist: What did you learn from this life?

Amber: I learned to look for the good times, even if most of it's horrible.

Therapist: What is your last thought, awareness, or feeling as you leave the body?

Amber: I feel lighter. Stars. Lots of stars. It's like I'm in space.

Therapist: Just keep on moving and tell me, are those stars other beings that you're witnessing or is it more…..

Amber: Yes, there are other beings, but they don't look like humans.

Therapist: Right. Just keep on moving and tell me if any of those star beings look bigger than others.

Amber: Yes, there's one.

Therapist: All right. Where is that one? Is it on the left or right, or in the middle?

Amber: It's in front of me.

Therapist: All right. Just move closer to that one as it comes closer to you. And as you approach, tell me what you become aware of.

Amber: Understanding.

Therapist: What do you notice about this being that has come to meet you?

Amber: He's black with a white outline.

Therapist: Does he have any features or is it more of an energy?

Amber: It's an energy.

Therapist: Does it feel like a guide, or does it feel more like somebody belonging to your own group?

Amber: Maybe a guide, there's nothing personal there.

Therapist: Does it feel like male, female, or more androgynous in nature?

Amber: Male.

Therapist: How do you feel in his presence?

Amber: I feel respect. It's wise.

Therapist: Beautiful. Does it feel like his light is sort of hugging you and embracing you, or does it feel more like it takes you by the hand?

Amber: The hand.

Therapist: Does he want to take you somewhere or are you just meeting here together?

Amber: Just meeting here together.

Therapist: Take a moment and feel, as he's holding your hand, his energy, his love, his power. I understand that most communication here takes place at a mental telepathic level. So is there anything coming from him that you become aware of?

Amber: Yeah, that human suffering is part of life.

Therapist: Does he say that regarding your life as Mika that you just lived?

Amber: Yeah.

Therapist: Does he say anything about how did in this life? Does he have any comments about it?

Amber: You did the best you could.

Therapist: How does it make you feel?

Amber: Validated.

Therapist: What was the intention of living this kind of life as a slave? What did you need to learn from this life?

Amber: That suffering exists, and it may not seem like it's fair, but everyone has to go through it.

Therapist: Why did your soul have to go through that? What did you get from that experience?

Amber: To learn what true loneliness feels like, so you can appreciate people in other lives.

Therapist: Beautiful. So, you feel that you learned that lesson well in that life?

Amber: Yes.

Therapist: In other words, if I understand it correctly, you went through this experience to understand the depth of human suffering and loneliness, so that your soul could develop sympathy and gratitude for having beautiful people around you in other lifetimes?

Amber: Yes.

Therapist: Amazing. Beautiful. Now, when we compare that life with the life of Amber, what are some of the parallels between these lives?

Amber: Feeling lonely.

Therapist: Why does Amber have to go through that again?

Amber: I don't have to because that was when I was a kid. I'm not lonely now.

Therapist: How do you feel that the experience as Mika helped the young Amber?

Amber: To be open to people and their differences and to accept them.

Therapist: You think that Amber gained a lot of depth and sympathy and openheartedness from the experience of Mika?

Amber: Yeah.

Therapist: What are the differences between Mika and Amber?

Amber: I've never had to experience the amount of loss that she experienced.

Therapist: As we're here with your guide, what do you think

was the intention of this life as Amber? Because we had a big theme in your past life as Mika, right? What is the main learning theme that is set up for this life?

Amber: Just make people feel warm and welcome in my life. To be the change, be the opposite.

Therapist: This is a life of expanding that heart towards others?

Amber: Yeah.

Therapist: That's quite amazing, right? Mika was kind of a victim, yet she used that experience to lay the groundwork for the love, openheartedness, and change that Amber is able to manifest.

Amber: Yeah.

Therapist: What does your guide say about that?

Amber: He's proud of me. It took me a while in this life to get where I needed to be.

Therapist: Is there anything else that he wants from you? Something you haven't thought about. Something more that perhaps you can do?

Amber: I don't know. I don't know.

Therapist: Tune into him a little bit deeper. As you're holding his hand and feeling his love and energy, what does he want for you in the grand scheme of things?

Amber: He wants me to show love and forgiveness. He wants me to forgive.

Therapist: Does it apply to anybody in particular or just in general?

Amber: Yes.

Therapist: Is your soul ready to let that go?

Amber: No.

It is interesting to note that even when a soul is in an astral sphere, it still has a personality and in most cases displays only a partial level of evolutionary awareness. The soul is still growing and is not a completely free and enlightened being yet. We reincarnate for this reason. In this instance, the therapist may need to help a bit and encourage the soul to dive deeper and face the underlying issues.

Therapist: No? But now that he suggests that you do that, is there any way he can help you with that?

Amber: I don't know.

Therapist: What if you could try to do that? Because isn't it a burden that you're carrying?

Amber: Yes.

Therapist: Could it be that we have come to meet him today to help you with this issue? Could you perhaps, together with him, go to another place, somewhere higher up in this realm, where it becomes easier for you to let go? Would you like to do that?

Amber: Yes.

Therapist: Why don't you ask him what would be a good place to go to right now? And let us go there so we can work on this forgiveness. Just follow him along and tell me where you go.

Amber: Going up a stone mountain. It's dark.

Therapist: What happens next? Share everything so I can stay with you.

Amber: There's something bigger.

Therapist: A bigger energy you mean?

Amber: Yes, it's very bright.

Therapist: That energy is here on that mountain?

Amber: Yeah.

Therapist: Tell me what happens next.

Amber: They tell me that everybody's going through their own journey and that I have to respect that person's process.

Therapist: Is that your guide saying this or is it the other energy saying it?

Amber: The other energy.

Therapist: How does it make you feel when it says that?

Amber: It makes me feel better.

Therapist: How does this energy help you to let go of that pain? To help you forgive. To let go.

Amber: Perspective. Just because she survived, it doesn't mean that she's reached her end-of-life purpose.

Therapist: Whom are you talking about?

Amber: My aunt. She's still growing and changing too, even though I don't see it.

Therapist: Now, that you're seeing and feeling this, do you think it will help you to let it go now?

Amber: Yes.

Therapist: Just take a moment with them, these two powerful energies. And with their help, let it completely leave your system, your heart, your soul. Take your time. And when you're done, let me know.

Amber: I think I'm done.

Therapist: How does it feel?

Amber: Peaceful.

Therapist: What can you tell me about this energy on this mountain?

Amber: It's the big energy. It's what makes us all work.

Therapist: The source energy?

Amber: Yes.

Therapist: You're fortunate to connect to the source energy. How does your soul feel in its presence?

Amber: In awe.

Therapist: Now, that we are here with this source energy, and we look at your soul, just as a beautiful entity, not as Amber, nor as Mika, not in any birth, what can this great source energy tell us about who you really are, the nature of your being and your destiny?

Amber: It's love, respect, forgiveness.

Therapist: And as you see that about yourself, seeing the beauty of who you are, that love, that kindness, that respect, how does it feel?

Amber: It feels really empowering.

Therapist: Remember, this is who you are. You're not Amber. You're not Mika. You are this love.

What does this source want you to do with that, in this life of Amber? When one day Amber's life has come to an end, many, many years from now, and you come back after that life here in front of this source, what is it that it wants you to have accomplished during that lifetime?

Amber: I don't think it wants anything more for me.

Therapist: Just love?

Amber: Yeah.

Therapist: That is the most beautiful answer you could have been given, right?

Amber: Yeah.

Therapist: Manifest love. Is there anything that your soul wants to ask from this source energy?

Amber: Did my dad survive? Is he happy?

Therapist: What is he saying?

Amber: He's very happy.

Therapist: Can we go and see him right now?

Amber: My dad?

Therapist: Yes.

Amber: Yeah.

Therapist: Ask the source and your guide to take you there right now and tell me what happens when you meet him.

Amber: He's happy.

Therapist: You see him now?

Amber: I do. It doesn't look like him, but I know it's him.

Therapist: That's right. What does he look like right now?

Amber: He's just light.

Therapist: Take your time. And tune in for a moment. Just merge into that light, that love. s he communicating anything with you?

Amber: He's telling me he loves me. He'll see me again. But it's all okay.

Therapist: Is he part of your eternal soul family?

Amber: I don't know.

Therapist: Why don't you ask him?

Amber: I don't know.

Therapist: What does your guide tell you?

Amber: He's telling me he's not.

Therapist: No?

Amber: Sometimes love is letting go. We're all part of the same thing.

Therapist: The same source?

Amber: Yeah.

Therapist: So from that perspective, there isn't really any separation?

Amber: Yeah.

Therapist: What else is taking place as you're meeting your dad?

Amber: That's it. It's just me and him. By ourselves.

Therapist: Would you like some quiet time with him alone?

Amber: Yeah.

Therapist: Take all the time you want, and when you're ready, just let me know, okay?

Amber: I'm ready. I'm ready.

Therapist: How do you feel?

Amber: More at peace, accepted.

Therapist: Now, tell me about your soul family. You're with your guide, with your dad, the source is everywhere. Would you like to have a look at who's part of your soul family?

Amber: Yeah.

Therapist: Now why don't we go there and tell me what you discover?

Amber: I haven't seen them before this lifetime.

Therapist: Are there many?

Amber: It seems there are eight.

Therapist: Nobody you recognize from this lifetime?

Amber: No.

Therapist: What makes them your family? Are there any similarities between the souls?

Amber: I don't know.

Therapist: Why don't you just go near them and connect to them? Is there anybody stepping forward to connect with you?

Amber: There's... she looks like an elderly lady.

Therapist: What does she say?

Amber: Regarding the good things that have happened, she's been instrumental in the positive changes in my life. I'm not alone.

Therapist: This group of eight people, including yourself nine, these are your divine companions?

Amber: Yeah.

Therapist: And she's been helping you from here?

Amber: Yeah.

Therapist: What about the others? What are you picking up from them?

Amber: That we're all looking for the same thing.

Therapist: Is that what binds you together as a group?

Amber: Yeah.

Therapist: What is it that you're looking for?

Amber: Enlightenment.

Therapist: This is a group that is all about enlightenment?

Amber: Yeah.

Therapist: Beautiful. What more can you tell me about that?

Amber: That though we've had our own lives, we all have the same goals, and that's what brings us together.

Therapist: Beautiful. Now that we check in with them, what do they say about Amber and her efforts toward that goal of enlightenment?

Amber: They see a lot of positives, but I got to let go of a lot of stuff. It keeps me from loving others.

Therapist: Right. We're here with your group and your guide, is there anything they can do to help right now, to help let go of all of this stuff?

Amber: Just know that everyone has their own journey. Just because I don't see it, doesn't mean it's not there. And I have to be patient through the process.

Therapist: Is there anything that Amber can do in her day-to-day life that would encourage her to let go, helping her toward enlightenment?

Amber: Let go of control.

Therapist: Controlling what?

Amber: I can't control other people's thoughts, or opinions, or actions.

Therapist: She needs to detach from that?

Amber: Yeah.

Therapist: What should she attach to instead?

Amber: What I do have control over. Making sure my family knows I love them.

Therapist: It is really love then that matters, right?

Amber: Yeah.

Therapist: And the struggle towards enlightenment.

Amber: Yeah, and if someone behaves in a way I don't agree with, it doesn't mean I can't love them.

Therapist: Right. Now, in what way is your group able to help you while you're living this life of Amber?

Amber: Support.

Therapist: What kind of support? Are they doing something behind the scenes, like helping?

Amber: Just validating my feelings.

Therapist: Is there any way that either your guide, the source, or any of your group members can come and check in with Amber more consciously? That she will have a way to commune with everybody? So that she's not feeling alone and spiritually disconnected, and helping her to remind her of that journey towards enlightenment?

Amber: Yeah.

Therapist: In what way can they do that?

Amber: To mediate.

Therapist: And then what will happen when Amber meditates?

Amber: I'll feel their acceptance, their wisdom.

Therapist: So they can channel through her?

Amber: Yeah.

Therapist: Beautiful. Is there any encouragement coming from the group now?

Amber: It's good that I'm wanting to change. Change can't happen if I don't look for it.

Therapist: How do you feel in their presence?

Amber: I just feel secure and comfortable, welcome.

Therapist: Is there anything that you want to ask from them or that you need?

Amber: No.

Therapist: Do you want to take a moment in their presence?

Amber: No.

We slowly end the session here.

Case 2: Amelia
The lightworker

This is a beautiful case of a very sensitive and advanced soul, who took several lifetimes to be able to express her true nature and develop the strength and awareness to shine in her own light. Amelia is a 32-year-old counselor from California.

Therapist: Tell me, is it daytime or nighttime?
Amelia: Daytime. I see two different lives, but I'm now moving into one.
Therapist: Good. Is it daytime, you're saying?
Amelia: Yes.
Therapist: Are you inside or outside?

Amelia: Inside.

Therapist: Are you alone or with someone?

Amelia: Alone in the room.

Therapist: Looking down at your feet? Tell me what, if anything, you see on your feet.

Amelia: Pointy shoes.

Therapist: What are they made of these pointy shoes?

Amelia: I'm not sure. Possibly some sort of leather.

Therapist: What are you wearing?

Amelia: A dress.

Therapist: Is it like one piece or made from multiple pieces?

Amelia: It's two pieces and it's very frilly.

Therapist: When you say frilly, would you describe it as a fancier type of dress?

Amelia: Oh yes. Very fancy.

Therapist: Can you describe the room to me?

Amelia: Yes. It's a beautiful room, with marble, and a fireplace to my right. There are brick walls. The floor looks wooded, with some holes in the floor, but almost as if they're meant to be there. And as I look around there's a table. The table is like an end table with some glass and is very antique-like.

Therapist: So it is a pretty fancy room?

Amelia: Very fancy, very light colors.

Therapist: What's your relation to this room? Is this where you live or what are you doing here?

Amelia: Yes. I have a glass of wine in my hand.

Therapist: What's your age right now, approximately?

Amelia: Similar age to now, the thirties, early to mid-thirties.

Therapist: Looking at the color of your skin, what do you observe?

Amelia: It's white.

Therapist: What does your hair look like?

Amelia: Brunette.

Therapist: Now looking around you or within yourself, what would you say is the most significant observation about this moment?

Amelia: Not happy here.

Therapist: No? What can you tell me about that?

Amelia: Feeling trapped in this space? Lonely. Very lonely.

Therapist: Can you tell me more about that?

Amelia: I think I have a husband. He's in a different room in this big house. I'm starting to feel very nauseous.

Therapist: Let me count from three down to one, and at the count of one we're going to move to another significant moment in your life as this lady, who will now be slowly getting a bit older, at, three, two, one. And you're there. Tell me what is happening now?

Amelia: (Smiling) I am watching a band, it's music. It's inside this wooded building.

Therapist: You say there's a band of music and you're sitting inside. Help me understand. What does that mean? Are you looking through the window?

Amelia: I'm inside sitting at a table.

Therapist: And there's a band passing by?

Amelia: They are on stage with a banjo and yeah, there's lots of singing and laughter. My heart's coming down a little bit.

Therapist: How old are you now?

Amelia: A little younger, in my twenties. I'm enjoying myself. Happy here.

Therapist: Do you have a nickname or any name you go by?

Amelia: Alice.

Therapist: So Alice, where do you feel you are?

Amelia: I feel like it may be in Europe.

Therapist: What time approximately?

Amelia: I'm getting something. The numbers four and zero. I'm not sure what that means.

Therapist: No? It may come to you in a moment. Just tell me whenever this becomes clear. You're telling me that you're a little younger, in your twenties. Can you look around a little bit and tell me what this place looks like and how you feel here?

Amelia: It's wooded. The tables are wooded. There's a keg of beer over in the corner. People laugh, drink, enjoying themselves. Everybody's having a good time. It's kind of living in the country.

Therapist: This is like a country inn of some kind?

Amelia: Yesh, it's a country inn. There are places you can stay upstairs. For some reason it's making me shake a little, I feel a little cold.

Therapist: Is it due to the cold climate?

Amelia: Yes, but it's sunny outside.

Therapist: Are you alone here? Are you visiting this place by yourself or is there anybody with you?

Amelia: There are a lot of people around me, but I am at the table by myself. I have beer on the table and I'm drinking.

Therapist: What can you tell me about your life situation, where you come from, and what's going on with your family?

Amelia: I come from a very rich family. The family has a lot of money, but I'm not very close with them. My parents are still together, but they don't love each other. I'm an only child.

Therapist: Are you married or are you alone?

Amelia: Now, here, I am unmarried. I choose to. I want to travel. I want to enjoy my life and my parents don't approve. I want to be here. I want to enjoy my life and get to see the world and have a good time.

Therapist: Why don't they approve?

Amelia: They want me to get married. Settle down. They said that as a woman, I wouldn't amount to much without a man.

Therapist: How do you feel about that?

Amelia: (Deep sigh) I'm angry. Very angry about that. I feel frustrated. I want to rebel. I feel so rebellious, and it makes me feel happy to rebel. My parents don't know I'm here.

Therapist: Can you move a little bit forward in time, between the moment we visited before when you were in your thirties, and this moment, and tell me in broad terms how your life unfolded during these 10 years or so?

Amelia: I started feeling guilty in my later twenties. I was traveling and meeting people and having a good time and feeling free and realizing that my parents were getting older and sicker, and I felt that I needed to care for them. And in that way to do their bidding and to marry and to settle down so that it would be their one last wish for me as their only child to do that.

Therapist: As you are now 32 years old sitting in this house, not being very happy, is that the outcome of that decision?

Amelia: Yes, it is.

Therapist: How do you feel now, having made that decision?

Amelia: Miserable. It makes me feel nauseous, a little nauseous again now. Feeling like I made the wrong choice. I'm shaking.

Therapist: I'm going to count again, from three down to one, and we're going to move forward in your life as Alice, to a time after the age of 32, to another significant moment in your life. At 3, 2, 1. And you're there. Now tell me Alice, what is happening now?

She ignored my request and went back in time instead.

Amelia: I'm younger, much younger, and wearing a dress. It

looks pink and has lace underneath. I have shoes that are black, and they have buckles on them, white socks, or stockings. And my parents are beside me, my dad to my left and my mom to my right.

Therapist: How is your relationship now with your parents?

Amelia: Right now, it seems to be fine. They're teaching me how to be more well-to-do, how to have manners, how to be good. We're in public. We're in a small town with horse carriages.

Therapist: How to be a lady?

Amelia: Yes, how to be a lady.

Therapist: How does it make you feel?

Amelia: Proper.

Therapist: You like that?

Amelia: Yes, I like that now. Yes.

Therapist: What else is significant about this moment, either within you or around you?

Amelia: I'm just amazed at the beautiful shops around me.

Therapist: Can you describe the area a little bit?

Amelia: Yes. There are cobblestone streets, and it seems that the homes around me are very sturdy, very strong, and very small.

Therapist: What country are we in right now?

Amelia: Germany is what comes to mind.

Therapist: You said earlier the 40-ies. Which century, which decade?

Amelia: 1800 comes to mind. The 1840s or something like that.

Therapist: What kind of landscape are we in, is it a big town or a small town, and what does the area look like? Is it flat or mountainous?

Amelia: It's very mountainous. There are a lot of hills. It's beautiful. And this is a very small town I'm in. It seems to be summer and I'm shaking. I'm not sure why, but it seems to be summer where I am.

Therapist: Do you like it here?

Amelia: I do. I'm actually excited. I'm happy to be with my parents.

Therapist: Shaking out of excitement?

Amelia: Possibly, yes.

Therapist: Good. Now Alice, what else can you share with me about this moment?

Amelia: I feel happy. I feel at home within myself. I feel like my parents really care about me and really love me.

Therapist: As we project forward to your early thirties and you made this decision to look after them and you look back at your childhood. What has changed in the mind?

Amelia: The joy has gone (weeping).

Therapist: What happened?

Amelia (emotional): I made a big mistake by not following my heart, not living my dream. I wanted to help people and be in the world. Now I'm stuck at home with someone I don't love.

Therapist: In what way did marriage impact your freedom?

Amelia: He wants me to stay home, told me that's where I belong. He's not cruel. He's not violent. He's just not someone I love, not someone I connect with.

Therapist: As a young woman of this age, what power does he have over you to make such decisions?

Amelia: He decides everything for me.

Therapist: Is that the norm where you are?

Amelia: Yes. He decides what I do during my day when I get to go out and spend time with the other women. They are supposedly friends, but not really. I just feel like I lost my true friends when I was traveling. To live this life feels like a lie.

Therapist: Now, Alice, I'm going to count again from three to one, but this time we're going to move beyond the age of 32. When you get a little older, to another relevant moment in your life and on the count of one, be there 3, 2, 1. And you are there now. Tell me what is happening now.

Ignoring my request again.

Amelia: I'm even younger, still with my parents, sitting in a meadow outside and having a picnic. There's a windmill in front of me. We're on a blanket, with a picnic basket. And my mom is smiling. She's older, she's an older woman. And she's handing me food.

Therapist: What does she look like?

Amelia: She has her hair tied tightly in a bun, dark hair, but there's some gray.

Therapist: What does her outfit look like?

Amelia: It's very hard to describe. It's almost like she has an apron over her long dress. And she's got stockings.

Therapist: Ok.

Amelia: And my dad's there too.

Therapist: What do you think is her internal state like?

Amelia: I think she's at peace.

Therapist: As we move along the years and you get older into your thirties, how would you describe her mental state over the years?

Amelia: Hmm. Very different. It's all about being in the world, showing up as somebody important.

Therapist: Is that her choice or is that the way she is supposed to behave?

Amelia: I'm not sure. Seems as if it's not quite her choice. It seems like she's more like me deep in her heart. She seemed like she wanted to be more like me, but she lost that somewhere.

Therapist: And now as you're getting older, you're repeating the pattern. Is that it?

Amelia: Yes. Yes.

Therapist: Hmm. How does it make you feel?

Amelia: (Sigh) Like a failure, like a huge failure in my life?

Therapist: Were you aware of her internal struggle along the way? Or is it something you're discovering now?

Amelia: I think I didn't discover it until I got older, until I looked back maybe in my thirties, and saw that I had become like my mom in some ways, but even worse because the person I married is so far off from whom I would have chosen.

Therapist: Was that arranged in a way that marriage?

Amelia: Yes, it was. Was not chosen at all? I was forced into it.

Therapist: What is your financial status? Is it still very good?

Amelia: It is very good. He makes very good money. He supports us. I'm supposed to be happy about it.

Therapist: Okay. How does the family make their money?

Amelia: He works outside the home. I'm not quite sure what.

Therapist: It'll come to you in a moment. Now, Alice, I'm going to count again from three down to one. As we move to another significant moment in your life at 1, be there 3, 2, 1, and you're there now. Tell me what is happening now.

Amelia: I met somebody that I really, truly love. Pictures are coming into focus now, but it's someone I met during my travels in my twenties. He was an amazing man.

Therapist: How old are you now?

Amelia: 23

Therapist: Tell me now what unfolds with him.

Amelia: He's so adventurous and fun. He's a great speaker and he speaks wherever we travel about inspirational subjects.

Therapist: Are you traveling together?

Amelia: Traveling together.

Therapist: Where are you traveling?

Amelia: All over Europe.

Therapist: Tell me more.

Amelia: Holland, Ireland.

Therapist: What is your relationship with him during this time?

Amelia: At first, we didn't have a title and then we decided we were partners and I feel very deeply for him. And unfortunately, he got sick on our travels.

Therapist: Were you in any way more romantically involved with him during his time?

Amelia: Yes. Romantically involved with him. I wanted to marry him. My parents never knew about him because they never would have approved.

Therapist: Hmm. What happened?

Amelia: He came down with some illness while traveling that affected his chest and he had a cough. (Deep sigh) And I watched him kind of deteriorate over time and he was very, very sickly to the point where he couldn't travel. We had no money. My parents weren't supporting us.

Therapist: Then what happened?

Amelia: I watched him die. Could I just sit there and cry?

Therapist: How did this impact you and what did you do afterward?

Amelia: I became very fearful of death, very fearful of death, which then made me fear my parents' death later. It impacted me a lot. I went into a depression.

Therapist: Is that when you decided to go back home?

Amelia: Not quite. It seems to have been some time that I spent between there and home. I had to sort myself out; a kind of spiritual journey, so to speak, within myself, communing with nature.

Therapist: Did that help?

Amelia: It did help.

Therapist: You say spiritual journey. Can you tell me more about that? How did it start, and how did it unfold?

Amelia: Yes. I started to recognize that I wasn't going to live forever and that after being with the love of my life, I would never love the same way again. That's what I felt in my heart at the time. And I didn't want to be around people. And then I was afraid of getting sick myself and dying. So, I went out in nature and lived in this little cottage. At first, with people I knew. And later, a little bit more by myself for a few years.

Therapist: Did you still have some family money to sustain yourself? How did you manage to take care of yourself?

Amelia: No, I didn't have a lot of money. I think it was the divine guiding me to meet the right people.

Therapist: It was looking after you?

Amelia: Yesh. I was guided.

Therapist: How was your internal being going through this phase of your life?

Amelia: Difficult.

Therapist: How so?

Amelia: Afraid of survival and whether I would make it. Part of me didn't want to make it because I missed him, and I wanted to be with him again. So, I was conflicted but knew that my path was to go forward. I knew I was meant to do more in my life and to make a difference, but I didn't know how.

Therapist: Move forward a bit to the culmination of this spiritual journey and restoration.

Amelia: It was this feeling that it was time to move on. Now I've had my time for travel. It's time to reconnect with my family. It's the only one I have. There's no one else out there with them. And mother was older when she had me. So I knew that they probably wouldn't live very long.

Therapist: Before you went home. Did you come to some sort of internal resolution?

Amelia: A little bit. Some yes and some no.

Therapist: In what way yes and in what way no?

Amelia: Yes, in that I came to a resolution that I was a spiritual being and knowing that I was able to make a difference if I wanted. So, I had a sense of enthusiasm and that I could go back to my home and kind of talk to my parents and see if there was any way for them to help me to inspire the world through writing, which was my goal at this time. I was to be a writer. And I wanted to write a book that would inspire the world. And so, I felt very connected to that. But when I got home, things were pretty dire with my parents and their health was declining. And I knew that my dreams would have to be put on hold to care for them. And to do what was right.

Therapist: Move forward in time and tell me how the story unfolds.

Amelia: After the first time in the home. Is that right?

Therapist: Yes.

Amelia: (silence and a deep sigh) I don't live very long in this life.

Therapist: Tell me what happens.

Amelia: (weeping) I ended my own life.

Therapist: I want you to move forward to the last day of your life and tell me what happens on this last day of your life. How old are you?

Amelia: I'm still in my thirties, late thirties. Writing a letter to those I loved in case they ever see it. That my soul was just suffocating, and I just couldn't go on any longer, living a lie, not able to live my dreams (still weeping).

Therapist: What do you think about this life that you just lived?

Amelia: Purposeless in some ways and in other ways, purposeful.

Therapist: What did you learn?

Amelia: I learned the truth about who I am and the way of the world and how cruel it can be. How hard it can be to make a difference and do what you wanted to do. Because there are always limitations and obstacles and it's hard to trust that there's anything out there helping you when you're stuck in that deep dark state.

Therapist: What is your last thought when you leave the body?

Amelia: I'm going home.

I'm helping her cross over.

Amelia: I am watching the body from below.

Therapist: Is there anybody near you at the time of your death?

Amelia: No, I'm all alone. I see the pen and paper on this kind of desk. I'm not sure what to call it. My body is on the floor in this lifeless state.

Therapist: How do you feel about your death?

Amelia: Sad. Just really sad and looking at my body. Because I basically poisoned myself. I had contemplated hanging myself and decided to hurt myself in this way instead. And there's liquid on the ground and broken glass.

Therapist: Do you wish to remain a while longer to say goodbye to someone or attend to other unfinished business on earth? Or do you prefer to leave now?

Amelia: I feel like because my parents have already passed, and I have no connection to my husband or anyone in the town I live in it's time to leave.

Therapist: All right, let us now go (I help her move on) describing everything that's happening so I can stay with you. Have you started to move? (Deep sighs of relief as we go through this process)

Amelia: Yes, I've moved through the light and there's almost like wispy sparkly elements within me and around me at this time.

Therapist: Are you moving towards those sparkly elements or are you already there?

Amelia: I am there. Everything slowed down. And then it's white wispy and bright and comforting.

Therapist: Is any of those lights larger or more intense than the others? Perhaps in a way, as if waiting for you?

Amelia: No, I feel almost encompassed by it, almost like a bubble of light.

Therapist: Does it feel like this bubble is embracing you or does it feel more like it's as if taking you by the hand? What does it feel like?

Amelia: Like it's embracing me. Like it's holding my entire being,

Therapist: Just take a moment and feel around and tell me what happens next.

Amelia: It's almost like these little sparkling energies or elements are like little fairies in some ways. They're just kind of circling around me. That's making me smile and feel connected and I'm just kind of walking forward now through the light. And now there's kind of a rainbow of light, so many colors ahead of me and I'm drawn to it. So, I moved forward and then I realized as I get towards this rainbow of light, the colors are almost see-through so I can walk through them and they become part of me and I just keep walking forward. And now I see that some guides are waiting for me. There's a main guide right in front and several behind.

Therapist: Can you describe them to me?

Amelia: Yes. The first guide in front comes to me as an older gentleman with a beard (smiling). He comes this way because he knows I like to see him like this. Kind of a state of wisdom and comfort. The guides behind him are more like monks, in white. Without any hair.

Therapist: Are they all male figures?

Amelia: They're all male figures.

Therapist: How many are there?

Amelia: Five behind my main guide. So, six in total.

Therapist: As the main guide steps forward, I understand that communication may be more of a telephonic kind or could be of any kind. Is there any initial contact communication we can start talking about?

Amelia: Yes, he comes forward and he places his hands like this (welcoming). That's a way of reminding me that he's here for me and to receive the information he's about to give to me as he comes forward. He then places his hand right here on my heart, and he smiles, and I smile. It's almost like I'm telepathically receiving love from him. I'm calling my guide male but he's not really male. He just appears that way.

Therapist: Right. Is he an entity that you know from before?

Amelia: Yes. He's helped me devise all my soul contracts.

Therapist: Does he have a name?

Amelia: (laughing) Ezekiel. And he's been with me in this life but shows up a little differently.

Therapist: Now tell me, as we're here with Ezekiel and he's sharing his love and his light with you, does he have anything interesting to say about this life you just lived as Alice?

Amelia: Yes. He tells me to relax. That all is well now. He gives me love and that there's no shame or blame or guilt around what happened. He says that he understands why I chose to leave and that in many ways it was what was best for my soul, which surprises me a bit.

Therapist: How does it surprise you?

Amelia: Because I feel as if I would have been punished for this, but he reminds me that it's not in any way a problem. That he can see that I was struggling. And I was in so much pain that I had no other choice.

Therapist: As part of this understanding and loving demeanor, is there yet a positive criticism that he could share with you?

Amelia: He tells me that the most important message along this path, the most important thing that I was to learn was resilience. An understanding that I write my own life story. And I have a choice of whether to let others write that for me.

Therapist: How did you do as Alice in that regard?

Amelia: I allowed my parents to write my story. I allowed my husband to write my story towards the end.

Therapist: What does he suggest you could have done differently?

Amelia: He tells me that my fear of death and dying and disappointing others was the main thing that led me away from doing what was important to me. The main lesson is to remember to be true to myself, regardless of what anybody else says or does. And that in this life I was supposed to learn that, yes, I have a light within me to share, but that it's more important that I share it with myself first. And that was something I had a hard time doing.

Therapist: What was planned specifically before starting life as Alice? Like, this is what we're going to try and accomplish? And to what degree did you, or did you not accomplish that? I know you already said it, but just to be more specific.

Amelia: I have an image in mind of writing the book to inspire the world. It was to be a book about nature and spirituality and about being completely in tune with all that is. No boundaries between forms. It would have been a challenge to get that out in the world, knowing that I had undertaken a big challenge in this life choosing to come as a woman and an author and be as widely known as I was hoping to be.

Therapist: So, you're getting a picture of what could have

been? How does it make you feel now being here with him and looking at the plan and knowing that you stepped out early? What do you realize?

Amelia: I realize it shows a hard path for myself and he agrees, and he says, we talked about this.

Therapist: You did?

Amelia: I did, it was kind of iffy. He said it was going to be a big challenge. And I said that I can do it. I can handle it. I've done tons and tons of this before. And he said: "I love your confidence and courage. And it'll be a challenge.

Therapist: Now taking that story forward to the life of Amelia. And if we look at her plan, I assume there is some sort of continuum in this realm. What had you planned for her?

Amelia: This is a life about being able to manifest what I was unable to manifest in that life, which is why I feel a sense of urgency now. What he hints at is that it's not a personal urgency as it was in that life, but more of a collective worldly sense of urgency to awaken the planet, to be a light worker in the world of sorts. And he tells me that being in this life, being Amelia is much easier. So that's part of why at this time I decided to go on this journey. Being female it is now much easier to write a book and to make a difference. But then also now there's a greater sense of urgency than before because it's not about me. I feel it's interesting. Cleansing almost. I feel there is a cleaning up of this feeling of personal motivation between lives that occurred. And now it's less about me.

Therapist: Do you think Alice was still in the bubble of her personal feelings and interests versus Amelia having become more altruistic?

Amelia: Yes, but she doesn't truly know that on all levels. She's concerned about the trappings of the ego mind and the potential of the trappings of achievement and success.

Therapist: So the true purpose of Amelia as specified by Ezekiel for your soul Self for this specific life then is, in a more altruistic way, bringing light and knowledge to the world? Is that correct?

Amelia: Yes. Yes, it is. That's Amelia's purpose. It's for her to transcend the personal self. And in many ways, there's still more to come.

Therapist: Amelia is now 32. What is the plan for Amelia's life?

Amelia: The plan is to help other beings recognize that they need not believe they are not stuck in the way that Alice was stuck. Though this human is limited in form, it can do and accomplish and be in the world. And to remind each human being who they really are and how powerful and divine they are on the deepest possible level. Spreading this to as many people as possible through love and light.

Therapist: Are you saying that Amelia doesn't quite fully notice that altruistic side of herself? Where is she now in the grand scheme of things on that spiritual journey? Her true purpose has now been clearly defined and articulated, yet in the contemporary world, Amelia is at this phase of her life. What needs to be accomplished to fully bring this plan to fruition?

Amelia: She's very close. She's at the edge of a new part of her life. At the breaking point so to speak. Moving through the personal self, into more of the unconditioned Self. And she knows that she feels that there's some part of her that's fighting that. A fear of losing Amelia.

Therapist: Why is she afraid of that?

Amelia: She's afraid she might lose what she's had. The whole idea of life, her understanding of it, her knowledge. She's afraid she'll lose it, but in truth, she's going to gain so much more.

Therapist: You mean, is it an attachment to the ego or more an attachment to a way of life?

Amelia: To both ego and the way of her life.

Therapist: You mean identity?

Amelia: Yes. control, and identity.

Therapist: That's an important point. So how can Ezekiel, for example, help Amelia to make that transition? What needs to change?

In the next part, it is her guide Ezekiel, and her higher Self taking turns speaking through Amelia.

Amelia: We've been trying to help Amelia live a more calm and peaceful life, where she can settle into her being, which does mean a little less contact with people and from circumstances. However, it's been difficult for her because of her urgency.

Therapist: On the one hand, she's driven to become the soul that she is with all her accomplishments and the tools that she needs to accomplish this. But on the other hand, there's a need for withdrawal and a contemplative meditative kind of life. Are you saying that she's seeking balance?

Amelia: That's exactly right. She's seeking balance. And it's been a constant theme for her, especially over the past few years. And she's had illnesses due to being imbalanced and now it's time to help her gain this balance.

Therapist: But in all fairness, as young as she was, she needed to get accomplished first, right? It was a required phase. You cannot expect her to be accomplished without spending a certain amount of energy and time on that.

Amelia: Right. But she is not young in spirit, and she knows deep within what comes next. It's just about taking that next first step.

Therapist: Is she aware that she needs to move more into that next contemplative phase?

Amelia: She is, she's contacted me about this several times, asking for guidance and support, and I'm here supporting her in this, but I cannot make the choice for her.

Therapist: Is there anything that could stand in the way? Because

Alice, you know, couldn't quite follow through. So, what is the distraction that could stand in the way of integration?

Amelia: It's her affairs, specifically her affairs of survival surrounding money and finances. She's afraid of taking a break from work and not knowing what that might mean for her finances.

Therapist: Is there something that she's not seeing in this contemporary California world?

Amelia: Yes. All these affairs are only karmic. They are not real. She is supported financially, and she knows this. At the same time, there's a deep intrinsic fear within her. And this is the fear that we're asking her to face and overcome.

Therapist: Isn't overcoming fear also a spiritual practice in itself? Learning to surrender to something bigger? I don't want to put words in your mouth, but is that a correct assessment?

Amelia: (Ezekiel smiles). He says the only path is surrender. That is the only path. And it is the path that you will be focusing on for now until the rest of your life.

Therapist: That's why I brought up surrender. Can we say it's a spiritual highway that is allowing them to work through you, rather than you being fearful and self-reliant?

Amelia: Right.

Therapist: If I summarize it, can we say that you being a lightworker really implies that the ego needs to go away, and by surrendering they can work through you?

Amelia: Correct. However, it's not a hundred percent that the ego needs to go away. It's more that the ego needs to step out of the way.

Therapist: Mature, not be in fear.

Amelia: Yes.

Therapist: The ego is the tool through which you act and express, right? It is not good or bad, it's just ripe or immature.

Amelia: You got it. And what it comes down to is that the ego right now is a little overstimulated, a little over-fearful.

Therapist: Is that because of the past momentum trying to accomplish, or is it due to the world she lives in, or is it due to the past life of Alice or all the above?

Amelia: Yes. Everything that you mentioned, all the above. As well as other karmic experiences of other past lives. But mostly that past life that was shown today to help you see that this is the one that is directly connected to this life right now.

Therapist: Right. This should help Amelia have a better understanding of the bigger picture.

Amelia: Yes. Helping her to see that we're here to help her every step of the way. She's never alone, she's never without help. In fact, the reason she's here is to be that channel that allows all of us here in the astral realms to move the energy down to the earth.

Therapist: But she's having a problem being here on this earthly physical dimension. Why is that?

Amelia: She's having a hard time being in this earthly dimension because she is connected to the higher dimensions in many ways. And part of her path is to learn that she is still meant to ground here on this planet, to be in the world, instead of trying to hide from it.

Therapist: What can you tell me about that true home?

Amelia: Her true home is noticing when her heart is open.

Therapist: Is that true home limited to the astral planes or is that something that she needs to channel here on this earth as well?

Amelia: Yes, she needs to channel what is her true home here on this earth. Amelia is a bit confused about that. She's struggling to recognize that as she reaches the higher realms it will allow her to ground here on earth. She must find a balance between being grounded versus reaching higher.

Therapist: Does it have anything to do with Alice trying to get out, finding this earthly plane uncomfortable? And instead, trying to find a home in the astral planes? Is there in Amelia some subconscious resistance to accepting this realm here?

Amelia: This is a very difficult dimension. It's meant to be a challenge, especially for Amelia because she's so connected to the higher dimensions. It's harder for her to feel as if she belongs here.

Therapist: So, there is a resistance to staying here and manifesting here?

Amelia: Yes, that is part of her soul's contract. And part of her challenge is to work, to feel at home within herself, despite the way the world appears.

Therapist: So, what is the key to achieving that?

Amelia: The key is to go further within and not seek outward. Time in contemplation and meditation is not only important but imperative for this journey.

Therapist: Beautiful, beautiful. Not to seek an escape in some way, but rather to awaken that within herself here and now.

Amelia: Correct. No more escaping.

Therapist: Now, regarding being here on this earth, there are two characters that Amelia has talked about in her pre-session questionnaire, namely her dad and her sister.

Amelia: (smiling) They're here now. Right before you said it they were appearing. I'm coming back to Amelia now.

What she means is that her guide steps back and her higher Self starts to talk again.

Therapist: What can you tell me about them in relation to your soul? Are they part of your soul group?

Amelia: Definitely part of my soul group. I see my dad. Interestingly, I see my sisters too. Hm. I don't see my mom just yet, but I see my dad coming forward and he's just full of light and peace and love.

Therapist: What can you tell me about this strong relationship between you two?

Amelia: (weeping) We're almost like one in many ways. He says I told you, so Amelia, I told you that this is real.

Therapist: Help me understand. What does that mean?

Amelia: (still very emotional) At the time in my early twenties, late teens, when I was struggling with moving out of the religion of Christianity, which my mother was so firmly trying to keep me in, my dad was open to my new understanding of spirituality and who I was as a spiritual being. And he let me and not just let me but opened doors for me into my true Self. And I asked him when he died if it was all real. He said then, "I told you."

Therapist: So, he's saying it again now.

Amelia: Yes.

Therapist: Hmm, beautiful, beautiful.

Amelia: He's saying it couldn't be more real. (laughing) Your world is not real.

Therapist: Regarding your dad and you and your sisters, if I would look like an objective observer of your soul group, what would I see you all have in common? What are your common tendencies?

Amelia: The first thing that comes to mind is playfulness. Very playful (smiling). Very joyful. Just kind of getting a sense of the energy of it right now. Mm. The number seven comes to mind. I feel like there are seven. Not sure who exactly the others are, but I see us all as light orbs for lack of a better word.

Therapist: Do you have a common purpose as a group?

Amelia: Yes. There's a word; 'enlighten'.

Therapist: Is that something that you have recently started

doing as a group? Or is it something that has been going on for a while as a group?

Amelia: My dad says a long time, a really long time.

Therapist: Is it something you also do in the astral plane or is that something that you primarily do on the earth plane?

Amelia: We've done a lot of work in both. Together, all of us have done a lot of work. But my dad's kind of speaking and saying that we've all found different paths along the way as well. At first, it was more cohesive. We all had extremely similar missions. Now it's a bit different, but we're still on the same path.

Therapist: If I look at the nature of your group, are there any common talents that you share?

Amelia: Yes. We're all very creative. My dad says (she's a bit shy here) that I'm very artistic and we all are very artistic in our own way. And he says that it's so important that you mentioned that because we're all meant to bring this sense of creativity to the world and to be creative in our way of enlightening the planet.

Therapist: Having a playful nature without laying it on so heavy?

Amelia: Right. Don't be so serious (laughing).

Therapist: The light is playful. It's artistic. It's creative.

Amelia: Yes. Have fun with it.

Therapist: Is that something that Amelia is aware of?

Amelia: Amelia sees this a lot in her dad. As Amelia, right now, I can say that I struggle with that sometimes on Earth.

Therapist: Is that something that she can try to connect with more, that fun-loving creativity and lightheartedness?

Amelia: Yes. And now I know why I keep getting messages as Amelia to have more fun and be lighthearted, to bring more joy into my life. And it all just sounds so simple. Profound.

Therapist: You know, the whole idea of surrender comes into play as well, right? Not to take control so much, and surrender and let the divine, in a playful way, guide you and play through you and with you.

Amelia: (Very happy and emotional) Yes. It's about bringing joy to the world, not being so serious.

Therapist: And enjoy yourself as well?

Amelia: Yes. By being joyful myself, I bring joy to the world.

Therapist: Yes. Beautiful. Beautiful. What about Amelia's sister? What is her role and why is there a sense of disconnect now?

Amelia: Yes, there is a disconnect. My dad's telling me something. He's saying it's on purpose. It's part of the path right now. He says she's learning more about the subjects and themes around being a mother and how to utilize that to learn to understand who she is as a person, as a soul and to be able to express love in that way. And because that is not my soul's path here in this life, I feel disconnected. We're experiencing love in different ways currently. And because of that, it feels as if the channels of love are separate. They're not, of course separate, but they feel that way and feel disconnected.

Therapist: Unavoidable in the conditioned self.

Amelia: Yes. Yes. My dad is saying that we'll get together again.

Therapist: So, what should Amelia's attitude be to help her not feel so sad about this?

Amelia: Be gentle with her. She's struggling a lot. What I'm getting right now is that she's really hurting in many ways. And on some levels doesn't realize how much she's hurting.

Therapist: Does the word surrender fit here also?

Amelia: Yes.

Therapist: For Amelia to kind of just let it be?

Amelia: To see my sister is innocent and she was innocently following what feels right to her on her path. And there was no right or wrong in any of it.

Therapist: At the end of the day, you're in the same soul group having the same purpose, right?

Amelia: Yes. We still have the same purpose, but I haven't seen that up until now and seen how love connects us. Her love for her children is her way of expressing that.

Therapist: Because if you look at your divine purpose as a group, which is one and the same, there are myriad ways in which we can express that. You said yourself that you have all gone different ways. And it finds its way into the world in its own unique way. We tend to project our own way up on everybody else, don't we?

Amelia: Yes. And my dad wants to tell me something. He's saying that my last life as Alice was important for us as a soul group too, and for him. I'm not sure how he fits into that life just yet. He's just telling me that he came into this current life and chose to struggle with his health and contemplated suicide and taking his own life. And he is saying that it was so important for me to recognize the struggle in him, to heal myself from that life and that there was a deep connection there from different lifetimes.

Part of why I became a counselor was a continuation of my previous life of suffering that I endured. Knowing that so many other people experience and suffer this stuff in the world and being able to be there as a light for them. My dad has a sense of humor. He says, you're welcome, for helping you to heal from this. He says that he knows it was hard for you to see me go through all that, but you needed to see that you went through this in other lives and it's part of your healing journey.

Therapist: Where does John fit into all of this (another pre-session question)?

Amelia: That's a good question.

Therapist: Is he in the same soul group? And is he a soulmate?

Amelia: I am looking into that now. Just kind of moving deeper and deeper into the soul group. He seems to be in a different soul group. He's part of a soul cluster (intertwining group). The wider sole group of 20 or so of us. He's in that group, not in my immediate group of seven.

Therapist: A circle moving within your circle, but still a separate circle.

Amelia: Exactly. Yes. He's there. And as far as soulmates go, yes. There's a very deep connection, and there are many lifetimes of helping each other.

Therapist: Does he share the same purpose that you as a soul group have?

Amelia: No. He has a different one. His purpose is different, but it's interesting because our purposes do connect in many ways. So, for me, my purpose in my soul group is to again, be the lightworker in the world. But to do that, I need help with grounding. And because of that, he's come forth as a way of helping me to ground out my energy.

Therapist: He's a support?

Amelia: In the process of it. He chose to be more of, in the play of life, in the background. A backstage person, not the actor on stage. He wants to be backstage. In some ways it suits him. He wants to support the players; the actors on the stage.

Therapist: You said that there are several guides. Can you tell me if there is just one main guide and the other ones are supporting, or whether they all have a particular task and come forward in their own way at their own time? How does the relation between you and your guides work and what is the function of each of them?

Amelia: Hmm. They all helped me with different themes of my life. Different things I struggle with. One guide is specifically here to help me with fear. All of them are very quiet. They're not like Ezekiel. They don't speak up and talk very much. I get a sense that their presence is supporting me. And one of them is helping me work through fear and giving me courage.

Another guide is helping me to remember the truth of who I am, specifically when I'm in nature and things like that. I have another guide who is helping me with things around my work. I have a guide helping me with family.

Therapist: Beautiful. Is there anything, if we asked them collectively, outside the paradigm that we haven't really discussed today, that we haven't really thought about today, that maybe have some real importance to your soul development?

Amelia: Ezekiel is reminding me that I have many different paths I can choose in this world to be a light worker and many different things that will interest me. And again, coming back to that urgency and desire to be on this planet, helping as much as possible, he's giving me permission, so to speak, to slow down and to choose as many things as I want to focus on. But concentrate on one at a time for now as a way of staying focused.

Therapist: So, if I understand this correctly, it doesn't matter which method you use because the end purpose is the enlightenment of the world. However, to really get it done, you need to focus on one thing at a time. Otherwise, it gets dispersed too much. Is that correct?

Amelia: That's correct. And as he is reminding me how important mindfulness is and how it's no wonder that I want to be more of a mindfulness teacher in the world as well. This has had a great impact on my life, and I like to be this kind of teacher in the world. And to focus, I'm going to need more downtime regardless of how many things are going to distract me. Ezekiel is reminding me about distraction, saying distraction is going to be the hardest part for me in many ways, and just stay focused as best as I can.

Therapist: To restrain that enthusiasm in a more contemplative integrated way and not be all over the board? What about the awakening online business (another pre-session question)?

Amelia: They want an awakened online business. Ezekiel is telling me about the potential of this portal through which my higher self can appear and serve in the world. And Ezekiel is also letting me know that he really understands that it's not as easy as I once thought it was. That being human, it's not easy to set up a business and not be concerned about finances and getting things right. Ezekiel is just kind of giving me some compassion right now and understanding that I don't have to get it right immediately and that I can just let it flow.

Therapist: What about Amelia's health? It is kind of a concern to her.

Amelia: Ezekiel says it's because I don't listen sometimes, and that I like to kind of push myself a bit past what my soul is telling me to do. So, after working a few hours, if I need a break, I won't.

Therapist: It's kind of the same theme running throughout today's experience, is it not?

Amelia: Correct. Yes. Yes. And reminding me that I can be as healthy as I want to be, and there's nothing in my self-contract that says otherwise.

Therapist: This is important to know.

Amelia: Yesh, that's good news.

Therapist: It's a dispersion of energy versus focusing on a singular way, a singular way of life, a singular mindset. When we talk about mindfulness, it has to do with finding a peaceful rhythm. Then the body will follow accordingly. But when you disperse it too much in different directions and restless behavior, then the body will take its toll. Is that a good summary?

Amelia: It is a good summary. It sums up the experience of being human. Sometimes you feel restless, and you need to rest. And a lot of the path right now is to listen to my body. And in the past, there have been some chronic illnesses. There still is some, but Ezekiel says it's better now because you're listening.

Therapist: It's understandable perhaps because of the urgency that was felt after cutting short Alice's potential. The spirit is trying to accomplish what was not accomplished last time and understandably feels a sense of urgency and angst.

Amelia: Guilt was a huge, huge problem, which led to a stomach condition in this life. It was the guilt that I was feeling that prompted this condition.

Therapist: Do you think that guilt is from Alice's premature death?

Amelia: Yes. Part of it is that.

Therapist: Arriving at this phase in her life, how can we bring it together? Looking at it in the big picture, looking at Alice, with an understandable sense of urgency, guilt, health, and enlightenment. How can this be integrated into the next phase of Amelia's life?

Amelia: The next phase is important now, which is why we were drawing Amelia to this work. We want her to know that she's on track with her purpose because she questions this often and she worries that she's not doing as much as she could be doing. And we want to extend our love and compassion to her around this. She's doing all she can in the way of the world at this current time of human history and not expecting so much from herself as an individual being in the world. She takes on a lot for herself, forgetting that here there is so much spiritual support for her.

Therapist: And as a footnote from what I heard earlier, it's not about doing more, but about doing one thing at a time.

Amelia: Less is more.

Therapist: Becoming more like a laser beam, focused on one purpose with more impact.

Amelia: And it's important to note too, that although she is afraid for her survival, she's had many lives connected to not having enough food or not having enough money. So we have not mentioned that there are still remnants of that coming up in this life now and we just want to extend some encouragement to her that she will always be supported financially, and emotionally on all levels.

Therapist: It's a very beautiful and cohesive story. The surrender and the focus part of it is highly important and the next phase where integration is allowed to take place. Where she can kind of retreat, not fearing survival, and focus on one thing, which in turn brings calm and peace to her mind, which in turn brings health to her body. So, it seems to be a domino effect once she gets to the core purpose.

Amelia: It is. And there are just a few more things to note about her, the lifetimes that she's chosen to live. In her soul group, right now, there is intensity and growth happening. And in some ways, there is a choice as well, around reincarnation in future lives on this planet. She knows that she gets to decide whether she wants to come back into this life into another body. But not to use that as part of the fear or the urgency, thinking what if I don't do it now, I will never get to it later. Rather try one step at a time knowing that there's always opportunity if she decides to come back later, but that she is towards the end of her incarnation cycle.

Therapist: And perhaps also to realize that along with your soul group, there are millions of other beings everywhere supporting that same mission. So, you don't have to take that cross upon yourself. That we are instrumental, but not responsible.

Amelia: Exactly, exactly.

Therapist: That would allow her some peace of mind as well.

Amelia: Right. And as she heals the fears and the worries in this life, specifically around being human, experiencing pain and suffering, she will no longer have the same kind of heaviness of urgency hanging over her because she will recognize that all that she does in this life is enough. And if she chooses to come back later, she can.

Therapist: A higher understanding is required, knowing that there are planes, levels beyond the astral planes. Perhaps Ezekiel and your guides come from that realm that perhaps even transcends the astral. Is that a place where perhaps for a moment, we can take your soul Self and plug into that light source for a moment? Can you have a moment of full divine connection? Is that something that you would like?

Amelia: Yes, that would be wonderful.

Therapist: Can we ask Ezekiel? You can ask him to see what can be done.

Amelia: I see that as Ezekiel is holding my hand, I'm now seeing other members of my soul group. Even those that aren't here in these realms. It's very interesting. I see my dad is more solid in this realm. My sister is here, but she's not solid in this realm. She's more of a shadowy, light color. Just an outline of her. Both my sisters are here. Hmm. I'm not quite sure my mom is here. And I feel like there's still something missing from my soul group. I'm not quite sure what it is, but it feels as if I don't quite have the full picture of who is here. And it feels important to know that a little bit deeper.

Therapist: Tune in a little bit deeper. Tune in to what lies beyond.

Amelia: Hmm. I don't think my mom is part of this immediate soul group. I get a sense she's part of the wider group, like John. But my sisters are. My dad is here and there are other people here too. I don't know who they are. I think one of them could potentially have been an ex-partner. My dad is telling me something important. About somebody in my soul group that I met. I met him on a retreat just a few months after my dad's passing and the retreat was planned long before my dad's passing. In fact, my dad's telling me that he got me in touch with him at that time as a way of helping me remember my spiritual essence, because I had such an incredible kind of spiritual connection with this person.

And I truly felt like I was connected to my higher Self again, after so much grief. My dad said that on purpose and I felt guilty for connecting with somebody, even if it wasn't necessarily romantic. Even though I was with my current partner, my dad is telling me that it was on purpose. So I could see there was somebody else in our soul group here that is on the same path because he was exactly where I am on my path. And he was just meant to show up at that time to help me through one of the darkest times of my life.

Therapist: Beautiful. He just showed up to show you that divine connection.

Amelia: Yes. My dad was there. Just kind of guiding me through. It feels like I'm supported by the soul group in so many ways, even though I don't know everybody in this life. There's a sense I'm going to meet some of them still. I'm not sure about my close friends, if they're in the soul group or not. It is almost like the clusters of soul groups are so connected to my immediate soul group. It's hard to tell who's in it directly versus who is not. I work with so many different souls.

Therapist: In retrospect, perhaps we can measure it by the intensity of the meeting. Like when you met this person with whom you connected deeply, there was a strong recognition, reminding you of your dad's connection and your soul's purpose. So perhaps that could be a criterion for making a distinction.

Amelia: Yes. Yes.

Amelia: I'm getting some very clear information that my good friend Zack is within the soul cluster group, as well as an old childhood friend of mine. We're not connected now, but she's on track. I get a sense that no matter what journey we take here as souls, we're still going to reconnect again in our soul groups. It feels good.

Therapist: We have covered most of the concerns and questions that Amelia had. Is there anything else missing or do you feel that we've covered most of what we needed to understand today? What do you feel at this moment?

Amelia: I feel connected. I feel good. There's still a question or wonder about how to work through these distractions.

Therapist: Well, let's ask Ezekiel very specifically about how to cross this bridge from being distracted towards this contemplative, one-pointed focus that is required to be effective and bring peace and health. What does he say? Be very specific.

Amelia: He says it's important to set time aside for mindfulness work. More specifically, make time for yourself in your own retreat. Even if it's only for short periods of time, leading up to longer periods of time, make sure to carve as much time as you possibly can in your daily life. As you're going through a very, very big energetic shift in your mind and body and be ready for this. Do not get caught up in the ungroundedness of the world. It's important. So important.

Therapist: That's an important message for everybody. Yes. There needs to be time. Purify and strengthen the nervous system so you can carry that enlightened current. It's a package deal. Is it not? It's the way you live, the way you eat, and the way you take time for yourself. Everything matters.

Amelia: It feels like I must make a life shift. And it's a permanent life shift. It's not a temporary one.

Therapist: Isn't that part of being aware? Because otherwise, these are just beautiful words, right? Being aware means, I've got to walk the talk regarding every aspect of my life and it's a permanent shift.

Amelia: Right (smiling). It is a permanent shift. And right now, it seems that I am on the right track. And it's important just to stay fully present.

Therapist: Could we say that on the mental and spiritual level, you've done all the groundwork to come to this understanding, but to bring this to actualization you need to be grounded as regards discipline, a diet, a way of life, to taking time for yourself?

Amelia: Yes. That's the next phase. The next phase is to integrate. It's like I'm standing on a diving board, looking down at the water and getting ready to jump in.

Therapist: Isn't that what a real yogi does, living the right way?

Amelia: Yes.

Therapist: And you have these lifetimes of understanding and experience like very few people have.

Amelia: Yes.

Therapist: It's that final coming together, living it.

Amelia: Yes, it is. It is. That's the rest of my life. Yes, exactly. It'll work. It will come together and it's all going to be much more beautiful than I ever thought was possible.

Therapist: Well, that's a very important answer that he gave you because, at the end of the day, unless we understand that, it just remains an idea and never gets actualized.

Amelia: Yes, exactly. Yes. It's moving forward. It's being in the beingness of it. Being there. And I sense that now and I feel that deep in my soul.

Therapist: And that distinguishes one from another where mindfulness is just a fancy idea. But the one who can integrate that into a living reality is the one that is becoming the real channel.

Amelia: Yes. And there's this message coming through that I will make this impact that I've been so determined to make, but not by force. But by being. It's happening. It's happening now. And they're telling me that it'll show up more readily as a manifestation in the future.

I wonder if there's just one more question I might ask, which I realize now I didn't write down. It's more connected to starting a family. It's something that I've never felt that I had to do necessarily, but wondering now if that might be a part of my journey. They tell me it can be a part of my journey if I decide to do that as a way of learning. Like my sister, to know what it's like to be a mother, but that it's not necessary.

Therapist: What does your heart tell you?

Amelia: My heart tells me it's fine either way. There's beauty in being a mother and there's beauty in the life path I've chosen to dedicate myself as a light worker. And since I've been a mother, many, many times in my lives I've had that experience and it's not a hundred percent needed. But it's also something that as Amelia I'd like to experience in this life. I feel like I have backing from my spirit guides on that. And of course, my dad, because he always said he wanted more grandchildren and that it was never enough.

Therapist: So how are we feeling about everything you've seen today?

Amelia: Feeling good, feeling like there are a lot of beautiful things to come in this life. A lot of positive changes and transitions that I'm really excited about.

Therapist: Do you feel that you have a good comprehension of the steps ahead of you and what to do?

Amelia: Yes. I do know that it's not something I could sidestep anymore. Something I have to make happen regardless of how many people say they need me; I need to put myself first in order to help.

We end the session here.

Case 3: Nicole
A deeper meaning behind loss

Nicole, 50 years old, recently lost her husband Bill. This is a classic example of how a past-life and life-between-lives combination allows us an insight into the continuation of grief, and how it can be reframed and healed, by realizing herself as a soul, and her higher purpose.

Therapist: Now tell me, is it daytime or nighttime?
Nicole: Daytime.
Therapist: Are you inside or outside?
Nicole: Outside.

Therapist: What do you notice, right in front of you?

Nicole: It's a pathway.

Therapist: What's the environment like?

Nicole: It's trees.

Therapist: Now looking down at your feet, tell me what, if anything you see or feel you're wearing on your feet.

Nicole: I'm barefooted.

Therapist: What are you wearing on the rest of your body?

Nicole: A dress.

Therapist: Is it a one-piece or a multiple-piece dress?

Nicole: It's a one-piece, it's blue and it's pretty.

Therapist: How old are you now?

Nicole: Like 11 or 12.

Therapist: What's the color of your skin?

Nicole: White.

Therapist: What about your hair?

Nicole: Blonde.

Therapist: What are you doing on this pathway?

Nicole: I think we're going to church.

Therapist: Who is all going with you?

Nicole: Dad's there, my mom, my brothers, and sisters.

Therapist: Is it a big family?

Nicole: Yeah.

Therapist: And preparing to go to church?

Nicole: Yeah. Dad's downstairs.

Therapist: How do you feel, ready to go?

Nicole: It's fun.

Therapist: What do your parents dress like? Can you give me a description of their outfit?

Nicole: Dad's tall with brown pants and suspenders. Mom's got a dress on, she's so pretty. It's Sunday.

Therapist: When you look at the environment of where you are right now, is it more like farmland or a city? Where are you?

Nicole: I live on the farm.

Therapist: Where, what climate? What place comes to mind?

Nicole: It's warm right now. But we have cold winters.

Therapist: Where in the world are we approximately?

Nicole: Pennsylvania.

Therapist: What year approximately?

Nicole: 18 something.

Therapist: You are here in Pennsylvania and you're going to church. Tell me what happens when you get there and how you feel. What's the place like and the community?

Nicole: It's small, but everybody knows everybody. And I don't quite understand though.

Therapist: What is it that you don't understand?

Nicole: Everybody's so strict, Dad's so loving.

Therapist: What kind of community are you part of?

Nicole: I mean, everybody's so nice, but you have to follow a lot of rules. It doesn't make a whole lot of sense.

Therapist: Is that coming from the church or is it coming from the community?

Nicole: I think from both.

Therapist: What can you tell me about your thoughts and feelings and what you observe around you?

Nicole: I'm happy. I'm very happy. Part of me has questions and doubts, but I don't want to because I want to be good. Daddy loves me and he's such a good man.

Therapist: What's your name?

Nicole: Beth.

Therapist: So, Beth, I'm going to count from 3 down to 1, and at 1 we're going to move forward in time a till you get a little bit older to another relevant moment in your life as Beth. Going to a time that shapes your mind, thoughts, and feelings as I go from 3, 2, 1, and you are there now. And tell me what is happening now, Beth?

Nicole: I'm married.

Therapist: Where are you now?

Nicole: We have our own place. He's a good man.

Therapist: Can you describe the place to me and what it looks like?

Nicole: It's small but warm. I keep a good house. At least that's what I'm told.

Therapist: And you say you have a good relationship with your husband?

Nicole: Yes. He's a good man.

Therapist: When you look outside the window or step outside, what do you see around you?

Nicole: There's a huge field. Lots of flowers. Well, grass and flowers.

Therapist: Is it like a farm?

Nicole: Yeah, we have lots of cows and horses.

Therapist: How do you feel in your marriage?

Nicole: I don't like always having to follow the rules.

Therapist: What are some of those rules that you must follow?

Nicole: He's the man. I have to be quiet. I'm not one for being quiet.

Therapist: Is that he who imposes that or is it part of the culture in which you live?

Nicole: It's the culture, I guess. But he tries to understand me, I guess.

Therapist: So, is this some sort of Christian community that imposes all these rules on you?

Nicole: It's Christian.

Therapist: How do you feel about all of that?

Nicole: I want to speak up and say something, but I keep thinking there's more because it doesn't always make sense.

Therapist: So, you're still questioning?

Nicole: Oh, yeah.

Therapist: How old are you now Beth?

Nicole: 33.

Therapist: In general, how do you regard your state of mind at 33?

Nicole: I'm loving. I'm kind.

Therapist: What matters to you now at this point in life?

Nicole: My kids are growing up. The oldest one has moved away. The youngest one is still around.

Therapist: So, you're married quite young then, huh?

Nicole: Yeah. Now I want more, there's got to be more.

Therapist: What is it that you're looking for?

Nicole: Connection.

Therapist: What kind of connection?

Nicole: I feel like there's more. Like oneness, a greater purpose, or more.

Therapist: So, you're looking for a spiritual connection, something bigger, a bigger meaning in life?

Nicole: Yeah. But I'm told that, well, you're not crazy, but, there's only just one way.

Therapist: How do you feel about that?

Nicole: I don't believe him, but I'm afraid to speak up.

Therapist: Right.

Nicole: And I pray, and I walk, and I talk to God a lot. But nobody will listen. I do have one friend.

Therapist: How do you feel about your connection to God? Is it good?

Nicole: Yeah. But I never feel like I'm going to be good enough.

Therapist: Why is that?

Nicole: Because I'm sinful. And if I'm sinful then how can you love me?

Therapist: Now, I'm going to count from 3 down to 1 Beth, and on the count of 1 we're going to move forward a few years in your life to another relevant moment. Something that shapes your heart, your soul, your mind, your inner being, something relevant, going from 3, 2, 1. And we are there now. Tell me what is happening now, Beth.

Nicole: (crying) My son died and I'm holding him.

Therapist: What happened?

Nicole: He got shot.

Therapist: Where are you now Beth?

Nicole: Up in the yard and I'm screaming.

Therapist: How did it happen? Who shot him?

Nicole: There are people that came to the house. My husband wasn't home. They wanted stuff and they were taking stuff and my son wanted to stop them and they shot him.

Therapist: How old is your son?

Nicole: 17.

Therapist: Was he still living with you?

Nicole: Yes.

Therapist: What happens next?

Nicole: I'm just holding him for the longest time until my husband comes home.

Therapist: Well, Beth. I want you to move forward away from

this incident to a time after this event. And tell me how you are now.

Nicole: Everybody tells me I need to move on and get over it, but I can't let it go.

Therapist: How do you feel?

Nicole: Angry, I should have done something.

Therapist: Such as?

Nicole: I should have stopped him.

Therapist: Stopped him from doing what?

Nicole: Stopped him from trying to save me.

Therapist: So, you're blaming yourself?

Nicole: Yeah. Yes.

Therapist: How does that make you feel when you start blaming yourself?

Nicole: I just don't understand how God could hurt me so badly. I was so good. I tried to do everything right. He took my baby.

Therapist: Is this infecting your life in any way as you move on?

Nicole: Yeah. I can't get out of bed.

Therapist: Depressed?

Nicole: Yeah. Yeah.

Therapist: How long will this go on, this state of mind?

Nicole: It's been going on for a long time. My husband's getting very tired of it. And I've got to find a way to pull it together.

Therapist: Now, I'm going to count again Beth, from 3 to 1, and on the count of 1 we're going to, again, move forward in your life till you get older to another relevant time. And tell me what is happening now.

Nicole: Life is just going on.

Therapist: How old are you now, Beth?

Nicole: Like 45.

Therapist: How are you feeling right now at 45?

Nicole: Still lost, but better. It's never been the same.

Therapist: No?

Nicole: No.

Therapist: You mean externally or internally?

Nicole: Both. When I finally got over it, I got out of bed and started moving, but life's going on, life moves on.

Therapist: How's your internal state right now?

Nicole: I'm detached. Not as loving as I was. I don't blame anybody anymore, but I'm definitely not going to get close and stay guarded.

Therapist: Does it affect your overall state of well-being?

Nicole: I've aged a lot. I remember people wanting me to just move on and get over it. I've got other kids. So, I eventually did. My husband got over it. At least I think he did.

Therapist: How's your relationship with your husband now?

Nicole: It's okay. Not like it was though.

Therapist: How do you spend your days, Beth?

Nicole: I clean. I help around the farm. There're no kids anymore, but we've got grandkids.

Therapist: What's your internal demeanor right now? Did you say detached?

Nicole: Yeah. Very detached. Part of me just wishes to die.

I move her forward in time again.

Nicole: I'm living in another house.

Therapist: What kind of a house?

Nicole: With my daughter, I think.

Therapist: Where's your husband?

Nicole: He's no longer around. He's gone.

Therapist: How old are you now, Beth?
Nicole: I think I'm like 60, but I feel a lot older.
Therapist: How do you feel in your mind and heart right now?
Nicole: Like I've wasted this life.
Therapist: In what way?
Nicole: I wish I would've questioned more. I wish I would've just done what I thought I was going to do.
Therapist: What is it that you wanted to go to do?
Nicole: I didn't want to get married. I wanted to live my own life.
Therapist: Doing what?
Nicole: I wanted to be a writer. I wanted to go off on my own, but that was not what Daddy wanted. I couldn't do that.
Therapist: How do you feel now being here with your daughter?
Nicole: Oh, I love her and she's good to me.
Therapist: If you look outside, what does the place look like?
Nicole: It's like a city almost, like a town, it's very busy.
Therapist: What do you think about this town life now at this age?
Nicole: Oh, everybody's busy. I just sit out on the porch.
Therapist: You don't work much anymore?
Nicole: Oh, no. My daughter takes care of me.
Therapist: How's the relationship between you two?
Nicole: It is good. It's good. She's obligated.

I move her forward to the last day of her life.

Therapist: Tell me how old you are on this last day of your life.
Nicole: 66.
Therapist: Is there anything going on around you or within you

to suggest that your physical death will come this day?

Nicole: I'm in bed.

Therapist: How are you feeling?

Nicole: Tired.

Therapist: Do you have any illness or disease?

Nicole: I have a hard time breathing.

Therapist: Looking back, what do you think about this life you lived as Beth?

Nicole: It was a good life. I just wish I would've made different choices.

Therapist: You regret some of your choices?

Nicole: Yeah.

Therapist: How come you didn't make them?

Nicole: I didn't feel I could.

Therapist: Now that you reflect on the fact that you think you couldn't, what do you feel now?

Nicole: I made the only choices I could, where I thought that I could. And even though they weren't exactly what I wanted, I still had a good life. I had five kids, and a good husband. It was a good life overall, but I wish it could have been more. I wanted it to be more.

Therapist: What did you learn from this life?

Nicole: Making choices is so hard. Loving is so hard sometimes, letting go.

Therapist: And what is your last thought or awareness as you leave Beth's body?

Nicole: I hope I was good enough.

I move her past her death.

There are just bright lights, it's so wonderful.

Therapist: How does it feel, this bright light?

Nicole: It's loving. I feel light.

Therapist: When you look at your own soul Self, what do you feel or look like right now?

Nicole: I am light.

Therapist: Beautiful. What is the energy of this light around you?

Nicole: Like a going under... it's white. It's hard to explain.

Therapist: Just feel it and enjoy it. How do you feel your connection to this light?

Nicole: It's joyful. Peaceful.

Therapist: Just enjoy getting deeper and deeper absorbed into this light that you are as well. And in the meantime, see if there's any guiding principle around you. Tell me how you feel, and what you become aware of. Take your time.

Nicole: I see wings. Angel wings.

Therapist: Beautiful. Is it one or more?

Nicole: There are so many. It's where the light's coming from.

Therapist: Are they guides of angels or who are these beings?

Nicole: I don't know if they're guides. They're very familiar.

Therapist: Can you go towards that light? Just move towards it or let it move towards you. Tell me what happens when you get there.

Nicole: It's just like a big rhythm, people everywhere. Like a party.

Therapist: Who are these beings that are here? Are they part of your soul group?

Nicole: It's my soul group because they're all very familiar.

Therapist: What is the energy as you enter the soul group?

Nicole: Very high energy.

Therapist: Is anybody stepping forward to welcome you?

Nicole: Everybody is there, saying hello and giving me hugs.

Therapist: Beautiful.

Nicole: Welcoming me back.

Therapist: Is there anybody you recognize?

Nicole: It's like I know them all.

Therapist: Is there anyone that starts a conversation?

Nicole: My son from the life before comes up. He's Charlie.

Therapist: Is he Charlie in this life?

Nicole: No.

Therapist: He was Charlie in that life?

Nicole: Yeah.

Therapist: How's the meeting as you see him again?

Nicole: I give him a big hug. He's okay.

Therapist: Just take your time with him.

Nicole: There's a lot of light. A white light.

Therapist: Are you getting a message or communication from the group as a whole?

Nicole: It's just all-encompassing. There're no words, it's overwhelming.

Therapist: Beautiful. Just enjoy it. Allow yourself to be fully engaged and absorbed in the light and power. Now, while you hold on to it, and we look at your soul group, what kind of beings are these? What kind of group is this in terms of talent and aspirations?

Nicole: We're like the fixers, the changers.

Therapist: What kind of things do you fix and change?

Nicole: We take on the hard lives usually to help people grow. Although this past life, I didn't do that.

Therapist: How come?

Nicole: I didn't feel I could. I was being held back.

Therapist: As fixers, what is your state of being when you're not incarnated?

Nicole: Almost like angels, but not angels. We're just like healers, but I know the truth of life. And we help to evolve spirits.

Therapist: When you say we know the truth of life, how does that relate to this group?

Nicole: We're all one. People don't understand that when they go to earth it's about the experience of love. Remembering and being.

Therapist: You as a group remind people on earth about these truths?

Nicole: Yes. Connecting to that heaven where we're at now, right here. It's right here. And I forgot that when Charlie died, I couldn't connect my soul, I put up a wall.

Therapist: What do you think caused that wall, that forgetfulness?

Nicole: I had to remember what people feel.

Therapist: Have you been doing this in many lifetimes, bringing this connection and love to others?

Nicole: I've been around for a long, long time.

Therapist: What is it as a soul and as a soul group that you are aspiring to? Is there an evolution in this group?

Nicole: Yes. We are trying to help souls move towards oneness. To bring oneness to the world, to bring oneness back. But it's kind of interesting because I don't know if it'll ever happen.

Therapist: Could it happen more on an individual level when some souls experience this truth individually?

Nicole: Oh yeah, yeah.

Therapist: So, in that way, it does happen, but it just doesn't happen all at once?

Nicole: Yeah. The Christians say that they're waiting for Jesus to come back. But it's really about the evolution of our souls because there's Christ in every one of us.

Therapist: Beautiful. Beautiful. Now that you're here with your group, is this a good place to discuss some of the issues regarding Beth's life or Nicole's life? Or do we need to go somewhere else or talk to somebody else?

Nicole: I think we need to go somewhere else.

Therapist: Where do we go for that? Do we meet a guide, or do we go to another place?

Nicole: Jonathan's here. He's my guide. He'll take us.

Therapist: What does he look like, Jonathan? Does he have a form or is he more like an energy?

Nicole: He's an energy here, but he's been around. He's worked with me for many lifetimes.

Therapist: Does he incarnate with you as well?

Nicole: He hasn't been incarnated in a looong time.

Therapist: Tell me about Jonathan. What is his energy when you are with him?

Nicole: He's a very soulful man. Well, spirit, but he comes across as a male.

Therapist: So, you have a long relationship with him?

Nicole: Yes.

Therapist: Now, what does he have to say about this incarnation of Beth?

Nicole: This was a pivotal lifetime for me because in many lifetimes I've just gone and experienced dark lifetimes and have come through to heal others. And in this one, I had a very loving upbringing. Although I knew that there was more, I made choices to make myself small on purpose.

Therapist: Why was that?

Nicole: To feel and to understand and have compassion for those souls who aren't ready yet to see and understand the light. I like being a lighthouse shining light for the boats to come in.

Therapist: When Jonathan looks at the life of Beth, does he give any positive criticism? How you could have done things differently?

Nicole: I could have made other choices, but I made the ones that were best for me at that time. And even though I closed my heart off, I had to. It was part of the contract for that lifetime.

Therapist: To what end? Why was that?

Nicole: To experience what that was like. Because normally I don't close my heart off.

Therapist: To learn that's what happens when somebody closes off their heart?

Nicole: Yes.

Therapist: Now that we are here with Jonathan and look at Nicole's life, are there any similarities between Beth's life and Nicole's life? You can ask Jonathan what he thinks about it.

Nicole: In a way. Nicole, even when young, always heard voices. My voice, me, and Jonathan.

Therapist: What about the loss that Nicole has experienced in this life very recently? How does that fit into the plan for this life? What is its purpose? How is Nicole to deal with this?

Nicole: Nicole made a choice to love Bill. She was fulfilling the contract, but she did so willingly knowing that it wouldn't last long. Though there was lots of heartache in between, she was a beacon for him.

Therapist: In alignment with the tendency of the soul group, did Nicole come to help him?

Nicole: Yes.

Therapist: How is Nicole going to deal with this loss? Because we saw in Beth's life that she closed her heart, withdrew within, and ceased to connect. How is it different this time?

Nicole: Nicole still hears Bill. Nicole still sees Bill. Nicole still knows that he's around. She still feels his spirit.

Therapist: She's not closing up this time around?

Nicole: No, there's more to this relationship.

Therapist: Is he part of this soul group family?

Nicole: Yes. They've spent many lifetimes together.

Therapist: Can we connect to Bill's soul right now?

Nicole: Yes.

Therapist: Take a moment. How do you feel?

Nicole: I feel...aaaah (long silence)…..

Therapist: Now that Bill is in the spirit world and Nicole's in this physical world, can the roles be reversed so that Bill can come and help Nicole?

Nicole: He does.

Therapist: How can he help Nicole for the rest of her life? What is the rest of this life about now and how can Bill help?

Nicole: Bill will be the bridge between this world and the other world across the veil. He will help her to share that with others who are ready to hear. And help others to hear from their loved ones.

Therapist: Through Bill, it will be easier for Nicole to stay in touch with this dimension, with this reality.

Nicole: Yes. He had to go the way he did when he did.

Therapist: This was all planned before?

Nicole: Yes. His son needed him to go at that time and she will help his son.

Therapist: Yet Nicole feels something is blocking her from allowing this to flow through her. What is that block?

Nicole: Charlie.

Therapist: Is it left from the last life?

Nicole: Yes. She had to feel today and let it go.

Therapist: Can we do that now? Now that we're here with Jonathan, we are here with the soul group, we are here with Bill. This could be a perfect healing circle to help the soul let go of this pain. Can we let go of this painful energy?

Nicole: Yes.

Therapist: You want to take some time to do this?

Nicole: Yes.

Therapist: Go ahead and tell me everything that happened so I can stay with you.

Nicole: (Speaking very slowly) Charlie is standing in front of me. Jonathan is to my left, he's always to my left. Bill is to my right, he's always to my right now. I can feel the oneness. There's light everywhere. They are showing me the moment Charlie's soul left his body in that lifetime and how he was still right there. And I choose love and know that this is my choice. Charlie is with me in this lifetime too.

Therapist: Who is he in this lifetime?

Nicole: He's David (her oldest son in this lifetime). I should have known.

Therapist: How does it feel now that you're choosing love over shutting down?

Nicole: Very open.

Therapist: The block is gone?

Nicole: Yes.

Therapist: Beautiful. Talking about blocks. Nicole must live in this world and is worried about abundance, finances, and things coming to her. What can this loving group around you tell you? Jonathan, Bill, the guides, the group? How can they console you and help you stay in touch with a sense of abundance and flow?

Nicole: Jonathan's laughing because he says she knows. She needs to be open and trust. There's a difference between working and loving what you do.

Therapist: Does he mean your work as a facilitator with Akashi records, and writing a book?

Nicole: Yes.

Therapist: What can the guide, Jonathan, and the soul group tell you about your writing and working as a practitioner, helping people connect to the Akashi record?

Nicole: Just to keep doing what I'm doing because I'm being prepared. And I don't need to worry about how to write the book. I just need to sit down and write it because the words are just going to come.

Therapist: What about the Akashi record work?

Nicole: There's is more to that. There's going to be more teaching and expanding, and people will come. They already are. But right now, she needs to just focus on healing and allowing and remembering.

Therapist: Should she be involved in the healing process of her two sons (who are grieving the loss of several family members)?

Nicole: Oh yes. She will be. She is.

Therapist: What can Jonathan say about that? To what degree she should be involved and what position should she take?

Nicole: Bill is going to open a door that he could have only done from the heavenly realms. He couldn't have done it from the earthly realm. And he's going to work through her to help her son.

Therapist: Are there any observations, advice, or encouragement that Jonathan or Bill may give to your soul before we return to Nicole's life? Something that perhaps we haven't discussed yet.

91

Nicole: Keep watching for signs, open your heart, and what I mean by doing that is continuing to be open-minded and breathe, follow the breath. That's where the answers lie, it's in the breath and the open-mindedness, and the space. Be outside more, allow the space to envelop you and fill you. In the quiet is where you'll find Bill and where you'll find me. In the silence of the night and the silence in the early mornings.

Therapist: Beautiful. Are there any questions that your soul has for Jonathan and Bill?

Nicole: No, I feel so at peace with them right now.

Therapist: Would you like to stay a few moments quietly with them?

Nicole: Yes.

Therapist: All right. Stay as long as you want. And when you're ready, just let me know. Okay?

We end the session here.

Case 4: Stephen
Scars from past lives

Stephen is a psychologist from California, who suffers from bouts of anxiety, depression, and neck and shoulder issues. As a coping mechanism, he self-medicates with too much cannabis and wants to understand the root causes of his suffering.

We first help him get back to a relevant past life:

Stephen: I'm in the wild west.
Therapist: What are you aware of?
Stephen: I can see some wooden buildings.
Therapist: Is it a big town or a small town?
Stephen: It is a small town.

Therapist: Is there a dirt road or is it more sophisticated?

Stephen: A dirt road. Just one street.

Therapist: How far are you from the town? Are you seeing it from a distance or are you there on the street?

Stephen: Right in the middle of the street.

Therapist: Look down at your feet and tell me what you're wearing on your feet.

Stephen: Field boots and chaps. Spurs.

Therapist: What are you wearing on up?

Stephen: A shirt. A hat. A white-rimmed hat.

Therapist: How old are you now?

Stephen: Thirties or forties? Thirties, younger man.

Therapist: How do you feel being in town right now?

Stephen: I feel a little on edge.

Therapist: Is anything going on that makes you feel on edge?

Stephen: Some kind of anxiety or danger.

Therapist: You think something is about to happen in this place?

Stephen: Perhaps yeah.

Therapist: Do you feel that you're involved or is it something that you're intuiting is going to happen in this place?

Stephen: I am involved.

Therapist: Do you think there's some sort of conflict with somebody?

Stephen: Yes.

Therapist: How dangerous is this?

Stephen: Very.

Therapist: Does it have anything to do with guns?

Stephen: Yes, I have 2 on my hips.

Therapist: Is your hand on it?

Stephen: Yes.

Therapist: I want you to move forward in time a little bit and tell me how this unfolds.

Stephen: I think I get shot in my neck.

Therapist: Is it terminal?

Stephen: Yes.

Therapist: Now, I'm going to count from 3 down to 1. Before we get into this last moment, on the count of 1, we're going to move backward in time, as this man. Now being a young child, back to a relevant moment in your childhood, arriving there at 1. 3,2,1. And you are there now. And tell me what is happening now?

Stephen: I'm on the porch of the house. In the middle of...not much.

Therapist: Can you give me a general description of what this place looks like?

Stephen: A log cabin with a log porch and there's dry grass around.

Therapist: What kind of landscape is it?

Stephen: Pretty flat with mountains in the distance and dry grasses. Must be later in the fall.

Therapist: How old are you now?

Stephen: Pretty young, maybe 7 to 10. Maybe even a little younger.

Therapist: Are there others near you?

Stephen: My family is in the house.

Therapist: Who is part of your family?

Stephen: I feel my mom, a sibling. That's about it.

Therapist: Your dad is not there?

Stephen: I don't think so.

Therapist: Is he just gone or is he like permanently gone?

Stephen: Dad is away.

Therapist: What's the general ambiance and the relationships between everybody?

Stephen: There's more fear again.

Therapist: What are you afraid of?

Stephen: Some kind of danger, maybe Indian invaders, something like that.

Therapist: Is the environment hostile?

Stephen: Well, the house isn't, but something is coming or going to happen.

Therapist: You're aware of that huh?

Stephen: Yea. It's unsafe. That's the first thing that brought back this memory.

Therapist: Is it always like that where you live, like it's just a dangerous place or is it something that's a randomly dangerous situation?

Stephen: Out of the blue.

Therapist: Up till now life has been pretty good?

Stephen: Yes.

Therapist: Did you have a nice relationship with your parents?

Stephen: Some sadness regarding my dad.

Therapist: What happened to him?

Stephen: He had to leave or was gone.

Therapist: Never came back?

Stephen: No.

Therapist: Do you have a nickname or a regular name?

Stephen: Gus.

Therapist: Tell me which part of the world we are in.

Stephen: We're in the Southwest of the United States.

Therapist: Any date comes to mind?

Stephen: 1875.

Therapist: Gus, I'm going to count from 3 down to 1, and on the count of 1 we'll move forward a few years in your life as Gus to another relevant time, at 3, 2, 1. And you're there now. And tell me what is happening now.

Stephen: I'm a late teenage boy and I'm working in a bank. I am dressed in nicer clothes. I feel happy. I feel like there's a good sense of responsibility or I'm doing the right thing.

Therapist: What do you do in this bank?

Stephen: Some kind of financial thing, greeting people. Counting money.

Therapist: How did you get this job, Gus?

Stephen: I was on my own and I started sweeping the floors and helping wherever I could. And the family took me under their wing.

Therapist: They trust you? They like you?

Stephen: Yes.

Therapist: You indicated that you're feeling pretty content at this point in your life, right?

Stephen: Yeah.

Therapist: Can you describe the most significant observation about this moment in your life, Gus, within or around you?

Stephen: I'm a good person trying to do the best I can.

Therapist: You're a sincere worker? A good character?

Stephen: Yes.

Therapist: Where do you live, Gus?

Stephen: Behind the store or bank? A small dark room.

Therapist: What does this room look like?

Stephen: It's small and dusty with a bed and a very small window. With some light that comes in through the window.

Therapist: When you look through the window, what do you

see?

Stephen: Mostly just desert.

Therapist: When you look at yourself, your features, what do you look like?

Stephen: I'm shorter than in this life. My hands are dirty.

Someone can be in a very deep state, completely absorbed in a past life, and still have an awareness of this current life and be able to talk about both lives simultaneously. This can be explained by the fact that to access a past life, one needs to be in a theta state, which is a state of high consciousness. This high consciousness will allow awareness of multiple planes of existence simultaneously.

Stephen: My clothes are different. I think I'm blond. Like a lighter blond. I'm male.

I'm asking him to move forward again in his life as Gus, to somewhere in his twenties.

Stephen: I'm having to fight. There are maybe 3 or 4 men. They're trying to take a woman I love.

Therapist: Tell me what is going on.

Stephen: I can see myself hitting somebody with the butt of a gun.

Therapist: Are they harassing her?

Stephen: Yes.

Therapist: Are you in a relationship with her or do you just like her?

Stephen: Yes, I love her.

Therapist: Is the feeling mutual?

Stephen: Yes.

Therapist: How many men are there?

Stephen: 3, 4 maybe.

Therapist: What is the setting? Where are you?

Stephen: In a dark place. Maybe it's night or inside at night.

Therapist: How successful are you in getting rid of them?

Stephen: I don't think,…. I think I get hurt and I lose consciousness. And she is taken.

Therapist: Let's move to the next day and tell me how this unfolds.

Stephen: Some pain and some anger.

Therapist: Are you still working at the bank?

Stephen: No.

Therapist: What do you do now?

Stephen: Nothing is coming to me about work.

Therapist: How old are you now, Gus?

Stephen: 28.

Therapist: Do you ever see her again?

Stephen: I don't think so.

Therapist: Are you still in the same town as where you worked earlier in the bank?

Stephen: Yes.

Therapist: Where do you live now?

Stephen: In a room above a business. I can see out onto the main street.

Therapist: How are you doing now, at 28?

Stephen: The day, a couple of days after the event, I am recovering, and I am half dressed in a white shirt and overalls.

Therapist: What's your emotional state?

Stephen: Angry and sad.

Therapist: Do you have any plans?
Stephen: Some kind of revenge.
Therapist: Do you know who they are?
Stephen: Vaguely. I can't just go find them.

I'm moving him forward in time again.

Therapist: Tell me what is happening now.
Stephen: I sense anger and guns. I am on the path of revenge.
Therapist: Do you think that this event with your girl has shifted something inside of you?
Stephen: Yes. I don't care anymore. I am doing crimes and whatever to survive.
Therapist: Did you become some sort of bandit?
Stephen: Yeah, more or less.
Therapist: Are you on your own or with a group?
Stephen: There's one other guy, but I'm not that close to him, emotionally.
Therapist: How do you spend your days?
Stephen: I guess we have a wagon and we're going from place to place. And I am hoping that someday I will find the people who did this to that woman.
Therapist: In the meantime, you say you're involved in crime? What kind of things do you do?
Stephen: Hold up places and use my knowledge of banks.
Therapist: What is your state of mind?
Stephen: Anger. Depression. Intoxicants.
Therapist: You don't really care anymore?
Stephen: Yeah.
Therapist: Is it about losing this girl and your pride?

Stephen: Yes.

Therapist: Which is more predominant? Is the pride that they took her from you? Or is it the loss of love?

Stephen: A feeling of how it is unfair. Like, how could they do this to me? I was a good person.

Therapist: Now, Gus, before we move on, what is the most significant observation about your life now, within you or around you?

Stephen: Don't let the fears and the injustice of the world take you off your path.

I'm moving him to the last day of his life.

Therapist: What is happening now?

Stephen: The first thing that comes to me is being surrounded by people in a fight and I feel myself getting shot in the side of the neck.

Therapist: What is this incident of being shot really about?

Stephen: I'm under the impression that I have found the people that have wronged me and that I foolishly jumped into the conflict quicker than I should have.

Therapist: You're outnumbered.

Stephen: Yes.

Therapist: How old are you on th s last day of your life, Gus?

Stephen: 33, 34.

Therapist: Is the setting familiar or is this a new place for you?

Stephen: It seems like a different, but similar dusty town.

Therapist: Now, before we move on, what do you think about this life you just lived?

Stephen: It was hard.

Therapist: In what way?

Stephen: A lot was taken from me.

Therapist: What did you learn from all of this?

Stephen: That I was so attached to others in my life. Their physical form.

Therapist: Because they can be taken away?

Stephen: No, you just don't have to let it ruin everything.

Therapist: He took it too hard, Gus?

Stephen: Yeah.

Therapist: What is your last thought, emotion, or awareness as you leave the body of Gus?

Stephen: Relief.

Therapist: In what way do you feel relief?

Stephen: I tried to bring justice and I didn't and it's okay.

I move him beyond the death scene into a higher place.

Therapist: What is the first thing you notice?

Stephen: I feel my solid color. So orange.

Therapist: How do you feel about yourself? Do you have a shape or is it more like a light or a frequency or an awareness or a combination of these?

Stephen: It's like a frequency, a pulsation.

Therapist: And it's orange you say?

Stephen: Yeah.

Therapist: How does it feel to be this beautiful light frequency?

Stephen: It feels great. Feels very relaxed and expansive.

Therapist: Regarding the energy in which you exist, what impression do you get?

Stephen: I feel it all. And all of a sudden, I sense my father.

Therapist: Does he have a shape or is he more of an energetic presence?

Stephen: I mean, he came to me as my dad from this life. I feel it's kind of purple.

Therapist: What is his energy?

Stephen: It's purple energy.

Therapist: How does he feel?

Stephen: I feel some guidance and some love.

Therapist: You say this life. Do you mean Stephen's life?

Stephen: Yes.

Therapist: Is he here to welcome you?

Stephen: Yeah.

Therapist: I understand that communication at this frequency could be more intuitive. What kind of communication do you get from him?

Stephen: I feel there is kind of a pulling sensation. Like, let's go this way, this way.

Therapist: Let's go with him and tell me where you're going and what it looks like and tell me everything that happens so I can stay with you.

Stephen: We were passing by clouds, and we're being sucked through a Stargate. We're traveling in the tunnel for a while.

Therapist: Is it beautiful, this tunnel?

Stephen: Well, we have now landed somewhere where it's beautiful. It feels like nature.

Therapist: Can you give me a description of what this place looks like?

Stephen: Lights and things are flowing.

Therapist: Are these lights other beings?

Stephen: Of in the distance, I can see other beings. Lots of beings.

Therapist: Is it just you and your dad right now?

Stephen: Yeah, he's bringing me to this place with all these beings.

Therapist: Just keep going and tell me what happens.

Stephen: Kind of flying about. And it's kind of like, I want to stop and chat, but no, he's almost dragging me at this point.

Therapist: You want to chat with some other souls or with him?

Stephen: No, we're above it.

Therapist: He wants to take you somewhere?

Stephen: I guess, and quickly.

Therapist: Tell me what happens when you arrive, where he wants you to be.

Stephen: All of a sudden it feels familiar.

Therapist: You've been here before?

Stephen: Yeah.

Therapist: Tell me about this place.

Stephen: It's hard to, I can't really see much and kind of feel and maybe sense others now.

Therapist: What is the purpose of this place? We're here for a reason I assume.

Stephen: Maybe just to be back with my friends and my soul group.

Therapist: This is a soul group gathering? Who's all here?

Stephen: I can sense my brother who died in Stephen's life: Robert.

Therapist: My mom.

Therapist: How does it feel to see everybody again?

Stephen: It feels like a weight has been lifted from my shoulders.

Therapist: In what way?

Stephen: Like there's no need to fight or to worry. We're all safe here.

Therapist: Is anybody stepping forward to welcome you?

Stephen: A guru-like presence.

Therapist: What does this guru look like? Does he have a name and a form or is he more of an energy?

Stephen: My mind right now is quantifying it like an Indian.

Therapist: Like a Rishi?

Stephen: Yeah.

Therapist: What's his energy?

Stephen: Very bright.

Therapist: Tell me about the guru. Is he a guide for the entire group or is he specifically yours?

Stephen: I feel he is the center and we're all circling around it. Like an atom and he is the nucleus.

Therapist: How does it feel to be in his energy, with all of you together with him?

Stephen: Vibrating, pulsating.

Therapist: How important is the guru to the group?

Stephen: It's like the sun of the universe.

Therapist: Beautiful. Is this a good moment to discuss what happened in the life of Gus? Is that what's being done with the guru and the group?

Stephen: I feel right now, we're just dancing and celebrating together.

Therapist: Yeah, just enjoy for a moment. Take as much time as you want. And when you're ready to take it to the next step, just let me know what happens.

There is a long silence.

Stephen: I am being reminded that everything is okay.

Therapist: Is that by the guru or by the group?

Stephen: It's a feeling. No one has to say it.

Therapist: How does it make you feel?

Stephen: During my life as Gus, I was very always on edge and scared and worried. So, it was a big sigh when it was over.

Therapist: Do you think that Stephen has carried over some of these energies and scars from Gus?

Stephen: Yes.

Therapist: Now that we're here with everybody, and with the guru, is there anything they can do to help us? We are having this pit stop, as it were, checking in. What can be done right now to help Stephen release some of these things?

Stephen: It's okay. Life is unfair and that's okay.

Therapist: What is it that Stephen needs to understand?

Stephen: That suffering is a part of life.

Therapist: What did he carry over from Gus?

Stephen: This feeling of being unsafe, having to fight, having to have a gun to fight.

Therapist: Being on the defense.

Stephen: Yes.

Therapist: Do you think that the shoulder issue of Stephen comes from this bullet?

Stephen: Yes. And also, being hit in the head when that woman was taken from me.

Therapist: We understand that these scars are obviously not as much physically transferred as they are energetic. Can we ask the guru and the group to help iron this out of his astral body?

Stephen: Stephen should continue with stretching and not be so fearful of things being taken away.

Therapist: Now that you understand where this is coming from, is there any healing place or room where your soul can be taken right now, somewhere where you can go and perhaps recover some of this wholeness?

Stephen: After requesting that, I've got the vision of being in a bath, some sort of cleaning area.

Therapist: Tell me about this and get into it a little bit deeper.

Stephen: It feels like when you're under the water in the ocean and you can feel the waves taking you back and forth. Like peeling off layers from my spine.

Therapist: Are they focusing on any particular area?

Stephen: Kind of in the middle of my spine, the heart chakra.

Therapist: Beautiful. Take your time here. No need to hurry….

After a while.

Therapist: What about Stephen's insomnia? Is that also a residue of the past?

Stephen: It is part of some fear, some on-guard feelings.

Therapist: Now that we're here. Is that something that we can also let go of into the beautiful ocean of healing?

Another long silence.

Therapist: How do you feel?

Stephen: They keep continuing to say that it is all right. And a vibration, in the front of my chest.

Therapist: Just take your time. Is the guru still nearby?

Stephen: Yes, but he's not really involved in the cleaning process at this time. Okay. I feel myself coming out.

Therapist: How are you feeling? Better?

Stephen: Lighter. Yes.

Therapist: Beautiful. What happens next?

Stephen: I'm noticing my colors, looking at myself, and seeing a lighter color.

Therapist: Is the energy also different?

Stephen: Yeah. Relaxed. More able to feel the Oneness and less of the last life.

Therapist: Looking at your soul and the birth of Stephen, what was the primary purpose of this birth? What was the main theme and goal to focus on? Is that something we ask a guru or is this something your own soul-Self remembers?

Stephen: I'm trying to put into words what I feel. It's about service. About awakening. About service and awakening others.

Therapist: What is the nature of your soul-Self, looking at yourself beyond Stephen, beyond Gus? Do you as a group, as souls, represent a common purpose, a common theme, and a common interest?

Stephen: One of the first things that came to my mind was that we were dancing around a pole or something. We're erecting something, we're dancing around a pole, like a Mayflower pole.

Therapist: What does this mean?

Stephen: It's almost like the medicine idea of two snakes around a pole, but that doesn't feel quite right.

Therapist: It is like a totem?

Stephen: We're trying to create stability, like a channel between the higher and the lower.

Therapist: You're trying to bring about a higher consciousness in the world, a higher frequency?

Stephen: Yes, something like that.

Therapist: Do you work on that together as a group or also as individuals?

Stephen: We all dance together.

Therapist: Do you do that only on earth, or do you do that work also in the astral plane between lives?

Stephen: I'm feeling we're doing it in the astral right now.

Therapist: Not necessarily on the earthly plane as a group?

Stephen: I feel that in this life, I have encountered some others that are doing similar things.

Therapist: What makes you take up these births, separate from what the group is doing?

Stephen: To grow and to learn and to know the struggles.

Therapist: How successful do you feel Stephen, who is 36 now, has been able to express himself regarding his highest purpose?

Stephen: I'm happy that I'm working in the right direction.

Therapist: Looking at the big picture, looking at Gus, looking at Stephen, looking at your soul purpose, looking at the group and your guru, what is important for Stephen to understand, so that he can serve better and use his talents and education in the best possible way?

Stephen: Use the pain to guide your path.

Therapist: Why is that important?

Stephen: The pain will guide me to the right solutions.

Therapist: Is there a way to transcend that pain into something higher, something more positive?

Stephen: Understanding the human experience. It's all like a roller coaster. Enjoying the dips and the rises.

Therapist: Being aware now of your disembodied Self, and just coming out of this healing and cleansing space, is there a way to bring that consciousness, joy, and lightness into the awareness of Stephen? Not to forget the pain necessarily as it could perhaps help him be compassionate to others, but to embody some of the divine joy that he can feel now on the astral level.

Stephen: Continue to serve and meditate, perhaps explore

some plant medicine, and not be afraid to take a different path.

Therapist: Is there a particular location on this earth that would be more conducive to his growth and his expression?

Stephen: I don't think he's found it yet.

Therapist: How can the guru help?

Stephen: Keep looking and trust your heart.

At this point, he started to lose his deep absorption into the high state of consciousness a bit and I helped him reconnect. It is not always easy for the client to maintain this state for a long time. It depends on training and preparation. Sometimes a strong emotional experience can also get one out of the experience.

Therapist: Go a little bit deeper again, and allow yourself to feel the soul group, the guru, and the teacher. The mind fluctuates now and then. It's okay. It doesn't matter. Especially now that we're going deeper and deeper, deeper, and deeper, and stepping from the head back into the heart space and from that heart into that astral Self, the divine consciousness. Find yourself shifting into that state automatically. Focusing on the joy of that light when you came out of this healing room. Experiencing that sense of relief that you felt. You're back in this infinite realm right now. Going deeper and deeper, deeper, and deeper into that joyful connection. Focusing on the guru and the energy of the group, knowing that what they want for you is the highest joy.

Therapist: Now looking at Stephen from a detached distance, and how he struggles sometimes with depression and insomnia, how can the guru and the group help him overcome some of these issues?

Stephen: Be okay with being sad. It's okay to cry.

Therapist: Do you think some of that comes from Gus? What is the original cause of the sadness?

Stephen: This is from before.

Therapist: From before Gus?

Stephen: Yes.

Therapist: Let's go back a little bit and have a quick look at where this originated.

Stephen: I'm in some kind of opium den, very skinny. A life with a lot of sadness.

Therapist: Where did this take place?

Stephen: Southern China.

Therapist: Was this a case of addiction? What was the root of that sadness?

Stephen: Once again, many things were taken, and more and more things got stripped away. And all there was left was the opium.

Normally, as therapists, we avoid initiating healing, as we prefer the client or the guide or group to initiate it. But I felt he needed some help here, a nudge.

Therapist: What if we all came together for a moment? The guide, your soul group, as if holding you and crying with you, going through this experience together, and showing you that you were never alone. And that you are not alone now. Realizing that this is something you had to go through, perhaps some karma. And that it is over now. That only the teaching remains.

Stephen: I can feel my girlfriend here. She's with the group saying it's okay.

Therapist: How does it feel?

Stephen: Reassuring.

Therapist: Do you feel that you can begin letting some of that go?

Stephen: Yes. My different lives have taught me different emotions. The more you feel like you're open, the wider and more expanded it gets.

Therapist: So, your soul has developed a lot of bandwidth to understand all the different nuances and variations of the suffering and pain of mankind?

Stephen: Yeah.

Therapist: Making you also a better tool, a better empathizer for the work that you do.

Stephen: Yes.

Therapist: But at the same time, don't you think that perhaps we don't want you to carry it? You understand it. You can feel, you can laugh, cry, you can sympathize, and empathize. That is your beauty. But at the same time, correct me if I'm wrong, there comes a point in your evolution that you can let it all go. You can be filled with love, joy, and grace.

Stephen: To rise above it.

Therapist: Do you think you're ready to take that step?

Stephen: Most of the time.

Therapist: Let's ask the guru. What do you want as a soul?

Stephen: I want to feel the unity and be connected to this central pole.

Therapist: Do you think we can take a few moments and step into that future, and step into the experience?

Stephen: It feels like it's beyond the soul group, beyond everything, like all expansive.

Therapist: Good, go into it all the way.

Stephen: I'm like, flying or suspended in mid-air. No gravity, no nothing.

Therapist: Just let it all go and give yourself permission to fully expand and merge.

Stephen: I feel drawn to how people feel this feeling.

Therapist: Take a moment and integrate it now consciously into the body and mind of Stephen. Can he feel that?

Stephen: Yes.

Therapist: Beautiful. Now, from this perspective, how do you look at cannabis?

Stephen: It's a temporary search for an eternal state.

Therapist: So how would you reframe this relationship with cannabis, now that you can feel the joy coming from a higher source?

Stephen: I can see how it's been helpful, especially when life is particularly challenging, but that it is not the solution.

Therapist: What is the solution?

Stephen: Getting to a less populated area. Continuing to find ways to help people and to have joy in my career or in my healing of others.

Therapist: The spirit world is wide open to you. Is there anything else we need to see or experience, or do you feel you've seen what you needed to today? How do you feel?

Stephen: I feel like this is an important shift.

We slowly end the session here.

Case 5: Derick
The mason

Derick is a 77-year-old retired dentist and ex-Mormon. During his past life as Nick, though he speaks in very short sentences, he is a very advanced and sensitive soul.

Therapist: Now, tell me. Is it daytime or nighttime?
Derick: Daytime.
Therapist: Are you inside or outside?
Derick: Outside.
Therapist: What is the first thing you notice?

Derick: Golden leaves in the forest.

Therapist: Is it Fall?

Derick: Yes.

Therapist: Look down at your feet. What, if anything, are you wearing on your feet?

Derick: Loose, soft shoes of some kind.

Therapist: What else are you wearing?

Derick: Loose shirt and pants.

Therapist: How would you describe this type of clothing? Nice, poor, or working class?

Derick: Practical.

Therapist: Are you a man or a woman?

Derick: I'm not sure.

Therapist: If you look at your skin. What is the color of your skin?

Derick: White.

Therapist: What is your age, approximately?

Derick: 13.

Therapist: I want you to look straight ahead of you and tell me what you see.

Derick: Deeper forest.

Therapist: What are you doing in the forest?

Derick: Exploring animals and plants.

Therapist: Is it for fun or do you have a purpose?

Derick: It's a purpose that's fun.

Therapist: Do you live nearby?

Derick: Not close.

Therapist: What can you tell me about where you live?

Derick: (sobbing) It's not good.

Therapist: It's not good?
Derick: No.
Therapist: What can you tell me?
Derick: The people I'm with are not good.
Therapist: Is that why you are in the forest?
Derick: That's why I prefer the forest.
Therapist: How are you feeling?
Derick: Free, temporarily.
Therapist: What can you tell me about your living situation and the people that are not good?
Derick: (sighing).
Therapist: Are you living in a town or in nature, in a city?
Derick: In nature.
Therapist: Your house is in a remote place?
Derick: Very.
Therapist: What does the house look like?
Derick: Wood, mud, brick, cobbled together.
Therapist: These people you live with are no good?
Derick: (sighing).
Therapist: Is it your parents, or are these other people?
Derick: I think they're other people.
Therapist: How did you end up living there with them?
Derick: I didn't have a choice.
Therapist: How come?
Derick: (with great difficulty) They....they took me.
Therapist: These people took you?
Derick: Yes!
Therapist: Like they kidnapped you?
Derick: Yes, against my will and my family's.

Therapist: How could they get away with that? They just stole you or were your parents aware of what happened?

Derick: I don't know. They (bad guys) were strong and overpowering.

Therapist: What do you have to do when you are living with these people?

Derick: Anything they want me to.

Therapist: Are you like a slave to them?

Derick: A servant.

Therapist: A servant. So what time are we living in? What is the date, approximately?

Derick: 1710.

Therapist: You are living far away in the countryside. What is the landscape like?

Derick: Hilly forest.

Therapist: What is the climate like?

Derick: Warm now.

Therapist: In what part of the world are we?

Derick: Not sure.

Therapist: It will come to you in a moment. I'm going to count from 3 down to 1. And we're going to move forward in your life, to a relevant moment as this person, but a few years older. Going from 3,2,1 and we are there now. And tell me what is happening now?

Derick: Trying to escape.

Therapist: How old are you now?

Derick: 15.

Therapist: Are you successful in escaping?

Derick: Yes.

Therapist: Tell me, what happens next?

Derick: Happy to be free. Afraid to provide.
Therapist: For your food and your lodging?
Derick: For survival.
Therapist: Right. Where are you going?
Derick: To water. A lake, a stream.
Therapist: How are you feeling?
Derick: Freer.
Therapist: How long have you been with these people?
Derick: Can't remember.
Therapist: A long time?
Derick: Several years.
Therapist: Move forward a little bit in time, till you get out of the forest and to wherever you are going.
Derick: (long pause) Not sure where to go. I want to be safe.
Therapist: I'm going to count from 3 down to 1 and you will move forward in time to a time when you're away from this place. You're arriving there at 1 and now 3,2,1 and you're there now. Tell me where you are now and what is happening.
Derick: I see a small village. Out of logs. Houses. Good weather. I'm safer.
Therapist: Are you going to stay in this place?
Derick: Until I can totally provide for myself. People help me.
Therapist: Somebody is taking you in?
Derick: Briefly.
Therapist: And then, what do you do next?
Derick: Learn a trade.
Therapist: You're a young man?
Derick: Yes.
Therapist: What trade are you learning?

Derick: Stones, stone mason.

Therapist: You like it?

Derick: Yes. It's creative. Helpful, Constructive.

Therapist: Is someone teaching you?

Derick: Yes.

Therapist: What does the place look like where you are learning?

Derick: Large building, several people. They care about teaching.

Therapist: Are you any good at it?

Derick: I enjoy it.

Therapist: You enjoy it?

Derick: I'm good at it. I can make things. I like to make things that will make people feel good.

Therapist: Does it take a long time to learn to do this?

Derick: I learn fast. It's natural to me.

Therapist: Are you able to stay there while you're being taught? Is it kind of a board and lodging?

Derick: Yes.

Therapist: You have a leader or a boss or somebody who is showing you? Like a mentor, or how does that work?

Derick: Yes.

Therapist: What kind of person is that, the one who is teaching you?

Derick: Kind, cares, sees my potential. And supports it.

Therapist: Are you safe now?

Derick: Yes.

Therapist: What is your inner state of being right now? How do you feel in general in your life right now in this place?

Derick: Hopeful, looking forward to the future. Providing for myself and finding friends of similar interests.

Therapist: Do you have a nickname or a regular name that comes to mind?

Derick: Nick. Like Nicholas but Nick.

Therapist: I'll call you Nick. OK?

Derick: Yes.

I'm moving him forward in time in the life of Nick.

Derick: Working with partners. Appreciated, successful.

Therapist: What are you building?

Derick: A large house. Everything is gray.

Therapist: Everything is gray? The stone or the place itself?

Derick: The stone. The building materials.

Therapist: With how many people are you working together?

Derick: Four.

Therapist: Do you know the people that you are working with?

Derick: Fellow masons.

Therapist: Do you have a good relationship with them?

Derick: Yes. Finally.

Therapist: Life is better now?

Derick: More secure.

Therapist: How old are you now, Nick?

Derick: 25

Therapist: Where are we? In which part of the world? If you look at the landscape, at the building you're making. Where are we?

Derick: Mountains, forests.

Therapist: Is it beautiful there?

Derick: It is.

Therapist: What is the weather like? Is it warm?

Derick: Four seasons.

Therapist: In what kind of style are you building? Is it a fancy place or more like a normal house?

Derick: Fancier than normal. More artistic.

Therapist: Do you carve each stone that you use to build the house? How does it work? Do you carve ornaments? What is your job?

Derick: I'm the artistic one.

Therapist: Yes? Do you do the ornaments?

Derick: Yes.

Therapist: Does it mean you get paid better; does it make any difference?

Derick: It matters. It matters to me.

Therapist: You like to make something nice?

Derick: Yes!

Therapist: How do you feel at this point in your life?

Derick: More peaceful.

Therapist: Where do you live?

Derick: Small house along the side.

Therapist: Do you live alone? Or is there anybody with you?

Derick: Partners.

Therapist: You live with the other workers?

Derick: Yes.

Therapist: You don't have a wife yet?

Derick: No. I'd like one. But I can't provide.

Therapist: You don't make enough as a mason?

Derick: It's not money. I'm not able to provide, somehow. It bothers me.

Therapist: In what way are you not able to provide? If it's not money?

Derick: I don't know what it is.

Therapist: You feel that something is obstructing you?

Derick: Yes, and I don't know what it is.

Therapist: Don't worry. It will come to you in a moment.

The client told me afterward that he realized that Nick was missing part or all of a leg. He couldn't climb the scaffolding. He did the carving, and his buddies carried the stone up and set it. Women saw him as a cripple and a savage from the forest. It's not uncommon for a client to remember more of these past life experiences after the session.

Therapist: If you could describe to me the most relevant observation about your life at this point, either within you or around you, what would it be?

Derick: I'm making progress. Overcoming something.

Therapist: What is it that you are trying to overcome?

Derick: Socially, to be accepted. Be worthy.

Therapist: You think it has something to do with the fact that you were taken away from your parents and the things that followed?

Derick: (crying) Yes.

Therapist: Your background?

Derick: Yes.

Therapist: Is it something that you feel or is it something that you feel others are judging you for?

Derick: Both.

I'm moving him forward in time again.

Therapist: Tell me Nick, what is happening?

Derick: Celebration. Some achievement.

Therapist: Tell me about it.

Derick: I can be proud of what I've made.

Therapist: What did you make?

Derick: A beautiful water fountain in the middle of the town square.

Therapist: It's kind of important in the context of the town. Right?

Derick: I'm appreciated.

Therapist: All the town folks are here to celebrate your achievement.

Derick: Yes.

Therapist: How does it make you feel?

Derick: Worthy, recognized.

Therapist: How old are you now, Nick?

Derick: Middle-aged.

Therapist: Who is all there with you as the celebration is going on?

Derick: Apprentices I can teach.

Therapist: Is this a milestone for you that you can teach now?

Derick: Yes.

Therapist: How does this feel to teach the youngsters?

Derick: I'm no longer the cast out, the wasted child. I can help them become providers, teach them, and be appreciated. So they don't have to go through what I did.

Therapist: You're very much aware of that?

Derick: Certainly, yes.

Therapist: How do they look at you, these boys?

Derick: Wiser.

Therapist: Do they love you?

Derick: Yes. So, I can finally love myself more.

Therapist: You are in a good place right now?

Derick: Yes.

Therapist: Are you still living alone, or do you have a relationship?

Derick: Still alone. But I'm appreciated. I can love myself. I can give to others. I can make beauty.

Therapist: Do you have a workshop where you work with your boys? Where do you work?

Derick: Yes, I am a master.

Therapist: Do you have a place where you live and work?

Derick: It's well conceived, well provided, furnished.

Therapist: Did you buy that yourself?

Derick: I earned it. From my first master.

Therapist: He gave it to you?

Derick: He passed it.

Therapist: Wow, he passed it on to you?

Derick: Yes.

Therapist: That's a great compliment. Is it not?

Derick: That's why I could appreciate myself more.

Therapist: Because he saw something in you, and he gave it to you?

Derick: Of value. I have a value.

Therapist: That is so beautiful. Now everybody is celebrating your beautiful creation.

Derick: Many people, everybody. There is opposition.

Therapist: Yes, why is that?

Derick: They feel threatened by my success.

Therapist: Jealousy?

Derick: Competition.

Therapist: Are you talking about other masons or just people in general?

Derick: It must be other masons.

I move him forward in his life to an elderly age.

Therapist: Tell me what is happening now, Nick.

Derick: (emotionally) I have people around me who love me. I'm older. I'm quite old. Getting feeble. But they comfort me. Show me love. Tell me I have value.

Therapist: Who are these people?

Derick: People I've served and cared for as they grew.

Therapist: Students?

Derick: They were students. And others who recognize that I've accomplished something to pass along.

Therapist: You're a respectable Elder in the town?

Derick: Yes, as I always wanted to be.

Therapist: How does it feel to arrive at this level of accomplishment and self-worth?

Derick: Successful. Overcame some great difficulties.

Therapist: Do you still live in the same place where you were teaching these youngsters earlier?

Derick: Same village.

Therapist: Still the same workshop?

Derick: I don't go there anymore.

Therapist: No, you don't?

Derick: They do the work.

Therapist: You're kind of retired?

Derick: I'm retired. They provide food, comfort, and a place to live.

Therapist: Is it still yours or did you give it to somebody?

Derick: (emotionally) I passed the business on to a worthy student.

Therapist: And they look out for you?

Derick: Yes.

Therapist: Beautiful. What's the most relevant observation that you have about this moment in life, Nick?

Derick: I'm weak in body, but strong in spirit. And wish I can teach others to grow.

Therapist: Is this important to you?

Derick: To be strong in spirit, to be strong in loving, in beauty and people.

Therapist: Beautiful.

Derick: They return the love. Almost more than I feel I deserve. I appreciate it. I allow them to serve me. Because they also need to learn to serve. Like I had to learn. To give service and now I must learn to receive their service. Both sides of the coin.

Therapist: Beautiful.

Derick: I don't have much longer.

I move him to the last day of his life.

Therapist: Tell me how old you are, Nick, on this last day of your life.

Derick: 80.

Therapist: Is there anything going on around you or with you that suggests that your physical death will come this day?

Derick: Peace.

Therapist: You're peaceful?

Derick: Yes.

Therapist: Are you ill or what is the situation right now?

Derick: I'm just through! Nothing more to accomplish.

Therapist: Where are you now?

Derick: I'm peacefully ascending. I'm free!

Therapist: Before you go, tell me what you think about this life that you just lived.

Derick: It was noble in what I accomplished compared to what I had to start with. It was a struggle. But it made me grow.

Therapist: In what way did it make you grow? What did you learn?

Derick: That I could create beauty. I found the strength that was in my inner self and spirit, that could overlook adversity and opposition. The nastiness and meanness in others. I could just let go. I learned to grow in the goal that I had in coming, to learn to be bigger in my spirit than what I saw in people around me. But see it without looking down on them. To see it in the way that I could be an example to some to whom it would matter.

Therapist: Beautiful. What is your last thought or awareness as you leave the body?

Derick: (deep sigh) Freedom. Freedom...release from the difficulties of mortality.

I move him through the death scene.

Therapist: Where are you now in relation to the body that you left behind? Can you still see it?

Derick: Very distant.

Therapist: Is there anybody near you at the time of your death?

Derick: I don't see any.

Therapist: What are you feeling?

Derick: Freedom.

Therapist: How do you feel about your death?

Derick: It was a step forward.

Therapist: In what way?

Derick: I bring with me the lessons I learned. I was able to serve, and I feel that was important to me.

I help him move beyond his past life and death into a higher place.

Therapist: What is the first thing you notice?

Derick: Waves of light. The contours and topography are interesting. It's like they are curves of light running from my right around to the left as there are ridges. Some lighter, some darker. But all leading to even more light.

Therapist: Do you have the feeling you are moving into space, or do you feel it is kind of unfolding around you as you connect better and deeper?

Derick: I don't feel movement.

Therapist: When you look at your own Soul-Self, do you feel you have a light body or is it more consciousness, vibration, or frequency? How would you describe your own divine identity?

Derick: A light, positive. It has so much of what I always wanted.

Therapist: This last life, was it one that helped you advance?

Derick: It was necessary...to experience struggle, to experience negativity. To know that I could rise above it...at any time. Untouched by it. Other than being stronger, caring more.

Therapist: Now that you're in touch with your true inner Self, is there anybody near you? Or do you feel it's more your awareness that is free and self-luminous? How do you feel in relation to this space in which you are right now?

Derick: I'm aware of being somewhere. I feel like I need society, but I don't know where it is.

Therapist: Just reach out and feel yourself connecting deeper and deeper. Perhaps soon divine help may come your way. Find yourself connecting deeper and deeper. See the beauty of your own Self as well as the energy around you. How would you describe the energy around you?

Derick: All positive...The light. I feel like I don't need people.

Therapist: Do you feel that your own Self is wise enough to assess your evolution so far?

Derick: I have learned that I can. I can receive light and appreciation without having to fight for it.

Therapist: Now that you're here in this frequency, where you say that you are receiving light, is there anything you do in terms of rejuvenation or recharging? What is it that you do in this realm when you arrive?

Derick: I might be recharging, but I feel connected. Connected to light. Beyond people.

Therapist: Beautiful. Just connect yourself even more to that light. To the divine essence, the Source. Give yourself the time to connect in the deepest way possible.

Derick: It's more peaceful, more appreciated. I have more to give. I love to give.

Therapist: When you look upon your past and perhaps some of the lives you have lived before, and look at your evolution, how do you feel things have been going so far?

Derick: I have been my own personal obstacle. My biggest challenge has been to accept myself. To accept who I am, what I am. It's not seen by others.

Therapist: How do you feel now, when you distance yourself from all these incarnations and you look at your divine essence? How do you feel about the nature of your true being as separate from these bodies?

Derick: It doesn't belong in any of those bodies. It's too big and powerful, strong. There are things it would burn. It's going home, (emotional) going home. I want so badly to be home. To go home.

Therapist: Just take a moment and feel you're home now. Your true Self, your true essence is here, is home. Does it feel like home now in this state of being?

Derick: I'm looking in. I'm looking in at ...I'm judging myself too strongly that I'm not worthy of it. But I do. I do belong. (very emotional) I do feel love. I feel light. As all things go around and around. I'm just starting on this beautiful journey around. Gaining...gaining more light. Learning to use it. Maybe now I can help others benefit from it. I feel what my own abilities are. There's so much I can give. So much I can teach. I love to teach. Not to be bigger or more advanced than others, but to see others awaken. Up to their potential, their knowledge. That's one of my abilities. To help others learn about theirs.

Therapist: Is that what your true spirit nature is? To bring light to others, to help others?

Derick: Yes! That's when I feel fulfilled. That's where I feel successful.

Therapist: How does that translate into the life of Derick? This capability to help and serve others. Is that what he has been doing in his life as well?

Derick: I could have done better.

Therapist: In the remaining phase of his life, if you could help Derick, what would you tell him?

Derick: There's so much. So much to say, to pass on. That those who didn't value me and who belittled me were not true, were not friends, were trying to step on me. Recognize that I am beyond that. That I find peace in not partaking in their negativity. But in focusing on the beauty that life really is. Despite the world that we are living in. It's so fulfilling to blend and meld with advanced people.

Therapist: Now that you see yourself in this astral plane and you see the grandeur of your own beautiful Self, the luminous One, whose nature is to love and to share, and you look at Derick at 77 years old, how would you like to inspire Derick to use those remaining years of his life in the best possible way?

Derick: I need to learn to be more social, to be less influenced by people around me. There are those who need my example, who need the energy that I have to transmit and show. There are those around me in this life who need to see the nobility of spirit. I need to be willing to show myself, my spirit.

Therapist: Why does he have difficulty being that leader? What stands in the way of that?

Derick: I just need to rise above it.

Therapist: Is it something from a past life?

Derick: I'm sure it is. Perhaps I've failed as a leader at some time.

Therapist: You were successful as a master, as a stone mason, where you shared love and knowledge to help many people. You were a leader in your own right in that life. How can we integrate the achievement and confidence of that life with Derick?

Derick: I think I need to see that telling other people what they should do is not controlling them. I have such an aversion to control. To being and having been controlled, so mercilessly. I do not want, in any way, to exert control over another person.

Therapist: You realize that by sharing light and love, like you are sharing it now in the astral plane, you are not controlling anybody, right? You're giving love and you're sharing light. It has nothing to do with control.

Derick: I understand that academically. I don't feel successful in sharing it. I need to share it. I need to give it. I need to be an example by my actions. By giving appropriate counsel at appropriate times to those who need it. And realize that, in so doing, I'm not controlling. I'm offering. I feel like I've sacrificed so much in the past, in my lives, in order to achieve recognition, that would grant me the right to counsel, to advise, to be a guide. Perhaps that is leadership.

Therapist: It's flowing because of your internal accomplishment. It's because of who you are. You have become that wise, loving soul that is full of light, love, care, and compassion. Who is aware and understands that he doesn't want to control. He just wants to love. Isn't that enough to qualify you? Because at the end of the day, your purpose is to help, right? To shine a light. Don't you feel that you are more than ready for that?

Derick: I feel that I'm filled with light and that I must share what I can. That I can overcome my reluctance. My fear of failure. My fear of hurting anyone.

Therapist: You can look at it in two ways. You can look at all the possible fear and pain that could come with that. Or you can look inside, and see the source of that love, which is that light within you, that divine being.

Derick: Yes.

Therapist: Would you like to take a moment to be in that light and see the beauty of that within yourself?

Derick: Yes

Therapist: Let's go a little bit deeper into the divine being and merge yourself in it completely for a moment. Take all the time you want and when you're ready to continue, just let me know.

Derick: Many of my soul group have given me support and shown me love. Have shown me in this duality of this world the negative in a loving way, that I could see to grow above it. I thank them for it. I give myself the right to be loved. To give love to myself, that I can show it to others.

Therapist: That's beautiful. Isn't it interesting, when we look at your last life as a stone mason you gave yourself permission to be worthy of respect as a mason and as somebody in society. And now, you are lifting it to a whole new level. Now, you're giving yourself permission to be a light worker. To be a giver of love and light. Isn't that beautiful?

Derick: And use that love to heal.

Therapist: Yes.

Derick: To be a healer.

Therapist: You're accepting yourself as a light being. You've changed your identity from being a physical being to a divine being.

Derick: I thank you. I thank you.

Therapist: That's who you are. You're not a human being. You're a divine being working in a human body. Once you accept that within yourself, then your service is just shining forth your true nature. You're not doing anything. You're just allowing that self-identity to express itself. Like an artist. Like a mason. Like you're sculpting reality around you in the most beautiful, poetic way.

Derick: I've known I had that light. I've known I had it within me. I've known I had that healing energy.

Therapist: You are that! It's not just happening.

Derick: I've known that's me. Somehow in this life, through my associations, I've let it be dampened. Unrightly, unrighteous.

Therapist: You've come to this turning point, ready to accept this in your life as Derick. You've come so far.

Derick: Thank you. I've been told many times, "Prepare yourself". "Prepare yourself". I have sought to understand that.

Therapist: Do you see it now? Can you feel it? It's more important to feel it.

Derick: (emotionally) Yes, yes, I feel it. And I'm close... to recognizing my potential. My ability. My real Self.

Therapist: It's not an ego thing. It's a divine thing. And as such, you don't have to worry. You just manifest that reality that is innate in you and innate in all beings.

Derick: Thank you.

Therapist: What do you feel?

Derick: It feels like I am becoming one with myself after being separated for a very long time.

Therapist: Just take a moment and allow the oneness.

Derick: Thank you.

Derick: I'm both! I'm both male and female. A complete androgynous spirit, with the best manifestations of each gender.

Therapist: Beautiful.

Derick: I'm a beautiful woman. I'm an awesome warrior. I'm thankful to be me. I have resisted for so long. Not wanting to accept myself, thinking I was too negative, too unworthy. And now I know I'm whole. I have nothing to be sad about or to be sorry for. But that I'm one to be proud of. Even for myself to be proud of.

Therapist: And to see that, behind this earthly manifestation, there is your divine essence. That is who you really are.

Derick: I've been touched by it, off and on, on different occasions. And I thank the energy for having reached through to me.

Therapist: It's a matter of your personal evolution. Do you feel you're ready for that?

Derick: Yes! I love the energy.

Therapist: And from this perspective, what would you tell Derick?

Derick: Don't be ashamed. Don't feel less. And always remember your strength, your spirit, and be willing to show it, to share it. That is your mission. To help some of your soul mates who are depending on you, rise to it, feel worthy of it, to do it. Help them. In so doing, you're helped. Love and service are inseparable.

Therapist: Beautiful. That's what you said as a mason, as well. Isn't it interesting? Is there anything that Derick would want to know or needs from your higher self?

Derick: Ahh, let me think. He needs to know that he's forgiven by anybody he might have hurt or harmed in any way. So he can rise, unfettered.

Therapist: What does your higher Self say in response to that?

Derick: (loudly) That I've been a fool! I've been a fool to think I was less. (emotional) I'm worthy. I am not that undeveloped body and mind, though it was intelligent. A learning ground from which I had to rise and be recognized. That this life that I chose is not me. I can leave it behind, feeling good and successful. And feel recognized by those whom I have lifted up. To whom I have been an example. I can feel, as Derick, successful in all the spiritual ways that matter to him.

Therapist: What does that final state of spiritual accomplishment look like?

Derick: I'm not sure I understand the question.

Therapist: How can we help Derick connect to that spiritual center for the remainder of his life? Why wait, right? See if you can go beyond Derick for a moment to connect to that highest realm.

Derick: Anything that Derick thought was the reward of goodness or the reward of being right, the physical, the sexual, the warmth, the companionship, is nothing compared to what's ahead. (pause) It is nothing to regret leaving, because what's ahead is such a complete total whole-body sensation of wholeness.

Therapist: Can you feel this now?

Derick: I feel that potential.

Therapist: I want you to go a little bit deeper and feel yourself going into that now. Go a little bit deeper, and deeper and lift yourself as high as you are capable of at this moment.

Derick: Yes.

Therapist: Just be natural about it and see yourself going deeper and deeper. So we can give Derick a little bit of a taste.

Derick: Ah, the world has no idea.

Therapist: You can feel it now?

Derick: I had uncovered brief glimpses in the past. And now ... validate them.

Therapist: Now remember this state. I want you to show Derick that this is his potential even while he is in the body. He doesn't have to wait to die. He can ascend to this consciousness. He can live and breathe this consciousness and he can share this consciousness.

Derick: It's a gift.

Therapist: Remember this.

Derick: (pause) Thank you.

Therapist: How do you feel?

Derick: Whole.

Therapist: Are there any more questions or anything else that we need to address?

Derick: Do I have a companion? Am I alone?

Therapist: Why don't you look around yourself in this state and feel?

Derick: (long pause) Derick has had a lonely life.

Therapist: What do you feel from this divine perspective?

Derick: He'll never be alone again. His soul mates will join him as it's necessary and appropriate. He'll join them as they need him. Him, or Her. The whole package. I'm not alone. And Derick should stop feeling that way. He should find society and should find it pleasing and wholesome.

Therapist: Is there anything else?

Derick: Only if you see anything that I can't.

Therapist: If you feel that this wholesomeness is the last beautiful memory of today, then we can bring it to a close here.

Derick: I just want to remember it. I feel whole. I feel like one. I want to always be able to recall this feeling of oneness whenever I need it.

Therapist: Now before we bring this to a close, why don't you just stay for a few minutes and let this be imprinted into Derick's mind, body, and soul.

Derick: Thank you.

We slowly bring the session to a close.

Case 6: Bianca
The sacrifice of self

Bianca is a 57-year-old woman from California, going through a painful divorce, without a job, facing great uncertainty about her future.

Therapist: Now, tell me, is it daytime or nighttime?
Bianca: It's daytime.
Therapist: Are you inside or outside?
Bianca: I'm outside.
Therapist: Are you alone or with someone?
Bianca: I'm not sure.

Therapist: That's okay. Looking down at your feet, tell me what, if anything, you see on your feet.

Bianca: They're a very simple sort of homemade, leather shoeing, boot.

Therapist: What else are you wearing?

Bianca: A long skirt.

Therapist: Is it a one-piece or a multiple-piece skirt?

Bianca: I feel like I have something underneath. It's simple. It's blue, but it's long and it's simple.

Therapist: When you say simple, does it feel like it's ordinary as in poor, or just simple as in middle class?

Bianca: No, I feel like it's ordinary and not poor, but ...

Therapist: But decent.

Bianca: Yeah, definitely not rich.

Therapist: Take a look at the color of your skin.

Bianca: It's white.

Therapist: And what is your age, approximately?

Bianca: I feel like a young woman. I feel like I'm 28.

Therapist: I want you to look straight ahead and tell me what you see there.

Bianca: I see open prairie space and the sky, and it feels like it's cold and grayish.

Therapist: When you look around, what else do you see behind you or on the side of you?

Bianca: I know I'm standing in front of my home and it's a wooden home. It's a simple wooden home.

Therapist: Is it one story or multiple stories?

Bianca: It's one story. I feel like my husband built that.

Therapist: What can you tell me about this place? Are you alone here or are there multiple houses in this area?

Bianca: No, we are alone here and there's a modest corral. Maybe some cows, some horses. I feel like we're in the middle of nowhere trying to eke out a living. I don't know why we're here at this place.

Therapist: How do you feel being here in this place?

Bianca: I don't like it.

Therapist: You don't like it?

Bianca: No, I don't like it.

Therapist: What don't you like about it?

Bianca: It's sparse. There are no trees and there's no green.

Therapist: Is it flat or are there mountains?

Bianca: It's flat. I can see mountains off in the distance. You can get to the mountains probably in a day or so. You can get to the town. It's not that far, but where we are, it's just out in the middle of nowhere and I don't like it. I don't like it.

Therapist: Is it just you and your husband in this place?

Bianca: Yep. Yeah.

Therapist: How long have you been here in this place, approximately? Does it feel like a long or a short time?

Bianca: It feels in between. It doesn't feel like a long time. It doesn't feel like a short time. It was long enough to build this house and be here. Maybe a year.

Therapist: Now, if you tell me, what is most significant either within you or around you about this moment?

Bianca: That I'm stuck here. I'm stuck here.

Therapist: Where do you feel this is? In which continent?

Bianca: I feel like it is in the North American continent. I want to say the plains.

Therapist: Ok.

Bianca: The plains. It's in the plains.

Therapist: All right, good. Now, I'm going to count from 3 down to 1. We're going to move forward in time to another significant moment in your life as this young woman getting older now, and on the count of 1, be there. As I count from 3, 2, 1, and you are there now, and tell me what is happening now?

Bianca: I'm holding a baby. I feel like I just gave birth. It's inside. Everything's very warm. Again, it's cold outside, and I have this baby, and I don't know why I want to cry.

Therapist: Allow your feelings to be as authentic as you want them to be. Are these happy tears or sad ones?

Bianca: I don't feel like they're happy tears.

Therapist: No?

Bianca: No.

Therapist: Why not? Tell me about it.

Bianca: I don't feel like I want this baby. I feel like there's nothing to offer this baby. It's a girl. It's a girl baby, and I feel like she'll be stuck like me.

Therapist: Are you still in the same place?

Bianca: Yeah. Yeah. I feel like it's the same place.

Therapist: Right.

Bianca: But we've done well.

Therapist: In what way have you done well?

Bianca: My husband has done well for us business-wise and whatever. We don't want for things, but I can't even see his face. I can't even see his face.

Therapist: How is your relationship with your husband? How do you feel?

Bianca: I don't think I love him.

Therapist: No?

Bianca: I don't even know if I know him. I feel like when I go to look at him, I don't see him. I see, ooh, I see a beard. I see a black beard and a masculine man, but I don't see his face.

Therapist: How come you got together with this man, to be in this situation?

Bianca: Ooh, I came with the land. I came with the land. I was a bargain.

Therapist: And you were part of the bargain?

Bianca: I think I was part of the bargain. I feel like my father bargained me.

Therapist: How do you feel about that?

Bianca: Sad. Just, what's the word? I have no say and I have no choice, but why don't I have a choice? Why don't I have a choice?

Therapist: I guess it's the time that you live in, right?

Bianca: Yeah. I don't like that. I don't like not having a choice.

Therapist: If you were to describe to me the most significant observation, either within you or around you about this moment, what would it be?

Bianca: That I have shut myself down to where I don't even really think. I just go through the motions of life.

I move her forward in time again.

Bianca: I'm standing erect. I'm older and I am dressed very fine, but hell, man, I don't like who I've become. I've become bitter, like pinched. Pinched and bitter, and I don't feel anything anymore.

Therapist: How old are you now?

Bianca: 68. 68.

Therapist: Where are you?

Bianca: Oh, standing on a porch. It's still an old wooden porch, but this is a much finer house. It's a much finer house. It's got two floors now, and I'm standing in front of it, sort of like, "This is mine."

Therapist: Is it in the same location or is it in a different place?

Bianca: It's in a different place. It doesn't feel so far, though. Maybe just in town. I still feel an attachment to that land. I feel very rich. I feel like I have a lot of money.

Therapist: So you did well for yourself?

Bianca: Uh-huh. Just I didn't do anything.

Therapist: Your husband made it?

Bianca: Yeah. But, yeah, it's all superficial. It doesn't matter, but it's the only thing that matters because I can't feel anything anymore.

Therapist: Right. Why do you think that is?

Bianca: Just because of the way I trained myself my whole life. I wasn't happy.

Therapist: When you say I trained myself, what does that mean?

Bianca: I didn't allow myself to feel sad and I didn't allow myself to feel all the frustration and the things that I felt, so I didn't feel any of the good things either.

Therapist: So, you hardened yourself?

Bianca: I hardened myself, yeah.

Therapist: What can you tell me about the place you live in now, this town? What does it look like?

Bianca: Like an old western town with just a dirt road for the center and wooden buildings everywhere. I feel like I may even own the general store. Yeah, I feel like I may own the general store.

Therapist: What do you look like now? How are you dressed?

Bianca: I'm wearing a very fine fabric. It's a brocade. It's very rich and has deep colors, like red and it's a ... Oh, my hair is gray and I feel like I have something over my head, like a hat or a cloak, but I feel draped. I'm draped in this fabric, and I have something very fine at my throat, some necklace, and it ... Oh, whew, it all just feels like material compensation for my life, for giving away my life. It's like it's all very fine, but it doesn't impress me.

Therapist: Are you yourself aware that it doesn't impress you?

Bianca: I am now. I am now. It took me this lifetime.

Therapist: Right.

Bianca: But I am now. I'm aware.

Therapist: But as this woman standing there, is she aware?

Bianca: Yes.

Therapist: She is aware.

Bianca: She is aware that she gave all of herself for this.

Therapist: Right.

Bianca: But she didn't know she had a choice. She didn't know how to make that choice. I think she knows now. She would've known now, but she didn't know then. So, it almost feels like her life was wasted.

Therapist: Right.

Bianca: Oh. Oh, geez.

I move her forward in time again, to the last day of her life.

Therapist: How old are you now, on the last day of your life?

Bianca: 89. So old.

Therapist: Is there anything going on around you or within you that suggests that your physical death will come this day?

Bianca: I'm ready.

Therapist: Where are you now?

Bianca: I am in my room. I feel like I'm in the bed.

Therapist: This is a familiar place, where you are?

Bianca: Yeah.

Therapist: Where is this place?

Bianca: This is in my home. It's in my house. It's in my room. This is my room.

Therapist: Is it the same house that you described earlier?

Bianca: Yes, it's that two-story house in town, and my room, again, is very fine. Oh, it's very fine. It's filled with beautiful, rich things.

Therapist: Is there anybody near you at this time of your passing?

Bianca: There's somebody here. This is my daughter, and I don't want to leave her. I think that's why I've stayed so long, because I don't want to leave her. She feels alone.

Therapist: I see.

Bianca: She feels alone. I don't know if she's alone or what.

Therapist: What do you think about this life that you just lived?

Bianca: I didn't get it right. I didn't get it right.

Therapist: In what way?

Bianca: I was not strong enough. I wasn't. No, I didn't know my strength at the time that it would've counted. At the time that it would've made a difference in my trajectory.

Therapist: At what time did you have a choice?

Bianca: When I was younger and I would say no to my father or to whoever, but I didn't say no.

Therapist: Why do you think that is?

Bianca: I didn't know that I could. I didn't know that I should. I didn't know my strength.

Therapist: In retrospect, do you think that you felt your strength at that time?

Bianca: No. I did not feel my strength at that time. I didn't know that I had it.

Therapist: Right. What did you learn from this life?

Bianca: That my strength is always in me and will always be in me, and that I can speak up for myself and make my choices and not let others make my choices for me.

Therapist: Now, what is the last thought that you have as you leave the body?

Bianca: I'm looking forward to what's coming because I'm curious. So, it's about the process, what's going to happen? I'm hovering above and I'm looking at my body.

Therapist: Is there anybody else there at the time of your death?

Bianca: Yes. There's my daughter on my side.

Therapist: What are you feeling?

Bianca: Relief. Relief, and I'm ready to move on.

Therapist: How do you feel about your death?

Bianca: I feel fine about my death. I'm in a place of flowers. There are just flowers. It's like heaven.

Therapist: Beautiful, beautiful. Just take your time getting acquainted with this place. Looking at yourself, what do you look like? Do you have a human form, or does it feel more like an energy form?

Bianca: Yeah. I have a woman's body again, but I don't feel like it's an earth body. I feel like it's just an image.

Therapist: Does it have a predominant color or some sort of light form? What does it feel like?

Bianca: It feels like a hologram. I feel like a hologram. Right now, I need to identify with a body, for some reason.

Therapist: That's okay. Just take your time and tell me about this place and how you feel, and what you're doing here.

Bianca: It's a place, it's like, oh, my gosh. It's like my heaven. It's a place of giant flowers, and I can put my face into them and they're all fragrant, and I can breathe in this fragrance and it fills me and it heals me, and it's just lovely.

Therapist: When you say it fills me and it heals me, does it feel like this place is some sort of place of restoration?

Bianca: Yes. Yeah, and I think that's why I feel like I need to identify with a body for some reason because it's like an in-between and it's a place for me to heal.

Therapist: To feel again.

Bianca: Yeah, yeah.

Therapist: Right.

Bianca: Oh, wow. Yeah. Wow. Yeah, and the fragrances and scents of these flowers are very important for some reason.

Therapist: Take your time. Just enjoy yourself in this place, and when you're ready to move on, just let me know, or perhaps somebody may show up. Just take your time and let me know what happens next, okay? Take all the time that you want in this place.

Bianca: There's someone that's saying, "It's time to go." There's a hand saying, "It's time."

Therapist: Good. Now, follow that hand and tell me about who is here to come and greet you.

Bianca: Oh, my gosh. It makes me laugh. It's like Prince Charming. It's like a cartoon Prince Charming, and he is saying, "We have to go," and he pulls me from my flowers, and we go through sort of opening, but he stays, so he takes me, and I go through the opening. Yeah.

Therapist: What's on the other side of the opening?

Bianca: It's dark, but not bad. It's like the universe. It's like the doorway was clouds, gray clouds, and now I am in the darkness of the universe, but it's got stars and some kind of light, and I'm just hovering, but I like it.

Therapist: Know that a loving power is guiding you home,

and tell me when you can see off into the distance to your destination. What does your form look like now? Is it still a human form or have you changed your form?

Bianca: Ah, no, I have no form now. I'm like an essence. Just an essence.

Therapist: Does it have colors?

Bianca: No.

Therapist: It's just energy?

Bianca: It's just energy.

Therapist: Or consciousness?

Bianca: Right, yeah, consciousness. It is just consciousness. I have no form.

Therapist: Right. Now, I can understand that being in this consciousness, we perhaps could interpret location in a different way. Perhaps there is no coming or going in this place. There is just you being here. Is it something like that?

Bianca: There are levels, and I have levels to go, but I am connected.

Therapist: Ok.

Bianca: I am connected, and I can expand myself and I can retract myself. It's all through my consciousness.

Therapist: When you say there are levels, does that mean these are levels that you're going to go to now or aspire to go to in the future?

Bianca: That's what I need to find out. I am not clear.

Therapist: Take your time. You have all the time in the world. As you're here in this beautiful, expansive consciousness, get a better sense of it and feel if there is perhaps another guiding principle here, or perhaps it is enabling you to guide yourself, whatever works best for you.

Bianca: It's like I have help, but I am going to try to do this on my own, and they are there to help me. The only thing is I am not really sure what I'm supposed to be doing, but whatever it is, I'm going to try to do it on my own, so I just have to sit with it. It's actually fun. It's like really being me and what can I do.

Therapist: Just take your time as you figure it out.

Bianca: Oh. Yeah, so I mistook the levels to mean you have to level up, but you don't have to level up. You have to settle into a level. You have to sort of match your frequency.

Therapist: Becoming attuned to a particular level?

Bianca: You have to just allow yourself to be, and that's how you match it.

Therapist: Which level would be a good one, where we can talk a little bit about your past life as this pioneer woman?

Bianca: I think this one.

Therapist: All right, so why did you need this particular experience? What can you tell me about living that life?

Bianca: I know it. I have to find the words.

Therapist: Take your time. Just express it from your heart, from your higher consciousness.

Bianca: Oh, we must not allow ourselves to become hardened if we have not accomplished what we set out to do. In that life, it was to discover my strength as soon as possible. To discover my voice as soon as possible. And in that life, I felt that I did not discover that soon enough and allowed the emotions attached to that, the disappointment and sadness and the things, to harden me.

I was hoping to not allow that to happen, but it did. It did, and it's okay. It's okay. That's how it turned out. I am grateful that in that life I was able to see it at the end, though. In that life, I felt like it was too little, too late, but it ultimately wasn't.

Therapist: It's very true.

Bianca: Ultimately, it wasn't. It felt like it, but it wasn't.

Therapist: Because at least you could feel the consequences of it, right?

Bianca: Yes.

Therapist: Which is also a lesson, isn't that right?

Bianca: Exactly, and I can bring that with me.

Therapist: Was the central theme the notion of choice?

Bianca: Voice, voice ...

Therapist: Ah, I see.

Bianca: Speaking, speaking truth.

Therapist: Right.

Bianca: Because it gets stuck here if you don't. So speaking truth, which speaks to choice.

Therapist: What stood in her way of not speaking that truth and expressing that choice?

Bianca: She wasn't awake. She didn't know.

Therapist: What does that mean, not being awake?

Bianca: She didn't know who she was. She wasn't awake to who she was as a person.

Therapist: She was more a body versus an individual spirit.

Bianca: Yes. She was just a woman. So she was not awake to her power as a woman in that time and place, which would've been so out of the norm. She would've been a maverick if she would've been able to recognize that. She would've been a pioneer if she would've been able to recognize that, but there was also fear that held her back. That stuff was too big for her. So she chose ... wow ...

Therapist: Submission.

Bianca: She chose to stay small, but then she got hardened because of that choice.

Therapist: If you compare that to the life of Bianca, what can we say about her current evolution and her voice, and her identity as, not only a woman but a spirit?

Bianca: Well, Bianca has chosen to face the fear and to find her voice, I think because of that experience, for sure.

Therapist: Is that applicable to the divorce, or was it already before?

Bianca: Oh, the divorce is so big. It's comparable.

Therapist: Standing up as an individual woman?

Bianca: Yeah. Well, it's definitely standing up as an individual woman. This is the choice of being the maverick and doing the unthinkable and facing fear and all of those things that weren't done.

Therapist: So can we say that this current situation of Bianca is the culmination or the fulfillment of what couldn't be fully actualized in the previous existence?

Bianca: Oh, yes.

Therapist: She does it now. She's able to do this.

Bianca: Oh, yes. And that's why she felt so compelled for so long, but there was so much fear. There was always, always so much fear. So much fear.

Therapist: What was the fear about?

Bianca: Not being able to ... if she chooses this, she may die because she doesn't know.

Therapist: Know what?

Bianca: What it is. She doesn't know how to do it.

Therapist: I see. But she finally made a choice to override fear because of principle, because of spirit, and identity.

Bianca: Yes.

Therapist: Is that a good assessment?

Bianca: That is, that is. Yes.

Therapist: Not thinking about consequence, but rather realizing the internal reward, which is standing up for your own true self, right?

Bianca: Yes.

Therapist: That is its own reward, is it not? Its own safe place.

Bianca: Yes, and trust.

Therapist: Why did it take so long though, till the age of 57?

Bianca: Just so afraid, and my mom is so afraid, and it's just all so scary, but I had to do it. I had to do it.

Therapist: How does it feel to take that step?

Bianca: I'm very proud of myself, and I feel that my ancestors are proud also.

Therapist: Right.

Bianca: I think I'm doing something really big that is more than me.

Therapist: In what way?

Bianca: I am changing the trajectory for those who came before me, as well as those who will come after me.

Therapist: The trajectory of your lineage.

Bianca: Yeah.

Therapist: You're standing up for individuality, for women, for the self.

Bianca: Yes.

Therapist: The soul. It's not just women, right?

Bianca: It's for all who need a voice.

Therapist: I love the idea of what you call the voice. Now, tell me, when we project this trajectory forward in the life of Bianca and beyond, what is the path forward in terms of self-actualization? How does she want to express that, what she's seeking to express? How would you express this voice?

Bianca: Well, for some reason, I see a star-lined path. This has been stuck for so long, and it is being freed and unstuck. So, this is a healing. It's like a big healing, and that healing goes forward, and it spreads out. So, I take my healing forward with me and I spread it out, and I share it, and I know that it gets shared energetically. Everything is affected, and I also get to share it to help those who may want to hear my story and who may be helped by it.

Therapist: Wonderful.

Bianca: Yeah.

Therapist: Could we say that this voice is the throat chakra, which is lifting you to another plateau of consciousness?

Bianca: Yes, yes.

Therapist: There's a different world at a different plateau.

Bianca: And I think that's what happens when it gets released and everything is affected energetically. I think that's what happens.

Therapist: You're in a different world.

Bianca: Yeah.

Therapist: You're in a different chakra, but it means also you're living in a different plane of consciousness. Is that a good assessment?

Bianca: Yes. Wow.

Therapist: How is Bianca doing releasing that voice? Could we say that this was her old block and that now she is unblocking it?

Bianca: Yes. Now it is unblocking. I feel like there's more work.

Therapist: What work is required for the further evolution of this life?

Bianca: Sound work.

Therapist: To open that voice properly?

Bianca: Yep. The sound. It's the sound.

Therapist: To become a truly autonomous being.

Bianca: Yes.

Therapist: Ok.

Bianca: Yes, and I feel there's someone out there that needs to place their hands there. That someone will come along.

Therapist: In order to help and to support?

Bianca: Yes. Yes, they have a particular energy that will help me.

Therapist: You mean helping you heal?

Bianca: Yeah.

Therapist: Beautiful. Now the spirit world is wide open to you, is there any other issue of concern?

Bianca: There's a money issue.

Therapist: Tell me more about that.

Bianca: See, this Bianca feels unsafe because she doesn't know how to earn money, but in that life, she had money and she was safe, but it wasn't hers.

Therapist: A money issue is very sensitive because it binds and subjects a woman to somebody who is a source of that money, the man, right?

Bianca: Yep.

Therapist: Move to that level now where we can gain some insights regarding this issue.

Bianca: I saw myself sitting on a treasure chest. I was sitting on it, and then I took a step up. "Step up, Bianca, step up", and then they say, "It is not to be revealed yet," and it's because I need to learn to trust and to surrender.

Therapist: What does it signify?

Bianca: That I'm okay.

Therapist: That you don't have to hold onto the treasure chest?

Bianca: Yes, and the stepping up means it's time for me to step up.

Therapist: And surrender to the universe that has a plan for you and guides you, right?

Bianca: Yes. Yep, yep.

Therapist: And that is the ultimate self-reliance, is it not? Reliance on the Self which is connected to the divine.

Bianca: Yeah, yeah. Yeah.

Therapist: Self-reliance is not relying on the ego, but relying on the spirit that expresses itself through your voice. Is that a good way of saying it?

Bianca: That is correctly said.

Therapist: Because otherwise, you tie yourself down to material security, like in your past life.

Bianca: Yes, exactly.

Therapist: And that is at the expense of everything that the spirit is trying to express, correct?

Bianca: That is correct.

Therapist: Do you understand that now?

Bianca: I do. I understand.

Therapist: Don't hold on to the illusion of fake security. Or your own idea that you're not good enough because that's not true, is it?

Bianca: No, it's not true.

Therapist: Because who are you?

Bianca: I am a part of the divine.

Therapist: Ah. That's right. Can that ever be lost?

Bianca: Never. Never.

Therapist: That's right. That is the way you surrender, by realizing that divine essence within, isn't it so?

Bianca: Yes.

Therapist: You're not surrendering into a vacuum, you're

surrendering to the fact that you are part of a higher intelligence, a higher reality.

Bianca: I'm actually very lucky.

Therapist: You are. I wouldn't call it lucky. I would call it becoming awakened.

Bianca: I am becoming awakened.

Now, tell me, is there anything else that needs to be added to this, or do you feel we've accomplished what we want to accomplish today?

Bianca: We have accomplished what we wanted to accomplish.

Therapist: How do you feel?

Bianca: I feel really good and happy and content. I feel content.

We slowly bring the session to a close.

Case 7: Karen
An instrument of light

Karen is a charismatic 62-year-old spiritual church leader, in search of a purpose and a higher spiritual unfoldment.

Therapist: Tell me, is it daytime or nighttime?
Karen: Daytime.
Therapist: Are you inside or outside?
Karen: In the mountains.
Therapist: If you look around you, what do you see?
Karen: It's like the Sound of Music. It's like the Alps or something

like that.

Therapist: If you look down at your feet, what if anything do you wear on your feet?

Karen: I'm just wearing sturdy shoes.

Therapist: What else are you wearing?

Karen: It's kind of like Bavarian, like a dirndl (traditional Bavarian dress). It has something to do with a cow. I think I have a cow there with me. I've got braids, blonde braids.

Therapist: You're a girl, it seems.

Karen: Yeah, I'm a girl.

Therapist: How old are you now?

Karen: Young, teenager.

Therapist: When you look straight ahead of you, what do you see?

Karen: I have this strong sense that Bella, my dog from this life, is with me somehow. I see light. It may not actually be on Earth, but it's some kind of light that's like a guardian.

Therapist: The guardian is with you?

Karen: Yes.

Therapist: And you can feel it as this girl. Do you feel this presence?

Karen: I feel this connection.

Therapist: It seems you're pretty much in tune with this guardian, even at that young age, isn't it?

Karen: Yeah. Yeah.

Therapist: Beautiful.

Karen: Yeah.

Therapist: You think Bella is the guardian?

Karen: Yeah, I think so.

Therapist: Beautiful. Beautiful. What is your experience like?

How do you feel when you are witnessing this as this young girl?

Karen: So much love.

Therapist: Are you psychic in this life as this girl?

Karen: I am.

Therapist: What's your name?

Karen: I don't know.

Therapist: What comes to mind?

Karen: Lorna.

Therapist: Lorna?

Karen: Lorna.

Therapist: I'm going to call you Lorna, okay?

Karen: Okay, sure.

Therapist: Now, Lorna, I want you to tell me what you're doing here in this field, in the mountains.

Karen: I'm breathing, enjoying. Flowers are beautiful. I love this cow.

Therapist: (Karen is very emotional) Here's a napkin.

Karen: Thank you. I love this cow a lot. She's really sweet. She's really tame.

Therapist: You have a good connection with the animals.

Karen: Yeah.

Therapist: You live nearby, Lorna?

Karen: Yeah. Yeah.

Therapist: Where do you live, and you tell me what the place looks like?

Karen: It looks like where Heidi would live. It's kind of like a little patchy hut type of thing.

Therapist: How many people are there in the dwelling?

Karen: Just my parents and me.

Therapist: How's the energy in the house, all of you together?

Karen: We're crowded, but it's good. We get on each other's nerves, but it's good.

Therapist: Now, at this point in your life, as a teenager, how do you spend your days? Do you go to school, work, or help out at home?

Karen: I don't think I go to school. I think I kind of learn from nature. I just go around in the fields. I can trust nature.

Therapist: What do you learn? You said you're intuitive? What do you learn from nature?

Karen: How beautiful it is, how it's so connected to everything and to me. Everything is so easy to take for granted, but it's so beautiful and so permanent, but impermanent.

Therapist: Lorna, at this point in your life as a teenager, what is the most significant observation about your life so far? Either within you or around you?

Karen: I have no need to get married, no need for approval. No need to be loved by anybody because I'm so deeply loved.

Therapist: When you say I'm so deeply loved, in what way do you mean that?

Karen: I don't really know. I just think it's nature that loves me.

Therapist: You're at peace with yourself and with nature.

Karen: Yeah, the cow. Still love my guide. It just loves me so much.

Therapist: It seems you live in your own bubble of love.

Karen: Yeah.

I move her forward in time.

Therapist: Tell me what is happening now, Lorna?

Karen: I'm 25 and I'm not as free. There's more darkness somehow. I have a memory of being that purity that I was, but it's not quite as present as it was.

Therapist: How come? What has changed, Lorna?

Karen: I think I had to be with people. I had to be with more people. I had to start relating to others and maybe some of their opinions.

Therapist: When you say I had to, why is that exactly?

Karen: Something about not being able to live at home anymore. Just having a feeling that I should get married.

Therapist: Are you married at this point?

Karen: I think sort of.

Therapist: Sort of in the process?

Karen: No.

Therapist: Sort of married, but ...

Karen: I'm legally married but not quite with the person.

Therapist: You said something about the Alps. Does any particular country come to mind?

Karen: I would think maybe Austria in the '30s.

Therapist: Lorna, are you implying that you don't live at home anymore? That you're now married and you're living differently?

Karen: I live in a city and I'm wearing more grown-up clothes, city clothes.

Therapist: What's significant about this stage of your life at 25?

Karen: I'm sort of resigned to a temporary inconvenience. I'm not being as free as I want to be.

Therapist: And by free you mean to be connected to spirit, the mountains, nature? Does it feel like an obligation, something that is expected of you?

Karen: Both. Obligation is a good word.

Therapist: What is making this an obligation? Is it something within you, society, or your parents?

Karen: Well, probably me just feeling like I should do it and I guess I learned that from society.

Therapist: Where do you live now, Lorna?

Karen: I live in a city. It's kind of a connected house.

Therapist: And with whom do you live here?

Karen: My husband sort of. He travels a lot.

Therapist: When you say sort of does that mean that you're not really connected to him?

Karen: Not fully committed.

Therapist: Was this a marriage out of convenience?

Karen: Maybe or just impulse.

Therapist: When you look outside on the street, in the town, wherever you are, what does the place look like?

Karen: It's all right. It's a city. It's kind of dark. It's not that clean.

Therapist: What do you do during the day?

Karen: I walk someplace, and I think I work in an office.

Therapist: How does that make you feel, kind of going through the motions? Sounds like you're not too enchanted by all of it.

Karen: No, I'm not enchanted.

I move her forward in time.

Therapist: Now, Lorna, tell me what is happening now.

Karen: Okay, I'm in my 40s now and I'm a little wilder and freer.

Therapist: Help me understand, what does that exactly mean?

Karen: I think I'm not married anymore. Something happened to my husband. I'm not sure what, but I'm doing more creative work. Some type of healing or art, more in touch with my inner self. I think I still live in the city, but I'm more in touch with my calling.

Therapist: What would your calling be?

Karen: It's about creativity and healing and joy and paradox and looking at the absurdity of life and making fun of it and just being a free spirit.

Therapist: Being a free spirit is important to you?

Karen: Yeah.

Therapist: What does that really mean to you? Being a free spirit?

Karen: I get to not dress up so much and I get to say what's on my mind. And I get to express love in unconventional ways.

Therapist: What does this mean, to express love in unconventional ways?

Karen: I have an absurd love of animals. Oh my goodness.

Therapist: You're living your own emancipated way, so to speak?

Karen: Yeah. I don't really like going to parties and shit. I just like to have fun. I like fun.

Therapist: Do you have a like-minded group around you or are you sort of an oddball in this society where you live?

Karen: I'm an oddball.

Therapist: An oddball. Is anybody understanding what you're doing?

Karen: Yeah, a few people?

Therapist: How do you feel now in relation to the society you live in?

Karen: I think it's entertaining, but I'm a step back from it.

Therapist: You don't really bother?

Karen: No, no. I bother in that it's a great source of comedy, but I'm not engaged. I'm not obligated, that's the word we used before. I don't feel obligated.

Therapist: What would be a significant observation about this stage in your life?

Karen: Freedom.

Therapist: What does that mean to you as Lorna, freedom at this time in the '30s?

Karen: I've got long hair. I'm not dressed up. I'm wearing pants. I'm working sometimes for money, but mostly working full time. Somehow the cow is back, some cow. Even now, Bella is still very connected.

Therapist: So, Lorna is all about freedom. And what's your state of mind, your state of consciousness at this stage in your life?

Karen: Joyful.

Therapist: Is it paying dividends for you, this sense of freedom and the way that you think and the way you live?

Karen: Yes, it works. Yes.

I move her forward in time again.

Therapist: Tell me, what is happening now?

Karen: I'm so free but calmer. Probably in my 60s. I still have long hair. Doing creative things. There's a lot of light around me and maybe darkness in the atmosphere, but there's a lot of light around me and I'm wearing light clothes. Golden clothes and I'm very, very peaceful. Peaceful, but still joyful.

Therapist: You say there's a lot of darkness around you. What does it mean?

Karen: Just the city itself hasn't changed. It just feels kind of dark and dirty. But I seem to be navigating it in a cloud of light and I don't really go to that many places.

Therapist: When you say light, what does it mean? Is it your internal experience of your inner state of being?

Karen: I actually see an aura around me, a golden aura. And it's also my inner state, but just very much at peace with what is and finding great joy and light in it.

Therapist: How is your intuition? Has it evolved over the years? You said for a while it kind of went away in your early 20s.

Karen: Yeah.

Therapist: Is it back or even more as it was before?

Karen: It's back and it's very present. Not so much concern about the future, but just being very present with the beauty and the light that is right now.

Therapist: And how does this intuition, this gift, help you in your day-to-day existence?

Karen: I don't mind what happens. I just don't mind about the future. I just am. I'm in love.

Therapist: You're always in a good state of mind.

Karen: Not with an object, but just in love, in the presence of love.

Therapist: What do you think you attribute that state of being to?

Karen: Love, being loved. Just relaxing and being present and being connected once again to my sweet guide, my source.

Therapist: How is that guide interacting with you on a day-to-day basis?

Karen: She's also light.

Therapist: You talk to her, or do you just feel her presence? What's the relationship?

Karen: I feel her.

Therapist: You feel her? She kind of goes along with you wherever you go?

Karen: Yeah.

Therapist: Like a companion so to speak.

Karen: Sort of, but she's also internal. She's present.

Therapist: Is she just light, love, and confirmation, or is there also some other form of communication happening?

Karen: She makes me laugh. She reminds me of the way she guided me in the current life that I have now. It makes me laugh, makes me remember that I didn't trust her in this life, but how trustworthy she really is, that she's been my guide for centuries.

Therapist: Beautiful. So, you're very much in touch.

I move her to the last day of her life.

Therapist: How old are you on this last day of your life as Lorna?

Karen: 87 or so.

Therapist: Is there anything going on around you or within you that suggests your physical death will come this day?

Karen: Yeah. Yeah. I'm in a bed and the dog is cuddled up next to me and she won't leave my side.

Therapist: How are you feeling at this moment?

Karen: Love. And the internal guide, Bella, is with me too and she's surrounding me. She's enfolding me and she's in my heart. She's enfolding me inside and outside.

Therapist: What do you think about this life you just lived as Lorna?

Karen: Oh, it was beautiful. It just was beautiful.

Therapist: What did you learn?

Karen: I learned to trust, and that darkness is light. Darkness is light in disguise, and it's all okay. It's all okay, even the period in my 20s where it wasn't great it was okay, but it was still just part of what had to be, and it was good. The weird marriage and I don't know how that ended up, even that was good.

Therapist: What is your last thought?

Karen: I'm grateful.

She's moving past her death.

Therapist: What's the first thing you notice?

Karen: So grateful. I don't know if this is the first thing, but it's not the rainbow bridge. It's the rainbow field. It's all animals. It's all the ones I've had and all the ones that I just love in theory and oh my God, they're just so beautiful. And Bella is the main one. She's right by me and she's no longer light. She's a dog, as she was in her physical form, and she's a nutcase because that's what she was. And she's running around and jumping up on me. Stop licking my face. I'm so excited. And it feels like there's something that could be beyond that. I don't know what that is yet.

Therapist: Just enjoy yourself for a moment here. There's no hurry.

Karen: I like that.

Therapist: This is just your beautiful welcome here.

Karen: Yeah, the kitty's there, Mira.

Therapist: Just take your time.

Karen: All the rabbits I've had, even Big, not the fake one, but my rabbit Big is there and he's saying it was not my fault that he died. And yeah, it's pretty good. Anna.

Therapist: They all come to welcome you?

Karen: Yeah, yeah. They're all over me.

Therapist: Feel the love. Stay here as long as you want. There's no hurry.

Karen: Well, of course, I can ask them to show me around. Because I think they're going to come with me wherever I go.

Therapist: Yeah, there's room enough for everybody. So now tell me, is there anybody guiding you? Is Bella guiding you or are there any other guides there?

Karen: Bella, Bella's mainly the guide.

Therapist: So where is she taking you first?

Karen: Well, I think she's taking me to somebody that looks an awful lot like Jesus and it's okay, and I'm sort of Christian.

Therapist: Yeah. Okay.

Karen: And he's hugging me. I don't have to be all holy and shit around him. He's hugging me and he's expressing delight in my irreverence and saying he was kind of irreverent too, that maybe he said the F word a lot. And something like God is there and I don't know, some of the Hindus.

Therapist: Beautiful. So, everybody's here receiving you?

Karen: Yeah, it's like a party. It's a cocktail party without the booze.

Therapist: Beautiful. It's like a spiritual hangout, so to speak.

Karen: Yeah, what's it called? A flash dance almost.

Therapist: Spiritual rave.

Karen: Yeah, rave. That's it. Yeah.

Therapist: Beautiful.

Karen: Flash mob. That's it.

Therapist: What's the energy here?

Karen: Oh my God. It's such a celebration. Like, you did it, you did another life. Holy fuck. You did another life. This is so cool. Here we are.

Therapist: What is your relationship with them? Are they your guides or do you belong to them?

Karen: Equal, like I'm on equal footing. I'm not intimidated by them. I'm sort of in awe, but not in awe of "You're better than me." Just in awe of the whole process.

Therapist: Do you think you're one of them?

Karen: Yeah, sure. I don't mean to sound like …..

Therapist: No, not at all. Not at all.

Karen: Everybody is, but I get to see it in this particular journey. I get to see how I'm just, wow.

Therapist: Do you have the feeling that, over the course of

these different lifetimes, you ascended to their level?

Karen: Kinship, just kinship.

Therapist: Right. Now, tell me, while you're having fun, without being dramatic in any way, do they have any comments about this life as Lorna? Anything they say about it?

Karen: I'm more interested in Karen (her current life), but they can tell me about Lorna.

Therapist: Well, they can do both. What about Karen?

Karen: Yeah, Lorna, you got it. You got it. Toward the end, you started to relax. You realized that a lot of what the world is, it's kind of just made up. It's bullshit. You don't have to let seepage into your consciousness. You can just sort of, without building a wall, allow it in and then allow it out. Don't give it any power. Just say, "Oh yeah."

Therapist: Be in your own light.

Karen: Yeah. Yeah.

Therapist: That was kind of the conclusion of the evolution of Lorna.

Karen: Yeah, I think so.

Therapist: Looking now at Karen, what's up with her? What do you have to say about Karen?

Karen: Oh, just your biggest doubt is that you think you're a goofball and that you don't trust your job and that you're supposed to be all holy and shit, and you're not. You are, but you're not, you know? You watched fucking South Park before you came here today and you thought, "Oh, maybe I'm screwing it up." But it was really funny. And so just trust your joy. And we like South Park too, and we like irreverence and we like that you can be so incredibly fucking spiritual and use the F word with spiritual. It's just amazing. It's who you're meant to be. Yeah, your church does inhibit you, inhibit it a little bit. It's not worth the fight sometimes to be exactly who you are, but you have plenty of people around you where you can be completely rowdy and deeply spiritual at the same time.

Therapist: When you look at this life of Karen and you look at Lorna and the way forward, what is it that they want for you for your further evolution? What state of mind do they want for you?

Karen: Joy, more joy. Just joy and more joy.

Therapist: What kind of joy? Because there are many kinds of joy.

Karen: Respectable joy. Joy that is appropriate to the situation, but also joy that is a secret joy that is unrepentant, and also joy that is incredibly loving. If I'm going to use unrepentant joy, it has to be for the purpose of love. It has to be to bring forth greater love.

Therapist: With an underlying higher consciousness.

Karen: Yeah, of love. Yeah. Yeah. Love beyond love, love that I can't explain right now, it's my state of body, but love that I know.

Therapist: Can you feel that love, now when you're with them?

Karen: Yeah. Yeah. It doesn't really have words. It's feelings, it's tears. It's tears and it's laughter. It's simultaneous tears and laughter.

Therapist: What's interesting, when you think about what my purpose is, it becomes almost superfluous, thinking about this state of joy, is it not? From this perspective, it's not about doing, right? Nevertheless, having said that, on a relative existence, is there anything that they say you could do in this relative world that could make some difference?

Karen: Well, I said the burning question is what am I supposed to do with my church? What do you want me to do with my church? Because it's pretty crazy right now.

Therapist: What do they want you to do?

Karen: Oh, God damn. They want me to stay. They want me to stay and continue to have fun, but just stay if it's fun, stay if it's joyful, and you can do that joy beyond joy thing, that love beyond joy thing, where you bring forth greater love in the group. Immediately I say, "I don't know how," but they say they know how, and they can show me how.

Therapist: Can they show you now?

Karen: I don't know if I can ask.

Therapist: Why don't you stay with them for a moment? We're here now with them and they can show you.

Karen: Okay, so show me what do I do? Do I do nothing? Do I do that? Okay, let me calm down for a second. Telling me just to calm down.

Therapist: Take your time and just have fun with them. Calm down. Go a little bit deeper within, deeper in their spirit.

Karen: Okay. What I'm getting now is to trust the laughter, bring all the tears, and trust the unknowing, that I may not get it in a single download, but that I can trust that I'm going to get it moment by moment, step by step and that I have a really good team of people assembled around me that I can share this consciousness with. At least share that we're not going to get it in one download, that we must trust step by step, and that we're going to have failures.

Therapist: What if for a moment, right here, right now, you could have a little download as a frame of reference for the future? Can they do that for you?

Karen: Yeah. I see the church, I see the light, the Lorna light coming out of the church into the community, and I'm standing in the center of it and light is coming out of me and light is coming out of almost everybody in the congregation, the people that will allow it. But there are some that will not. There are some that are going to continue to be in darkness.

And I get to embody that light, and that's part of the energy that's going to feed the church.

I get to see the light coming out of the church. I get to see the light coming out of me. I get to see the light coming out of all the people there.

Therapist: Beautiful.

Karen: Some of the people who drive me crazy, I get to see if I can find the light for them. Yeah, it's there. It's there. I guess the light draws the light. Yeah, it's good. It's good stuff.

Therapist: Now that you're here with them having this spiritual rave, is there anything that they could show you that is outside the box?

Karen: I would love it if that light was not limited to me standing in the church and that wherever I went, people could experience this deeper sense of love and joy without knowing that it's coming from me and me not having to take the credit for it. Me being able to let go of that part of my ego and say, "You know what? Light and joy are here."

It's like when I go to the grocery store and people can't find shit, and I just get out of my comfort zone and I say, "I can tell they're like old and they can't find stuff." And I say, "Let me help you find that." And as soon as I say that, they find it. And so to have that for bigger things, for just to be able to say, let me help you find that, but not have to do anything, that is so awesome. I'm trying to control my language, I'm sorry, but it's so awesome. It is just so incredibly awesome.

Therapist: What do they say about that?

Karen: They say that's part of my power, part of my light is generosity. Like talking to strangers and bringing light and love to the people at Starbucks. It brings me such joy and I have to think on some level, it brings others such joy. They're saying that generosity is one of my touchstones, that stepping out of my comfort zone to be generous is one of my touchstones to being that greater light in the world.

Therapist: Beautiful.

Karen: This human being is a little scared to give all my shit away. But just stop that. You don't have to do that.

Therapist: Isn't that what being an instrument of greater love and greater good is? It's not about you. It's just running through you. It's not about holding on.

Karen: There you go.

Therapist: It's not about calculating. It's about being that flow, that instrument of that abundance.

Karen: Yeah. Yeah. Absolutely.

Therapist: Then you must let go as well as be the instrument, which can be a scary thing.

Karen: I know. I know. And it's what you just said. It's the dualistic mind, sorting and counting and predicting. I need to let it be like Lorna, and let that life flow through me. Flowing through me, not attaching to it, but just letting it go out in one ear and out the other, in my mouth and out my butt, just letting it go. Not feeling that if I eat too much, I'll be poor.

Therapist: Eventually, even Karen's life is going to come to an end. Looking at your soul identity that is beyond Lorna, beyond Karen, what is the journey and state of being going to look like?

Karen: Well, two things. The bizarre one is that I get to eat whatever I want. The other one is that I get to be of service. I get to be a source of light and generosity from a different sphere.

Therapist: Okay. Are you going to work for beings on the Earth, or are you going to work with people that are beyond as well?

Karen: I don't know. I really don't know. I don't know anything.

Therapist: Have a look at it now.

Karen: Both then. Both.

Therapist: You were thinking of working from there, for the well-being of humanity?

Karen: Yeah, I was thinking that. For animals, also.

Therapist: What about those in spirit? It could be a different job.

Karen: Can I have two? I can have two.

Therapist: That's right. Ask your guides what destiny is going to be like.

Karen: My guides say that I can do both, that I can work on behalf of humanity and the animal kingdom and the Earth itself, that I can also be of service in the spirit realm.

Therapist: Is that your real nature, be that guide, be the one who helps others? What is your spirit identity like?

Karen: I feel like I often help others and other spiritual beings through joy, laughter, and clear seeing. On Earth, certainly, in the last year, it's been helping people to avoid extreme polarization, seeing both sides. You're a higher being and you don't dismiss humanity because humanity is spirit and matter. It's the same thing.

Therapist: We can even go beyond that, beyond even name and form, and see what that ascension looks like. Would you like for that moment, to check that out and see what lies beyond? Because at the end of the day, in the non-dual state, there may even be more to be experienced.

Karen: Yeah. I'm getting mostly color and light, mostly fuchsia and turquoise and purple and sort of gold, those colors kind of blending in a swirl, whatever that is.

Therapist: Would you like for a moment to be quietly absorbed in this and connect yourself to its essence? Take your time.

Silence.

Karen: I'm good. I'm done.

Therapist: How does that feel? I'm asking because there is engagement in service, both in the spirit world, the animal kingdom, and on Earth. But there is also a level that is beyond all of that, and one of Karen's questions is to understand surrender versus engagement. Can we help Karen understand this concept in a broader way than perhaps she has been thinking about up to this point?

Karen: When I was swimming around in the color and the light, I got this thought that relationships are secondary, that relationships are not the most important thing to me.

Therapist: What is the most important thing to you?

Karen: It's swimming around in the color.

Therapist: Yeah, that's why I was asking you. See, there's a reason I asked you to get into it because if we want refuge and surrender, there must be a way beyond all dualities. What do your guides say about that?

Karen: They're saying, "Give yourself permission to do that." Like in my relationship with my husband. I do love him very much, but it's also that we do have parallel lives, and both go our separate ways very easily, and that really works for me. But though people will tell me it's a bad thing, it's actually a really good thing for me because he has a deep respect for this journey that I'm on. He's on his own journey.

Therapist: How can your guides help you become a better leader? I want them to really answer the question for you.

Karen: I want them too, yes. We'll just continue to do the rave with them. The Christians say the communion of saints is around all the time, and to party with them, to celebrate with them. I'm not very good at meditating. I do it, but I kind of suck at it. And possibly, let me check in with them about this, to recognize that not everybody meditates in the same way and that perhaps my best form of meditation is being with the dogs and the other animals, but the dogs in particular.

Therapist: But that is meditation, isn't it?

Karen: Yes. Yes.

Therapist: When in the flow of joy, you're in the flow of saints, you're in the flow of animal consciousness. Then you are already in a state of meditation. Because at the end of the day, when you're flowing the way you do, and dancing with them, raving with them, you're already free.

Karen: The dogs are my meditation and the Guinea pig and the rabbit.

Therapist: Even those trying to meditate, are not always capable of achieving the flow that you're talking about, right? So as such, you're an instrument of that flow already.

Karen: Yea, I don't have to work so hard to meditate when I am in the garden or with my animals.

Therapist: How can they summarize this for you?

Karen: Just to love myself so much, and I don't know, I keep coming back to eating things. That food is filling some gaping hole that can be better filled by the joy of them.

Therapist: What is the gaping hole that needs to be filled?

Karen: Approval, but I don't need approval. That's what we just said before. I don't really need the approval of the world.

Therapist: Lorna didn't need approval, did she?

Karen: No. No. And I have instant approval when I'm raving around with the communion of saints.

Therapist: Is that perhaps a reason why we saw Lorna? Because maybe Karen needs to remember her irreverent sense of freedom, that she didn't need anybody or anything, and she was so connected to spirit, to her creativity, to her expression of joy.

Karen: Oh, yeah. I don't need to be important. And if I'm lusting after importance and I'm not getting it, then I feel like I'm not being approved, and I don't need to be important. In fact, I need to allow other people to be important, and that makes me important in secret. I get to be important in a way that really lights up, that never goes away. The other kind of importance is temporary, but this importance is permanent.

Therapist: Right. And you know, you don't have to be apologetic about being an instrument.

Karen: Yeah, yeah. I know. I get it. I'm an instrument. When people see me as an instrument and think that they need to glom onto me to get something from me, is when I start feeling the suck and when I would like to detach. I start feeling like I'm not a good person unless I let them suck the energy out of me.

Therapist: Self-preservation is required. The more you become powerful, the more distance is required, because it's a light that's very addictive to people. And that's perhaps how we can redefine meditation for you. Meditation is what keeps you free. Maybe that's why we saw Lorna because she's a good reminder for you on how to be free.

Karen: Yeah. That's why I think dogs are so appealing to me. They need stuff from me, but I can give it or not give it, and they're still going to love me no matter what.

Therapist: Is there anything that one of the sages wants to share with you, something that we haven't thought about?

Karen: Well, both Krishna and Jesus are telling me, don't be worried about having your Christian tendencies. A lot of Christians act like total dicks, but you're not that, you're a mystical Christian, and even though people in your church are terrified of Christianity, you can still rely upon your Christian framework. You were raised in an actually really loving Christian environment and the work that you've done in understanding mysticism will serve you well. And you can provide that in a way that feels safe for people. And even if they're scared at first, they'll be safe eventually. And you can also bring a lot of humor and joy into it.

Therapist: And though today's Christianity may be challenging, it's still a cultural vehicle in which we are born and raised, which could be a powerful way of helping people get used to new ideas.

Karen: Right. And they tell me to trust. Trust your intuition about the rightness of what has been said here and the rightness of what you brought in here, what you brought in already knowing, but had no idea you were going to say. That I'm already leaning in the right direction. I just need the confidence for it and find ways to build confidence in my life. Such as recognizing that meditation is being with the dogs, and recognizing meditation as my ability, when others are sucking the life force out of me, to not having to go along with that without feeling that I'm rejected. And that my ability to get away at that moment is actually not a bad thing but a good thing.

Therapist: To trust yourself.

Karen: Yeah, yeah, yeah.

Therapist: Being an upgraded version of Lorna. The spirit of Lorna is an acquisition of a beautiful state of evolution that, when integrated with Karen's life, could bring about a greater acceptance of yourself and a vision for how you can behave. Does it make sense?

Karen: Yeah, yeah.

Therapist: Is there anything else that we may need or want to see?

Karen: I'm so grateful for them. I think they just want me to be what I got in touch with today, to be who I'm intended to be, and to be them because I am them all. Yeah. We're all it.

Therapist: And that's perhaps the greatest gift you can give to them. To be you without apology, without restraint, without limitations. And then they will dance with you.

Karen: Yeah. Yeah, and if I can do that with others, that's really cool too, whether I'm in this body or in the next one.

Therapist: Realize that there are always going to be limitations of those around you who are not at your level. That doesn't mean that you stop being that way. But that there is an understanding of people's limitations.

Karen: It's not worth the fight.

Therapist: No.

Karen: It just detracts from the overall message.

Therapist: It's the art that we learned from Lorna. She didn't bother in any way. It didn't stop her from being the light, correct?

Karen: Yeah.

We slowly bring the session to an end.

Case 8: Clara
A civil war soldier

Clara is a 27-year-old nurse, who has experienced a lot of suffering.

Therapist: Tell me, is it daytime or nighttime?
Clara: It's nighttime.
Therapist: Are you inside or outside?
Clara: I'm outside.
Therapist: When you look ahead of you, what is the first thing you're aware of?

Clara: Just like distress.

Therapist: Distress?

Clara: War or something.

Therapist: I want you to look down at your feet and tell me what, if anything, you wear on your feet.

Clara: I'm in boots.

Therapist: What else are you wearing?

Clara: I'm in a uniform.

Therapist: Do you see any colors?

Clara: It's like a dark green, maybe dark gray. It's dark outside.

Therapist: And is there fighting going on around you, in the darkness?

Clara: No, but I feel like there has been.

Therapist: Are you alone, or is there anybody near you?

Clara: Yeah, they're hurt.

Therapist: Is this a battlefield?

Clara: Yeah.

Therapist: Are you walking around this battlefield?

Clara: Stuck frozen, scared.

Therapist: Give me a general description of the area where you are.

Clara: This is the woods, there are trees. This all happened in the South.

Therapist: Is it the civil war period?

Clara: Yeah, I think so.

Therapist: Do you carry any weapons with you?

Clara: I have a gun on my back.

Therapist: Are you the only one that is here walking around, or are there others?

Clara: I feel like there are people coming.

Therapist: Are they opposed to you, or are they with you?

Clara: They're with me. They're with me.

Therapist: This is after a battle?

Clara: Yeah.

Therapist: How does it make you feel witnessing all of this?

Clara: We got to get back to camp, we're not safe.

Therapist: How old are you now, approximately?

Clara: 22.

Therapist: What's your name? Anything that pops up in your mind is fine. Could even be a nickname.

Clara: George.

Therapist: George, I'm going to call you George. Okay? George, why don't you move back to camp and tell me what this place looks like? Go there now and tell me.

Clara: It's horrible.

Therapist: In what way?

Clara: People are injured everywhere, hungry, and cold.

Therapist: Where are you staying?

Clara: We have a tent, a cot.

Therapist: Are there many in the tent, or just a few?

Clara: There's a lot.

Therapist: So, it's a big tent.

Clara: There are a few tents, many beds, on the floor.

Therapist: Now, George, before we move on, what is the most significant observation, either within you or around you, about this moment?

Clara: There's so much injury, so much hatred. Distress, there's so much distress. Worry.

Therapist: Now, George, I'm going to count from 3 down to 1, and on the count of 1, we're going to move forward in time to a later time in your life as George to another relevant moment, to something that shapes your heart, your soul, your mind, your evolution. Going from 3, 2, 1, and we are there now. And tell me what is happening now.

Clara: I'm happy. I have a family.

Therapist: How old are you now, George?

Clara: 45.

Therapist: Okay. What can you tell me about where you are right now?

Clara: I'm in New York.

Therapist: In the city?

Clara: We live there.

Therapist: Do you live in a high rise, or do you have a house?

Clara: It's like a townhouse.

Therapist: Can you tell me about your family?

Clara: I have two kids.

Therapist: What about your wife?

Clara: She's beautiful. She's kind.

Therapist: What do you do for a living, George?

Clara: I work at the bank.

Therapist: Do you have a good position at the bank?

Clara: Yeah.

Therapist: What kind?

Clara: I'm trying to advance.

Therapist: You're trying to advance. Are you pretty good with numbers?

Clara: Yeah.

Therapist: Are you working in the city?

Clara: Yes. Yes.

Therapist: What has changed these last so many years after

the war?

Clara: My heart, I look at people differently.

Therapist: In what way?

Clara: I look past the trivial things of life. I see them for who they are. I listen to their stories and don't take them for granted.

Therapist: How did that change your life, George?

Clara: Because I watched so many people get taken away from their families, I watched them turn bitter.

Therapist: It's beautiful, George, that you didn't become bitter from the war, and you did the opposite. How did you do that, George?

Clara: I had help.

Therapist: From whom?

Clara: My wife. She's intuitive.

Therapist: She understood your soul, your pain.

Clara: Yeah.

Therapist: And you were able to work through it with her?

Clara: Yeah.

Therapist: That's beautiful, George. So, you're saying you're happy now at 45 years old?

Clara: Mm-hmm.

Therapist: What is the most significant observation about your life at this point?

Clara: Growing so much, I felt very weak in the war.

Therapist: Do you mean physically, or mentally?

Clara: Mentally. But it just made me stronger.

Therapist: Is that what you mean by I've grown so much?

Clara: Yeah.

Therapist: So where did all that growth and that strength come from after the war?

Clara: I had to find it within myself. Because I had so many reasons to just be depressed. I don't want to be depressed.

Therapist: So, you turned all this pain, hurt, and loss, into strength.

Clara: Yeah.

I move her forward in time.

Therapist: Tell me what is happening now, George.

Clara: We moved out of the city. I'm old.

Therapist: How old are you now, George?

Clara: 60.

Therapist: Where do you live now?

Clara: It's grassy. It's a farm. I've always wanted to be with animals.

Therapist: Do you like animals?

Clara: I love animals.

Therapist: Is it you and your wife? Are your kids still there? Are they grown up?

Clara: They're grown.

Therapist: Are they gone already?

Clara: Yeah.

Therapist: It's just you and your wife. How is life now here at the farm?

Clara: It's fun. It's beautiful. Simple.

Therapist: Is it a big farm, or a small farm?

Clara: It's not small. It's enough.

Therapist: Do you actively work on the farm, or is it more like a gentleman's farm?

Clara: I work. We do what we can. It's not big.

Therapist: How's your life been during these last 15, 20 years?

Clara: It's been good. I feel like I learned. I lived a hard life when I was young, for it to level out when I'm old.

Therapist: What constitutes a good life for you in these last few years? What is the meaning of a good life?

Clara: I'm comfortable and stable. I'm happy. I don't stress anymore. I don't find trivial things stressful.

Therapist: Beautiful. How did work at the bank go? Did you manage to rise in your career?

Clara: A little bit. Not as much as I would have wanted, but that's okay.

Therapist: It's okay?

Clara: Yeah.

Therapist: It wasn't your priority?

Clara: No.

Therapist: What was your priority?

Clara: I just want to be comfortable. Success is not always measured the same.

Therapist: What is the real measurement of success for you?

Clara: I just want to be happy, stable, loved. I have.

Therapist: You have? How is your relationship with your wife?

Clara: It's better than ever.

Therapist: Better than ever. Beautiful.

Clara: We grow old together.

Therapist: Beautiful. What, now in your sixties, do you define as most relevant in your life, George?

Clara: I just want to be happy. I want to level out.

I move her forward in time again, to the last day of her life as George.

Therapist: How old are you?

Clara: 72.

Therapist: Is there anything going on around you, or within you, that suggests that your physical death will come this day?

Clara: I can't get up.

Therapist: Are you in bed?

Clara: Yeah.

Therapist: Are you ill?

Clara: Yeah, I'm ill, got a cough and sweaty, fever.

Therapist: Is there anybody with you?

Clara: No. My wife died.

Therapist: Recently, or a while ago?

Clara: Two years ago.

Therapist: How has life been after she passed?

Clara: Not good.

Therapist: No?

Clara: I'm sad that she's left.

Therapist: Are you alone now?

Clara: Yeah.

Therapist: Looking back, what do you think about the life you lived as George?

Clara: It was a good life, I was strong.

Therapist: What did you learn from this life as George?

Clara: I can overcome more than I think I can. I'm mentally strong.

Therapist: Have there been certain things you have been able to evolve in this life as George?

Clara: Yeah.

Therapist: What were those things?

Clara: I evolved. I evolved my trust. I evolved my mind. I trust myself more.

Therapist: Now, George, what is your last thought, awareness, or feeling as you leave this body of George?

Clara: I'm ready. I know I'm going to be happy, I'm okay with that. It smells so fresh, it's crisp, just happy.

Therapist: Have you arrived at a certain place that smells this way?

Clara: I think I'm waiting.

Therapist: Is this a waiting place?

Clara: Yeah, I think so.

Therapist: Sure. And somebody or something will come to welcome you, just look around you and move to that point when somebody's there.

Clara: Yes. Someone's coming. Someone's coming.

Therapist: Who is this?

Clara: I think it's a guide.

Therapist: Does the guide have any form; does it look like something?

Clara: Just kind of purple.

Therapist: Are there any recognizable features, or is it just color and energy?

Clara: Just energy. I can feel it.

Therapist: Purple and energy. Beautiful. Does it feel male, female, or androgynous in appearance?

Clara: She's female.

Therapist: Beautiful. So let her come to you as you come to her. What does it feel like when you get close to her?

Clara: Familiar, so happy to see her.

Therapist: Have you known her before?

Clara: Yeah.

Therapist: Beautiful. Just take a moment and soak up this beautiful energy. Now in this meeting with your guide, how does the communion with her unfold?

Clara: Insight.

Therapist: What kind of insight?

Clara: She's just telling me I'm okay, I did good. Feedback, if you will.

Therapist: About George's life?

Clara: Yeah.

Therapist: What are other things that she really liked that you did in that life?

Clara: I didn't give up, but wanted to all the time when I was younger.

Therapist: But you didn't.

Clara: But I didn't.

Therapist: What goal was set for this incarnation as George before you took up George's life? I assume you discussed with her what this life was going to be about, what was important. What were some of these things that you tried to do, accomplish, and experience in this life?

Clara: My lesson was to see people, and listen to people, who they are, and to help them. It's always to help them.

Therapist: And how did you do regarding that lesson?

Clara: I did help them. Even though they took such a mental toll on me, I was still strong enough to hold on.

Therapist: So, you did well regarding what you had set out to do in this life?

Clara: Yes.

Therapist: Does your guide also offer some positive criticism as to what you could have done differently in this life as George?

Clara: She said I wasted a lot of time, after the war.

Therapist: In what way?

Clara: Mourning.

Therapist: Oh, yes?

Clara: Mourning. Too much time.

Therapist: What did she say about that?

Clara: That I was stronger than that, but it's okay.

Therapist: For a while you let it go down a little bit.

Clara: Yeah. Let it take me over for a little bit, but it's okay. I made it back.

Therapist: What was the main theme of Clara's life? What is the main emphasis for this incarnation?

Clara: I need to be reminded that I can overcome this, and I don't need it to be that long, like last time.

Therapist: The mourning.

Clara: That I can help people. Because I've already got that, I can help them.

Therapist: This life too is dedicated to service, to helping?

Clara: Yeah.

Therapist: What else does she want for your mental and spiritual evolution? What does she want from you in this life?

Clara: She wants me to teach. How to help other people.

Therapist: What form of teaching does she want you to do?

Clara: She wants me to teach how to care for people the way I care for people.

Therapist: In some professional setting, by means of doing what she's doing now?

Clara: I think both.

Therapist: Can she give us some more details about that and help Clara form an image of what that is going to look like?

Clara: I think I need to go be an instructor or a professor, to teach the nurses empathy and sacrifice.

Therapist: Beautiful. She wants you to continue your studies to elevate yourself so that you can share knowledge and love with others.

Clara: Yeah. Because what I know can't be taught by books.

Therapist: Right. So, you need a platform as a teacher to do this. A nursing career is good, but you need to elevate it to something higher, like a teacher.

Clara: Yeah.

Therapist: Looking at the first 27 years of Clara's life, what can your guide tell you about how you've been doing so far, and whether we are in alignment with this idea?

Clara: We're in alignment. I'm already doing what I'm supposed to do. She's told me that, she keeps telling me to listen because I'm so stubborn.

Therapist: This pit stop here today is to remind you to move on, not to keep stuck where you are now.

Clara: Yeah.

Therapist: Are we still seeing an overly long mourning process, or is she doing better with that this time around?

Clara: She's telling me not to mourn as much as I did last time. I have the tools.

Therapist: What should be the right attitude? Instead of mourning, what should that mindset be? Can she give an example of how that can be done differently?

Clara: I need to let it go as it's happening, mourn for short periods, not days and months. It's okay to mourn, but not like I have been doing.

Therapist: Not to hang on to it.

Clara: Correct.

Therapist: In other words, you can feel it, you can be aware of it, but then snap out of it and move on constructively, is that it?

Clara: Right.

Therapist: Beautiful. What can we do to make the communication with your guide clearer and more real?

Clara: She knows that I talk to her.

Therapist: But she doesn't really believe it all the time, correct?

Clara: I'm telling her, this will remind her. She knows. She's always known. She just doesn't want to believe, and now she does.

Therapist: So, her intuition is correct?

Clara: Yes. She's always known.

Therapist: Are there any specific signs or symbols that would alert her to your presence?

Clara: I send her number patterns. Tell her that she's on the right path.

Therapist: She just needs to be more convinced and live in tune with it.

Clara: Yes.

Therapist: Going a little higher, by detaching from Clara and George even more, and looking at the nature of the Self, what is it that you are as a soul? What is it that you aspire to express?

Clara: She likes acts of service. She likes to help. She's also pure and wise. She's smart. Funny. She's very helpful. She likes to help.

Therapist: How could she manifest these qualities as Clara?

Clara: I think she needs to learn how to be reminded of her true Self. She's got to connect with me more, she's so stressed out by worldly things.

Therapist: Is there anything in her day-to-day routine, or thought pattern, that could de-stress her and allow her to be more in tune with this pure Self?

Clara: She can take better care of her body. She can work out; she likes to do that. And she can meditate more and go sit in the grass and listen to the outside noises. She likes to connect, but she doesn't have time, and she needs to make time.

Therapist: We get so busy forgetting to connect to that highest reality.

Clara: Yeah.

Therapist: She needs to prioritize.

Clara: She needs to realign and reconnect.

Therapist: Right. Because her job here is to express love and compassion through teaching and sharing. But if she's not manifesting love and light, then how can she share that? She needs to rearrange her life fundamentally, to be more in alignment with who she is and what she's here to do. Is it the correct way to summarize?

Clara: Yes, that's exactly what it is.

Therapist: Asking your guide, is there anything else?

Clara: She says I found my people. I'm so worried that I don't have the right people with me. I do.

Therapist: What can she say about these people?

Clara: That they're on their own journey, but we're all supposed to be here together.

Therapist: Are some of these characters that George was connected to also in this life of Clara?

Clara: Yeah.

Therapist: Who was there?

Clara: Bella, my wife. She's my wife now.

Therapist: She was the wife of George as well?

Clara: Yeah.

Therapist: The love continues in this life.

Clara: Yeah.

Therapist: Beautiful.

Clara: John, my best friend, was one of my friends in the war. He was really sick then. And Carrie, she was one of my kids. Well... I think my dog was one of my animals.

Therapist: Interesting.

Clara: I need more animals.

Therapist: George loved animals too.

Clara: He loves animals.

Therapist: What else? How do you feel?

Clara: She's telling me that I need to remember what I went through in the war, and how I was so strong, that I'm kind of doing that now, kind of in a war again. But I'm stronger now, and I can't waste any more time mourning. We already did that. I have to go teach people. I have to show them.

Therapist: Beautiful. Do you have any questions for your guide that we may have forgotten to ask? Something that comes to you right now? Anything you need from her? Anything you want from her?

Clara: She just wants me to stop being stubborn and listen to her. And listen to my intuition, it's so strong.

Therapist: If you could surrender some of that stubbornness to her, and in a beautiful way connect with her, surrender to her, be in tune with her, how would you go about doing that?

Clara: She can feel my emotions. She knows that I'm telling her I'll listen to her. She knows that I'm telling the truth, she knows I'm doing my best. She says she made me come here.

Therapist: To remind you of your story.

Clara: Yeah. That I'm much more than this.

Therapist: Can she give you an idea of what that's going to feel like, as a frame of reference?

Clara: Peaceful. Accomplished.

Therapist: Step into that for a moment, so we can burn that feeling into the nervous system of Clara. So she knows what she is going to be, allowing her to start feeling that already. Can you feel that?

Clara: Yea.

Therapist: Remember this feeling. This is who you are, and who you will be. Be in alignment with this.

Clara: She's telling me that I have the tools, I know, I just need to do it. She'll be there along the way. It's kind of funny, because if I told you everything, there's no fun in that, you have to do it on your own, with the right tools.

Therapist: Right. Otherwise, there's no more point in living, right?

Clara: Right.

We slowly bring the session to a close.

Case 9: Barry
A conduit of infinity

Barry is a financial planner from the East Coast. He has a son who has severe autism and suffers from a lot of physical and mental issues.

Therapist: Now tell me, is it daytime or nighttime?
Barry: Daytime.
Therapist: Are you inside or outside?
Barry: Outside.
Therapist: When you look down at your feet, what, if anything, do you wear on your feet?

Barry: Cowboy boots.
Therapist: What else are you wearing?
Barry: Jeans and a shirt.
Therapist: Are you a man?
Barry: I am a man.
Therapist: What's your age?
Barry: 25 or 26.
Therapist: What is the color of your skin?
Barry: It's white, but it's tan.
Therapist: Are you wearing anything on your head?
Barry: A hat.
Therapist: What kind of a hat?
Barry: Like a dusty white Stetson.
Therapist: What are you aware of straight ahead of you?
Barry: I see buildings on either side of the street, like a dirt street that leads out into the countryside.
Therapist: Can you describe those buildings to me?
Barry: They're false fronts. It's a false front.
Therapist: Like a movie set?
Barry: What was that?
Therapist: Like a set. You say a false front, what does that mean?
Barry: Like a big, western building.
Therapist: But why do you call it false?
Barry: Because the boards are higher than the roof. It's behind it.
Therapist: What kind of stores are there?
Barry: There's a bar saloon.
Therapist: What are you doing here looking out over this town?

Barry: I'm walking toward the edge of town on the boardwalk.

Therapist: Any reason you're going there?

Barry: I don't know.

Therapist: How do you feel right now, walking here?

Barry: I feel like I've got something to do.

Therapist: Important or just important to you?

Barry: It's just a normal day.

Therapist: Just a workday?

Barry: Yeah.

Therapist: What kind of work do you do?

Barry: I work on a ranch.

Therapist: Is it your ranch or are you more like a ranch hand?

Barry: I don't think it's my ranch.

Therapist: Do you like that work?

Barry: I do.

Therapist: What can you tell me about your work on the ranch?

Barry: I like the smell of the trees in the mountains.

Therapist: Are you in the mountains?

Barry: When I go away from town, I am. And I like the camp and I work with cattle.

Therapist: So, you go on these cattle runs, is that what you do?

Barry: Yeah.

Therapist: Is that when you camp?

Barry: Yeah, but I'm alone up there. It's like I'm finding cows, but there's not a lot around me in this.

Therapist: Oh, okay. You're just trying to keep the herd together?

Barry: No, it's like I'm in a different scene now.

Therapist: What scene are you in right now?

Barry: I'm out of the town and I'm up in the mountain and I'm rounding up like stray cattle, but there's not a big herd right now.

Therapist: Oh, okay. What's your name?

Barry: Tom.

Therapist: Ok, Tom, at this point in your life, 25, 26, doing this work, what would you say is the most relevant observation about your life?

Barry: I'm alone.

Therapist: How do you feel about that?

Barry: Somewhat free.

Therapist: Do you like camping and being out with nature and such?

Barry: Yeah.

Therapist: Now, Tom, I'm going to count from 3 down to 1. On the count of 1, we're going to move a few years forward in your life as Tom, to a relevant moment in your life. Something that shapes your heart, your soul, your destiny, your mind. At 3, 2, 1, and you're there now. And tell me what is going on now, Tom?

Barry: I'm 28. And I'm at a dance social, and I see a beautiful girl.

Therapist: Tell me more.

Barry: And when I look at her, it's magical.

Therapist: Do you think she feels the same way?

Barry: Yeah.

Therapist: Ok.

Barry: She has green eyes.

Therapist: Tell me what happened between you and this girl.

Barry: I dance with her and she's laughing and I'm laughing, and I don't feel alone anymore.

Therapist: How is the connection between the two of you?

Barry: It's really strong.

Therapist: What does the place look like where you are now dancing together?

Barry: It's outside. There's a lot of people, maybe 25 people, and there's music, but it's a box lunch social.

Therapist: What does that mean?

Barry: It's where you get to have a dance with girls and then they've all made some food and you get to bid on the box. It's a fundraiser. And you get to bid on the box lunch, and everybody is trying to make sure that the girl they like, they know what box she brought.

Therapist: Did you get the right box?

Barry: I did. I was real careful about that.

Therapist: Now what happens next after you've met this girl?

Barry: I start dating her and her family gives permission even though I'm older. She's younger, like 17.

Therapist: That's almost 10 years younger.

Barry: 18. I'm on a buckboard ride with her and we go down to a stream and have a picnic that she packed, and the wind is blowing her hair at the street. I reach out and touch her face and she smiles at me and pulls my face. She's so beautiful.

Therapist: Are you happy now Tom?

Barry: Very.

I move him forward in time.

Therapist: Tell me what is happening now, Tom.

Barry: We're in a cabin that I built. We're married. She's giving birth.

Therapist: Move forward a little bit and tell me what happens.

Barry: I'm really concerned.

Therapist: Why is that?

Barry: Because I don't know what's going on in the house. I'm outside.

Therapist: Is there anybody with her?

Barry: Yeah, the midwife.

Therapist: Just move forward a little bit in time and tell me what happens next.

Barry: She's okay. We have a little girl. We call her Mary.

Therapist: How are you feeling?

Barry: I'm happy again and I have my own little place. I'm not with the ranch anymore.

Therapist: How do you survive? What kind of work do you do?

Barry: I farm. Have some vegetables, raise corn, and I have some sheep and some pigs.

Therapist: Are you managing all of that?

Barry: Just a small farm. It's a simple life. I see her holding Mary.

Therapist: So where in the world are we exactly, Tom?

Barry: I'm out west.

Therapist: Any idea where West?

Barry: Feels like Wyoming.

Therapist: You like it here?

Barry: I love it here.

Therapist: Are there many others around you or are you pretty isolated?

Barry: We're pretty isolated, but we can go into town with the buckboard.

Therapist: What year is it approximately, Tom? What date? Whatever pops up in your mind is fine.

Barry: 1888.

Therapist: What can you tell me about your life with your wife, your daughter, and your farm? How is it all going?

Barry: It's hard work, but we're happy.

Therapist: What is it exactly that makes you happy now, Tom?

Barry: Coming in at the end of the day, seeing those lanterns flickering off the faces of my wife and daughter.

Therapist: That makes you happy?

Barry: Yeah.

I move him forward in time again.

Therapist: What is happening now Tom?

Barry: (very depressed) We lost the house.

Therapist: What happened?

Barry: I see char burns, and there's smoke. My cabin burnt down.

Therapist: How did it happen?

Barry: Something was wrong with the chimney.

Therapist: How old are you now, Tom?

Barry: 35.

Therapist: How are your wife and your daughter doing?

Barry: I can't feel them anymore.

Therapist: How come? What happened?

Barry: They're gone.

Therapist: How is it possible? What happened?

Barry: (emotional) They got sick. They got sick.

Therapist: They died? When did this happen? Is it long ago or is it recent?

Barry: Two years ago.

Therapist: And now the cabin burns down?

Barry: I didn't care about life anymore.

Therapist: What happens next, Tom?

Barry: I drank heavily.

Therapist: Is that how the house burned down?

Barry: I drank after they passed and wasn't very careful, didn't really care. They didn't die in the fire. They died of sickness. I see their tombstones.

Therapist: What are you going to do now, Tom, now that the house is burned down?

Barry: I don't know.

Therapist: How do you feel?

Barry: Pissed.

Therapist: Let us move a little bit forward in time and tell me how this unfolds.

Barry: For a while I leave, and I go out to the mountains.

Therapist: What do you do in the mountains?

Barry: I live off the land, hunt. I don't drink anymore.

Therapist: No? What made you stop?

Barry: My wife.

Therapist: How is that?

Barry: She did. I felt she wouldn't want me to do it anymore.

Therapist: So, your love for her made you stop?

Barry: It was to heal, rather than to avoid. Or to heal rather than to feel all the pain. To escape the pain with alcohol. So, I moved out into the wilderness.

Therapist: To heal?

Barry: To heal.

Therapist: You said you were there for a while?

Barry: Yeah.

Therapist: And then what did you do afterward? Did you feel better?

Barry: Found a cave and I smoked weed that I killed. And my hair is long and it's a hard, rough life, but I am getting softer inside. When I look out from the cave at the entrance, I see the land and it heals me.

Therapist: I see.

Barry: And I'm old and I stay there.

Therapist: All in all, how long have you stayed in the cave, Tom?

Barry: I move from one section to the other. I don't stay in one spot, but I live that life. I'm older, 50. But it's peaceful and I hear her whisper in the wind.

Therapist: You're still living in the wild right now, Tom?

Barry: It's a lot wilder here.

Therapist: Do you still think about your wife?

Barry: Every day.

Therapist: You have so much love. Are you feeling better now that you're 50 years old? Have you healed?

Barry: It doesn't hurt as bad. And being alone, she's still with me and I talk to her.

Therapist: Go on.

Barry: It sustains me.

Therapist: How would you describe your mental and spiritual state right now?

Barry: I live closer to God, the God of nature. I see. I find peace in the trees or in the streams and in the wind, for the animals.

Therapist: Beautiful. Are you becoming more at peace internally?

Barry: I am.

Therapist: You are?

Barry: I don't want to go back to civilization.

Therapist: You just want to stay this way.

Barry: I will stay this way.

I move him to the last day of his life as Tom.

Therapist: Tell me, how old are you now on this last day of your life, Tom?

Barry: I'm 67.

Therapist: Is there anything going on around you or within you that suggests that your physical death will come this day?

Barry: I've broken my leg.

Therapist: Where are you now?

Barry: I'm in my cave and I have a fire.

Therapist: And how is this broken leg going to cause your death today, Tom?

Barry: I've been... I can't go and hunt and I'm all alone.

Therapist: Is it a lack of food that causes your death or is there an infection of some kind?

Barry: It is an infection and a sickness, but it's also hunger and starvation.

Therapist: When you look back on this life of Tom, what do you think about it?

Barry: I see my wife's face in the flames of the fire and I'm happy to join her.

Therapist: What did you learn from this life?

Barry: The cost of love.

Therapist: What does that mean? Help me understand.

Barry: When you give yourself deeply, you could hurt deeply to the extent that you block out all else.

Therapist: You mentioned the word cost. Do you consider that to be something negative?

Barry: No. I'm spinning right now.

Therapist: What is your last thought or awareness as you leave the body?

Barry: I'm going in circles by clouds. I'm going through the clouds.

Therapist: Just keep on going and know that the loving power is guiding you home. Keep telling me what you're aware of until you arrive so I can stay with you.

Barry: I'm kind of dizzy. A little dizzy.

Therapist: Just give it a moment. As you're adjusting to the out-of-the-body state, allow it a moment. You'll find yourself slowly becoming more centered. The higher you go, the more centered you'll be. The more centered you'll be, the better it feels. Keep on going. Let this loving power guide you home.

Barry: Oh, there she is.

Therapist: Who's here?

Barry: Virginia. That was her name.

Therapist: She waiting for you?

Barry: Yeah.

Therapist: Tell me about this meeting.

Barry: She looks Beautiful. She looks like she did at the box dance.

Therapist: Oh, beautiful.

Barry: And I see her holding Mary's hand.

Therapist: Mary's there too?

Barry: Mary is.

Therapist: Tell me about his meeting and how you feel.

Barry: I give them a big hug, but it's not a hug. It's something different. It's like a hug, but I'm not able to hug because I don't have arms.

Therapist: It's like an energy hug.

Barry: There.

Therapist: How does it feel to have this connection again?

Barry: Oh, I feel so happy. I feel the weight of the loneliness and sorrow dropping away.

Therapist: Is there anything that she says to you as you arrive?

Barry: She doesn't have to.

Therapist: Tell me more.

Barry: We're one. That we are really.

Therapist: Is Mary part of that oneness too?

Barry: Yes. We, all 3 of us. It's like a big family hug where everybody's leaning in without arms.

Therapist: Tell me what happens next. Is she taking you somewhere?

Barry: Yeah, we're walking together. We're in a meadow and we see birds. We're laughing at them. All of us are walking through the meadow together.

Therapist: What is this meadow about? Why here?

Barry: Because it's what we did on earth in our last… before they passed. It looks very similar, but it was the happiest time of our life.

Therapist: You're recreating it again now?

Barry: Yes. We're going under a tree. We sit down.

Therapist: Can you ask her why she had to leave so early?

Barry: Wants to teach me. So that I would remember or learn how it felt to love that deeply, but not be able to act on it.

Therapist: How does she feel about your life in those years after her passing? Was the lesson learned?

Barry: She was compassionate about how much pain I was going through. But I went off by myself and I never moved past it.

Therapist: What does she say about that?

Barry: Well, I found healing by being alone and I connected to peace. I didn't do anything with that for other people. It was just me.

Therapist: Does she suggest you could have done it differently?

Barry: I could have gone back and found the other woman that she was going to have in my life. And to have found love again and maybe another family. But I didn't want to do that. I only wanted her. But she's laughing too because she's like, "But yeah, but it is me after all." It was a joke. It was a little joke there.

Therapist: Tell me about the connection you have with Virginia and Mary. Is this a connection that is running through multiple lifetimes?

Barry: Yeah.

Therapist: Who is she? Is it anybody you recognize?

Barry: Oh, it's my wife.

Therapist: And who is Mary?

Barry: My son.

Therapist: What can you tell about this birth and the plan that was made for this incarnation? What is the theme of this birth? Why did you all come back together again?

Barry: It's the same theme. It's still love. It's a choice to leave or to stay.

Therapist: Help me understand what does that mean?

Barry: Except this time, it's my choice.

Therapist: What does that mean? To stay or to leave?

Barry: They chose to leave, to help me have a greater capacity for love.

Therapist: As Tom?

Barry: As Tom. And now in this life, I was given the choice to leave.

Therapist: When was that and how?

Barry: It was when my son was two years old and there was a lot of pain. And I tried to get away from the pain and I was asked to leave. I was given a choice to be part of the family if that's what I wanted, or to not be part of the family. To see if the love I had learned in the previous life was enough to take the pain or not.

Therapist: You stayed.

Barry: Yes

Therapist: Go on.

Barry: And I came back because I realized that the amount of pain that I had meant that I had a lot of love and I learned to choose the pain for love.

Therapist: You learned to see love through pain?

Barry: No, not exactly. I realized that the pain was there with the love. And that I couldn't have one without the other.

Therapist: When the look at the life plan of Tom, centered around love, are we experiencing that same theme again in this life, as if exploring different ways of deep love?

Barry: Yes.

Therapist: When you're in the spirit world, where you're neither Tom nor Barry, what can you tell me about your true soul identity? What do you do in the spirit world?

Barry: Between lives, I visit different places.

Therapist: What can you tell me about some of these places and see if you can go there?

Barry: They're wild and empty places, but beautiful.

Therapist: Tell me more, and how you travel.

Barry: I fly.

Therapist: You fly there?

Barry: Yeah.

Therapist: You like to travel in the astral worlds, and see different places?

Barry: Yeah.

Therapist: Is that something that you always do between births?

Barry: Yes.

Therapist: You do that alone or do you do that with the spirit of your soulmates?

Barry: I do it by myself. I don't see them with me.

Therapist: Do you sometimes visit guides and wise ones?

Barry: Yeah. There is a pool of blue shimmering water. And there's someone in a white robe at the left of it kneeling, doing something at the edge of the water. And I'm walking toward them.

Therapist: Is it one or are there multiple?

Barry: It's one.

Therapist: Is it a male, or female?

Barry: It's a male.

Therapist: Okay. Does he have facial features?

Barry: Looks a little bit like Gandalf. But yeah, a lot like Gandalf.

Therapist: Tell me, what is the energy of the wise one like?

Barry: Soft and loving.

Therapist: How does his presence make you feel?

Barry: They know everything about me.

Therapist: Has this guide been with you for a long time?

Barry: Yes.

Therapist: Is it okay if we sit down with your guide for a bit and ask him questions?

Barry: Yes.

Therapist: When we look at your soul trajectory through these different births, as Tom, as Barry, what is it that your guide wants for you through and even beyond these births? What is the main mission?

Barry: A place of peace.

Therapist: What does that mean?

Barry: It means feeling like the current. It's raising my vibration. It's raising something inside of me.

Therapist: A higher state of consciousness, a higher state of awakening, is that what he wants for you?

Barry: Yes.

Therapist: To what end? What should that evolve into? What does it become?

Barry: More understanding of what others feel without judgment. It's showing me a place of no judgment, a place where there's no wrong.

Therapist: What he wants for you through all these lives is to come to a place of deep inner peace where there's no judgment, just love.

Barry: Yes.

Therapist: Now, how is Barry doing in that regard, in this incarnation?

Barry: Well, he chose to stay. That was a big choice for him. And he worked through his anger. He's working through loneliness. And he does seem to be looking with more compassion.

Therapist: He is doing well then?

Barry: He is doing well.

Therapist: Now in relation to your wife and son, what is the main mission of these three souls together in this incarnation? What can your guide tell us?

Barry: We have a deep love, and with that love is an opportunity to go deeper. But we all have our own choices to make as to how deep we want to go and how much pain we are willing to take.

As a footnote, Barry's son is severely autistic with a tremendous number of issues.

Therapist: What was the meaning of your son taking on this challenged body and mind? What can your guide tell us?

Barry: He's opening his hands and I see this beam of light coming out of his hands and the light is my son. And it is pure. Pure light. Pure. Oh, he is pure light. He is pure light. It's like a waterfall of light coming out of his hands and that light is my son.

Therapist: What is his task in this world?

Barry: He's a lot. He's like a plane of water, a smooth plane of water. This is one part of him here. And there are lots of other parts of him.

Therapist: Here means where? In the astral world or on Earth?

Barry: There is a little portion of him here, but he is in a lot of places at once.

Therapist: Is it comparable to the idea that an iceberg is also part of that ocean? The ocean exists in different forms, such as waves, icebergs, and planes of water, yet is the same ocean.

Barry: Yeah, it's like a little plane of lava and there are these little bubbles that pop up. And the plane of lava as well as the bubble is my son. But as he is with me today, he is a little bubble popping up out of that plane.

Therapist: Why, this time, is he in this challenged body and mind?

Barry: Helping other people see the world differently.

Therapist: Are you saying that the true nature of your son is not an individual, but of the nature of universal light?

Barry: Yes.

Therapist: He came down to create understanding and compassion in the hearts of other people.

Barry: Yes. But he's also doing lots of other things. This is just one little part of him and there's a whole lake of him.

Therapist: You mean is he doing things in other bodies and in other lives and other worlds?

Barry: I can't see, but yes.

Therapist: So, are you saying he's actually a very large universal consciousness?

Barry: Absolutely.

Therapist: He doesn't have an ego consciousness, and he's more of a universal kind.

Barry: Yes.

Therapist: Well, that's incredible, isn't it? It's like God, right?

Barry: Yes. Like God.

Therapist: Barry believes that his son may not have taken enough energy with him in this incarnation. Looking at this issue from this perspective, does Barry need to understand it in a different way?

Barry: Yes.

Therapist: How would you help Barry understand?

Barry: The liquid can flow back and forth, and it has. It flows back and forth and it's not Barry's responsibility to worry about that.

Therapist: Would it be correct to say that the very fact that your son has a challenged body is the purpose of this birth? And that it's not about having more energy, it's about accepting that this is why he came.

Barry: He came this way because the amount of love that he brought with him is what we can handle at this time. People can't handle more of him than this right now.

Therapist: Can we say that he took this form for the sake of mankind, but that he works this time through this limited form because that's all people can take?

Barry: Exactly.

Therapist: But could he theoretically, even in this birth itself, increase his energy?

Barry: Absolutely.

Therapist: All that he would need to do is open the channel and allow more of the universal consciousness to flow through.

Barry: He can control that.

Therapist: It's not something Barry needs to worry about.

Barry: No.

Therapist: What about the energy levels of Barry and his wife? Is that something that needs adjustments? How much did they take with them?

Barry: Enough.

Therapist: What does the guide have to say about that?

Barry: He's smiling. We're both very strong-willed people and we both have had issues with that in the past.

Therapist: Are you implying that if you would've taken more energy, it would not have ended well and that you would've been too forceful for each other?

Barry: We would've burned each other up.

Therapist: Can we ask the guide to provide Barry and his wife some encouragement and advice on proceeding in life in the best possible way?

Barry: The gift is the moment. To learn to be in the moment. To simply be in that moment and not keep looking ahead or back, just to be in the moment.

Therapist: That's beautiful.

Barry: And they haven't learned that yet, but they're learning it. They still have too much care about the future.

Therapist: That's beautiful advice. Is there anything else that the wise one wants to share?

Barry: I see him raising his hands over us and filling us all with a big bubble of love. There's a big smile and lots of compassion and love.

Therapist: Are there any other souls that are part of this soul group of three?

Barry: No.

Therapist: Is there any predominant color that radiates from your soul?

Barry: There's a greenish color with my wife. My son is pure white, and Barry is yellowish with a little blue.

Therapist: Do you have separate names in the astral plane?

Barry: Aziza. Aziza.

Therapist: Aziza. Who's called Aziza?

Barry: Aziza. I'm Aziza.

Therapist: You're Aziza. What about your wife?

Barry: Starts with an I? Iz, Iz... They sound the same, but one's with an I and one's with an A. They sound very similar.

Therapist: Iziza or something like that?

Barry: Something like that.

Therapist: What about your son?

Barry: He doesn't have a name.

Therapist: From what you described earlier; he seems beyond names.

Barry: He just is.

Therapist: That's incredible. Beautiful. Now, the spirit world is wide open to you. You're here with your guide, you're meeting your soul family again. You know what your purpose is and what you need to do. Is there anything else that we need to understand?

Barry: It is to have fun and enjoy. Being in the moment means it doesn't all have to be big and grand. It's simple. It's the little things. It's the little moments. It's right there. It's not out there. It's right in front of them.

Therapist: Isn't that what you meant earlier? By just being, living in love and gratitude.

Barry: Yeah, but it's a little different. It's even simpler than they think. Oh, I see. It's simpler than they think.

Therapist: Who's they? Do you mean Barry and his wife?

Barry: Yeah, Barry and his wife.

Therapist: How would you help them understand it if it's even more simple?

Barry: That's what their son is doing. He's teaching them simplicity.

Therapist: To just be?

Barry: To just be, to just be.

Therapist: I like what you said. It's not something grandiose because just to be is to become that ocean that your son is.

Barry: Exactly.

Therapist: That is really beautiful. That is really high and yet so simple. How does it make you feel when you see all of that?

Barry: A lot of peace. They think too much.

Therapist: You mean Barry and his wife?

Barry: Yeah.

Therapist: Maybe you can send them over some of this peace. Why don't you let that peace run through the body and brain of Barry right now and integrate it? What are you feeling?

Barry: (weeping) Love. It's him.

Therapist: You are so fortunate to have a manifestation of this love as your son. It is incredible.

Barry: (weeping) He's so big. He's so big.

Therapist: Just take your time with this. Sit with him for a while. When you're ready, just let me know.

(Silence) How do you feel?

Barry: Peaceful. I see him. He is beyond anything and everything.

Therapist: This is incredible. Do you realize how amazing this is? It tells us something about these special children that we think are challenged, but who in reality may have come here as messengers and as conduits of love.

Barry: It explains so many things.

Therapist: Right. These are special children. They're not even of this earth. They're beyond name and form.

Barry: And that's why he doesn't fit in his body.

Therapist: No, of course not. The body cannot contain this power.

Barry: Yes.

Therapist: Beautiful. You're so blessed to see and understand this and to have this in your life.

We slowly bring the session to an end.

Case 10: Reina
A trail of karma through lifetimes

Reina is a 47-year-old Latin American woman, who struggles with her husband and her daughter and doesn't seem to be able to find love in her life. She hardly speaks during the session, but experiences a profound insight into her situation.

Therapist: Tell me, is it daytime or nighttime?
Reina: There's a bright light. I can't see.
Therapist: Is it light everywhere?
Reina: Yes.
Therapist: Are you in the body or are you out of the body?
Reina: I don't know.

Therapist: Is the light everywhere around you or do you feel you are the light?

Reina: There's light around.

Therapist: Are you in the body?

It seems she's hanging around in a white-light space without much going on. She's not very responsive to further questioning. At this point, I must decide to either move her up into a higher out-of-the-body state or make another attempt to get her to go into a past life. It can happen, though rarely when trying to get into a past life that the client instead wants to go higher. This could be due to several reasons. Either the client intuitively anticipates some difficult past life memory or the client has an extremely strong pull to the divine realms. I decide to go ahead and try to get her into a past life.

Therapist: Tell me what is happening now.

Reina: I'm looking at trees.

Therapist: Is it a forest?

Reina: It's a forest.

Therapist: Can you look straight ahead of you and tell me what it is that you're seeing in this forest?

Reina: A bunch of trees.

Therapist: Is it a very dense forest?

Reina: Yes, very dense.

Therapist: In all directions?

Reina: There's nothing behind me. I'm walking towards a dense forest.

Therapist: You're walking towards the forest.

Reina: There's a field behind me.

Therapist: Okay. Look down and tell me what if anything you wear on your feet.

Reina: I'm barefooted.

Therapist: What else are you wearing?

Reina: A dress.

Therapist: What kind of dress?

Reina: Simple.

Therapist: What age are you approximately?

Reina: 12.

Therapist: What is your skin color?

Reina: White.

Therapist: What about your hair?

Reina: Long.

Therapist: Now, you said you're walking towards the forest, right?

Reina: Yes.

Therapist: What are you doing? Are you playing or do you have any purpose?

Reina: Just walking.

Therapist: How do you feel walking toward the forest?

Reina: Fear.

Therapist: Are you running away from something?

Reina: I don't see anything.

Therapist: Hmm. Now tell me, is your house nearby?

Reina: No.

Therapist: Where is it?

Reina: I don't know.

Therapist: Have you run away from your house? Or escaped? Why are you so far away from home at 12 years old? Can you help me understand that? Just trust yourself. You're going to know all the answers.

Reina: Somebody left me there.
Therapist: Really? How did that happen?
Reina: I don't know.
Therapist: Like parents or family members?
Reina: Yes.
Therapist: Do you have any idea what year it is?
Reina: 1800
Therapist: Do you know where you are?
Reina: Somewhere in Europe.
Therapist: What is your name?
Reina: I don't know.

As I'm not getting a lot of information, I move her forward to a later time.

Therapist: We are there now and what is happening?
Reina: I'm older. My name is Nikki.
Therapist: What's your age?
Reina: 20.
Therapist: What can you tell me about where you are right now?
Reina: It's nice. Looks like a tavern.
Therapist: Are you inside the tavern?
Reina: Yes.
Therapist: What are you doing inside?
Reina: Entertaining.
Therapist: In what way? What are you doing?
Reina: Flirting, talking to men.
Therapist: Is that part of your job?
Reina: Yeah.

Therapist: How do you feel doing that kind of work?

Reina: It's okay.

Therapist: What exactly does this job entail? What is it that you need to do?

Reina: To live.

Therapist: To live? Help me understand.

Reina: Pay my bills.

Therapist: Do you live in the tavern?

Reina: No.

Therapist: Where do you live? Why don't we walk there and tell me what the place looks like?

Reina: Looks like an old seedy and nasty place.

Therapist: Do you live there alone?

Reina: I don't see anybody.

Therapist: Do you have a room or something?

Reina: Yes.

Therapist: At 20 years old, how do you describe your life now?

Reina: It's my life now.

Therapist: Your work in a tavern?

Reina: Yes.

Therapist: Do you ever get to go away or is your life only here?

Reina: That's my life.

Therapist: How did you get into this tavern life? I mean, after the age of twelve, what happened?

Reina: It was hard.

Therapist: I bet. Can you tell me in just a few sentences what happened, how you ended up alone in the forest and now in this place?

Reina: A woman. She helped me.

Therapist: A woman helped you?
Reina: Yes.
Therapist: And has that the woman something to do with this tavern?
Reina: She works there too.
Therapist: It's more than entertaining, I assume, or not?
Reina: Yes.
Therapist: Do you work as a prostitute in this place?
Reina: Yes.
Therapist: Has this been going on for a long time?
Reina: Yes. Yes.
Therapist: You said you're used to it now.
Reina: I'm resigned to it.
Therapist: Looking within you or around you, what is the most significant observation about this moment in your life at 20 years old?
Reina: This is a sad life.

I move her forward in her life as Nikki.

Tell me, Nikki, what is going on now?
Reina: I'm older.
Therapist: How old are you now?
Reina: 40s.
Therapist: Where are you now?
Reina: I'm sitting.
Therapist: You're sitting?
Reina: I'm in a room. Living in the same city.
Therapist: Where are you now exactly?
Reina: In a house. I'm older and fatter. I don't like myself.

Therapist: You don't like the way you look?

Reina: No.

Therapist: Are you still working in the tavern?

Reina: No, not making a living like that anymore.

Therapist: No? So, how do you survive now?

Reina: There's a man that lives with me.

Therapist: What can you tell me about this man?

Reina: He uses me. I use him.

Therapist: I see. Can you describe to me the place where you live?

Reina: A brick building, with a window. He's sitting by the window, smoking. With a smirk on his face.

Therapist: Why do you think he has that smirk on his face?

Reina: He's mean to me.

Therapist: And he uses you for his comfort and you use him for his house. Is that what it is?

Reina: And protection.

Therapist: So, not exactly like a loving relationship.

Reina: No.

Therapist: What is your state of mind now in your 40s?

Reina: Resignation.

Therapist: Do you do any work?

Reina: Very little.

Therapist: How long did you work in the tavern?

Reina: For a long time.

Therapist: Did he get you out of that place?

Reina: Yes. I couldn't do the work anymore.

Therapist: Why not?

Reina: I'm fat.

Therapist: Nobody wanted to be around you anymore?
Reina: Not like before.
Therapist: Right. Are you sad about it?
Reina: I just don't like it.
Therapist: Right. What is he doing for a living?
Reina: He steals.
Therapist: Is he a thief?
Reina: Yes.
Therapist: How do you feel about that?
Reina: That's life. He does what he wants. I do what I want.
Therapist: What is it that you do?
Reina: I con people on the streets.
Therapist: What is it that you do? How do you do that?
Reina: Tell them stories and get money from them.
Therapist: And these are lies?
Reina: Yes.
Therapist: How would you describe your mind now?
Reina: I'm wondering, am I going to keep doing this?

I move her forward in time again.

Therapist: Tell me, Nikki, what is going on now?
Reina: I'm sitting on a porch in a rocking chair.
Therapist: How old are you now, Nikki?
Reina: 80.
Therapist: How are you feeling?
Reina: Ok.
Therapist: What is this place like where you are sitting?
Reina: Looks like the countryside.

Therapist: Are you still with the same guy?

Reina: No.

Therapist: What happened to him?

Reina: He died.

Therapist: Have you been in for a long time?

Reina: For quite a while.

Therapist: What happened after he died? How did you manage all these years, Nikki?

Reina: I got his money, then moved here.

Therapist: He left you some money and that's how you survived, and this is how you got to the countryside.

Reina: Yes.

Therapist: As you're sitting here in this rocking chair and you look around, can you tell me what the place looks like?

Reina: Looks old and dirty. Nobody takes care of it.

Therapist: Is it a house?

Reina: It's a house.

Therapist: What about the landscape?

Reina: It's an open field.

Therapist: Are there any other houses nearby?

Reina: No.

Therapist: So, it's very remote?

Reina: Yes.

I move her forward to the last day of her life.

Therapist: Tell me Nikki how old are you on this last day of your life?

Reina: 86.

Therapist: Is there anything going on around you or within you that suggests that your physical death will come on this day?

Reina: I can't breathe.

Therapist: Where are you now? Is this feeling familiar?

Reina: I'm in bed. All wood paneling.

Therapist: Is there anybody near you?

Reina: No.

Therapist: Is it the same house we were in earlier?

Reina: Yes.

Therapist: Now looking back, what do you think about this life you just lived?

Reina: I didn't do much.

Therapist: What are your thoughts about the fact that you didn't do much in this life?

Reina: It was a bad life.

Therapist: What did you learn from this life?

Reina: Not to use people.

Therapist: You are aware of this at the end?

Reina: Yes.

Therapist: Now Nikki, what is your last thought, feeling, or awareness as you leave the body of Nikki?

Reina: I'm going to leave now.

I move her past her death.

Therapist: Where are you now in relation to the body you are leaving behind, can you still see it?

Reina: I see it.

Therapist: Are you floating above it?

Reina: I feel sad for her. She died alone.

Therapist: Look at that body and realize that you're not this body and that you are now a in soul state.

I move her further away and into a higher state of consciousness.

Therapist: As we're now awakening to your true divine Self and the life between life worlds, what is the first thing you notice?
Reina: There's a lot of light.
Therapist: Is it one light or multiple lights?
Reina: Many.
Therapist: Is one light stronger or brighter than others?
Reina: Yes.
Therapist: Why don't you move toward that one while it moves toward you? Know that a loving presence has come to greet you. And tell me what happens next. What kind of feeling do you get when you are coming closer to this light?
Reina: Warm.
Therapist: Is it a guide that has come to meet you or is it a loved one, a soul group member? What is the nature of that light?
Reina: A guide.
Therapist: Does it have a male or female energy or is it more androgynous in nature?
Reina: Male.
Therapist: Beautiful. Just take your time and connect to this male guiding energy.
Reina: Getting closer.
Therapist: Go ahead and do that. Tell me what happens when you do this.
Reina: I'm home.
Therapist: How does it feel?
Reina: It's beautiful.
Therapist: I can understand that communication here perhaps

takes place telepathically. Do you start receiving any sort of communication from your guide?

Reina: I started complaining right away.

Therapist: You did?

Reina: Yes.

Therapist: Why?

Reina: I don't want to go back again.

Therapist: Are you complaining to your guide about this life as Nikki?

Reina: Yes.

Therapist: What does he say about that?

Reina: We'll talk about it.

Therapist: Why did you have to live through this life of Nikki? What does the guide say?

Reina: I needed that.

Therapist: Why did you need that?

Reina: I was bad before.

Therapist: In a life before Nikki? What did you do?

Reina: I was mean and abused women.

Therapist: Were you a man in that life?

Reina: Yes.

Therapist: You were abusing women and you had to experience it yourself this time. Have you learned your lesson?

Reina: Yes.

Therapist: What is it that you have learned based on this last experience?

Reina: Compassion.

Therapist: Very good. How would you describe your heart right now, how do you feel?

Reina: I need to understand what it was like.

229

Therapist: Can you now feel for these women that are abused?

Reina: Yes.

Therapist: In retrospect, how do you feel about Nikki?

Reina: It was a hard life. A failed life. A failed story for her. A failed story.

Therapist: A lesson that you had to go through.

Reina: She suffered a lot. She was never happy.

Therapist: Looking back with your guide to the life before Nikki, where you abused women, do you feel you have learned the required lessons?

Reina: It was necessary.

Therapist: Do you feel that this aspect of that journey has been completed?

Reina: I think so. But the guide thinks otherwise.

Therapist: He does? What does he say?

Reina: I could have used more compassion. Even the moments of despair, I could have been compassionate to other people, but I wasn't. I was consumed in pain.

Therapist: You were self-centered?

Reina: Yes.

Therapist: Now, does this have any consequences for the next life as Reina? What does your guide say?

Reina: He smiles and thinks I'll do fine.

Therapist: Does he feel that this theme must be continued in your current life as Reina?

Reina: Yes.

Therapist: How is it playing out in Reina's life?

Reina: Be compassionate. She needs to learn compassion.

Therapist: And how are you supposed to learn that? What circumstances have been put in place to teach her compassion?

Reina: Her husband.

Therapist: Help me understand.

Reina: It's difficult. She needs to be compassionate to him.

Therapist: How has she been doing so far?

Reina: Not so good.

Therapist: Has she been too focused on her own pain, rather than learning to be compassionate to others instead?

Reina: Yes.

Reina: She's unhappy and she must learn to be aware of it.

Therapist: And use suffering to become more compassionate?

Reina: Yes.

Therapist: Would you say that this is one of the most important themes of this incarnation of Reina, or is there something else as well? You can ask your guide if you don't know it, or maybe you do know it as you remember discussing it with your guide before taking up this birth of Reina. Go back to that moment before you took up this birth. What did you decide you needed to develop in this life?

Reina: You will seek love and you will not find it.

Therapist: Help me understand what this means.

Reina: You will seek love and you will not find it. And that is my purpose. No physical love but developing self-love instead.

Therapist: Are you saying that in this life of Reina, she needs to learn to become self-reliant, and find love within, in her higher self?

Reina: Yes.

Therapist: In other words, this is the beginning of a spiritual awakening. Is that correct?

Reina: Yes.

Therapist: Could we say that this is a turning point in her evolution, where these karmas seem to unravel, and she instead starts finally to turn the journey within? By becoming awakened to the search within, instead of being engaged in looking for love outside in physical relationships.

Reina: That's it.

Therapist: Does your guide agree with that or have anything to add to that?

Reina: Rely on yourself and you'll be fine.

Therapist: Once she starts relying on herself, what is going to happen? What is the next step?

Reina: Learn to move forward.

Therapist: And what does moving forward look like?

Reina: She will stop this search for love.

Therapist: What is your soul looking for?

Reina: Joy.

Joan. Tell me more about that joy that you're seeking. Are you talking about the search for physical love that you must overcome, and must turn into the love of your own true Self?

Reina: Yeah.

Therapist: Is there anything that you want to ask your guide?

Reina: Where is my tribe?

Therapist: What does he say?

Reina: You'll find it soon.

Therapist: Is there anything he can tell us that would help give Reina some courage?

Reina: Be patient, it will come.

Therapist: It's not something that you should worry about?

Reina: No.

Therapist: Any other questions for your guide?

Reina: My daughter.

Therapist: What does he say about that difficult relationship?

Reina: You've seen her before.

Therapist: In a past life, who was she? Are you aware of who she was?

Reina: (very emotional) Yes.

Therapist: Who was she in the past life?

Reina: My husband.

Reina: She hates me.

Therapist: But didn't you use each other?

Reina: Yes.

Therapist: So why is this karma continuing in this life?

Reina: I think I killed him to get his money.

Therapist: And this is why the karma continues in this lifetime?

Reina: Yes.

Therapist: What can Reina do to neutralize this karma?

Reina: Be ready to forgive.

Therapist: In what way should she bear this?

Reina: Be strong.

Therapist: Now we understand why this girl acts this way, yes?

Reina: (still very emotional) Yes.

Therapist: Perhaps now you also understand why compassion is important.

Reina: Yes, I see it now.

Therapist: But the guide said you will be able to overcome, right?

Reina: Yes.

Therapist: And at the end of this life, you will be able to free yourself from this karma.

Reina: Yes, he says I can be free from it.

Therapist: So, you have something good to look forward to.

Reina: I will, I can be free. I have to work my way through it.

Therapist: Do you see now how this karma moves through at least three lives?

Reina: I see it.

Therapist: That actions have consequences?

Reina: Yes.

Therapist: Are there any other questions for your guide?

Reina: My sister.

Therapist: What can he tell us about her?

Reina: She was my friend.

Therapist: When?

Reina: In another life. Before.

Therapist: During your life where you were the abuser?

Reina: Yes.

Therapist: What was your relationship during that life? Did you work together?

Reina: We were friends and lovers.

Therapist: Is that karma still active in this lifetime?

Reina: I hurt her.

Therapist: You hurt her in that lifetime? What did you do?

Reina: She wanted to be closer to me and I didn't like it. I hurt her.

Therapist: And now she's hurting her back in this lifetime by not loving you?

Reina: She wanted to marry me, and I never did.

Therapist: And you're experiencing rejection this time?

Reina: I must learn to love her, even though she never loves me back.

Therapist: So, there is a kind of payback from that life.

Reina: Yes.

Therapist: What is your conclusion, looking at all of this?

Reina: You get your goals and finish this life.

Therapist: Let's detach ourselves for a moment and look at your soul-Self beyond these births. Who are you beyond all these births? What is your real nature like?

Reina: I'm energy.

Therapist: Beautiful. What is it that you want as a pure energetic being when all these lives come to an end?

Reina: Experience all the emotions.

Therapist: And what will that lead to?

Reina: To be one with the Master.

Therapist: And who is that master?

Reina: The one that created it all.

Therapist: And how close are you?

Reina: Not close, no.

Therapist: Do you have some lives to go?

Reina: Yes.

Therapist: Can we, if even for a moment, get a glimpse of the master? Maybe your guide can take us there.

Reina: I'm eager. But he says I must wait.

Therapist: Why wait?

Reina: I'm not ready.

Therapist: Can you at least, for a moment, truly embrace your own divine Self? Can you feel the divine aspect of yourself in the astral world?

Reina: (deep sigh) Yes, I can.

Therapist: And how does it feel?

Reina: (very deeply emotional, yet calm) Eternal. Eternal.

Therapist: Just stay with that for a moment and let this beautiful eternal feeling flow through the body and mind of Reina as well, so she can start to feel it too.

(silence). Can she feel it?

Reina: I'm one.

Therapist: Beautiful. Now remember this feeling. And remember that you're perfectly capable of inviting this into your life, as you are showing yourself now. Remember that all these karmic events are just theater performances. That the eternal part of you is not affected by this. Feel the difference. And allow Reina to invite this eternal energy into her life. Now, the spirit world is wide open to you. Is there any other being we need to connect to or any other place we need to go to, or do you feel that we've seen what we needed to see today? How do you feel?

Reina: I'm okay.

Therapist: Would you like to stay a moment longer in this eternal energy?

Reina: Yes.

We slowly end the session here.

Case 11: Kelly
Love and loss

Kelly is a 57-year-old woman from the East Coast, and has, to use her own words 'a thirst for knowledge of what life here on earth is all about.' One of her sons, Shane, passed away prematurely and the family, each in their own way, it trying to deal with it the best they can. You can find the story of her other son Hank here as well, in the next case.

Therapist: Is it daytime or nighttime?
Kelly: Daytime.
Therapist: Are you inside or outside?
Kelly: Outside.

Therapist: Looking down at your feet, what, if anything, do you feel you wear on your feet?

Kelly: Black shoes.

Therapist: What else are you wearing?

Kelly: Black clothes.

Therapist: Does it strike you as fancy, formal, rich, poor, or somewhere in between?

Kelly: Plain.

Therapist: Plain and all-black. Are you a man, a woman, a boy, or a girl?

Kelly: Man.

Therapist: What is the color of your skin?

Kelly: Brown.

Therapist: Now what is your age approximately?

Kelly: 30s.

Therapist: Look straight ahead of you, what are you aware of?

Kelly: A town.

Therapist: Can you give me a general description of this town? What does it look like?

Kelly: There are dirt roads.

Therapist: What kind of houses?

Kelly: I see a general store.

Therapist: Is it a small town or a big town?

Kelly: A small town.

Therapist: You say dirt roads. What's the climate like?

Kelly: It's dry.

Therapist: Where in the world are we? What comes to mind?

Kelly: America.

Therapist: What part of America?

Kelly: The South.

Therapist: Now, are you in the middle of town or are you kind of looking at the town?

Kelly: I'm looking at town.

Therapist: How do you feel looking at it?

Kelly: Not good.

Therapist: No? How come?

Kelly: Pain.

Therapist: What kind of pain?

Kelly: Unjust.

Therapist: Injustice?

Kelly: Injustice.

Therapist: How come? Does it affect you in any way?

Kelly: Yes.

Therapist: How come?

Kelly: The skin.

Therapist: Because of your skin color?

Kelly: Yes.

Therapist: Are you treated unfairly?

Kelly: Yes.

Therapist: What year is it, approximately?

Kelly: 1900s.

Therapist: Are you here alone looking at this town or are there others with you?

Kelly: I'm alone.

Therapist: What are you doing here?

Kelly: I'm standing here.

Therapist: Do you have any plans? Are you going somewhere?

Kelly: I don't have a plan.

Therapist: Where do you live? Do you live near this town?
Kelly: I think so.
Therapist: Do you have a family?
Kelly: No, not anymore.
Therapist: What happened to them?
Kelly: Bad things.
Therapist: Can you share with me what happened?
Kelly: They were killed.
Therapist: How do you spend your days now?
Kelly: I don't know.
Therapist: What is your name?
Kelly: Abel.
Therapist: How would you describe to me your most significant observation about this moment?
Kelly: Lost.
Therapist: In what way? Can you share?
Kelly: I don't know what to do next.
Therapist: Why is it that at this moment, you're feeling lost?
Kelly: I don't have anybody.
Therapist: Did this all happen recently?
Kelly: Yes.

I move her forward in time.

Therapist: Tell me what is happening now, Abel.
Kelly: I'm stuck there.
Therapist: In the same place?
Kelly: Yes.
Therapist: How old are you now?

Kelly: I didn't move. I didn't change.

Therapist: You're still there? Is there anything else that you need to share with me about this moment? Have they been treating you so badly?

Kelly: Yes. Murdered.

Therapist: Your family was murdered?

Kelly: There's nobody.

Therapist: No support anywhere?

Kelly: No.

Therapist: Now tell me, Abel, in your younger years, what can you tell me about yourself? What kind of work do you do? How have you been living?

Kelly: I was with my family.

Therapist: In the same area?

Kelly: Yes.

Therapist: And with family, you mean your wife and children or your parents?

Kelly: My parents.

Therapist: How was your life growing up?

Kelly: More joyful.

Therapist: What did your father and mother do for work?

Kelly: Mother's home. Father goes to work.

Therapist: What kind of work was he doing?

Kelly: Shoes, repair shoes.

Therapist: And how many brothers and sisters do you have?

Kelly: A lot. Three.

Therapist: Where are they now?

Kelly: Dead.

Therapist: They're all dead. It's the family that got killed?

Kelly: Yes.

Therapist: Did you have a wife as well?

Kelly: No.

Therapist: I'm so sorry that you must go through this, Abel, but what I would like to do is count from 3 down to 1, and I want us to go beyond this moment, okay? We're going to move forward till you get a little bit older and you can jump forward as far as you want till you arrive at a relevant moment in your life, going from 3, 2, 1. And you are there now. Tell me what is happening now, Abel?

Kelly: I don't think Abel makes it.

Therapist: Then let us go to go to the last day of Abel's life. How old are you now, Abel, on this last day of your life?

Kelly: Maybe the same.

Therapist: Is there anything going on around you or within you that suggests that your physical death will come this day?

Kelly: No.

Therapist: What happened? How is Abel going to die?

Kelly: Hung.

I'm trying to avoid the gory details of his death.

Therapist: I'm so sorry. Now, before we move on, looking back at this life, what are your thoughts about this life that you lived as Abel?

Kelly: I don't understand.

Therapist: About why people do what they do?

Kelly: Yeah.

Therapist: What did you learn from this life, Abel?

Kelly: Love.

Therapist: It's very remarkable, Abel, that going through the things that you go through, you develop love. Now without necessarily going through this traumatic death, I want you to tell me what your last thoughts, feelings, or awareness are when you leave this body.

Therapist: I want to see my family.

I move her past her death.

Therapist: Can you still see your body?
Kelly: I'm floating.
Therapist: How do you feel about your death?
Kelly: I'm happy.

I move her even further up.

Therapist: What do you notice?
Kelly: A bench. It's bright. A bench. I want to sit on the bench.
Therapist: How do you feel sitting here?
Kelly: Peaceful, secure.
Therapist: What does the place look like when you look around you?
Kelly: It's nature. It's like a forest. The sky is blue. The trees are green.
Therapist: Beautiful.
Kelly: There are animals in the forest.
Therapist: Beautiful.
Kelly: It's peaceful.
Therapist: When you look at your own soul-Self, what do you look like now?
Kelly: Like light.
Therapist: Any particular colors?

Kelly: Light.

Therapist: Do you have a form?

Kelly: It's kind of like those wood models, just no face, no hair, just a form, and light.

Therapist: Just made out of light. Beautiful. How do you feel being this light?

Kelly: I want to feel this way always.

Therapist: Now what is this place? Is this like a welcoming place or a place of restoration?

Kelly: I feel like it's my spirit home.

Therapist: Beautiful. Take some time and enjoy being here, being back home again after all the events of this last life. Now tell me, do you have a spirit name?

Kelly: I don't think so.

Therapist: Are you alone in this spirit home or are there others as well?

Kelly: Just animals.

Therapist: You like animals?

Kelly: I do.

Therapist: Take your time and enjoy this place. You can stay as long as you want. What we also can do, whenever you're ready, is ask a guide to come and visit you or we can go to visit some ancestors or wise ones, whatever you feel like. Whenever you're ready. Okay. You tell me what you like to do when you're ready.

Kelly: I want to see a guide. My guide.

Therapist: Do you normally invite the guide to your place, or do you go to the guide?

Kelly: I don't know.

Therapist: Well, you know what? If you like it, we can invite the guide to come to you. Would you like that?

Kelly: It feels like this is where we meet.

Therapist: All right, look around you and know that the guide is already here and when you see the guide, let me know.

Kelly: It might be the deer. It came over to me.

Therapist: Oh, beautiful. Now tell me, what is the energy of this deer guide?

Kelly: It's peaceful, loving, kind, good.

Therapist: Oh, beautiful.

Kelly: Yeah.

Therapist: What is the first communication you're receiving from your guide?

Kelly: It's giving me peace. Telling me it's going to be okay.

Therapist: Ok.

Kelly: It gets behind me.

Therapist: Why did your soul have to go through that experience? What did you need to learn from this lifetime as Abel?

Kelly: I have to learn. I can get through it. Don't give up.

Therapist: Before you took up this life of Abel, when you were discussing with your guide the next challenge, what was decided the life plan of Abel was going to be?

Kelly: The challenges of skin color.

Therapist: And what did you learn?

Kelly: We were not lesser or equal, we're not worthless, we're worth just as much.

Therapist: So, what did Abel learn from this life then? Self-worth and self-value?

Kelly: Don't give up.

Therapist: Strength.

Kelly: Abel gave up.

Therapist: You gave up. What did the guide tell you about how Abel did in that life?

Kelly: Abel gave up.

Therapist: I see.

Kelly: Abel didn't believe he was going to be okay.

Therapist: What could he have done differently had he stayed?

Kelly: Lived.

Therapist: I see.

Kelly: Lived by himself until he found somebody.

Therapist: So, he also gave up on love then?

Kelly: Yes.

Therapist: He gave up on life and gave up on love. Now, before starting the life of Kelly, what was the assignment for this life?

Kelly: I don't really know, but I have to think... I think it's faith, humility, strength.

Therapist: How is Kelly doing?

Kelly: Kelly's doing okay. Kelly's doing great, I'm proud of Kelly.

Therapist: Are there some lingering issues from Abel's life that are yet to be worked out in Kelly's life? Or has Kelly kind of accomplished what Abel couldn't do?

Kelly: Kelly did accomplish what Abel couldn't do.

Therapist: So, there's a huge progression then in Kelly's life. Is the guide proud of Kelly?

Kelly: Yes.

Therapist: Looking beyond where Kelly is now, and looking at her potential, what does the guide want for your soul?

Kelly: Hm. I think I'm supposed to learn.

Therapist: And what is the culmination of that learning? What does your guide tell you? What is your destiny? What does he want for you?

Kelly: I think I'm going to keep coming back.

Therapist: Is there anything that you want to do coming back?

Kelly: I would want to help people, spiritually.

Therapist: Beautiful. Is that's why you want to keep learning so you can give back more?

Kelly: Yes.

Therapist: What do you want to become as a spirit? Everybody has their own different ways. Some people want to just become an instrument of knowledge, some as instruments of love, others instruments of light. What does appeal to you in your highest form?

Kelly: I think love, it's all about love.

Therapist: When we ask your guide about Kelly at this moment in her evolution, what does he have to say about love?

Kelly: I'm learning.

Therapist: Is there anything that can be improved? Something that the guide can share with your soul-Self so you can take it back to Kelly?

Kelly: Just give. Don't want anything back.

Therapist: Beautiful. Can we define that the purpose of your soul-Self is to give back, to love, to share that with others, to enlighten and to help others, or is there more?

Kelly: Yes. I think that's it.

Therapist: How does it feel knowing that about yourself?

Kelly: It feels heavy.

Therapist: Yeah? Why so?

Kelly: It's hard to do.

Therapist: It's the highest, is it not? That's the highest sacrifice. Is there anything your guide can give you that will help you?

Kelly: The guide is saying: one day at a time. One day. No rush.

Therapist: Is there anything that you need from the guide right now?

Kelly: Knowing. I need to know.

Therapist: What is it that you need to know from the guide?

Kelly: That one day I'll get there.

Therapist: Do you need a confirmation from the guide?

Kelly: He can tell me.

Therapist: So why don't we ask him? What does he say?

Kelly: One day.

Therapist: You will get there, right?

Kelly: One day. One person.

Therapist: Wonderful. Now, that we are here with the guide in your spirit home, would you like to meet Shane?

Kelly: Yes.

Therapist: Why don't you invite him to come over as well, or if you need be, you can go to him, whatever you feel like. You lead the way, okay? And tell me what happened so I can stay with you. Is he there?

Kelly: Yeah.

Therapist: How is he doing?

Kelly: He's great.

Therapist: What does he look like right now?

Kelly: He looks handsome. He's happy.

Therapist: Would you like to stay a few moments alone with him?

Kelly: Yes.

Therapist: Stay as long as you want with him, okay? And when you're ready, let me know?

Kelly: Okay.

(silence)

Therapist: What did he say?

Kelly: He's happy. He's going to stay with us. He was showing me some signs and kissed me.

Therapist: How do you feel seeing him?

Kelly: He's with our dog right now while he was with me, and he said he knows and he's taking care of us. He's showing his tricks. He's happy.

Therapist: Is there anything that he needs to tell you that he hasn't told you yet?

Kelly: Don't worry about me, I'm ok.

Therapist: Now the spirit world is wide open to you. Is there anything or anybody else we need to visit?

Kelly: I'd like to see my father.

Therapist: You lead the way again because you know your way around. And tell me what happens when you meet him so I can stay with you.

Kelly: He can't come down.

Therapist: No?

Kelly: No.

Therapist: Why is that?

Kelly: He's still reviewing his life.

Therapist: Is there anything you'd like to share with him?

Kelly: Yeah, I told him that it's okay.

Therapist: Is there anything else you need to discuss with your guide that we may have missed?

Kelly: Let's just see if there's anything he needs to tell me before he goes.

Therapist: Take your time. Are you still sitting on your bench?

Kelly: Yes.

Therapist: Beautiful. Take your time with him. Enjoy his

presence. Feel his energy so you'll never forget. You can always connect back to him later as well. We want to make sure that we are not missing anything.

Kelly: Oh, it said one day at a time again.

Therapist: He wants you to focus on the now, right?

Kelly: One at a time.

Therapist: To love now, to live now and not to worry about the future, right?

Kelly: One person at a time. It doesn't have to be something big. I don't have to change the world.

Therapist: Just love one person at a time.

Kelly: One person at a time.

Therapist: That's significant because what it means is that you love now, right? It's not about quantity, it's about quality. Where you go, you love. It's an expression of who you really are. It's not a task, it's about being.

Kelly: Just accept.

Therapist: Yeah.

Kelly: Just accept it.

Therapist: Accept yourself as love, the source of love.

Kelly: Just accept that simplicity.

Therapist: It's not a job.

Kelly: It's simple.

Therapist: Isn't that very liberating? Because before you felt this to be heavy. But when you look at it this way, the way he says it, that's not heavy. You're not responsible. You just love.

Kelly: That's it.

Therapist: Isn't it beautiful what he's telling you?

Kelly: Yes.

Therapist: It's very profound.

Kelly: It's easy.

Therapist: And he sets you free.

Kelly: It's too easy.

Therapist: Yeah. It's only easy when you know how to love, which you know how to do, right?

Kelly: He showed me the Dalai Lama. He's showing me his kind face.

Therapist: Yeah.

Kelly: Go read his books.

Therapist: Beautiful. How does that make you feel?

Kelly: It makes me feel great. It makes me feel secure.

Therapist: Is there anything you want to share with your guide, to express to your guide?

Kelly: I want to see him more.

Therapist: So how can we do that?

Kelly: I want to talk to him more.

Therapist: Is there anything that he can share how you can accomplish that?

Kelly: Meditate more, like today.

Therapist: Because you have the gift. You see, you can easily do this.

Kelly: Yes.

Therapist: Once you open this channel you can easily do it. Just trust that about yourself, knowing you have this beautiful gift of divine connection, of love, and purity.

Kelly: And trust myself.

Therapist: Trust yourself. Remember this feeling, because it is undeniable, is it not? Any other questions you may have for your guide?

Kelly: No.

Therapist: How do you feel?

Kelly: I feel connected to spirit.

Therapist: Would you like to stay a moment quietly with spirit?

Kelly: Yes.

Therapist: All right. Take all your time and when you're ready, let me know, okay?

We slowly end the session here.

Case 12: Hank
A royal mystic

Hank, age 27, is the son of Kelly, whom we saw in our previous chapter. His elder brother Shane passed away prematurely.

Therapist: Are you inside or outside?

Hank: Inside.

Therapist: Looking down at your feet, tell me what if anything, you wear on your feet.

Hank: Sandals.

Therapist: What kind of sandals?

Hank: Four straps.

Therapist: What about the rest of your body?

Hank: A white garb.

Therapist: Is it a one-piece or multiple pieces?

Hank: Maybe two pieces with the top piece that is pretty long.

Therapist: When you look at this garb, what does the style remind you of?

Hank: Something I'd wear to relax.

Therapist: Is it more like an inside dress?

Hank: It is.

Therapist: Are you a man or a woman?

Hank: A man.

Therapist: What age approximately?

Hank: Maybe 30.

Therapist: What is the color of your skin?

Hank: White.

Therapist: You said you're inside, right?

Hank: Yes.

Therapist: Can you give me a description of what this room is like?

Hank: It's books everywhere on bookshelves. Out the window, you can see water.

Therapist: What kind of water?

Hank: Maybe a lake.

Therapist: Is it a big lake or a small lake?

Hank: I can only see part of it.

Therapist: Is this a library of sorts?

Hank: It feels like it.

Therapist: Does it have a desk as well or is it just books?

Hank: It has a desk. It's well-lit.

Therapist: What kind of desk? Is it ornate or is it simple?

Hank: It's wooden.
Therapist: What's the energy in this library?
Hank: Light.
Therapist: Do you like it here?
Hank: I'm happy. Yes.
Therapist: Is this your library?
Hank: It feels like it's somewhere I think by myself.
Therapist: Is this where you come to think?
Hank: It feels like it.
Therapist: What is it that you are thinking about?
Hank: Something important.
Therapist: Is it regarding your work? Or is it more about politics or your family? What is it?
Hank: A life event.
Therapist: Ok I see.
Hank: Maybe family.
Therapist: Does it pertain to you?
Hank: It feels like a divorce.
Therapist: Do you think it's your divorce?
Hank: I think so.
Therapist: How does it make you feel?
Hank: I think I'm depressed.
Therapist: How come?
Hank: I feel like I don't know why it happened.
Therapist: Has the divorce already taken place?
Hank: Yes.
Therapist: You didn't see it coming?
Hank: It could be death.
Therapist: Is it about separation?

Hank: Yes.

Therapist: Where are we in the world, looking around you, what comes to mind?

Hank: It feels like somewhere in Europe.

Therapist: What year comes to mind?

Hank: The 1800s.

Therapist: What is your name? It could even be a nickname.

Hank: I'm not sure.

Therapist: It may come to you in a moment. Now, what would you say is the most significant observation about this moment, either within you or around you?

Hank: I think it's beautiful outside.

Therapist: Is it a nice place?

Hank: It looks like there's a tree and then you can see the lake after it. The water is glistening.

Therapist: Beautiful. Do you think this is an affluent area where you are?

Hank: It feels like a castle.

Therapist: Oh, okay.

Hank: I'm in a town.

Therapist: Can you describe this town to me?

Hank: It looks like there are cobblestones on the ground. There are people selling stuff.

Therapist: What kind of buildings are here?

Hank: Stone-like castles.

Therapist: So this is a nice-looking town.

Hank: It is.

Therapist: Where are you now in relation to this town?

Hank: I'm by the boats.

Therapist: Is there a marina? Or what does it look like?

Hank: I think people have brought food.

Therapist: I see.

Hank: They brought food for the town.

Therapist: Say that again?

Hank: Like I'm overseeing something. Boats came in. Merchants.

Therapist: With food and items?

Hank: Yes.

Therapist: Are they offloading things?

Hank: Yes.

Therapist: What kind of boats are those?

Hank: They look like traditional boats.

Therapist: Are they sailing boats?

Hank: Yes, with sails.

Therapist: They come off the lake?

Hank: It must be the sea.

Therapist: Is your job somehow involved with this or are you just looking? You said you're overseeing something.

Hank: It feels like I'm involved.

Therapist: Are you at the top of the food chain, in between, or at the bottom?

Hank: It feels like I'm on top.

Therapist: Are these your boats or is it your company? Or are you more like a supervisor?

Hank: It feels like it's my town.

Therapist: You must be an affluent guy.

Hank: I think I might be a king or a prince or something.

Therapist: How does it feel to be in this position?

Hank: I think I'm just trying to do a good job.

Therapist: What is your relationship with your people?

Hank: I think they like me.

Therapist: Are you hands-on, or are you supervising from a distance?

Hank: Hands-on.

Therapist: What else can you tell me about this moment? Just look around you and see what's going on.

Hank: I think I'm wearing armor.

Therapist: Oh, really? Is this wartime or is there a conflict going on?

Hank: I think it's a formality.

Therapist: Like a pose?

Hank: Yes.

Therapist: What else can you tell me? Just give me a description of what this marina looks like.

Hank: There's a wall. I'm on the other side of the wall. And then stone all over the grounds, and wooden docks for ships. And people are coming off the ship with wheelbarrows.

Therapist: They're taking stuff down?

Hank: Yes.

Therapist: How far is your place from this marina?

Hank: I think it's about a 20, 30-minute walk.

Therapist: What is your age right now?

Hank: I must be 35, 40.

Therapist: Any idea what your name is? What do people call you?

Hank: Patrick.

Therapist: Patrick, are you in a relationship?

Hank: I don't know.

Therapist: It will come to you later. Now, Patrick, what is the most interesting observation about this moment?

Hank: I see that all the people from the town are looking at me.
Therapist: How does it make you feel?
Hank: Like they need my help.
Therapist: What do you do with that awareness that they need your help?
Hank: Help them.
Therapist: Are you able to?
Hank: Yes.
Therapist: How does it make you feel when you help them?
Hank: It feels good. It's just like I'm doing everything.
Therapist: All right.

I move him forward in time.

Hank: It all went dark.
Therapist: Did something happen?
Hank: I'm in a jail cell.
Therapist: Tell me about it. Just look around you.
Hank: It's dark. There's one window. It's very small.
Therapist: How old are you now?
Hank: 50 or 60.
Therapist: Have you been long in this place?
Hank: Maybe five years.
Therapist: What happened?
Hank: I lost a battle.
Therapist: Where did this battle take place?
Hank: The town got taken over.
Therapist: This cell, where is it exactly in relation to where you used to live?
Hank: It feels like it's underground.

Therapist: Is it the same place? You're held captive in your own place?

Hank: I think so.

Therapist: Who are these captors? How do you feel right now?

Hank: I feel like I'm used to it.

Therapist: Do they treat you well despite being locked up?

Hank: I feel it's peaceful.

Therapist: I see.

Hank: I meditate a lot.

Therapist: What is your state of consciousness after all these years of meditation?

Hank: I'm feeling indifferent if I live or die.

Therapist: You're not necessarily in a bad state of mind then?

Hank: No. I've actually come to like life.

Therapist: You like the life of quietness and meditation?

Hank: Yes. There's this bird that comes to the window.

Therapist: You have a relationship with that bird?

Hank: It feels like it.

Therapist: Beautiful. Do you have any experiences while you're in this meditative state?

Hank: When I was in the library room, somebody died. And in the jail cell, I've been able to get a lot closer.

Therapist: To the spirit of the one who died?

Hank: Yes.

Therapist: Who died?

Hank: It feels like my wife.

Therapist: And you have been able to connect with her?

Hank: Yes.

Therapist: In what way? Do you actually see her or feel her or

connect to her soul?
Hank: I come out of my body. What is it? We intertwine.
Therapist: That's beautiful. You must be pretty advanced then?

I move him further ahead in time.

Hank: I think I'm about to get my head chopped off.
Therapist: Right about now?
Hank: It feels close.
Therapist: Where are you now?
Hank: I'm in front of a crowd.
Therapist: Is this still in the same town?
Hank: Yes.
Therapist: Are the captors doing this?
Hank: Yes. I can see a guillotine. People are screaming.
Therapist: How do you feel?
Hank: I feel at peace.
Therapist: Now looking back on this life as Patrick, what are your thoughts about it?
Hank: I feel good about it.
Therapist: In what way?
Hank: I feel as though I was a good king, I was a good husband, and I progressed spiritually.
Therapist: What did you learn from this life as a king?
Hank: What it feels like to help people, be responsible.
Therapist: What is your last thought or awareness as you leave this body?
Hank: I'm excited to see my wife.

I move him past his death.

Therapist: Where are you now in relation to the body you are leaving behind? Can you still see it?

Hank: I am floating up.

Therapist: Can you still see the body or are you going away from it?

Hank: Drifting away.

Therapist: All right. Just keep on drifting and tell me how you feel about your death.

Hank: I feel like I was ready to die. It's white.

Therapist: Is it white light everywhere?

Hank: Yes.

Therapist: How do you feel in this white light?

Hank: Carefree.

Therapist: What's the energy of this light?

Hank: I feel like I'm floating.

Therapist: What about your soul-Self? When you look at yourself right now, do you have a form or are you formless? Are you light, frequency, vibration, or a combination of these?

Hank: Like a light with a little bit of trail.

Therapist: Do you have a color or are you just white light?

Hank: Feels like a few different colors.

Therapist: Can you identify some of them?

Hank: Red, purple, and yellow.

Therapist: Beautiful. Just keep on moving. And as you find yourself expanding into the highest level of your being, what are you aware of?

Hank: I see other lights, but nobody's coming to me.

Therapist: Keep on going until you can meet them.

Hank: Okay. I think they're following.

Therapist: What can you tell me about who this is?

Hank: It is a purple light.

Therapist: Is it a loved one or is it a guide?

Hank: Maybe a loved one.

Therapist: Do you recognize who it is?

Hank: I think it's somebody I haven't met.

Therapist: You said there are multiple beings here, right?

Hank: Yes.

Therapist: Is this a group, a soul group of some kind?

Hank: Maybe.

Therapist: What kind of communication are you getting from this purple being who's here with you now?

Hank: Surprised.

Therapist: Why is that?

Hank: They think I'm on vacation.

Therapist: They didn't expect you here right now?

Hank: No.

Therapist: Is this because it's a premature kind of departure?

Hank: Unsure.

Therapist: Take a moment and find yourself tuning in to these beings until you find a situation, a vibration, a frequency where you can communicate with ease and clarity.

Hank: It seems like they're all in groups.

Therapist: There are different groups?

Hank: Yes. It's about 20.

Therapist: 20 different groups?

Hank: 20 different lights.

Therapist: Oh, there are different beings in this group. But is this your group or not?

Hank: I don't know. Nobody's coming over to me.

Therapist: All right. You have a choice to either go to them or go somewhere else.

Hank: I think I'm in the wrong place.

Therapist: You can depart here if you want. You can go wherever you want just by thinking about it. Where would you like to go? We can meet a guide, or we can meet your loved one.

Hank: Maybe meet a guide.

Therapist: All right. With just the intention of your mind, project yourself to where the guide resides, and tell me what happens.

Hank: They have just seen me.

Therapist: Are there multiple guides?

Hank: There are multiple, but one is talking to me.

Therapist: All right. Tell me what goes on between you two.

Hank: It's a red light.

Therapist: How do you feel being near this guide?

Hank: It's asking me about my life.

Therapist: Tell me about that as you discuss the life of Patrick.

Hank: I said it was a good life.

Therapist: What did they say about it?

Hank: They say I grew a lot. Made a joke about my head getting cut.

Therapist: How does that make you feel?

Hank: I think it's funny.

Therapist: They don't think it was a big deal?

Hank: No.

Therapist: What is it that they wanted you to accomplish in that life?

Hank: They thought that this life had multiple purposes.

Therapist: Can you elaborate on what those are?

Hank: They thought that this life had the experience of true love matched with grief and the opportunity to help other people.

Therapist: How did they think you did in this life as Patrick?

Hank: They thought I did well.

Therapist: Do they also offer some positive criticism as to what you could have done differently?

Hank: They seem to think that I'm going to go somewhere and relive part of that life.

Therapist: Help me understand. What does that mean?

Hank: It's like I connect with them, but I have to go somewhere after that is going to be a closer view of my actions as Patrick.

Therapist: Okay, so after the discussion with the guides, we're going to go and have a closer look at some things. Is that what they're saying?

Hank: Yes.

Therapist: Now, is there anything else the guide wants to share about Patrick?

Hank: No.

Therapist: Now, there are different things we can do. We can have a closer look at some of these actions in this other place or, we can ask some questions about Hank's life. What would be the right sequence?

Hank: We can ask questions about Hank's life.

Therapist: What do the guides want? After having lived this life of Patrick and having lived it well, what was the plan regarding Hank's life?

Hank: To break from tradition and to follow the heart.

Therapist: How is he doing in that regard?

Hank: Just still got ways to go.

Therapist: This is a life of breaking away from that which is traditional and becoming more authentic within himself.

Hank: Yes.

Therapist: Being still of relatively young age, does that mean he's barely scratching the surface of this theme?

Hank: Yes.

Therapist: What can the guide tell us about the similarities between Patrick and Hank?

Hank: They are similar.

Therapist: In what way?

Hank: Caring, loyal, and understanding.

Therapist: Beautiful. What are the differences between these two incarnations?

Hank: I think Patrick never moved on from grief, so maybe it was his second shot.

Therapist: Are you suggesting that the grief of Hank is a do-over, where he can develop a more spiritual approach to dealing with this grief?

Hank: Yes.

Therapist: What can the guide tell us about this journey through grief through these different lifetimes?

Hank: The guide says that although grief is hard, it makes for the most progression.

Therapist: Help me understand.

Hank: It alters life in beneficial ways.

Therapist: Are you saying that just like Patrick used grieve to spiritually advance himself while in jail, enabling him to get out of his body and connect to his loved one, in the same way, Hank can use his grief too and advance himself even more spiritually.

Hank: Yes.

Therapist: Does the guide have anything to add to that?

Hank: He says, in the next life, you won't have grief.

Therapist: So, this theme of grief and what can be learned from it is coming to an end in this life.

Hank: Yes.

Therapist: Well, that's beautiful then, right?

Hank: Yes.

Therapist: How does it make you feel?

Hank: Believing.

Therapist: Beautiful. Now, looking at you as a soul that is neither Patrick nor Hank, what is it that your soul really wants to be, to express, to become?

Hank: All-knowing.

Therapist: Beautiful. How do you see that unfold? What kind of state is that?

Hank: The soul has lived different types of lives as we learn specific lessons that help in accumulating wider knowledge.

Therapist: And then what happens with this acquired knowledge and realization?

Hank: Maybe you become a guide.

Therapist: In this world or outside of this world?

Hank: Outside of this world.

Therapist: How far has your soul progressed toward the realization of this?

Hank: Relatively close.

Therapist: Not too much longer, not too many more lives?

Hank: Not too many lives.

Therapist: How does it make you feel when you see that as your final goal?

Hank: Good.

Therapist: Now, still dealing with the grief in this life, losing Shane, is there a way we can connect with him?

Hank: I don't know.

Therapist: Would you like to meet him?

Hank: It feels like he can't meet with me.

Therapist: Why not?

Hank: He seems like he's busy.

Therapist: But if you insisted, could you meet him or not?

Hank: Yes.

Therapist: Let us insist and ask the guide to help us.

Hank: It feels fuzzy.

Therapist: Just take your time and allow the connection. Can you feel it?

Hank: Yes. I can't see anything, but I feel something in my heart.

Therapist: Okay. Let him decide how he likes to connect. If it's not visual, perhaps he prefers the heart. How does it feel?

Hank: Warm.

Therapist: They say that the heart is the bigger brain. So perhaps he wants to tell you something through your heart and share something with you.

Hank: He says you're doing great. Keep working hard. Keep going.

Therapist: Is there anything you want to tell him?

Hank: Just that I love him.

Therapist: Beautiful. Is there anything you need from him?

Hank: Strength.

Therapist: What does he say to that?

Hank: He says I got you. He knows what I'm trying to do.

Therapist: Is he going to be there with you and help you?

Hank: Yes.

Therapist: You're not alone. Beautiful. How does it make you feel to connect with him?

Hank: Good.

Therapist: You see, sometimes we must insist.

Hank: Yes.

Therapist: We are grateful that he's coming down though he's busy, to help, to support, and to strengthen you. Is there anything left unsaid or unresolved?

Hank: He just said, you know what you must do, and left.

Therapist: He left?

Hank: And I think he means that for spiritual progression, to meditate, and to raise my vibration so we can talk.

Therapist: Beautiful.

Hank: Ecstatic.

Therapist: Maybe he's deliberately holding back a bit because he wants you to develop more and open the channels.

Hank: I think he's saving it for when it's the right time.

Therapist: Yeah, maybe there is some work to be done, right?

Hank: Yes.

Therapist: How beautiful. The spirit world is wide open to you. Is there anybody else we need to connect to? Any place we should go and visit? What would you like to do?

Hank: I feel like my work is done.

Therapist: What about your loved one who was there in the prison cell? Where is she?

Hank: I think I haven't met her, or I just met her.

Therapist: Do you think you may have just met her in that life?

Hank: I think so.

Therapist: Is she what you consider to be a soulmate?

Hank: Yes.

Therapist: Well, this is important too.

Hank: Yes.

Therapist: That would explain why she's not very present here

in the in-between-world right now.
Hank: Yes.

As we could not connect to his soulmate, who most likely is incarnated at this time, we slowly ended the session.

Case 13: James
The struggle to surrender

James is a gentleman from the East Coast. Born into wealth in ancient Crete, we follow his journey through time and space.

Therapist: Now tell me, is it daytime or nighttime?
James: It is bright. Bright.
Therapist: Are you inside or outside?
James: I feel like I'm outside.
Therapist: Are you alone or are there others with you?
James: Alone.
Therapist: Look down at your feet and tell me what, if anything,

you wear on your feet.
James: Sandals.
Therapist: What else are you wearing?
James: Some kind of white robe, almost like a gladiator kind of outfit. Like a sheet kind of thing.
Therapist: Is it kind of heavy?
James: No, it's light.
Therapist: What is it made of?
James: It's like cotton.
Therapist: You're a man?
James: Yes.
Therapist: What's your age approximately?
James: I feel like I'm in my thirties.
Therapist: What's the color of your skin?
James: Black.
Therapist: Do you wear anything on your head?
James: No.
Therapist: I want you to look straight ahead and tell me what it is you're aware of.
James: I'm looking at our valley.
Therapist: What are your thoughts when you're looking at this valley?
James: That's where I live.
Therapist: Do you live in the valley?
James: Yes.
Therapist: How far away are you from your home?
James: Pretty far.
Therapist: What are you doing here?
James: Coming home.

Therapist: Where are you coming from?

James: I don't know.

Therapist: Are you alone or are there others with you?

James: I'm alone.

Therapist: Did you come back from a journey?

James: I feel like it, yeah.

Therapist: How do you feel looking down over the valley at your home?

James: I haven't been there for a while.

Therapist: Have you been on a long trip?

James: Yeah.

Therapist: Can you describe the valley to me and the way your house is located? Is it a village, a city, or a town?

James: It's really wild. Really fancy.

Therapist: What are the houses made of and what does it remind you of?

James: I'd say like a really fancy Roman church kind of thing. A lot of white buildings, very bright, very cold.

Therapist: Is it very affluent?

James: Yeah.

Therapist: There are streets?

James: Yeah. Yes.

Therapist: So where in the world do you think we are exactly? Did you say Roman?

James: It feels almost like a kingdom; like I'm looking at a king's castle.

Therapist: Like its own little kingdom?

James: A lot of little buildings around it that look very similar.

Therapist: What kind of climate is it? Is it dry or hot or wet?

James: It's all gold. It's just shiny. Like the sun is just gold,

273

everything's gold. I don't see any color.

Therapist: It is beautiful then?

James: Yeah, it's gorgeous.

Therapist: What date comes to mind?

James: A little after medieval.

Therapist: Like 14, 1500s, or something like this?

James: Yea.

Therapist: I want you to move from where you are now and go to your home and tell me what the place looks like.

James: It's a castle.

Therapist: You're living in the castle. Is it your castle or you're just part of the castle?

James: My father's.

Therapist: What is the position of your father?

James: I don't know. I think he's... I don't know.

Therapist: Is he a king or some kind of ruler?

James: Maybe.

Therapist: How does it feel to have your father in such a position?

James: He's well known. I left.

Therapist: You left?

James: I left.

Therapist: Why did you leave?

James: We didn't get along.

Therapist: And now you're back after a long time.

James: Yes.

Therapist: How's the reception been?

James: My mother's happy.

Therapist: Your father, not so much?

James: He doesn't know how to deal with it.
Therapist: How are you dealing with it, coming back?
James: Same thing.
Therapist: You don't feel comfortable either?
James: Standoffish.
Therapist: Is it a cold relationship?
James: Yes.
Therapist: How does this situation make you feel?
James: I don't want to be upset, but I don't want to deal with him.
Therapist: Is he hard or just cold?
James: Cold.
Therapist: Why is this?
James: He doesn't understand me.
Therapist: What is different about you?
James: He thinks I'm too much of a dreamer.
Therapist: Are you?
James: Yes.
Therapist: What do you want? What do you care about?
James: Whatever I want to do. I do whatever I want.
Therapist: You're more like a free spirit.
James: Yeah.
Therapist: You're not interested in ruling a kingdom or anything like that?
James: Not really.
Therapist: Do you have any other siblings or not?
James: I don't see anybody else.
Therapist: It's just you and your mother and your father?
James: Yes.

Therapist: Tell me the most significant observation about this moment in your life, either within you or around you.

James: I just feel glad that I went back.

Therapist: I see. What have you been doing all these years?

James: Roaming around.

Therapist: What did you learn from roaming about?

James: I wasted a lot of time and energy.

Therapist: You don't feel it was a successful operation?

James: No. I didn't need any of it. I didn't do that great.

Therapist: Did you have different jobs? What did you do to survive?

James: I did a lot of rock working, hard labor.

Therapist: What is your name?

James: I believe it's David.

I move him forward in time.

Therapist: Tell me what is happening now.

James: We are in a busy village, a lot of stuff going on, a lot of debauchery, and just real busy, rowdy.

Therapist: What are you doing here?

James: I don't know, I don't know.

Therapist: Are you just passing through or are you living here?

James: I feel like I'm kind of passing through, but I'm heading to a tavern or something.

Therapist: How old are you now, David?

James: It seemed pretty close to the same age.

Therapist: Is this far away from home or is this part of the same city?

James: No, its far.

Therapist: Did you leave again?

James: No. It's the same journey.

Therapist: When you say the same journey, is this part of the journey home?

James: I feel like when we first started, I was on my way back. This is part of my trip.

Therapist: Tell me about this tavern. What does the place look like?

James: A lot of wood, and muddy streets.

Therapist: What about the houses?

James: A lot of grassroots.

Therapist: This is unlike the shining city?

James: No. It's very different.

Therapist: Does it look more like a poor village?

James: Exactly.

Therapist: How does it feel being here?

James: I feel like nobody knows me.

Therapist: Is that a good thing or a bad thing?

James: It's a good thing.

Therapist: You don't want to be known.

James: I don't want to be known.

Therapist: Why are we stopping here at this tavern, in this town?

James: Just to come for some excitement. Have a drink.

Therapist: Is that what you like to do? Get excited?

James: Yes, I do.

Therapist: What excites you?

James: Girls.

Therapist: Ah I see.

James: I like to make people laugh.

Therapist: Is that one of the reasons why you left to begin with?

James: Yes. I wanted to prove that I didn't need anybody and that I could make it on my own.

I move him forward in time again.

James: We're back on the same hill. The castle's not there though.

Therapist: The castle is not there?

James: There's nothing there.

Therapist: What happened?

James: I don't know. It's just grass.

Therapist: How old are you now?

James: I feel like I'm an older guy. Sixties maybe.

Therapist: You're looking down and the whole city is gone.

James: Yeah.

Therapist: Has it been destroyed?

James: It looks like it was never there.

Therapist: How is that possible?

James: I don't know.

Therapist: You mean there's not a trace left of it?

James: I see a little bit of rubble.

Therapist: It seems it's been gone for a long time.

James: It's been gone for a long time.

Therapist: What have you done in these last years?

James: Nothing of significance.

Therapist: You were just wondering about?

James: Wondering about.

Therapist: What made you leave your hometown again?

James: I got bored.

Therapist: What have you been doing all these years? Nothing of significance?

James: Nothing. Working.

Therapist: Just working?

James: Working and floating around.

Therapist: Looking back at it now, how does this make you feel?

James: A little bit wasteful. I know I could have had something good, but I would have to give up who I was.

Therapist: Your dad wanted you to follow in his footsteps.

James: Yes.

Therapist: And you didn't oblige?

James: No.

Therapist: In the meantime, this whole city has crumbled. What happened?

James: I feel there was a war.

Therapist: What happened to your parents?

James: Rubble now. I think they've passed.

Therapist: How does it make you feel seeing this whole city in shambles?

James: Bad.

Therapist: Tell me more about that.

James: I should have been there. Yeah.

Therapist: Is that when your parents were killed?

James: I believe so.

Therapist: But you most probably would've been killed as well, don't you think?

James: Most probably, but I'm strong.

Therapist: Do you mean you could have fought?

James: Yes.

Therapist: Would it have made a difference?

James: Maybe.

Therapist: What do you think happened? Were you aware that this happened or were you taken by surprise?

James: Taken by surprise when I came back, that there was nothing there.

Therapist: You not only come back after so many years, but you didn't know what happened.

James: Maybe I knew and that's why I came back to check.

Therapist: Now what?

James: I'm disgusted and take off again.

Therapist: You're disgusted about what?

James: The whole thing.

Therapist: How so?

James: I'm disappointed in myself.

Therapist: Is there any family left or are you alone now?

James: I'm by myself. Totally by myself.

Therapist: Is that by design or is that by accident?

James: Yeah, it's by design.

Therapist: Why is that?

James: I don't want anybody around me.

Therapist: Do you like to be free?

James: Yes. I'm not tied down.

Therapist: Is that important to you?

James: It seems like it was at the time.

Therapist: It seems that this notion of freedom has been governing your life.

James: Yes.

Therapist: What are your thoughts about it now?
James: I'm going to change.
Therapist: In what way are you going to change?
James: I'm going to stop working and start a business.
Therapist: What makes you take this decision?
James: I want to have something. I want to have money.
Therapist: Why now?
James: Because I've been broke for so long.
Therapist: Does it have anything to do with the destroyed city?
James: Just to prove that I was right, that I could do it on my own.
Therapist: You waited all this time till now.
James: Yes.

I try to move him forward in time, but he goes backward instead.

James: I'm inside the building, inside the castle.
Therapist: Ok.
James: I'm eating. My last meal.
Therapist: Who's here with you?
James: My mother, who is always with me.
Therapist: How old are you now?
James: 13.
Therapist: How do you feel?
James: Comfortable.
Therapist: Describe the scene for me, what does the place look like?
James: This is a gigantic table. It's a big open room. A lot of wooden beams. There are people serving us.
Therapist: Are you sitting next to your mother?

James: I feel very confident and calm, very happy. I can see myself running around. I don't see my father, just me and my mother.

Therapist: Where does your confidence come from?

James: Just knowing I'm safe between these walls.

Therapist: Safe in the city?

James: Yeah.

Therapist: And you said your relationship with your mom is very good?

James: Yes.

Therapist: This is just the two of you kind of hanging out?

James: Yes. Yeah.

Therapist: What do you like best about your mother?

James: She's warm and very loving.

Therapist: At this point in time, was your relationship with your father already deteriorating?

James: My dad wasn't around much.

Therapist: No expectations now?

James: No.

Therapist: Was it a happy childhood?

James: Yes.

Therapist: Are you being educated here in this place as well?

James: Very much so.

Therapist: You're well-educated.

James: Yeah. I can see people around me with parchment paper. Scrolls, and they're white.

Therapist: They're white?

James: They're white. They're well-dressed.

Therapist: Are you privately tutored?

James: Yes.
Therapist: Do you like that?
James: I don't like it.
Therapist: You don't?
James: No.
Therapist: You don't like to be educated?
James: I want to play.
Therapist: Okay. You want to play.
James: Yeah.
Therapist: Are you a pretty good student though?
James: When I apply, I can be.
Therapist: Are you applying yourself?
James: No.
Therapist: I see.
James: I know I don't have to.
Therapist: Why is that?
James: Because my parents have money and I'll be fine.
Therapist: You're a successor, is that why?
James: I don't know about that, but I know they have money. I don't have to worry about it. I can fail.
Therapist: You're already aware of the fact that you don't really have to do anything?
James: Exactly.

I'm trying again to move him forward in time to an older age.

James: I'm old, really skinny. Not in good health.
Therapist: You're older?
James: I look very, very skinny.
Therapist: Where are you now?

James: Well, laying in the woods and in the grass.

Therapist: What are you doing here?

James: I'm getting ready to die.

Therapist: How did the last few years of your life go after you decided to start your own business? Did you succeed?

James: I worked hard, but I think I ended up broke.

Therapist: Ah.

James: I worked really hard.

Therapist: It didn't quite work out.

James: It did not. I squandered it. Just squandered the money.

Therapist: You squandered it?

James: Yeah, I looked like a bum.

Therapist: Your resolution to be successful was short-lived.

James: Yes.

Therapist: I want you to move forward to the last day of your life as David and tell me how old you are on this last day of your life.

James: I feel like I'm 70.

Therapist: Is there anything going on around you or within you to suggest that your physical death will come this day?

James: There's a haggard woman standing over me.

Therapist: Where are you?

James: Still laying in the grass.

Therapist: What's this woman doing here, looking out over you?

James: I can't really tell, she's in torn clothes.

Therapist: What is happening just now?

James: I feel like she's looting me, going through my stuff.

Therapist: How's the body feeling?

James: Skinny, sickly.

Therapist: What do you think about this life you lived as David?

James: Got some regrets. I should have stayed at home. I should have followed the rules.

Therapist: Why?

James: My life would've been easier. I suffered. But I did it my way.

Therapist: What did you learn by doing that?

James: A lot of lessons. A lot of hardships. Learning how to manage and learn how to be fast on my feet. Learn how to adapt, learn how to deal with situations, and get out of situations. I'm very good with my hands. Very skilled.

Therapist: Looking at it that way, you don't really regret all the things that you learned?

James: I never would've learned it.

Therapist: On the one hand you feel like you should have stayed, but on the other hand you feel like you learned so much.

James: Absolutely. Life experience.

Therapist: Now, what is your last thought or awareness as you leave the body of David?

James: My mother.

Therapist: How do you feel about her?

James: I think I'm going to see her. Yeah, I'm up above it. Looking down at it.

Therapist: How do you feel about your death?

James: I feel like I wasted this life.

I move him passed his death and into the life-between-lives world.

Therapist: What is the first thing you notice?

James: Everybody's all white.

Therapist: Who is all here?

James: I can't see the faces, but everybody's very white and glowing. I see my mother. She's in a white dress.

Therapist: Tell me about your meeting with your mother.

James: She's hugging me. She missed me. I see my father.

Therapist: What about him?

James: He's saying he should have done it differently. He caused a lot of problems between us.

Therapist: How does it make you feel when he says that?

James: Good, makes me feel good. He didn't understand me, but he understands now.

Therapist: Is he part of your soul group?

James: Yeah. Yeah.

Therapist: Who else is there?

James: I feel like God and Jesus are there, and a girl.

Therapist: What about his girl?

James: She smiles.

Therapist: What is her role?

James: Well, she's my friend now. God, she knows me very well.

Therapist: Is she your personal guide?

James: I believe so.

Therapist: Can you tell me about her?

James: She's coming to me.

Therapist: Tell me what happens when you meet her.

James: We hug each other. It's been a while.

Therapist: What is her energy like?

James: Clean, pure. She works there.

Therapist: What does she say about this life you just lived as

David?

James: She's told me I had one hell of a ride. She's glad to see me.

Therapist: How's the energy between the two of you?

James: Even. We have similar energy. It's like neither one else is any better than the other.

Therapist: She's part of your group?

James: Yeah. She's definitely part of me.

Therapist: Are you also part of these guides?

James: I believe I am. I'm part of a group.

Therapist: Tell me about this group.

James: I've been there before, and I left that group too. I chose to come back.

Therapist: Back where?

James: Earth.

Therapist: What can you tell me about this group? What is the nature of this group?

James: Awfully strong. Very clean.

Therapist: What do they have in common?

James: They're related somehow. Family, ancestors. I'm seeing some faces and they know me, but I don't recognize them.

Therapist: Are the father and mother of David also part of this group?

James: They're standing off to the side.

Therapist: Like a subgroup of some kind?

James: Exactly. The other group is on the right. My parents are on the left. I'm standing with the other group on the right.

Therapist: This group where this girl belongs to, is this a very powerful group?

James: It is.

Therapist: What do they do? What is their job?

James: To help people.

Therapist: They're like angels?

James: Exactly.

Therapist: Do they mostly work in the astral plane, or do they work on Earth as well?

James: They work on earth.

Therapist: Do they take bodies, or do they help people with bodies?

James: They're guides, they help.

Therapist: So, they generally don't take bodies.

James: No.

Therapist: But you choose to take a body.

James: I chose to take a body and come back.

Therapist: Why is that?

James: I feel like it was part of a plan.

Therapist: What was the plan? Why these experiences?

James: I feel like it was part of some kind of plan, and I deviated somehow from the plan, again.

Therapist: Let us ask that girl, maybe she can help us understand what this plan was.

James: I left the group, and I became James.

Therapist: What is it that you were supposed to do in this life?

James: I was supposed to be like an undercover guide, guiding but not being known.

Therapist: And are you fulfilling that task?

James: No.

Therapist: How come?

James: Same old reasons. Women, alcohol. I don't follow the path I'm supposed to be on.

Therapist: David's tendencies are continuing a little bit in the lives of James.

James: Yes, absolutely.

Therapist: Now, what does your group say about that?

James: They're pissed.

Therapist: Yeah?

James: Yeah. They're not happy with me.

Therapist: What do they say you should be doing?

James: There's still time to get back. I can straighten this out. The girl's standing there telling me, you still have time. There's another guy with her.

Therapist: What exactly do they want you to do?

James: I'm going to finish this life and I'm not coming back here. This is it.

Therapist: This is the last life?

James: This is it. They want me to clean things up.

Therapist: Is there anything from the life of David and James that he needs to do to clean it up?

James: Get his act together, start being cleaner, and pure. So, when I cross back over, I don't have to spend a lot of time and energy to straighten things out. They want me to go from one time right to another. Right to work there.

Therapist: They want you to work with the angel group.

James: Yes. They want me back in the group.

Therapist: They don't want you to waste time cleaning up in the astral plane.

James: Exactly.

Therapist: And they want you to use the rest of James' life to clean up?

James: Yes.

Therapist: Is there any work that he needs to do now? Apart from cleaning himself up?

James: I think I'm doing it.

Therapist: You're already doing it?

James: Not what this body, but with my spirit, my soul. I feel like it's doing stuff besides what I'm doing right now in this time and place. I feel like my spirit is doing other stuff.

Therapist: So, it's in the spirit world that this part of your soul is working?

James: I'm in the same time, but I'm not doing the same thing.

Therapist: Right, right. So, it's like a parallel existence.

James: Exactly. Exactly what it is. I can see it.

Therapist: Is there any part of that higher astral Self that can help James integrate with that aspect of himself to clean up faster and better?

James: They've been trying. They're with me right now.

Therapist: Is there anything we can do right now with the help of your group?

James: They are telling me to follow my heart. It always tells me where to go. Just listen to my heart.

Therapist: You'd think that the life of David has taught you to follow your heart? Although you deviated a little bit, you were strong in following your own calling.

James: Yeah. They're mad I keep repeating the same thing. I've been here a lot. I've been here a lot. They're mad.

Therapist: You've been on Earth a lot, you mean?

James: They've had it. I keep refusing to stay.

Therapist: What do you feel now that you're looking at this whole scene?

James: I'm ready.

Therapist: You're ready?

James: I'm ready.

Therapist: What causes the change? Why now?

James: I'm just tired. My body is tired. I'm tired. My head's tired. I just want to be home.

Therapist: You've lived enough?

James: Yeah.

Therapist: What do they say, now that you say that?

James: They're happy. They are happy to hear. They're actually very happy to hear that right now.

Therapist: What about Jesus? You said he is here also? Can we connect?

James: I see him in the distance looking down. We're separated now. I feel like I'm in between.

Therapist: Can we connect to him a little bit more now?

James: They aren't here. He loves me. He's ready for me to come home.

Therapist: Is he kind of the guide of your group?

James: He sent them.

Therapist: I see.

James: He sent them. They know me. They know me in and out. He sent the girl, and he sent the guy. The girl wasn't doing it.

Therapist: He's the one behind it all?

James: Absolutely

Therapist: The spirit world is wide open to you. Is there a higher council we can go to? Or is your group part of that council?

James: I can't get to the council. I'm not clean enough. They're going, they're mediating for me.

Therapist: But you belong with them. I mean, you are one of them.

James: I am one of them.

Therapist: That is important to understand.

James: I'm not alone.

Therapist: There may be some superficial dust on you, but your core belongs to them.

James: Absolutely.

Therapist: Remember who you really are, that is a very powerful thing.

James: Yes. They know that. They know. They know it.

Therapist: Is there anything else we can do with your soul group, a healing or a cleansing?

James: We're running around in the group putting hands on each other, and Jesus is looking at the circle smiling.

Therapist: Beautiful.

James: It's getting brighter.

Therapist: They're all around you?

James: It's just getting brighter and brighter.

Therapist: Okay.

James: They're trying to transfer it to me.

Therapist: Beautiful. Just take your time. Let it unfold. How are you feeling? What's happening?

James: The light's fading. The scene's fading.

Therapist: Did they transfer it to you?

James: They transferred what they needed to.

Therapist: How are you feeling?

James: I feel good. I feel like it sank in a little.

Therapist: Beautiful.

James: My girl's telling me she must go. She came for today.

Therapist: You said that you're all the same. Why has she been stepping forward?

James: We may have been together at one time.

Therapist: Like a special kind of soulmate?

James: I think we were supposed to connect, and we never did for some reason. She was there, back in the king's time, the girl that I was supposed to marry. And it didn't happen because of me taking off. But she loved me and made me aware of what I was doing wrong.

Therapist: Looking at the whole journey, what are your thoughts?

James: I keep repeating the same pattern over and over and over and over. It's time to break the pattern and go home.

Therapist: Do you think this is the moment this is changing?

James: I feel like I'm halfway there. I'm getting hung up.

Therapist: But you just said that you're ready to change.

James: I am ready. My heart's ready to go.

Therapist: All right. So, we have turned the corner.

James: Yes, sir. I finally surrendered.

Therapist: That word is beautiful. Surrender.

James: Surrendered my soul, turned it back over to them so they can work with it. It wasn't mine.

Therapist: You can see the resistance to the surrender. That's what stood in the way, right?

James: Absolutely. It took me a long time to get me to admit it.

Therapist: It's hard to comprehend surrender until you're ready for it. This tells us that you're ready.

James: Absolutely.

Therapist: I guess this means that you're going to stay there and you're going to work from there.

James: That's what they're telling me.

Therapist: How does it make you feel now that you understand this?

James: I can't wait. I want to do the job. I can't wait to get to work.

Therapist: Beyond that, is there a goal even higher than that?

James: I'm going to be strong in the group, and I'm going to end up being a leader of that group. They're waiting for me. If I'm patient.

Therapist: They want you to take that role?

James: An important part of it. All very important part.

Therapist: You're ready to accept it now.

James: Accept it for sure, yes. It's time to go. It's time to do my job.

Therapist: Beautiful. Now, the spirit world is wide open to you. Is there any other area we need to go to? Any other beings we need to visit?

James: I'd love to get to see the council, but they don't want to see me.

Therapist: What if you just try and knock at the door because now you've surrendered? They're, at the end of the day, very compassionate beings.

James: They tell me I'm on the right path, but they won't talk to me because I'm not fulfilling my part of the deal down here. I'm not doing something I've promised to do.

Therapist: What if from the bottom of your heart you say, "No, I am changing. I already have changed. I have surrendered."

James: They know. They know I'm changing.

Therapist: Perhaps that will give us a few minutes of access to them. Let us not give up now. Let us see right here, right now, if we can make this happen.

James: They say they're going to step aside and let me in. Not far. Not far.

Therapist: That's okay. Just step inside.

James: Right in the doorway.

Therapist: Step inside. Don't be afraid.

James: It's 2 rows of people sitting, one low. I feel like there are 6 of them. They're facing me. They're illuminated, but the rest of the room's dark. I can see that.

Therapist: Just tune in.

James: They're very strong and are kind of smirking. They are looking at me looking in there. They'll tell me that I'll be back. I'll be able to go in there.

Therapist: What do they say, now you have made the change?

James: They said that I know what I have to do. There's one person talking in the middle. It's a lady. She's saying, you know what you have to do.

Therapist: What is their demeanor, their energy? How do you feel?

James: I feel they're distant with me. They want to talk to me. They want to give me the right attention, but they just don't feel they can trust me. That's why I'm standing at the doorway. They want to let me in and put me in a chair that's in the middle. But they told me I can't, I'm not ready.

Therapist: What if you say that you are ready right now?

James: They just told me you're far from ready, but that I can get there.

Therapist: What do they want you to do?

James: Live a cleaner life. Clean up my act. Less swearing, less debauchery. Less partying. Less doing what I want. Be more conforming. Listen to what I'm hearing. Do what they tell me.

Therapist: Will they guide you from there?

James: They have to guide me every day. They're here every day. They're here. They know. They know I'm on a banana peel. I'm close to screwing it all up.

Therapist: But you've learned your lesson, right? As David and in these first years of James.

James: I still haven't fully taken it seriously.

Therapist: But that is about to change now. Is it not?

James: It is.

Therapist: We're here today to surrender to them. Would you like to take a moment in front of them to truly surrender to them? Would that help, you think?

James: They know. They know. They know I surrendered. They saw it, they were there. They know. They're glad to see the change of heart. They've been chasing me for a long time.

Therapist: Well, that's all that matters, right?

James: To get my attention.

Therapist: It's beautiful that they're allowing you to be here.

James: This is my last chance.

Therapist: Is there anything you want to tell them?

James: I'm going to get there. I'm going to finish it. They're glad that I'm acknowledging it. They're very happy about that.

Therapist: You don't have to do it alone.

James: No, they're there. They're there.

Therapist: Your soul group is there too.

James: They can't interfere, but they can bend things. They can make things happen. They can't interfere though. It has to be me.

Therapist: Right, but your soul group is there as well. They can help as well.

James: Exactly. They can be around. They can help, but they can't influence.

Therapist: It took all these lifetimes to come to this point. This is called evolution. There comes a point in our evolution that we are ready and now you're ready.

James: I am.

Therapist: Understand it's not that you've done something bad. It's a matter of evolution.

James: Absolutely.

Therapist: It takes time.

James: I need to go through it to make me stronger. They knew.

Therapist: And maybe, because they want you to be a leader, you need to have experience.

James: Going through it has made me stronger.

Therapist: You could develop relatability.

James: That's what I'm going to be doing. I'm going to be teaching and helping others.

Therapist: Don't be hard on yourself.

James: No.

Therapist: This is all part of growth.

James: Yes.

Therapist: Is there anything else that needs to be said?

James: It's time. My time is done. My time is up and we're backing back up.

Therapist: All right. Beautiful.

James: I need to step up.

Therapist: Is there anything else that we need to do?

James: I want to say I'm sorry.

Therapist: To whom?

James: God. Jesus. My family. My ancestors, the council.

Therapist: Yeah. Go ahead. Do you want to take a moment?

James: No. They know. They know me inside and out. They know me very, very, very well.

Therapist: Beautiful. Is there anything else you want to share with your group?

James: Just tell them how much I love them. I appreciate them praying for me. Every day, every night. I feel like I have a sister now. I see her.

Therapist: Never forget her. Take a moment to really imprint that on your mind.

We slowly bring the session to a close.

Case 14: Henry
The guilt of the Father

Henry is a 61-year-old IT specialist, who had a hard life and struggles with loneliness. He struggles to have meaningful relationships with women.

Therapist: Look down at your feet and tell me what you notice on your feet.

Henry: I have sandals on, standing on uncovered ground, undisturbed.

Therapist: What else are you wearing?

Henry: I think I have a robe on.

Therapist: What kind of robe is this?

Henry: I believe just one single piece, like a holy man.

Therapist: What is your skin color?

Henry: I'm Caucasian, but tan.

Therapist: What's your age approximately at this moment?

Henry: 30. 30 years old.

Therapist: What gives you the impression that you're a holy man?

Henry: People come to me for guidance.

Therapist: You say you are standing on untouched soil. Can you describe the area to me?

Henry: It's in a small village, with dirt roads, a farming community.

Therapist: What kind of houses are here? What are they made of?

Henry: I think wood.

Therapist: What's the climate like?

Henry: It's warm. It's summer.

Therapist: Where do you think you are?

Henry: I'd have to say the Mediterranean.

Therapist: How does it feel to be a holy man? What is your state of mind?

Henry: I'm at peace. I happen to be a good person that helps people. But it feels like I have something personal, disturbing.

Therapist: Help me understand.

Henry: Yes. I believe there's a woman, and I'm a priest and it's becoming too personal.

Therapist: You're not supposed to have a woman as a priest?

Henry: Right.

Therapist: What kind of priest are you? Some kind of church?

Henry: Yeah, I'm Catholic.

Therapist: What year is it approximately?

Henry: 1200 comes to mind.

Therapist: Are you saying that you feel conflicted? On the one hand, you're feeling very much at peace being a holy man and on the other hand you're getting too close to a certain woman.

Henry: Yes.

Therapist: Is she near the village where you are now?

Henry: Yes. She lives in the village. I live in the village.

Therapist: Are you the parish priest of this area?

Henry: That's my impression.

Therapist: What can you tell me about this place?

Henry: It's quiet. It's been peaceful. It has enough to sustain the community. It's a quiet, peaceful time.

Therapist: If you would describe to me the most relevant observation about this moment, either within you or around you, what would it be?

Henry: That I have this woman that I'm not sure how to handle. I'm torn. I have my human, normal feelings, but I'm a priest. It is not allowed. I get the feeling that she either has a man or a family. One of the two would have a very difficult time if I engaged with her.

Therapist: Right. You're longing to be with her, but your situation doesn't allow it or approve of it?

Henry: Correct.

Therapist: Right. Can you tell me about your relationship with the church and your faith?

Henry: With the church, it's in general, very good. I'm respected. I'm wise. I'm compassionate. I have no other problems. Everything else is good.

Therapist: Where do you live in the town? What does your place look like? Can you walk me there and tell me what it looks like?

Henry: I have a humble room in the church.

Therapist: Is there an actual church building?

Henry: I think so. I think it's stone. I think I have a small room of my own, a simple bed, very few luxuries.

Therapist: Which country comes to mind?

Henry: What is now Israel or Jordan.

Therapist: Are there any more priests where you are, or are you the only one overseeing this village?

Henry: I'm the only one.

Therapist: What's your name?

Henry: I think everybody just calls me, Father.

Therapist: I'll call you Father too, ok?

Henry: Yes.

I move him forward in time.

Therapist: Tell me what is happening now.

Henry: (very emotional) I'm being punished. I gave in to the woman. And I'm out. And now I've lost my position and am no longer loved or respected and may no longer be a priest. I've lost everything.

Therapist: Where are you now?

Henry: I lost my home. I've lost my respect. I'm living alone in the wilderness. I have no home, no friends, no companions.

Therapist: What happened to the woman? Where is she?

Henry: I don't know. She's gone.

Therapist: How old are you now?

Henry: I'm no longer in the village. I don't know what happened to her.

Therapist: How old are you now?

Henry: Just 40.

Therapist: Are you wandering around in the forest, you're hiding out there? What are you doing?

Henry: Yes, yes, I'm out in the wilderness alone, hiding from everybody that might know who I am or what I did.

Therapist: How do you survive?

Henry: Just wandering around, finding food, and water when I can. I don't have much desire to live. Just existing, waiting to die. Sad that I've lost everything I had, everything I loved.

Therapist: You said earlier that you're a holy man and you were very content. This contentment, was it an actual inner acquisition, or what it the result of your position and circumstances?

Henry: I think it was my position, my position in society. I was a productive member, respected if that makes sense.

Therapist: That explains why you're feeling so sad right now.

Henry: Yes, I lost all I had.

Therapist: What is the most relevant observation about this moment, either within you or around you?

Henry: It's about the woman. It's about how I took a woman and lost everything I had.

Therapist: What are your thoughts about that?

Henry: It explains a lot of the fear that I have of starting another relationship. I equate a relationship with the loss of everything I hold dear.

Not wanting him to go into an analysis of his current situation right now, I move him forward in his life as the Father.

Therapist: Tell me what is happening now?

Henry: It's not much beyond 40 and I'm dying.

Therapist: Go to the last day of your life.

Henry: I'm weak. I'm in a cave, I'm weak and I'm dying, just waiting to die.

Therapist: What do you think about this life that you just lived?

Henry: I am so sad. What had started as a wonderful life was all lost.

Therapist: What did you learn?

Henry: That I should have been strong, that I should have held out, that I should not have given into her. I should have followed my vows.

Therapist: What is the last thought before you leave the body?

Henry: I forgive her except it was my own choice. I'm still in the cave but above the body.

Therapist: How are you feeling?

Henry: Out of pain, at peace.

Therapist: How do you feel about your death?

Henry: I'm glad that it's over. I feel like the mental strain is fading.

Therapist: Take your time.

Henry: Feeling the freedom.

Therapist: Tell me more.

Henry: Feeling free, free of worry, free of regret.

Therapist: Does it feel like you're traveling, arriving, or do you feel you're already there?

Henry: (emotional) Some traveling. It feels very intense, the energy.

Therapist: Are there any visuals amidst this energy, or is it more of an intangible sense of expansiveness?

Henry: Just a sense of being an energy being.

Therapist: What is your energy like? What does it feel like, your own sense of Selfhood?

Henry: It feels like energy.

Therapist: I see.

Henry: Yeah, like I'm just a field of energy.

Therapist: And around you?

Henry: I sense other energy beings. We all look like an egg shape of light.

Therapist: Do you feel like you're able to connect to one or multiple other beings?

Henry: I feel like it's nonverbal, that they're around me, helping fill me with their energy to strergthen me. I sense I've had a difficult incarnation. I sense their love.

Therapist: Would you like a moment alone with their energy and love?

Henry: Yes.

Therapist: All right. Take all the time you want and when you're ready to continue, just let me know, okay?

(silence)

Henry: Okay. Okay, I'm ready.

Therapist: How are you feeling?

Henry: Much better.

Therapist: Tell me what is the best way to get some answers? Is this something we can ask your higher Self, or do you feel there is a consciousness around that can help us and may even work through you?

Henry: Either way.

Therapist: Looking back at your life as a Father, from the perspective of your spirit Self at this frequency, what are your observations?

Henry: It was the biggest challenge in my life, and I failed. I was supposed to resist, and I did not.

Therapist: Is that affecting Henry in this lifetime?

Henry: It no longer matters I was not allowed to be in a

relationship then. Henry still fears it. I'm still paying for it in my own mind. I'm not allowing myself to have a relationship because of that failure.

Therapist: Is there a different way of looking at this? Perhaps from the perspective of the Father, it was a failure. But looking at it from a more elevated perspective, away from the Father's belief system, is it actually a failure?

Henry: No, I don't think so.

Therapist: How would you reframe this for the sake of Henry and arrive at a resolution?

Henry: I was human. Humans have desires. We all have sexual desires. I believe a part of me was trying to provide the woman with what she needed as well. I was trying to be compassionate.

Therapist: Could we also say that the notion that a spiritual man is not allowed to love in that way is a narrow way of looking at spirituality? It's the church's way of looking at it.

Henry: Yes.

Therapist: The Father subjected himself to that viewpoint and thereby restricted himself. But we could say that in the modern world, it is possible to be highly spiritual and pure, while at the same time still loving somebody intensely and having a beautiful relationship with them.

Henry: Yes.

Therapist: By looking at it this way, could you help the Father free himself from his own judgment that he imposed upon himself and his desires? What would you say to him?

Henry: I would say, "Father, the requirement of the church to be celibate was wrong. It should never have been. We're human beings. To ask a human being to shut off a normal need is insane. Whatever the church leaders were at the time, for whatever their reason of requiring priests to be celibate, it doesn't fit human experience."

Therapist: Right.

Henry: "You had desires. They were normal. You were trying to deny them because of the church and because you believed you had to do this to be a good priest, to be a good man."

Therapist: Do you see how your soul has carried this guilt for all these centuries?

Henry: Yes.

Therapist: Regarding celibacy, may have to keep in mind that celibacy may be suitable for some people. Even when in a relationship, there may come a time when the soul craves a different kind of relationship. In this case, celibacy is a natural outcome. Love gets transformed into something different. But it cannot be forced upon anybody. It should be natural.

Henry: Yes.

Therapist: Integrating this understanding, what would you say to Henry?

Henry: You should welcome feelings of love. You should welcome a relationship. You should make sure to communicate a lot.

Therapist: Beautiful.

Henry: You are free to be in a relationship. There is nothing wrong. There's nothing spiritually wrong. There is nothing God would do to stop you."

Therapist: That's right.

Henry: You should feel free to experience your humanness.

Therapist: Right. And still be spiritually minded.

Henry: Yes.

Therapist: They're not exclusive, they're inclusive.

Henry: They're not truly exclusive.

Therapist: How quickly you're coming to this realization. How does it make you feel?

Henry: On the one hand, I'm happy. On the other, I'm so sad for all the time I've spent alone.

Therapist: Indeed.

Henry: All the wasted time, all the unneeded loneliness and sadness.

Therapist: But there's a new day tomorrow.

Henry: Yes.

Therapist: Henry had asked the question, "Are my troubles and loneliness the result of a karmic debt?" Isn't it interesting? Even this question contains an element of guilt as if somehow you did something wrong.

Henry: There was a karmic debt. I believe that I had a previous life with my ex-wife. I think that she made me jealous, and in my jealousy, I harmed the other man.

Therapist: I see.

Henry: I castrated him.

Therapist: That was in another life?

Henry: Yes.

Therapist: How can we help Henry free his mind? What can we do?

Henry: I need to release the guilt of sexual feelings. I need to release the guilt of how I may have harmed that man in another life.

Therapist: Take a moment to elevate your awareness above Henry, the father, and the life before that, and step into that divine aspect of your true Self. Would you like a moment alone for that?

Henry: Yes.

Therapist: All right. Take your time.

(silence)

Therapist: How do you feel?

Henry: At peace. I'm ready to accept my innocence.

Therapist: Isn't that just the most amazing realization?

Henry: It is.

Therapist: I want you to integrate that innocence and divine beauty into Henry's body and mind, letting go of guilt and shame. Would you like a moment for that?

Henry. Yes, I'd like that.

(silence)

Henry: I need to continue to remind myself that I'm a spiritual being, having an experience. That I'm free, that I'm free to experience everything that life has to offer. As long as I'm respectful of other human beings and communicate, I should enjoy the rest of my time to the fullest. Though Henry is troubled by the socio-political situation of today.

(In his pre-session questionnaire, Henry expressed grave concern about the political climate at the time this session took place)

Therapist: At the time of the Father, your soul was unable to elevate Itself above the church culture of your time. The Father was identified with the rules and social customs of his time and his church. Now that you are here in the life between lives world, is there another way you could look at this?

Henry: I'm having a hard time putting it into words.

Therapist: You want me to help you and you tell me if that's right or wrong?

Henry: Yes.

Therapist: Could it be that though the Father was living a spiritual life, he wasn't able to transcend his soul beyond his times, whereas Henry is much more awakened? He can transcend his awareness beyond Henry, as we are experiencing now. He can see the temporary nature of his life on Earth. Not to let the ways of the world overwhelm your soul. Is that a good assessment or not?

Henry: Yes.

Therapist: What an incredible journey. What a journey it has been.

Henry: Very overwhelming feelings.

Therapist: Now, tell me, is there any issue that we may have missed?

Henry: I think we have covered what was disturbing my soul.

Therapist: Isn't it amazing?

Henry: I think I'm going to be able to carry it with me. If there's anything left, it has to do with my sister.

Therapist: What about her?

Henry: Right now, we aren't talking. I shut her out maybe nine years ago, but then about four years ago, I opened back up and let her back into my life. But unfortunately, she doesn't know how to have a relationship either, and I basically had to let her go again. I know I can't fix her.

Therapist: From this higher perspective, how could you look at this relationship differently?

Henry: I see now that both with her and my ex-wife, these relationships were required to get me to this point. I have no negative feelings. I don't feel like I have to forgive them, that there's nothing left to forgive. I guess, I just pray for her.

Therapist: Could you look upon this as something you don't really have to try to fix?

Henry: Yes, I do see that now. I need to recognize that it's not my responsibility, that I need to let her go.

Therapist: Always keep the door and the heart open.

Henry: It's okay for me to love my sister, but it's also okay for me to let her go and not feel any more guilt.

Therapist: That's right. Because?

Henry: Because I've done the right thing. I've been loving. I've been kind.

Therapist: That's right.

Henry: I should protect myself. I should not allow other people to hurt me.

Therapist: That's right.

Henry: And I am love. I am innocent.

Therapist: First and foremost, we need to realize who we are, what we are. Accepting your own divine nature and knowing you are love and innocence. That's who you are. How does that feel?

Henry: Very much loved and at peace.

Therapist: Is there anything else that we may have missed?

Henry: No. You have my gratitude.

We slowly bring the session to an end.

Case 15: Iris
Near the sacred mountain

Iris, at the time of this session, is a 35-year-old nurse from Russia. For the longest time, she tried to please others, ignored herself and her needs, and went through bouts of depression and deep sadness. She has recently started to discover her spiritual nature.

Therapist: Tell me, is it daytime or nighttime?
Iris: Daytime.
Therapist: Are you inside or outside?
Iris: Outside.

Therapist: Are you alone or with somebody?

Iris: Alone

Therapist: You're alone. Looking down at your feet, tell me what if anything, you see on your feet.

Iris: I'm above the ground.

Therapist: You're above the ground? Tell me about that. What is happening?

Iris: (Crying) I'm floating.

Therapist: All right.

Iris: It's cold.

Therapist: How are you feeling?

Iris: There's snow everywhere.

Therapist: I see.

Iris: (Continue crying) Oh my God, I can see my body.

Therapist: Where's your body?

Iris: (Very excited) It's down there.

Therapist: Just calm down. It's okay.

Iris: There's a wound.

Therapist: You're wounded?

Iris: Yes. And there's blood. Not too much blood, but-

Therapist: What's the condition of the body?

Iris: Oh, it's dead.

Therapist: I see. How old is the body?

Iris: No. Not too old. About 40 years old.

Therapist: It's a male or female?

Iris: It's a male.

Therapist: All right. Now, we're going to count from 3 down to 1. On the count of 1, we're going to move back in time to when this body is still alive, when you're much younger. Going from 3, 2, 1. And you are there now. Tell me what is happening now?

Iris: I can see a boy, happy, playing with arrows.
Therapist: With a bow and arrows?
Iris: Yes.
Therapist: What does he look like, this boy?
Iris: Funny and cute.
Therapist: What does his outfit look like?
Iris: It's old. It's from an old epoch. I mean, I can't explain. He's wearing tights.
Therapist: And what epoch, what date comes to mind?
Iris: 1500 comes to mind.
Therapist: Where is it? Which country?
Iris: Definitely somewhere in Europe.
Therapist: Is he playing?
Iris: Northern Europe, cold country, snow again. Cold. Fall.
Therapist: What does his skin color look like?
Iris: White.
Therapist: He's outside playing?
Iris: He's playing. This is so nice. And I can see his house made from wood, a little house. His mom is there. She's a very good woman. It's in the village, a very small village.
Therapist: What's the house made from?
Iris: Wood.
Therapist: How many people are living here?
Iris: Just a few. It's about three houses in there.
Therapist: What does the landscape look like?
Iris: Very beautiful. Beautiful mountains, forests, lakes.
Iris: Yeah. This is what I dreamt about in this life.

As a footnote, though somebody can be completely absorbed in a past life or life-between-life, they still have an awareness of themselves in their current life. Clients are in a theta state, which is an elevated state of consciousness. Rather than losing awareness, they gain awareness of levels of consciousness they are not aware of in their normal day-to-day state of consciousness. It's important to understand that gaining an awareness of a past-life or life-between-life, doesn't go at the expense of the awareness of this life.

Therapist: Beautiful.

Iris: It makes sense now.

Therapist: Is your dad here as well?

Iris: No.

Therapist: It's just you and your mom?

Iris: Yes. And other ladies from the village and their kids.

Therapist: You're all together?

Iris: Kind of like a family.

Therapist: You all live together, like a little community?

Iris: Just a community, but very close to each other.

Therapist: If you would describe to me the most significant observation about this moment, either within you or around you, what would it be?

Iris: That I'm really happy.

Therapist: Wonderful. Is there anything else about this scene that we may have missed?

Iris: I don't think so.

I move her forward in time.

Therapist: Tell me, what is happening now?

Iris: I see an army. Yeah, I have to fight. I don't want to.

Therapist: Are you there already?

Iris: Yeah.

Therapist: How old are you now?

Iris: 24 comes to mind.

Therapist: What is your name?

Iris: Eric is the first thing that came to mind.

Therapist: Let me just call you Eric. Eric, tell me where you are. Describe the place to me.

Iris: Something royal. I was called, but by someone royal to fight for my country, like my dad.

Therapist: Is that the reason why your dad wasn't home earlier?

Iris: I think so.

Therapist: Is this like a royal army?

Iris: Yeah.

Therapist: What does the place look like where you are now?

Iris: There are a lot of young males. Everybody came here to fight, but nobody wants to.

Therapist: Have you any idea what this fight is about?

Iris: Just to protect our land.

Therapist: And you don't feel like it?

Iris: No, not at all.

Therapist: What do you look like right now? Look at your outfit. What are you wearing?

Iris: Everybody's wearing the same thing. It's brown in color.

Therapist: Describe it to me. Give me some details. What does it look like?

Iris: It's hard for me to see the details. I don't see the details. I know it's brown and it's comfortable. I don't mind it.

Therapist: What are you going to do next?

Iris: We are supposed to go somewhere.

Therapist: Move forward in time a bit and tell me what happens next.

Iris: There's a fight, and I didn't want to.

Therapist: You're fighting?

Iris: Yeah.

Therapist: How do you feel when you're going through this experience?

Iris: I hate it. I don't want to.

Therapist: What do you observe?

Iris: I see the bayonets. They are everywhere. I can't even see who fights who.

Therapist: There are many people here?

Iris: Many people. It's a battlefield.

I move her forward again.

Therapist: Tell me, what is happening now?

Iris: I can see the mountain. That's the mountain where my home is, and that's the mountain where I saw my dead body. Everything happens there.

Therapist: Where are you now?

Iris: I'm just in the field, in front of this mountain. It feels like I'm talking to the mountain as if it's a God. I think it is a God. That mountain is something special to me.

Therapist: How old are you now?

Iris: 28.

Therapist: You came back from the war?

Iris: Yes.

Therapist: Are you back home again?

Iris: War wasn't too far from here either. I'm on my way home.

Therapist: You're looking at the mountain and you're talking to the mountain. Is this on the way home from the war?

Iris: I think so, yes.

Therapist: How are you feeling now?

Iris: I'm grateful to be here.

Therapist: You survived the war.

Iris: Yeah.

Therapist: What do you like best about this place?

Iris: Everything is so beautiful. There are red trees. And this mountain is so magical. It has snow on top. And all the people regard this mountain as God.

Therapist: So, there's a collective feeling, a culture about this mountain?

Iris: Yes. And when I talk to this mountain right now, I feel something special.

Therapist: Tell me more about that.

Iris: I believe it's a God.

Therapist: Beautiful. What does it do for you when you connect to the God of the mountain?

Iris: It gives me power.

Therapist: Beautiful. What kind of power?

Iris: Healing power. It gives me strength. And calmness. Oh, this is so weird.

Therapist: Tell me.

Iris: I just thought that I'd like to die here, and I did.

Therapist: I see.

Iris: As if I asked for it.

Therapist: And the mountain gave it to you?

Iris: And it happened. But I'm happy.

Therapist: Do you sometimes go to the mountain, to worship or to connect more intimately with it?

Iris: Very rarely, yes.

Therapist: You do it yourself or as a community?

Iris: Some people go there alone, and I think I did it once, maybe twice. It was amazing.

Therapist: What can you tell me about that experience?

Iris: It was magical. I felt God.

Therapist: Beautiful. How come everybody has this feeling about this mountain?

Iris: Oh, yeah, there's a power that everybody knows about, and it helps us live.

Therapist: You feel it is a blessing to live at the foot of this mountain?

Iris: I think so, yes.

Therapist: Wonderful.

Iris: I went there, and I felt God, I felt the presence. That's why I didn't want to go to war.

Therapist: Right. You didn't want to leave your God. You're living very close to a living God.

Iris: Yes. Why did they send me to war? I didn't want to fight.

Therapist: But now you're back, right?

Iris: Yes, but I'm still thinking about it.

Therapist: Is there any way the mountain can help you with this?

Iris: Yeah. That's why I'm here. I want the God of the mountain to erase that memory.

Therapist: Move a little bit forward in time and see what happens.

Iris: When I was 18, I went there, and on that mountain, something happened over there inside the forest. Oh my God, it's enlightenment.

Therapist: Enlightenment?

Iris: Yes.

Therapist: Tell me about it.

Iris: I didn't expect that.

Therapist: Tell me everything about it.

Iris: When I was about 18 years old, I went there, and I was fulfilled.

Therapist: Go back to that moment. Experience it again.

Iris: I was alone there for a long time. I was searching for something, and I found it, but it wasn't what I expected. Yes, I knew something that nobody else knew.

Therapist: Tell me about that moment of fulfillment, the enlightenment.

Iris: I don't know how it happened, but I was searching for something for a long time, and then something happened for a moment, and I felt fulfilled as if someone told me a secret.

Therapist: Was it coming from the mountain?

Iris: Yes. I felt special at that time. I felt special, and I realized this is what I was looking for.

Therapist: You got a real glimpse of it?

Iris: Yes, exactly. I went home and my life was changed.

Therapist: After that experience?

Iris: Yes.

Therapist: In what way?

Iris: It became so much brighter and more beautiful. I understood people, everybody.

Therapist: You had an awakening?

Iris: Yes.

Therapist: It wasn't just one experience; it was a transformation.

Iris: Definitely. I had so many friends. I could understand everybody. Women, children, other men. I saw through them. People loved me.

Therapist: That is so beautiful.

Iris: Yes. It was, until that war.

Therapist: You lost it a bit after the war?

Iris: I was forced.

Therapist: What happened to that state of mind when you came back from the war?

Iris: Oh, you know what? I think it was just my ghost. It wasn't me. Oh, I didn't come back to the village.

Therapist: You didn't?

Iris: I didn't come back to the village. It sounds weird, but just my ghost was there.

Therapist: Your spirit came back.

Iris: My spirit came back to look around, and make sure everybody's safe.

Therapist: The scene of your death, was it during the war then?

Iris: Not exactly. I was killed after the war was finished, on my way back. Not in battle. I was alone and somebody just killed me.

Therapist: Near the mountain?

Iris: Yes. On the way back home.

Therapist: Just randomly?

Iris: I never made it. Yes, it was random. I didn't expect it either.

Therapist: Tell me, what did you learn in this life?

Iris: Oh, I think someone wanted to rob me. That's why. Yes, just stupid. I know what I learned.

Therapist: What did you learn?

Iris: It's so hard to explain.

Therapist: About enlightenment?

Iris: Yes.

Therapist: You don't have to explain.

Iris: I was so happy.

Therapist: Beautiful. Just hold onto it.

Iris: As if I didn't need anything else, just this. Just the light around me, and the light around other people.

I move her past her death.

Therapist: Now, where are you now in relation to the body you leave behind?

Iris: I'm flying.

Therapist: Are you still seeing the body or are you gone already?

Iris: No.

Therapist: You're gone already?

Iris: Yes.

Therapist: What is happening now?

Iris: I'm in a hall, just standing. I'm just standing in the hall.

Therapist: What does that mean?

Iris: It's just someplace. Looks like an old castle or something. Just a huge hall.

Therapist: Are you waiting for someone?

Iris: Yes. Looks like I'm waiting for someone.

Therapist: Is it like a place of welcome?

Iris: Yes, it is.

Therapist: Are you alone or is someone there?

Iris: Oh, someone is coming.

Therapist: Tell me about who's coming and what they look like.

Iris: Like a gypsy.

Therapist: Is she a guide?

Iris: I think so.

Therapist: Is it your guide or is it a general guide?

Iris: It's my guide.

Therapist: Do you recognize her?

Iris: Yes.

Therapist: Tell me what happens.

Iris: I feel so strong and she likes it.

Therapist: Does she say or express anything? I understand that not all communication is verbal, maybe telepathic.

Iris: She takes me by my hand. She's smiling. She's happy. She looks very weird, very, very old, but very funny and active.

Therapist: Where is she taking you?

Iris: Up the stairs.

Therapist: Tell me everything that happened so I can stay with you. What happens next?

Iris: Going up long stairs. There's another room, big and beautiful. There's a fountain in the middle. Here they are.

Therapist: Who are they?

Iris: Others, the Council.

Therapist: How many are here?

Iris: Eight.

Therapist: What do they look like?

Iris: Oh, very powerful. But they're kind to me.

Therapist: Are they saying something?

Iris: They don't say anything, but they send me the understanding that I did well. They send me the understanding of their gratitude. They're just happy for me. I did well.

Therapist: What did you do well?

Iris: That I didn't like the war.

Therapist: They're happy that you didn't like the war?

Iris: Yes.

Therapist: What else?

Iris: I shared my enlightenment with others. I didn't keep it inside. I didn't feel proud. I just shared every little thing. So they are very pleased.

Therapist: Wonderful.

Iris: And my guide, the old lady, this is how I call her, the old lady. She is very pleased too.

Therapist: How does it make you feel, to be here with them?

Iris: I'm proud and strong. More strong than proud. I just feel really strong, I've never felt that strong before.

Therapist: Why do you think you feel strong this way?

Iris: Oh, because of my life.

Therapist: Your enlightenment, your accomplishments.

Iris: Yes, everything.

Therapist: Is this a good place to talk a little bit about Iris as well?

Iris: I think I'm ready.

Therapist: Iris has some very important questions, and they are a little bit about enlightenment and identity. Because she is looking for her identity in this life.

Iris: She's weak.

Therapist: What does the Council say about that?

Iris: I've got to do it. I want to be a man.

Therapist: Why take up this female body? What is the task?

Iris: I need to feel weak this time.

Therapist: Why is that?

Iris: I don't understand. I don't know why.

Therapist: We'll ask the Council. You're here. Ask them. What do they say?

Iris: I don't hear an answer.

Therapist: Just listen with your heart and your intuition.

Iris: I need to know the way, how to make it from weak to strong. It's easy to be strong when you are born strong.

Therapist: This is another challenge.

Iris: Yes.

Therapist: What about the enlightenment that was achieved in the previous life?

Iris: Yeah, it was so beautiful.

Therapist: How is Iris able to retrieve that sense of divine identity?

Iris: She's not too far.

Therapist: Is she going to awaken that again?

Iris: If she tries. She needs to try harder. She's going round and round, but she can't see it and it's right there.

Therapist: Because the attainment had already been achieved previously, right?

Iris: Yeah.

Therapist: How come it's not manifesting now?

Iris: She needs to find her way.

Therapist: What does that mean?

Iris: It's like she needs to pass through it to get it. She needs to learn something very important before she gets it.

Therapist: What does she need to learn?

Iris: It has to do something with other people, she's too hidden.

Therapist: Help me understand.

Iris: She needs to be strong enough to open up to people. And when she opens up to people, she'll find enlightenment.

Therapist: Why is she not opening up?

Iris: I don't know. She's just like that, stubborn.

Therapist: What advice can the Council give, to help her to open up?

Iris: Oh, listen to your dreams. But so far, she has never got anything in her dreams about opening up.

Therapist: Maybe now that she hears about it, she will receive some information.

Iris: Yeah, but it's mostly about relatives. No. Sometimes she has dreams about others, but she's scared to share them. She needs to be more open. Share things.

Therapist: Can she learn from her previous life as a soldier who was enlightened?

Iris: Yeah. He shared everything that he had.

Therapist: So maybe Iris can learn from him, right?

Iris: She should.

Therapist: Is that why we saw his life today?

Iris: Yes.

Therapist: In a way you have already achieved that. It shouldn't be too hard to retrieve that because it's not somebody else's achievement, it's yours.

Iris: Yes.

Therapist: Doesn't that make it much easier?

Iris: Definitely.

Therapist: Why does Iris feel sorrow, even though she has a good life?

Iris: That's because of me.

Therapist: Why?

Iris: I didn't want to be a female.

Therapist: She resists being female.

Iris: I guess so.

Therapist: How can that be changed?

Iris: I feel male.

Therapist: Are there certain female qualities that Iris should learn? Is that why she came with this female body?

Iris: Actually, she does learn a lot, working in the maternity unit. That's beautiful. And having her husband and giving birth.

Therapist: So, she is learning these female qualities?

Iris: Yes.

Therapist: Were those qualities lacking in previous births?

Iris: I don't know.

Therapist: Well, you'll figure it out. In general, is Iris on track? Is she on the right path?

Iris: Yes.

Therapist: What is the goal that she needs to achieve?

Iris: Get enlightenment. Make it from weak to strong.

Therapist: The first step is to develop strength.

Iris: Yes.

Therapist: The second step is enlightenment.

Iris: Yes. She should be more open to people. She's trying hard, but it's so hard for her.

Therapist: What is the role of her husband in this life?

Iris: To support her in everything.

Therapist: What is the goal of that relationship?

Iris: It's funny. Her husband has a feminine nature, so he provides what is missing.

Therapist: When I hear this, your primary theme is to develop strength. This also includes integrating female qualities, that perhaps previously had been lacking. That balance is what provides the basis for enlightenment. Is that correct?

Iris: Yes.

Therapist: Is that a good summary?

Iris: I think you got it right.

Therapist: Who are the other people in your soul group?

Iris: There are not too many.

Therapist: How many are there?

Iris: Three.

Therapist: Do you know who they are?

Iris: My husband and my friend.

Therapist: Do you all share the same goal?

Iris: Yeah, we're working on something.

Therapist: Where does Iris' need for solitude come from?

Iris: It's the mountain.

Therapist: I see.

Iris: It is. She needs to be in nature more. She needs to go up North.

Therapist: Now that we understand Iris' goals on Earth, what can you tell me about her goals in between lives?

Iris: I'm strong and I have powers. I'm experienced. They won't let me see it.

Therapist: Maybe that's all you need to know right now, knowing who you really are.

Iris: I am enlightened, and I am strong. I need to do something else. My goal is to do some kind of task, not there on earth, here. An important task. Provide protection. Protect something beautiful. Oh, it is so beautiful. I am so happy. I don't want to go back to earth.

Therapist: Is this your real home?

Iris: Yeah. And I have a real task there.

Therapist: What is that task?

Iris: Protecting the force. Like a guardian.

Therapist: Do you know what that means?

Iris: It's a very important task. I'm so proud to be there. I did it earlier.

Therapist: You did?

Iris: Yes.

Therapist: Is this your spirit identity and your spirit role?

Iris: Yes.

Therapist: Why then did you have to come back as Iris?

Iris: To feel weakness.

Therapist: Why is that important?

Iris: Everybody has to do it.

Therapist: Why? In order to understand it?

Iris: Yes. Not to be proud.

Therapist: So, it's training?

Iris: I think so.

Therapist: What is the reason that Iris has so many different experiences? She lived in many different countries, coming from a Christian background, living in a Muslim country, and marrying a Jewish man. What is the purpose behind this?

Iris: Because it's been a while.

Therapist: To incarnate, you mean?

Iris: Yes.

Therapist: Was the last life the soldier's life?

Iris: Yes.

Therapist: There have been centuries in between.

Iris: Yes.

Therapist: When you say it's been a while, does that mean that she's just recapping all these experiences in one lifetime?

Iris: Yes. I want to see what's going on.

Therapist: I see, like an accelerated training process, so to speak.

Iris: This is so funny. This was one of the things that I chose before I came. There will be more.

Therapist: Many more?

Iris: Not too many, but yes. More experiences. I crave them.

Therapist: Why do you crave them?

Iris: It's been too long. I like to be a protector of the source, but I want to fool around too.

Therapist: In this life, you just took a refresher course, so to speak?

Iris: Yes.

Therapist: Well, how does Iris feel? Perhaps now that you see this, it may help detach Iris from her life a little bit.

Iris: It's a little bit of a bother for her now because she doesn't know I'm playing.

Therapist: She is used to being a forceful protector, and now she's a girl.

Iris: Yeah.

Therapist: How ironic. It would help to remember, don't you think?

Iris: Yeah.

Therapist: The voice she is experiencing, telling her about future events, who is that voice?

Iris: It's the source. It's the source telling me.

Therapist: What should she do with these visions and this information?

Iris: It's somewhat important. Listen to them and share.

Therapist: Is she sharing them now?

Iris: No.

Therapist: So, she should?

Iris: She should. It's scary for her. So much pressure.

Therapist: But isn't there a reason why the source is sending this information?

Iris: There is.

Therapist: You're like an instrument of the source, of the voice.

Iris: Yeah. She's got to listen.

Therapist: Iris has a strong desire to help people. She became a nurse to help those that suffer. However, now she's in a corporate environment. Why does he at this moment turn to the spiritual and the esoteric?

Iris: It's been a while. She needs to reach enlightenment.

Therapist: Has she been too casual about it thus far?

Iris: She needs to get to the point. It's not too far off.

Therapist: Other than this old lady, do you have other guides?

Iris: No, I'm partly on my own.

Therapist: As a protector, you don't need many guides?

Iris: She comes to me very rarely. That's why she's so old. She used to be my guide. She's just a good friend now.

Therapist: You don't need a guide anymore?

Iris: Sometimes I need her advice.

Therapist: How can you Iris contact her?

Iris: I don't think she can.

Therapist: She cannot?

Iris: I never did that before.

Therapist: Are you saying that there is no need?

Iris: I get the voice coming to me in visions and dreams. I just need to listen to that.

Therapist: The guide is more for the in-between world when you're the protector.

Iris: Yeah. She is just a friend now.

Therapist: Does the Council have anything else to share with you?

Iris: Yeah. As we were talking, one of the Council members told me that I needed to find my own group somewhere up North.

Therapist: Do you have to move there?

Iris: I need to move up North. Like in my other life, the North will give me power.

Therapist: This current environment is not conducive to your development?

Iris: It's too dry and too hot. My powers are not the same when it's hot.

Therapist: Oh, that's important information, isn't it?

Iris: It is very important. A geographical location for the soul.

Therapist: Okay, that's good. Now, the spirit world is wide open to you. Is there any other place we need to go? How are you feeling?

Iris: I want to stay with the Council.

Therapist: You want to stay with them quietly for a little bit?

Iris: Please.

Therapist: Yes, stay as long as you want.

Therapist: Yeah. How are you feeling?

Iris: I'm good.

We slowly bring the session to a close.

Case 16: Iris
A view of heaven

This is the second session of Iris, whose first session we described in the previous chapter. Iris is a labor-and-delivery unit nurse and enters a past life at birth. This was a special request, which we gladly honored as we knew her to be a wonderful and intuitive soul.

Iris: (Crying and breathing rapidly and heavily, immediately after birth).
Therapist: How does it feel being born?
Iris: Air (breathing deeply).
Therapist: Does it feel good to get air?

Iris: Yeah.

Therapist: Now your mommy is going to hold you.

Iris: Thank you (sigh of relief).

Therapist: Your mommy is going to hold you, loving you. And you're being washed. All clean now (deeper sigh of relief). How does it feel to be in this new little body?

Iris: I'm happy.

Therapist: Good. How was the birth process?

Iris: It was wonderful.

Therapist: What did you experience?

Iris: No pain.

Therapist: You didn't feel any pain at all?

Iris: Nothing at all.

Therapist: What was the experience like leaving the womb and entering the light?

Iris: It's just a very tight tunnel. Very, very tight. And there are no thoughts when you go through it. You're just being squished, squished, squished, squished, and then the air.

Therapist: How does it feel, this first breath of air?

Iris: It is so good.

Therapist: Yeah?

Iris: It is so exciting.

Therapist: Are you excited to be born?

Iris: Yes.

Therapist: Beautiful. What we're going to do now, is move forward in time a little. Are you a boy or are you a girl?

Iris: I'm a girl.

Therapist: Let us move to where you're a little girl, to a relevant moment in your early life.

Iris: This is a very, very wealthy household. Very wealthy.

Everything is opulent.

Therapist: Tell me, how do you look? What are you wearing?

Iris: Very pretty. I'm wearing a very pretty pink and white dress. My hair is done properly. I'm a very well-cared-for child.

Therapist: Where are we?

Iris: It's hard to say, but it's somewhere in Europe again. Yes, it is. Oh my God, I live in a castle-like mansion.

Therapist: Look out of the window and tell me what you see outside.

Iris: Very big windows. Oh my God. Am I a princess or something? I don't know. Very, very wealthy. Everything is gorgeous. Everything is so beautiful.

Therapist: Do you like it?

Iris: Me, as a girl, I don't appreciate it because I've never seen anything different. This is all normal.

Therapist: Tell me a little bit about your parents and who they are and what is going on in your day-to-day life. Do you get to see your parents?

Iris: Yes, a lot. My mom is a beautiful lady. Yes, it is Europe and I'd say maybe 1800 or 1700.

Therapist: What about your dad? What does he look like?

Iris: He's a nobleman.

Therapist: I see.

Iris: But he is not a king, no, he's just a nobleman. Very, very wealthy and powerful too. He's in politics.

Therapist: How old are you now?

Iris: I want to say four or five.

Therapist: Do you have any brothers and sisters?

Iris: Yes, I think I have a younger brother. I don't see him very often though.

Therapist: What is your name?

Iris: Belle.

Therapist: Tell me, Belle, is there anything interesting you'd like to share about this moment in your life?

Iris: It feels like I'm having a very good childhood. Very loving, very wealthy, no problems, but I don't know it yet. It's just very normal to me.

I move her forward in time.

Therapist: What's your age now Belle?

Iris: I'm 17.

Therapist: How do you feel?

Iris: I'm thinking of someone I love. I fell in love.

Therapist: Where are you now?

Iris: Some very fancy apartment.

Therapist: Is it in the same castle or somewhere else?

Iris: It's a different place. It belongs to the family and it's also very gorgeous and opulent.

Therapist: Where is this apartment?

Iris: It is in the city. Oh, I think it's Paris.

Therapist: When you look outside the window, what do you see?

Iris: Yes, I can see the streets of Paris. It's so beautiful. I see the people walking on the streets. My apartment is on the second floor.

Therapist: Do you like it here?

Iris: It's a city place and I like it because I grew up outside of the city in the big castle. This is an apartment in the city, and I like it.

Therapist: Do you live here alone or is there anybody with you?

Iris: There is a nanny, somebody who's taking care of me and watches over me.

Therapist: Do you have a lot of freedom?

Iris: I don't.

Therapist: Is it the nanny who is controlling you or social customs?

Iris: Yeah, there are several people who are controlling me.

Therapist: How do you feel about that?

Iris: They want to be noble.

Therapist: You're not allowed to just go outside and do things?

Iris: No. I always ask.

Therapist: Are you able to see your loved one, your boyfriend?

Iris: No.

Therapist: Do you have a relationship with him or are you just in love with him?

Iris: I don't have a relationship, no.

Therapist: You just love him?

Iris: Yes, I fell in love, and he loves me too, but he is not nobility like me.

Therapist: Is that a problem?

Iris: Yes.

Therapist: How did you meet him?

Iris: He is a soldier. He's fighting a war somewhere. He's not in Paris. I don't know how I met him. I can't see it.

Therapist: Are you waiting for his return, is that what you're doing?

Iris: He occupies my entire mind. I worry he gets killed.

Therapist: What is the most significant observation about this moment in your life at 17 years old in Paris?

Iris: I've learned a lot since childhood. I know the difference between rich and poor.

Therapist: How did you discover that? Because most rich people don't learn that.

Iris: My lover is poor.

Therapist: Your lover is poor?

Iris: Yes. Someone who I love is poor. He's a very simple man, and he showed it to me. He's the only one who showed that type of life to me. I didn't know before.

Therapist: How does it make you feel when you realize that difference?

Iris: I kind of like it better.

Therapist: Why?

Iris: Because the rich, their souls are not right. The poor have good souls. They seem to be better people.

Therapist: You've become aware of other people.

Iris: Yeah.

I move her forward in time again.

Iris: There's a war on the streets of Paris. There's a war. It's very dangerous everywhere. I don't have rich clothes anymore. I'm dirty and I'm running and I'm trying to hide.

Therapist: How did that come about?

Iris: I never knew this could happen to me. I was so spoiled. It's a civil war.

Therapist: Is it the French Revolution?

Iris: I want to say yes. And I'm hiding and I'm running.

Therapist: Why are you hiding?

Iris: I don't want to be killed.

Therapist: Who is after you?

Iris: A lot of people. I don't know who. It's not one particular person.

Therapist: Why are they after you? Is it because you were wealthy?

Iris: Yes.

Therapist: They're coming for the rich people.

Iris: Yes.

Therapist: Where's your lover? Is he still a part of your life?

Iris: Oh, I know nothing about him.

Therapist: You've forgotten him.

Iris: I'm just trying to save myself.

Therapist: Are you alone now or is there anybody else with you?

Iris: No, my nanny is with me. The woman who takes care of me. She's very, oh, what is the right word? She takes good care of me even though it's a Revolution. She could easily leave me, but she's with me.

Therapist: Does she love you?

Iris: She promised my dad that she would take good care of me.

Therapist: Where are your parents?

Iris: I think they were killed.

Therapist: Really?

Iris: Yeah.

Therapist: Are you destitute now?

Iris: They were killed in that house.

Therapist: Due to the Revolution?

Iris: People came and killed them.

Therapist: Did you lose all your wealth as well?

Iris: I think I have something left.

Therapist: And now you're running.

Iris: But I'm not rich anymore and I'm running and I'm trying to hide, and I pray, and I pray to find a place to hide.

Therapist: Move forward in time a little bit till this running is over and tell me what happens next.

Iris: I'm 30. I have kids now. I have a boy and a girl.

Therapist: Where are you now?

Iris: I'm in a very small apartment. I'm poor, but I am so happy.

Therapist: Are you still in Paris?

Iris: The suburbs.

Therapist: Tell me about your husband, how you met him, and what life is like.

Iris: He's a simple man. He was a soldier too. He helped me. He saved me. He helped me when I needed help.

Therapist: Are you happy with him?

Iris: He fell in love with me. I did not for a long time.

Therapist: What about now?

Iris: I accept him.

Therapist: But you're not in love?

Iris: I adore him because he gave me my kids and my kids are what I love most.

Therapist: What can you tell me about your house and your day-to-day life? Are you a housewife?

Iris: I am a housewife. I cook. I'm so proud of myself.

Therapist: Why is that?

Iris: Because I like this life better than my rich life.

Therapist: Why is that?

Iris: I'm free. My soul is so free. It makes me so happy.

Therapist: Was wealth restricting your emotions and freedom?

Iris: I never needed that.

Therapist: I see.

Iris: I understand now that my parents were not as loving as I thought they were. I just didn't know the difference. Having my own kids, I see the difference.

Therapist: You are much more loving?

Iris: Yes.

Therapist: Beautiful.

Iris: I spend so much time with them. I play with them. I teach them. I talk to them. I do all that stuff that I never had. I just had my nannies. Yes, I saw my mom and dad, but it wasn't right.

Therapist: I see.

Iris: Being poor changed my life for the better.

I move her forward in time again.

Iris: I'm 50 and my hair is gray. I'm mostly in my chair. I'm not healthy.

Therapist: What's going on?

Iris: I think that I'm old and sick.

Therapist: Are you still in Paris?

Iris: I didn't know.

Therapist: Are you still in the same house you were in before?

Iris: Yes, it is still the same house.

Therapist: Where are your children?

Iris: I have grandchildren now. Maybe somewhere else. Not too far.

Therapist: What about your husband?

Iris: I see him from time to time, but not often.

Therapist: How come?

Iris: He works, and lives somewhere else.

Therapist: Are you separated?

Iris: No.

Therapist: Is it due to work that he lives somewhere else?

Iris: We never really loved each other.

Therapist: I see. Like a separation without an official divorce?

Iris: We just have our own lives, but he comes and visits me very often. Maybe twice a week.

Therapist: I see. What is your mental state right now?

Iris: I'm ready to go.

Therapist: You're quite ill then?

Iris: No.

Therapist: You're just mentally ready to go.

Iris: Mentally. I'm exhausted mentally. I don't want to do anything. I just knit.

Therapist: Tell me about the room you're in. Describe it to me.

Iris: It's gray. It needs repair.

Therapist: What kind of furniture do you have in here?

Iris: There's almost no furniture. There's just one bed and my chair.

Therapist: Is it just a single room? Do you have a separate kitchen?

Iris: There is a little kitchen. It's like a very, very small apartment.

Therapist: If you look outside the window, what do you see?

Iris: I see children playing.

Therapist: Are these the suburbs or is it in town?

Iris: No, it's in town.

Therapist: Are the houses connected?

Iris: The houses are all connected, with very narrow streets and the roads are bricks. The children are playing.

Therapist: Do you like it here in Paris?

Iris: Occasionally, a horse with a wagon comes by. Do I like it? I don't care.

I move her to the last day of her life.

Therapist: How old are you on this last day of your life?

Iris: 52.

Therapist: What is going on right now to suggest that your physical death will come this day?

Iris: I'm in bed. I'm in bed and ready to go. Everybody's in the room.

Therapist: Who is everybody?

Iris: My family. My kids, my grandchildren.

Therapist: How do you feel?

Iris: Some neighbors.

Therapist: How do you feel?

Iris: I don't even care.

Therapist: Are you in pain or not?

Iris: No. I don't feel anything. I think it's…… I just have a problem breathing.

Therapist: What do you think about this life you just lived as Belle?

Iris: It's very vivid. I made a very good choice in this life. I had to choose between rich and poor and I chose poor because it cleansed my soul.

Therapist: What did you learn from this life as Belle?

Iris: I don't need to be rich. I don't need that kind of money. And that's true because all my lives after this one were poor.

Therapist: What else did you learn from this life?

Iris: Maybe not really poor, but not rich. I enjoy that. I don't like money. It's dirty.

Therapist: What else did you learn from that life as Belle?

Iris: I made a mistake marrying my husband because I didn't

love him. Love is a force for good in a family.

Therapist: Did it affect your life afterward?

Iris: Yes.

Therapist: In what way? What did you learn from that?

Iris: He loved me in the beginning, and he made me marry him and he saved me, but I never loved him. I just did it because he saved me. But as time went by, he realized it and became cruel. He was cruel to me and to my kids too. It was a mistake, but this is something that I needed to learn.

Therapist: What did you learn from that decision to marry out of obligation, not love?

Iris: I just thought I had to do it.

Therapist: What is your last thought or your last awareness as you leave the body?

Iris: It wasn't the most wonderful life I've ever had.

I move her to her life-between-life.

Therapist: What is the first thing you notice?

Iris: A castle.

Therapist: What can you tell me about this castle?

Iris: I think it is the same castle I saw last time, but it's from the outside now.

Therapist: Is this a castle in some lifetime or is this in an astral plane?

Iris: The astral.

Therapist: Tell me about this castle.

Iris: It's beautiful. It's purple in color. Each brick of this castle has a purple light, and this is what I saw last time too.

Therapist: Are you looking at it from a distance?

Iris: Yes, this time from a distance.

Therapist: Are you alone or is there a guide or anybody else with you?

Iris: Yeah, I think it's my guide. My guide.

Therapist: What does the guide look like?

Iris: My old gypsy.

Therapist: Tell me about her.

Iris: I don't see her as clearly as I saw her last time.

Therapist: It will come. Just give yourself a little time to see things more clearly. Go a little bit deeper. How do you feel now?

Iris: She loves me so much.

Therapist: How does she welcome you this time?

Iris: She gives me a hug.

Therapist: What does she have to say about this last life as Belle?

Iris: She always tells me I did well.

Therapist: Does she say anything different now than she did last time?

Iris: She didn't talk to me last time. She just grabbed my hand and looked me in the eyes.

Therapist: The last time?

Iris: Yes, but this time she actually talks to me.

Therapist: What does she say?

Iris: She gives me several pieces of advice.

Therapist: Such as?

Iris: Always choose love. Never fight back. She says I did well in that life.

Therapist: Wonderful.

Iris: The only mistake I made was to marry that man, and now I learned my lesson.

Therapist: What did you learn from that? What does the guide say?

Iris: I learned that I will always marry for love.

Therapist: Right. Follow your heart. No other considerations.

Iris: Always. Because things change all the time, but love will never change. It was a good lesson in that life.

Therapist: How are things different now? Compared to the last time when we exited your life and now, a few centuries difference, in what way have you evolved?

Iris: Yes. This experience was prior to my last experience. I wasn't as mature as now. And I know much more. Even when I entered my life, as I saw during the last session, I was more mature than in this life.

Therapist: As Belle?

Iris: As Belle, yes. Belle is still dealing with simple things.

Therapist: What was the main intention for the life of Belle? Before taking up that birth, what needed to be worked out karmically?

Iris: Two lessons. First, I don't need money. I don't like being nobility. I will never choose it again in my other lives. And the second lesson is to always marry for love. Always choose love. Always choose love.

Therapist: What were the main themes in the other lifetime we visited earlier?

Iris: As Eric?

Therapist: Yes.

Iris: Oh, it was so much deeper.

Therapist: What was that about?

Iris: I was enlightened in that life. I didn't deal with issues most people had. I dealt with something higher. Life as Eric taught me to be enlightened, to be close to the source, to have extra powers. Eric was so much deeper than Belle.

Therapist: Belle was more elementary regarding her issues.

Iris: Very.

Therapist: Before we discuss more, and you're with your gypsy guide now, looking at the castle, is this where we're going to stay, or do we need to go somewhere else?

Iris: No, we entered.

Therapist: Where are we now in the castle?

Iris: We're just walking through the castle. I think she's taking me to the Council again. We're going somewhere.

Therapist: Tell me when you get there and describe to me what happens so I can stay with you.

Iris: It's the same room I was in the last time. With the same people.

Therapist: What's different this time?

Iris: There are fewer Council members.

Therapist: Why is that?

Iris: Because of Belle's life.

Therapist: There are not so many required?

Iris: No. It's very simple.

Therapist: What's being discussed in the Council?

Iris: I see that person again. He makes me so happy. One of the Council members, the one who gave me a medallion the last time. I recognized him again.

Iris remembered after her first session more about what the Council member gave her before departing. It was this medallion.

Therapist: Why don't you ask him why he gave you that medallion?

Iris: (Crying). I knew that.

Therapist: What was the nature of that medallion?

Iris: It's my daughter Anna. She's so important.

Therapist: Was he indicating at the time that he was giving her to you with that medallion?

Iris: It's not just her. It's that she's going to be something very important in my life.

Therapist: What does he say about her? What is your soul connection?

Iris: She's bigger than me. She's going to teach me something like I taught my mother.

Therapist: Can they share with us what that will be?

Iris: She's going to take me to the other world. I don't know what that means.

Therapist: Ask him. What does that mean? To another level of consciousness? To another reality?

Iris: I'm ready for another world. But I'm scared.

Therapist: Ask him. He will help you understand. Don't be afraid. What is he trying to tell you?

Iris: That I shouldn't be scared. That I'm ready for another world.

Therapist: What does 'another world' mean?

Iris: Oh, something higher than this world.

Therapist: Do you mean after the life of Iris or during the life of Iris but on another level of consciousness?

Iris: After this. I should finish this life.

Therapist: Then she's taking you to a higher place?

Iris: Yes.

Therapist: What does that mean? You don't have to be born on this earth again?

Iris: No.

Therapist: Is this your last birth on this planet?

Iris: He said that I can return if I want to, but I'll enjoy the other place better.

Therapist: What is unique about the other world?

Iris: That's the thing. That is why I'm scared because I don't know.

Therapist: What can this Council member tell you?

Iris: He says it's divine. He says there's going to be no lying.

Therapist: It's a higher world?

Iris: There's going to be no talking too. Everybody just reads minds.

Therapist: So, it's a very high world. And Anna is the one who is going to prepare Iris for that life this time?

Iris: She's so powerful. I can't believe it.

Therapist: She's here to prepare you for that higher life. Is that it?

Iris: Yes, she'll take me there. (Crying) I can't believe it.

Therapist: Are you seeing her soul, her real soul?

Iris: I can't believe it because I felt it the entire time during pregnancy.

Therapist: Tell me about that.

Iris: It's a miracle.

Therapist: Now that we're here with the Council, why is Iris remembering Eric so much?

Iris: He was very close. Eric taught me. Eric brought me to that stage.

Therapist: The higher stage?

Iris: Yes. He was very close to the higher being.

Therapist: What lesson is Iris to learn from connecting to Eric in this lifetime? Why does she keep seeing that so intensely? What does the Council say?

Iris: Yes. I have to remember even more. I'm not trying hard enough to change it.

Therapist: Rather than thinking it's an obstacle, they want the opposite. He wants you to be more like Eric.

Iris: Yes. Eric could give up a lot to be close to the higher being. I cannot. Iris cannot.

Therapist: What does the Council say about that?

Iris: That's why they gave me my daughter. Oh my goodness.

Therapist: Is your daughter doing for Iris what Eric could do himself?

Iris: Yes and No. Anna is going to do more. Anna is very powerful.

Therapist: What progress the Council says has your soul made now that it's in Iris's body?

Iris: I should work harder. I don't work hard enough. I should just think of myself. I think too much about others. I create too many problems for myself and everybody else. Too much thinking that doesn't need to be done. I just need to focus. Just focusing will help me.

Therapist: On her own evolution?

Iris: Yes.

Therapist: What karma needs to be worked out to come to that freedom?

Iris: I need to learn to let go.

Therapist: Of what?

Iris: Stuff of the world. What's the right word for it?

Therapist: Worldly distractions and attractions.

Iris: Yes, the world's distractions. I must learn to let it go. And I know it, but I can't.

Therapist: What does the Council say when you say you can't?

Iris: He says just learn.

Therapist: Why is it so hard for Iris to let go of things?

Iris: I think that's how my parents taught me.

Therapist: You are here with the Council, not as Iris, but as your individual soul.

Iris: Yes.

Therapist: I want you to have a look at the big picture. At Eric, at Belle, at Iris, but now also as your soul. When they talk to you as a soul and want you to move towards that enlightenment, what advice do they give?

Iris: I need solitude. I need to be away from the city.

Therapist: To live in a more solitary place?

Iris: Yes. I need nature around. I need to meditate, and it will come.

Therapist: You need a different lifestyle?

Iris: Yes.

Therapist: Iris is wondering whether to proceed with nursing or be a midwife. What does the Council advise?

Iris: Nursing is wrong for me. Midwifery maybe, but it depends.

Therapist: How can the Council help?

Iris: Anything that's more natural. Stay away from the hospital, stay away from corporations, and stay away from the places where money is the main motive.

Therapist: In other words, she can reinvent herself as a midwife or a doula who works in a more natural and organic setting.

Iris: Yes.

Therapist: To be your own person and not be part of a corporation.

Iris: Yes.

Therapist: Well, that's very beautiful.

Iris: Anything I do that's natural will help me. Just, don't work in a money-dominated work environment.

Therapist: Sometimes Iris feels that she has healing powers, but in a corporate environment she's not able to really express that. What does the Council say?

Iris: Working in a hospital can of course be done, but she won't be as effective as it will drain her energy.

Therapist: Does the Council have anything to add to that?

Iris: Yeah, he's telling me what to do to use my powers for women in labor. I need to place my palms on the belly button, and I need to say a prayer, but I don't know what prayer.

Therapist: Ask them. They are here now. They will tell you everything.

Iris: He says there is a Viking song that he'll teach me later. He'll show it to me later. I should find it somehow.

Therapist: He will guide you. Is that it?

Iris: He will guide me, yes. It is a very old song that is actually a prayer. But people don't know that it is a prayer. This is a prayer for people going through labor helping them to have a beautiful experience.

Therapist: Beautiful.

Iris: It will help them be calm and relaxed. This prayer also provides energy for the baby. I should find out about it very soon. Within 6 months.

Therapist: Should she start making a career change and a lifestyle change in the meantime? Is that what the Council suggests? Living a different way, in a different place. How urgent is that?

Iris: He says half a year.

Therapist: Okay, beautiful. Is there anything we may have missed that they want to share with your soul?

Iris: He tells me to be stronger and do things the way I want to do them.

Therapist: Be more assertive. Is that what they want?

Iris: Be more assertive, yes. I don't have enough courage.

Therapist: Is there anything you want to tell them?

Iris: I just want to thank them.

Therapist: Now I don't know if they can do it, or if you want to, but is there a way the Council can give you a little glimpse of that new beautiful world that you could be going to next time?

Iris: Yeah, he just showed it to me.

Therapist: He did?

Iris: Oh, I don't know how to describe that. I just want to be absorbed in it.

Therapist: They already read my mind before I even asked a question.

Iris: So cool. I don't know how to describe it.

Therapist: You don't need to. Just enjoy it. Just stay here for a moment.

Iris: It flows through me.

Therapist: Stay as long as you want and just enjoy.

Iris: You don't have a body in that life. You're just spirit. But it is another world. It's not like in between lives.

Therapist: Is it higher?

Iris: It's kind of a life, but it's not a physical life. Not at all. I can see my own spirit without body, and I can see buildings and castles. It is very, very beautiful, but it's all transparent. And I can see the sky. We don't have colors here. I cannot even say what color it is. And there are spirits everywhere. Very smart, very experienced.

Therapist: You're going to be there too.

Iris: Yes. But I will feel very new. I'll be very new there.

Therapist: How does it feel in your heart and soul when you're there?

Iris: I'm very happy, that's true, but I miss the physical world a lot. Some of my friends are going to be there in the physical world and I'm a little bit lonely.

Therapist: But that is because you're just visiting now, but by the time you go there, perhaps you're more evolved. You still have the rest of Iris's life to prepare.

Iris: Oh, yes.

Therapist: That's not something you need to worry about now.

Iris: I could not ever imagine this. I never thought about it. I can't believe it.

Therapist: You're blessed that you're being shown this today. Something to think about as Iris and to meditate on.

Iris: Now I feel a lot of responsibilities.

Therapist: For yourself, yes, to get there.

Iris: Heaven is different from what we see in the life between lives.

Therapist: Is heaven a much higher consciousness?

Iris: Yes, but it is also a world. It's a higher world. What people call Heaven is not where you go after you die. You still need to be born there too.

Therapist: Are you saying that you need to qualify to get there after many lifetimes on Earth? You need to grow into it.

Iris: The Council tells me that if I miss Earth too much, I can always come back for a life or two.

Therapist: You don't have to make a quick transition if you don't want to.

Iris: He says it will take time to adjust.

Therapist: What do they want for you beyond the life of Iris? What do they want you to evolve in?

Iris: He says, I don't need to know right now.

Therapist: No?

Iris: But it's going to be an important task.

Therapist: Is there anything else that the Council wants to show?

Iris: He says I don't need a spirit guide.

Therapist: What is the most important thing they wanted to show you today?

Iris: Yes. Yes. Another world.

Therapist: That is the most important?

Iris: Yes. Yes. I needed to see it.

Therapist: Why?

Iris: I need to work a little harder to get there.

Therapist: You need to prepare yourself.

Iris: He says that I needed a little push. "Don't be scared. Don't be scared. Don't be scared."

Therapist: Think of it as beauty, as possibility.

Iris: It's another type of learning over there. There's no karma. There's intense learning, but a different kind of learning. Very, very spiritual.

Therapist: They want you there. They say you're ready. How does it make you feel when you see that?

Iris: I don't know if I'm ready.

Therapist: Not now.

Iris: I'm hesitant.

Therapist: Not now, because Iris is only 37, but they want to prepare you, isn't that so?

Iris: Yeah.

Therapist: You have a life to live as Iris.

Iris: Yes.

Therapist: To prepare. Isn't that what they want to show you today, to help you get ready?

Iris: Yes.

Therapist: Does the Council agree to that?

Iris: Oh yes. That's true. Yes.

Therapist: They showed this to you today because they believe in you. They know that you can do it.

Iris: He said that he's waiting for me there.

Therapist: There you go. Do you see that? They wouldn't show this to you unless you're ready. How do you feel now after everything you've seen?

Iris: I have more courage now.

Therapist: That's important. It gave you a bigger picture.

Iris: This is amazing.

Therapist: It is. It's amazing. Is there anything else from the Council and your guide?

Iris: No, that's it. Oh my God, it's going away.

Therapist: Ask your guide if she can come and show herself to you in your day-to-day life.

Iris: She doesn't want to talk to me.

Therapist: She doesn't?

Iris: She says that I know everything. She says she cannot help me with anything else because I already know everything that I need to know.

Therapist: Isn't that what the Council just told you, that you don't need a guide anymore?

Iris: Yeah, that's true.

Therapist: How do you feel?

Iris: Oh, he just told me. "Remember the image of the new world."

Therapist: Beautiful. Do you want to have a last look around?

Iris: It's disappearing. Yeah, it's gone now.

We slowly bring the session to a close.

Case 17: Marianne
Permission to be free

Marianne is a successful 43-year-old design business owner from the East Coast.

Marianne: I see a centurion. A man. There's a lot of construction and buildings. He's overseeing slaves. There are a lot of buildings. Thousands.

Therapist: Where are we now?

Marianne: Tens of thousands of people are building things.

Therapist: Where are we now?

Marianne: The desert.

Therapist: What country comes to mind?

Marianne: Maybe it's Egypt. I don't know what they're making, but he's got one of those uncomfortable helmets with the flappy thing on the top and sandals.

Therapist: How do you feel standing here overseeing these workers?

Marianne: It's not his home.

Therapist: No? Is he on assignment here?

Marianne: Yeah.

Therapist: How does he feel doing this work?

Marianne: He's proud of his job. He's not really happy, but he's proud that he's elevated this high above all these people. He's literally standing up high overseeing. It's very high.

Therapist: What else do you notice?

Marianne: He's got a sword. He keeps his hand on his sword a lot.

Therapist: Do you think he likes his sword? Is it a symbol of power?

Marianne: He's proud of it but he hates it. He hates being like that. He hates hurting people. But he's also proud of how high he's come because otherwise, somebody would fuck with him.

Therapist: He's aware of it. Now, what's your name as this centurion

Marianne: I don't know.

I move her forward in time as this man.

Therapist: Tell me what is happening now.

Marianne: More power, but he doesn't have to hurt people now. He's in a government palace, plush, and he hates that too. People are so boring. It's still better than most of the people who live terrible lives. He's very lucky. He lives very plush.

Therapist: How did he get to be in such a position? Was it due to family connections or his own effort?

Marianne: It's a combination. He's a determined person. Intelligent. Shrewd, even. Knows when to speak, knows who to speak to, when to speak and not to speak, when to act and not to act, when to be secretive, and when to make moves.

Therapist: Very clever?

Marianne: Yes. Kind and good, but he hides that. He has to hide that. It's not seen as a virtue at this time.

Therapist: Now, look around you. Can you give me a general description of the environment?

Marianne: It's plush. There's furniture. It's inside a castle, sort of, but it's brighter. There are tapestries on the wall in colorful forest greens and blues, and they drink from gold, and silver-type metal chalices.

Therapist: How old are you now?

Marianne: 65.

Therapist: What is your state of mind at this point in your life?

Marianne: Most of these people are full of shit, and he'd rather just be at home with his creature comforts.

Therapist: Where do you live?

Marianne: Looks like in the castle, in a well-appointed room where he can lock the door.

Therapist: Is he married, or does he live alone?

Marianne: He's alone.

Therapist: How come he's alone?

Marianne: Maybe there was somebody who died very young, and he never wanted anyone else. He thinks everybody's full of shit.

Therapist: Is he a cynical personality?

Marianne: Yeah, but it's just because he's so good.

Therapist: Does it have anything to do with a previous lover?

Marianne: I think she was killed violently.

Therapist: How did it affect him?

Marianne: He just shut down. He refused to really love again. He just focused on his work to take his mind off it. It's so sad.

Therapist: At 65 years old, what is the most significant observation about your life, either within you or around you?

Marianne: That there's more than all of this and everybody around here is so wrapped up in their bullshit.

Therapist: Tell me more about this.

Marianne: There's beauty and there's real love in the world and it's just not where he is. None of these people can experience it and understand it.

I move her forward in time as this man again.

Therapist: Tell me what is happening now.

Marianne: He's just old. He's very old.

Therapist: Where are you now?

Marianne: In a chair in a ragged nightshirt. I'm going to die soon, but I'm so happy finally because nobody expects anything of me, and I don't have to be fake anymore.

Therapist: You're retired?

Marianne: No, I'm almost dead. I still live in the same place, but they have somebody taking care of me. I was very high-ranking, so I've got a nice nurse that I like. She brings me comfort soup and I don't have to be something I'm not anymore because I'm old and there's comfort in that.

I move him to the last day of his life.

Therapist: How old are you on this last day of your life?

Marianne: I don't know.

Therapist: Pretty old?

Marianne: Yes.

Therapist: Is there anything going on around you or within you that suggests that your physical death will come this day?

Marianne: Just peace. I'm ready to go.

Therapist: Where are you? Is the setting familiar?

Marianne: Yes. I'm in my room. I'm just laying on my bed. I'm just ready to go. Just ready to go.

Therapist: What do you think about this life you just lived?

Marianne: It was hard. There's so little love and so little joy. I'm really cut off.

Therapist: What did you learn from this life?

Marianne: I learned how to fit into this society all while knowing that this society isn't important and knowing that there's something bigger. Knowing how to keep that under wraps because that's not the "reality" that I'm in, though I knew there was something else. I learned how to fit in and how to succeed, even though I had a secret the whole time, knowing that everybody was full of shit, just knowing that they were disconnected, they were wrong. I was happier when I was older, and I didn't have to do that anymore.

Therapist: What is your last thought or awareness as you leave the body?

Marianne: Home, finally. Truth, beauty, love.

I move him past his death into a higher region.

Therapist: How do you feel about your death?

Marianne: Oh, I'm fine. I'm ready to be home. I want to float around in space.

Therapist: What is the first thing you notice?

Marianne: Just so free. It feels so rich and warm just to move through the air. The air is thick but it's just free.

Therapist: When you look at your own soul Self, what do you feel you're like? Are you light or energy? Frequency? Do you have a form?

Marianne: I'm a woman. I know that I can be anything, but I like to be a woman. I feel my energy trailing behind me like a beautiful gown. It's like a big, thick, full gown flowing with energy behind me and I just swoosh around. It feels so nice.

Therapist: Where are you now? What does the energy around you feel like?

Marianne: Oh, just like space, heaven, and potentiality.

Therapist: Beautiful. Are there any other beings or guides nearby that we can invite?

Marianne: There can be if we just think it.

Therapist: What is the first thing you do when you reach this place? Are you just going to float around happily?

Marianne: Dissolve into it.

Therapist: Take some time and enjoy yourself. When you're done playing around and you want to go to the next phase, just let me know. How are you feeling?

Marianne: Good. You just dissolve.

Therapist: Now, tell me what you do next after you play around and enjoy the freedom.

Marianne: I must go to the hall with the higher ... not higher, but ...

Therapist: The Council?

Marianne: Yeah. We must talk about it.

Therapist: All right, why don't you go there and tell me what the place looks like as you arrive?

Marianne: It's all energy. It could look however I want, but

I like it to look like purple stone, imposing, like buildings on Earth, but it's not cold even though it's stone. It's still warm and loving there.

Therapist: How many Council members are here?

Marianne: Well, there's eight and then there's me, but we're all equals, so I would also be one, too. It's not like they're my bosses, we come together. I would be the ninth.

Therapist: Is there anybody stepping forward to welcome you and start a conversation?

Marianne: Yeah. A Dumbledore-looking dude.

Therapist: What is the first thing that he says or wants to show you?

Marianne: A big hug.

Therapist: Beautiful. Like, "Welcome home?" How does it feel to be with them now?

Marianne: So nice. They're my friends. They're perfect friends, where you don't think you're bad anymore, you know that you're all good and you're all different, but you're all together and you're all good.

Therapist: When looking back on the life of the centurion, what are their thoughts about this life?

Marianne: They're just empathizing that life on Earth is hard, but it's necessary, and they're thanking me.

Therapist: What was the plan for this life? What is it that your soul wanted to experience?

Marianne: To have power. It wanted to have power.

Therapist: How did you do, wielding that power in that life?

Marianne: I did okay.

Therapist: Do they offer any sort of positive criticism as to what you could have done differently in that life?

Marianne: I don't know. I'm not really connected to that life anymore.

Marianne: It's not hard. It's a lot easier than we make it. We make it so hard, but that's the Earth school. That's what's going on here. We put a veil over ourselves.

Therapist: What if you look behind the veil and you look at your intention as a soul? What are you about?

Marianne: A jokester. She's so funny. She just went, "Peekaboo." Laughter. Very childlike, very childlike, but knowing from a higher wisdom place, from the highest wisdom place, we're so childlike. It's beautiful.

Therapist: You just want to be joyful?

Marianne: Yeah. So much laughter.

Therapist: Divine joy, that's what you are about?

Marianne: Yeah.

Therapist: Beautiful. How is Marianne doing in that regard, expressing that in her life?

Marianne: I think very well. She wrote a book and published it. Didn't really do much with it, but that's because she's not putting too much pressure on it because she's about having fun. She was like, "That'll be fun. Put that out there." Didn't make it a big deal. Just have fun. It's fun here. Every second is a miracle, a cornucopia, smells, sounds, sights, feelings, and friends. It's amazing here. It's like the world's greatest concert for years every day. It's really cool here.

Therapist: In her daily life, she has many talents that she feels she's not using. What is the best way that she can express her highest purpose?

Marianne: Just joy. Just joy.

Therapist: What about the five guides that she sees in her meditations? Are they here also now?

Marianne: They're here all the time with her. She's always with them.

Therapist: What do we need to know about the guides?

Marianne: All of this, she already knows. She talks to all of them. None of this is new because she already knows all of this.

Therapist: Well, we're checking in with the Council now and we are here for a purpose today. What is it that they want to show you, share with you, or remind you of?

Marianne: They're loving me, but they're like, "You do this in the bathtub twice a week. It's not hard for you. Stay connected." Their love is always available there for me, and the more that I stay tapped in, the lighter and happier my life is, and the lighter and happier my life is, the more I show other people how to be light and happy. I'm a source of light for my son and for my employees. I can infuse light into every transaction or relationship that I have and that's beautiful, just to create joy for other people.

Therapist: It is beautiful. Now, she has this desire on this Earth for a Spanish house. Why does she have a desire for this place?

Marianne: She's just creating challenges for herself that she can rise up to. She's just so smart. She likes to play with manifesting reality around her on this Earth plane. Earth is so easy for her, so she makes up these little challenges, like when you're running a marathon and you're like, "I'll go a little faster than the guy in front of me." It doesn't matter. She's just having fun.

Therapist: What about a soulmate? She's alone now, at this moment. Is there any sort of residual block from the Centurion's life where he closed himself down? Is there perhaps a first chakra block due to some of these experiences? What does the Council say when we look at the centurion's life, how he hardened himself, closed himself off from love, and became almost cynical? Let the Council answer that one.

Marianne: I could have a soulmate, but I have to vibrate even higher. I have to be even more joyful than I am.

Therapist: Is there a block of some kind coming from the past?

Sometimes, it's easier to let the Council look at these things objectively and just listen to what they have to say.

Marianne: No human relationship is perfect. That's the nature of human relationships.

Therapist: What should be her attitude towards it?

Marianne: Every human relationship is perfect because that's what it's there for. All the challenges therein, it's all perfect.

Therapist: What does the Council suggest she do with the remainder of her life? What is important for this incarnation?

Marianne: Whatever you want, babe. Garden. Fuck it. Just have fun. Just have fun. Just relax. Keep reading your books. Floating, happy. None of it matters. All of it matters, but none of it matters. It's just joy. Just have fun. Be a joyful and official presence in all your interactions and do whatever you need to do to be that.

Therapist: It's beautiful what they are saying because it's such a simple yet such very difficult thing to do. The fact that your soul is so bubbly and able to do that is a sign of tremendous inner freedom and a sign of great evolution. I'm sure that's why you are part of the Council, so happy and free.

Marianne: Three or four years ago, I was asleep, just waking up, and one of my guides came to me that I'd never met before. He just whispered in my ear, "You never have to worry about money." I was like, "What?" "Yeah, just stop worrying about money." I go, "Okay." Never had to worry about money again. It always just comes.

Therapist: Beautiful.

Marianne: I just started tithing. Now, I'm giving away more money and I have started making lots more money. I used to want a lot more money but now, I realize I'm at the top, where any more you have might just create more problems. You can have more. That's fine. That's more to give away, but I certainly don't need more to be the happiest, most joyous person I am, which is nice. That's nice.

Therapist: That's a state of great freedom. During Marianne's meditation, she sometimes feels that she's choking and gagging, which seems to be a little bit different from the happiness that she could be experiencing in meditation. Where is that coming from?

Marianne: It's just all the garbage from this life. That's why she cries, too. Once the spirit gets in there that stuff must come out. It's like cleaning the counters of the kitchen. It's like when the counters are white you can see every little stain.

Therapist: The whiter the counters are, the more sensitive you are to any sort of gunk that is there, which will make you cough it out, basically, flush it out with the tears. Beautiful. Is there anything else they may want to share with you?

Marianne: Well, they're sharing with me that this person, this soulmate, is really happy and we could really make a lot of people very happy. But I have to maintain my glow and be hypervigilant about it with diet, exercise, meditation, and with whom I hang out. They're saying we can do so much together to pump up the vibe everywhere we go and raise the vibration of the planet. Through our joy.

Therapist: Anything else?

Marianne: I want to know how to stop my back from hurting. I don't know if it's emotional.

Therapist: Ask them and see what they say. Maybe they can do something for you now.

Marianne: Oh, I'd like that. Where am I being inflexible? Just keep working on that. I don't care what happens to me.

Therapist: Is there some inflexibility somewhere that manifests as that back pain?

Marianne: Yeah.

Therapist: Can we find out what it is?

Marianne: I don't care what happens to me. That's how I'm going to find all the magic of life. I can't care what happens to me. It doesn't matter. It's all fun. It's all fun.

Therapist: It's a great way of looking at yourself in a more detached way.

Therapist: Can they help you heal a little bit now?

Marianne: Oh, that would be nice.

Therapist: Ask them. They do it so often. How's it going?

Marianne: It's good. I'm just chilling.

Therapist: Are they able to help you with your back?

Marianne: I think some, yeah.

Therapist: How do you feel?

Marianne: I keep thinking about my son. He's very happy, too. How can I be the best mom to him? Just love him and be happy. Just try to keep him and his vibration raised. Should I be doing anything larger scale to raise the vibration of the planet? Doing that's counterintuitive because it creates stress that I'm not doing enough and then, that lowers my vibration. No. Just have fun. Just have fun and be kind. Be kind. Raise people's vibration by being kind.

Therapist: It's very subtle and significant. This is how the saints live. They just are. They're just happy and they shine a light. They don't have any plans or ambitions. They don't worry about money. They're just free. You are like that. It's really extraordinary. It's easy to misunderstand. It takes great intelligence to be so simple. It sounds like a paradox, but it's not.

Marianne: Just like the centurion. He was forced to be caught up in everything and he had to pretend to be caught up in everything.

Therapist: What a world.

Marianne: But, in this life, I don't have to because I'm free.

We're in America and I'm an upper-middle-class lady. I can do whatever I want. It's so freeing.

Therapist: If you project this trajectory of evolution forward and you see this life coming to an end, what would you want to be, to become, to express in this incarnation and beyond?

Marianne: Just to be light, to be happy. I can embody that, and I can share it with anyone who will listen. Then, they're going to share that with their children. Just lighten up. It's not that hard. Life is much easier than we make it.

Therapist: That's beautiful. I've seen that, throughout this experience today, you're very consistent in who you are and what matters. Now that we're here with the Council, would you like to stay a few moments quietly with them and just be happy?

Marianne: They're telling me my vibration is my superpower. It's my gift, it's my purpose, it's my responsibility. It's my reason for waking up. I always wake up in a good mood, but the first thing that I do, the first thought I have, is check in with myself because I'm different every day. My purpose is just to be that light and it's so fun to be that light. It's cool.

Therapist: All you must do is keep that light finely tuned.

Marianne: They want me to say it out loud: drinking wine and alcohol is detrimental to my overall vibration. It's going against my purpose and it's also not helping me have my happiest life. It dulls my shine. You don't have to be like everybody else like the centurion did. You can be however weird you want. Just because your friends drink doesn't mean you have to. We can still have fun with them.

Therapist: It's an important point. Your nervous system needs to be clear, pure, and shiny. Alcohol dulls it down.

Marianne: I've got to get rid of it at some point because it just dulls my shine.

Therapist: How do you feel?

Marianne: I feel good. I knew all of that. They talk to me and tell me, but it's really nice to say it again a little louder and realize how lucky I am because I can be whoever I want.

Therapist: Maybe that's why we saw the centurion today as a reminder of how grateful we can be for this birth under these circumstances because it does make a difference in which time, which place, and with which body you're born. Otherwise, you have to spend so much energy dealing with these things that prevent you from being just free.

Marianne: I just asked the Council, "Why did I have parents that made me so sad and why did I have such a sad childhood?" They said, "You had to teach yourself joy." I started doing a gratitude journal when I was 17. I realized I could take my joy into my own hands and then book after book after book followed, books like yours and experiences like these. I would've never had that if I had a loving family.

Therapist: It makes you more aware of what matters and, once you have it in your own hand, nobody can take it away. It's an acquisition. It's not a circumstance, it's an acquisition.

Marianne: It's a skill I had to learn.

Therapist: It is a skill, yes. It's an awareness, but it comes after many lifetimes.

Marianne: This body is so healthy. I'm so lucky.

We slowly brought the session to an end.

Therapist: That's ok.

Marianne: It's just that I keep coming back to this life. I'm sorry if that's wrong.

Therapist: No, that's fine. Let's talk about that.

Marianne: There's this higher tribune of higher souls that I will talk to. Sometimes, they watch my inner child for me so she's not sad anymore and they play with her and that's where she stays. It's these guys.

Therapist: Well, why don't you just play with them? Rather than having all these heavy discussions, just enjoy being with them and their playful energy.

Marianne: She's separate from me, but they watch her and she's so happy with them. Once a week or so, I check in on them in this life.

Therapist: Is that the soul Self who you really are, this happy child that is playing in the divine realm?

Marianne: Probably. I don't know why I keep crying.

Therapist: It's okay. As you are now with these beautiful beings, have a look at yourself, at who you really are, the beauty of your Soul, and your real nature. Just appreciate yourself. Isn't that what the divine is about, a simple, childlike love?

Marianne: It's purple light. Again, it's dark, it's not daytime. It's always night but it's always bright.

Therapist: Is that who you are, that purple light, or is that what you see around you?

Marianne: No, that's what I see around me.

Therapist: All these beings and yourself, you're in this purple light?

Marianne: Yeah.

Therapist: Now, tell me: through these different births, what is it that you're trying to achieve?

Case 18: Carry
A council incarnate

Carry is a 46-year-old TV producer from Hollywood, who recently lost her son and is grieving deeply, and searching for meaning in her loss.

Therapist: Now tell me, is it daytime or nighttime?
Carry: It's nighttime.
Therapist: Are you inside or outside?
Carry: I'm inside.
Therapist: As you look down at your feet, what, if anything, are

you wearing on your feet?

Carry: I've got some kind of strappy sandals on.

Therapist: What else are you wearing?

Carry: A robe. A brownish robe.

Therapist: Is it a one-piece or a multiple-piece robe?

Carry: No, two pieces.

Therapist: Does it strike you as very simple, fancy, very cheap, very poor, or rich? What does it look like?

Carry: It's worn. It's worn.

Therapist: Are you a girl.

Carry: No, I'm a male.

Therapist: It's a male kind of robe.

Carry: Yeah, the parachute kind.

Therapist: What is the color of your skin?

Carry: Tannish, brownish.

Therapist: What about your hair?

Carry: It's brown, curly.

Therapist: When you talk about a robe, what comes to mind? Where would such a robe be worn?

Carry: A farm or something.

Therapist: Is it kind of rough?

Carry: Yeah, like I'm working in the field. Like I'm on a farm or something.

Therapist: What do you see straight ahead of you?

Carry: I now see the house.

Therapist: Is it your house?

Carry: Yeah, it's familiar.

Therapist: What does it look like, this house?

Carry: It's stone, and it's got a chimney. Actually, it's small, and it's cozy.

Therapist: And the general environment around you, what does the landscape look like?

Carry: I'm on a hill.

Therapist: What's the weather like as you're outside?

Carry: Kind of cold. It's winter. It's just sort of chilly.

Therapist: What are you doing outside here this time of the day?

Carry: I'm getting an animal delivered. A horse.

Therapist: How old are you now?

Carry: 30, 37.

Therapist: How do you feel here on this farm?

Carry: I feel good. This is my land that I'm never leaving.

Therapist: Yeah, you feel comfortable here?

Carry: Yeah.

Therapist: Go inside your house and give me a description of what it looks like.

Carry: It's small, and there's a fire in the fireplace and there's a pot.

Therapist: Is there anybody else in this house, or is it just you?

Carry: No, there's my wife and she's pregnant.

Therapist: How do you feel about your wife?

Carry: I love her so much.

Therapist: You have a good relationship?

Carry: Yeah, I love her very much.

Therapist: Does she also work on the farm, or is she more confined to the house?

Carry: We work the land pretty much by ourselves, but she can't do so much of it now, because the baby is coming soon.

Therapist: If you were to describe to me the most significant observation about your life now what would it be?

Carry: I'm uneasy about something outside. I think it's the government or something, something that wants to take this away. Everything is so good inside, and I just want to be in this bubble.

Therapist: You're worried about something in your environment, politically or otherwise?

Carry: Yeah, my land could be taken away.

Therapist: What's the year we're in?

Carry: 1400 something.

Therapist: Can you tell me your name?

Carry: Yeah, John or Johann.

Therapist: Can I just call you John?

Carry: That's fine.

I'm moving her forward to a later time in the life of John.

Carry: I'm arguing with somebody in a building in Charlottesville. It's in town, and I'm arguing with some man about the money I owe him. And he's threatening me.

Therapist: Is this about your land?

Carry: Yeah.

Therapist: How bad is the situation?

Carry: It's pretty bad. I don't want my wife to know about this event, and I'm afraid. But it's pretty bad, I think.

Therapist: Did you get in debt in some way or other?

Carry: It's taxes of sorts, but they don't make sense to me. And I don't understand why. I don't understand why suddenly they need this amount of money. I got this on my own with hard work, and so I thought I was doing everything right, and somehow, it's not enough. They don't want to hear it.

Therapist: How old are you now, John?

Carry: Still 36 or 37.

Therapist: Around the same time?

Carry: Yeah, before it. It's about a year before it.

Therapist: What does the place look like where you are now?

Carry: It's in a town. It's got stones and arches, and there's a guy at a table.

Therapist: What does he look like?

Carry: He's got a cape on. He's the leader of the church or something. He's got a beard, and he's graying, red and gray hairs. He's writing, just writing with a pen.

Therapist: What's the mentality of this guy?

Carry: He's a cold man. Cold, he just seems cruel. He doesn't care, and there are so many people he's dealing with, and I'm the last of them.

Therapist: Do you feel that the fact that they want money from you is reasonable, or is this some sort of setup or corruption? How do you feel about what's going on?

Carry: I just don't understand it. I don't understand. Why do the right thing when I don't understand? I don't understand why they need this. No one can seem to explain it to me, and I want it to be explained to me. And nobody cares to explain it to someone like me. We don't really matter in their world.

Therapist: They don't care about you, a farmer?

Carry: No.

Therapist: Is it very class-oriented?

Carry: Yes, it's class-oriented, but it's also centered around the city and the church and the government. They want what we bring in, but they don't understand that we need to live, too. We're just so insignificant, and then they just tell us as much. If I die, it doesn't matter, and you can tell. It really doesn't matter if my wife dies.

Therapist: How does it feel to be a farmer in such a time and such a place? Do you like being a farmer?

Carry: I do like it. It would be wonderful if I didn't have to deal with this. I feel at home with my land, and my wife, and my home, and my animals.

Therapist: Your wife doesn't know anything about this?

Carry: She understands that something is happening. I tell her as much as I can about it.

I move her forward in time again.

Carry: My wife is dead.

Therapist: She is?

Carry: She's dead.

Therapist: What happened?

Carry: She was just really unwell, and she had blood coming out of her mouth. The doctor came and saw her last week, but there was just nothing he could really do, so she's dead. We had a son. She's gone, and I'm looking at where she's laying in the bed at our house.

Therapist: Are you still in the same place?

Carry: Yeah.

Therapist: How old is your son right now?

Carry: He's three.

Therapist: What happens now that your wife is dead?

Carry: I'll have to bury her.

Therapist: Have you known her for a long time?

Carry: Yeah, since we were little.

Therapist: Was it a real love marriage?

Carry: Yeah. We ran away together. She was younger than I was.

Therapist: Move forward in time a little bit until after your wife is buried. Tell me, what goes on now?

Carry: My son has become a very strapping young man and is helping me. It's getting harder for me, and he's good, and I train him.

Therapist: Is the financial issue with the land resolved?

Carry: Yeah, it was solved a long time ago. The people in power were taken out, and it turns out, they didn't pay much attention to us if we didn't go into town and alert them to us. Nobody wants to come out here, so I plan not to go there unless I need to. We have to go and sell things from time to time, in the market in town, but I avoid certain registries.

Therapist: Basically, they don't even know you exist?

Carry: Not really. The man from before died, so he doesn't come specifically looking. The man that's currently there, we've sort of fallen off the records, I guess.

Therapist: At this age, what is the state of your farm? Is everything going well?

Carry: It's hard. I still love it.

Therapist: How old are you now?

Carry: I think about 50.

Therapist: How is life without your wife?

Carry: I'm not without her. She's buried further up the hill, and I go see her every day.

Therapist: Did you ever remarry?

Carry: No.

Therapist: Why not?

Carry: I loved my wife.

Therapist: You love her that much?

Carry: Yeah.

Therapist: Like a soulmate.

Carry: Yeah.

Therapist: Beautiful. How's your son without a mom? Do you get along well with him?

Carry: I do, he's a good boy.

Therapist: Do you work together?

Carry: I do. He helps me. We go into town together.

Therapist: What is your state of mind right now, at 50?

Carry: I'm peaceful. I'm very old, but I've got this.

Therapist: What constitutes peace to you? What does that mean?

Carry: My land. I love my land. I love nature, the trees, and the fields. I love the bugs. I love the smell of it. I love the earth.

Therapist: That's bringing you peace, to be connected to all this?

Carry: Very much so, but it can be stressful sometimes.

Therapist: Right.

Carry: But I'm teaching him, and he loves it too. He loves it so much.

I'm moving her forward in time again.

Carry: I'm there, and I'm lying in bed. It's in the fall, it's nighttime, and there's a fire in the fireplace.

Therapist: Are you still in the same place?

Carry: Yeah.

Therapist: Are you ill, or are you just tired?

Carry: Just tired.

Therapist: Is your son still living with you?

Carry: He is, but he's married. He has a place, but he still comes here all the time.

Therapist: Is his house also on your land, or is it somewhere else?

Carry: Yes, it's near this land. It's not on this land, but he settled nearby.

Therapist: How are you feeling now?

Carry: I'm just tired.

Therapist: Are you still able to work your land?

Carry: No, it's grown over right now.

Therapist: Your son doesn't look after it?

Carry: He does. He does his best, but he has a wife, and she wants what she wants. She's demanding. I love her, but...

Therapist: So, your land is a little neglected right now?

Carry: A little bit, but that's okay.

Therapist: Are you able to feed yourself properly?

Carry: I'm eating a bowl of soup right now.

Therapist: What's your state of mind at this point in your life?

Carry: I'm at peace. I find everything kind of funny.

Therapist: Yeah? How so?

Carry: I just don't understand people. I don't understand them.

Therapist: What is the difference between how you think and the people around you?

Carry: Everybody gets very caught up. They're very caught up in all the comings and goings and the drama, and the money, what they have, and what they need. Everyone forgets to look for the simple stuff. Air, nature.

Therapist: Is that what you've been able to do in your life?

Carry: I think for the most part, yeah. I think I saw it a little in John, a little earlier when I was younger, but never entirely. Never swept up in it like so many.

Therapist: Your mental, and spiritual state is light and detached in that way?

Carry: Yeah.

Therapist: How does it feel to be in that kind of space internally?

Carry: Peaceful.

Therapist: Now, John, I'm going to count from 3 down to 1, and on the count of 1, we're going to move to the last day of your life as John. 3, 2, 1, and tell me how old you are on this last day of your life?

Carry: 84.

Therapist: Is there anything going on around you or within you that suggests that your physical death will come on this day?

Carry: My stomach is not right. My stomach feels like it's caving in.

Therapist: Where are you? Is the setting familiar?

Carry: It's in my home.

Therapist: Are you in bed?

Carry: I'm in bed.

Therapist: Is there anybody near you?

Carry: My son is on the way. He's not here yet.

Therapist: When you look back at your life, what do you think about this life you lived as John the farmer?

Carry: I think I didn't contribute much to this world, but I do think I appreciated this world.

Therapist: Do you feel you should have contributed something?

Carry: I wonder sometimes if I should have, yeah.

Therapist: What could you have done?

Carry: Tell somebody good stories. I tell good stories, and I could teach.

Therapist: Do you mean the knowledge and the experience that you have gained?

Carry: Yeah. I have grandchildren, and the grandchildren grew up hearing the stories.

Therapist: What did you learn from this life?

Carry: Not to have a fulcrum point, because I based everything on her death. And as much as I loved her, and as much as I was sorry to see her go, I never really lived again.

Therapist: You had your sense of identity, your sense of self, your emotional and mental state, wrapped around her existence?

Carry: I did.

Therapist: You mean you shouldn't have hung it up all around her?

Carry: The truth is, I wanted to get in that ground with her when she was buried. I think in many ways, I did.

Therapist: What was the result of that decision, unconscious though it may have been?

Carry: The relationship with my son became estranged.

Therapist: You couldn't give him what he needed?

Carry: He hurt. I wanted him to stay with me there. I wanted him to be a part of it. I wanted him to just want to be on the land with me, but he couldn't understand. He didn't understand that he needed it to get well.

Therapist: How is that related to you having that fulcrum point around your wife's death, and her existence?

Carry: He didn't have the same life. He didn't remember her.

Therapist: Now, what is the last thought or emotion or awareness as you leave your body?

Carry: He was a good man. John was a good man. He was a bit of a mystic. He didn't really ever leave his head, he just sort of communed on that small property his whole life. But he still, somehow, lived a full life in his head.

I move her beyond her death.

Therapist: Can you still see the body?

Carry: It's amazing.

Therapist: How do you feel about your death?

Carry: It's like going home.

Therapist: Before moving on, is there anybody you'd like to say goodbye to?

Carry: I'd like to see my son.

All right. Tell me how you reach out to him.

Carry: He's kind of a prisoner. He's on the way back to see me. He's going to find me. He'll be relieved and sad. I have wrapped my arms around him.

Therapist: Does he feel it?

Carry: He does.

Therapist: How does it make you feel that he feels it?

Carry: I'm grateful he feels it. I'm grateful that he knows something, even if he doesn't understand. We had a love. He and I had a love. We didn't understand each other sometimes, but he's a good guy.

Therapist: Is there anything else you would like to communicate to him?

Carry: I'm telling him in my head that I love him, and I'm not letting him go.

I move her to the life-between-lives world.

Therapist: What is the first thing you notice?

Carry: There are beings around.

Therapist: Are they everywhere, these beings?

Carry: They're everywhere. There are so many.

Therapist: Are you gravitating toward a particular group or a particular being?

Carry: Yeah, the angels on the left.

Therapist: Is it a group you're going to, or a guide?

Carry: It's a group.

Therapist: Tell me what happens when you reach the group. Is it a big group or a small group?

Carry: It's a big group. I see my wife from my last life.

Therapist: Is this your soul group?

Carry: Yes.

Therapist: Is there anybody else you recognize?

Carry: I just know them.

Therapist: I see.

Carry: I just know them all. I just know.

Therapist: Is there anybody kind of stepping forward to initiate some sort of welcome?

Carry: My wife.

Therapist: Do you have a different kind of relationship with her within the group?

Carry: Yeah.

Therapist: In what way?

Carry: She's been around him.

Therapist: Is she your primary soulmate? How do you feel about her as a spirit right now?

Carry: It's all white, so I feel a smile. I don't see a smile. I just feel full and light in my heart and all around me. I feel enveloped in a giant hug of light.

Therapist: You can connect to her at the deepest level here in the spirit world. Can you feel that?

Carry: Yeah.

Therapist: Now, without losing that connection, when you look at your whole group, how would you describe the temperament of this group?

Carry: We're all old. Feeling old.

Therapist: Old souls, you mean?

Carry: Yeah. I picture, for some reason, pointy ears and crazy, old, wispy, not really men, not really women. Androgynous, just old, wrinkly people.

Therapist: Do you have a common goal as a group?

Carry: Yeah.

Therapist: What brings you together?

Carry: Yeah, we actually have our club. It's like we have specific assignments.

Therapist: Do you share a common vision or a common spiritual goal?

Carry: Yeah, we're meant to be teachers. We're meant to be ascended teachers.

Therapist: Beautiful. Do you share any talents?

Carry: We each have different skills that we bring to it.

Therapist: Do you feel everybody in the group is at the same level?

Carry: Yeah. We serve as each other's guides.

Therapist: Beautiful.

Carry: I'm actually here to come and check in with them.

Therapist: What do they have to say about this life you lived as John?

Carry: They're congratulating me.

Therapist: What was the plan for John's incarnation? What was it that needed to be experienced or developed in that life?

Carry: It was a meditative life. It was supposed to be very long, and very quiet.

Therapist: To what end?

Carry: Getting used to a physical body.

Therapist: Help me understand.

Carry: To be really in a body, without all the distractions.

Therapist: When you say 'getting used to a physical body', do you imply that you were not really incarnating all that much?

Carry: We did different things.

Therapist: Such as?

Carry: We've incarnated but it's been more with visions? We're not used to living in bodies, and we're starting now with those bodies.

Therapist: When you say 'as visions', what do you mean? Did you create your own vision, or did you create visions for others?

Carry: No, for others. We were there for others.

Therapist: Like manifestations?

Carry: Yes, yeah. We had to be light bodies for early people on Earth, and our group planned to lead others as we became light bodies to them. We taught in that way, and it became obvious that we had to start incarnating, so we started coming into bodies. The first few lives were long and still, just so we could get to know the bodies and the Earth.

Therapist: That's interesting. So, as a group, you don't really incarnate forced by karma.

Carry: No.

Therapist: You are incarnating to serve and to help.

Carry: That's right.

Therapist: Are your origins of a divine kind?

Carry: Yes.

Therapist: Is this realm where you are now your true home, or is there still another place at another level?

Carry: There is another level, but we've been here for so long, I can't remember anything else.

Therapist: Beautiful. Now, when we talk about the life of Carry, what can say about how this ascended master consciousness is manifesting in her life?

Carry: At this point I've lived so many lives, and I came to Carry because the planet needs some people who know how to speak.

Therapist: In what way does she speak as a spiritual teacher?

Carry: Carry is very smart and she's a seeker because of her brain. And so, coming into this body we merge well. Values have changed, and minds have changed, and living at this time as Carry is the most merged way I have before.

Therapist: This body is well-suited.

Carry: It's a lot, but yes. It's a lot. It's very busy, but it's supposed to be. I knew it. I was ready for it.

Therapist: Is Carry in tune with her soul group's mission to teach and share spiritual truths?

Carry: More and more, yes.

Therapist: In what way is she manifesting that?

Carry: She's writing. She's been writing. And she can't help when she interacts with people, but to guide them.

Therapist: Carry has gone through a lot of suffering, though she's an ascended master, through the loss of her son. What was that all about? Why does she have to go through this?

Carry: That's just the plan. She's experiencing deep grief so that she can lead others through deep grief. He was the wife.

Therapist: In the past life?

Carry: Yeah. He was the wife.

Therapist: Is he in the soul group?

Carry: Yeah. He's a teacher, and it was their plan.

Therapist: Is he here now?

Carry: Yes, he is working with me from the other side. We work together every day.

Therapist: And the wife that you just hugged, is it the current wife, or is it a wife of the past life?

Carry: The wife that I have now, she was my son.

Therapist: Who is the primary soulmate?

Carry: It's the son.

Therapist: So it's him you just hugged?

Carry: Yes.

Therapist: How are you going to move forward now? Why don't you spend some time with his soul to help Carry move forward in a very loving, sweet, constructive way, without feeling that his loss is in some way a fulcrum point as happened in that past life?

Carry: He showed me a vision when he first died. I was reaching our hands together down into a terrarium, and that's how I must remember every day. This is part of our plan to work together. But I must keep planting, teaching, and dreaming.

Therapist: Is there anything we can do right here, right now? Take your time. That's right.

Carry: We're supposed to be such a beautiful unit. We have a very close connection to the other side. There is so little that separates us. And we've had to go through death again and again because I'm supposed to learn it very, very deeply. I'm supposed to learn it so deeply that I learn to walk over and have a complete connection. There's no staying behind.

Therapist: That's right, it's just as if it's a door into another room, and you can go back and forth. Rather than being depressed that there is another room, you acknowledge there is a door that you can go in and out of any time you need to.

Carry: Yeah.

Therapist: He's here right now?

Carry: Yeah.

Therapist: Can you feel him?

Carry: Right here.

Therapist: Right here. Beautiful.

Carry: I miss him much.

Therapist: Being here with him now, and looking at how Carry has been carrying this weight with her, can you help her let go of the burden of grief?

Carry: I understand the need for grief for the body. But I also understand that I picked a body that knew how to let light in so that we could start to demonstrate. Because that's what's happening on Earth. Everyone is afraid of both places. Carry's life needs to demonstrate some of these experiences.

Therapist: Why did this happen in Carry's life?

Carry: If you picture a slingshot, and you put the stone, which is Carry, in the pocket, these experiences pulled the cord back, engaged it, if you will. It was a heaviness. It was a need to exercise the purpose of that cord. The cord is there to pull what needs to be pulled, but it also needs to be released. It was to prime Carry for, and to release from it, what she thought was real.

Therapist: It propelled the stone forward.

Carry: Yes.

Therapist: It's to gain more depth, to understand deeper feelings, to learn relatability. And teach how to release it as well. Is that a good way of summarizing it?

Carry: That's perfect.

Therapist: A beautiful example.

Carry: Carry had to live a life of so many diverse emotions.

Therapist: Right.

Carry: So many possible human experiences have been packed into this very small life.

Therapist: It had to be relatable and grounded, to help her teach.

Carry: Yes.

Therapist: And yet the beauty is the flight of the stone, right? The Ascension.

Carry: Yes.

Therapist: Is working in TV the appropriate path moving forward, as the stone starts to ascend?

Carry: For the time being, it's not the TV she's producing, it's the people she's around. But there's more coming. There's more to be written down. Her life needs to have a large audience for this purpose. Not on TV.

Therapist: Working with and through it.

Carry: Working with and through it.

Therapist: Being on top is relevant to reach more people?

Carry: You have to go with it.

Therapist: Going through so many human emotions packed into one lifetime, what can be said about the pain Carry's body is carrying and how to release it?

Carry: Carry has put a lot of pain in different pockets of her body.

Therapist: What can we do right now to help your energy body? Perhaps you want to consult with the group and work together.

Carry: We're all laying our hands on her. We must take the pieces of the heaviness and disperse them through the group. She's advanced as a human, and she thinks she can do it, because she doesn't understand that she's a part of this whole group, so they're trying to take it from her.

Therapist: Go ahead and let it unfold, and when it's done, just let me know. Okay? Take all the time that you all need. How does it feel, the body?

Carry: Cherished.

Therapist: Beautiful. Now, when we talk about further growth and further manifestations of the qualities of this ascended soul, working through this body and mind of Carry, what can this body and mind do to advance the conductivity of this highest spiritual power?

Carry: She's been given glimmers of this, and that it is good so now we can directly download. She needs to regulate her meditation practice. She needs to continue to listen to the drum in her house when she meditates. She needs to practice yoga, which is something she's fought against because she doesn't trust her body.

Therapist: Can she do a gentle form of yoga, rather than a violent form of yoga?

Carry: Yes. She's always understood movement to mean violent movement.

Therapist: There's such a thing as restorative yoga, which is very soft and gentle.

Carry: Yes.

Therapist: If I understand this correctly, and correct me if I'm wrong, in order to have your group, the ascended masters, work through the body and mind of Carry, which is required to function at a high level because that's how the most impact can be made, there needs to be some form of daily connection, some form of gentle yoga, in order to help this body and mind tune. We want it to be grounded and it to be plugged in correctly. Is that a good way of putting it?

Carry: Yes, that's correct. She is yearning to lighten the load, really. There needs to be an integration of fluid movement with fluid thought, and she gets there sometimes, and sometimes she locks up. She's been locked up since the death of her son.

Therapist: Get back into the flow. Do you feel the flow now that everybody's here?

Carry: Yes.

Therapist: Beautiful. Remember, this flow is going to stay with you. And to strengthen it daily, you can do your practices, and feel the joy. Now, when we talk about family members, the daughter and the mother, what observations can be made about these two souls?

Carry: The daughter is also part of this group. Or she's part of a nearby group. They've been together many times. In many of these times, she has been a child of hers. She's of a new generation. She's observant, because her generation is actually going to be the new way of this world, and they have been prepped for it.

Therapist: In what way is her nature different than that of your soul group?

Carry: She's a receptor. She receives. They open up. We come in from elsewhere, and she's supposed to be here. She'll be here for a while longer, to live at a higher consciousness.

Therapist: Do you think your incarnations are coming to an end? Will you keep coming?

Carry: It may. We'll have to see, but they're not going to be much longer here. They have work to do in other places.

Therapist: Other places, you mean other realms?

Carry: Yeah, there are other places.

Therapist: What are your highest spiritual aspirations?

Carry: What I'm picturing is splitting apart so that all of the parts of me become a new creation. That from me, come new worlds.

Therapist: What will be the essence of these new worlds? What would you want it to be, as it comes out of you?

Carry: Love. A physical world. In a sense, the beauty of Earth, but with all love. And in that, there's pieces and pieces upon pieces upon pieces and pieces that come from me. And then I come for others. But that's the next phase, afterward.

Therapist: Beautiful. Now, is there anything you need to do regarding your mother?

Carry: She's really stuck. I'm going to teach her.

Therapist: How come she's so stuck?

Carry: She's in a little rut, and she isn't young. She's old. And she's very self-conscious.

Therapist: What can Carry learn from this experience, with that type of mother?

Carry: Patience and love. How to love someone that is always looking for the worst, even though there's so much love there. She can't see the forest for the trees. And Carry has had to reconcile her own deep love with that frustration, and the fact that the two of those can coexist. And in fact, the polar opposite is what creates the reality of that relationship.

Therapist: What about the wife?

Carry: She is a partner that is on this mission with her. She's a new body. She's not in my group, or she's moved on. A newer group. She and I do well together to advance each other. We do well, and so we have to incarnate together. Sometimes we're women, sometimes we're siblings, and sometimes we're daughters and sons.

Therapist: Now, focusing back on your soul group, what is it that they could share for the benefit of Carry's body and mind, to help her move through these remaining years in the most beautiful, gracious, enlightened way?

Carry: I'm picturing a mud pit at a concert when someone surfs across. They've all got me, and they're laughing about it. They're laughing and saying, "No matter what, we actually all are working together." And it feels like I'm alone, but I'm not the only one on this mission. My son and I incarnated. I live apart from the group for a while, now he's gone back. They're holding me, and this is part of the plan. And It's okay.

Therapist: Beautiful. Now what is it that you want from the group, as support, and a reminder?

Carry: Signs. More signs.

Therapist: How can they give them to you? What can they promise you?

Carry: Listening. Music. My son is with music. He's a musician. Meditation will help Carry try to pause better. She tries to classify it. It doesn't serve her because she's so busy.

Therapist: Instead, she should connect, right?

Carry: Yes.

Therapist: Flow with it. Beautiful. How do you feel?

Carry: Like I'm in touch with this love after, all the real joy. I have a really kind of silly bunch. You would think this many old ones would somehow be more serious, but it's the opposite.

Therapist: Because they're free.

Carry: They're free. They're free, and this is where Carry's humor will help her.

Therapist: This is what Carry needs to remember, that we are, at the end of the day, an enlightened, free bunch, and never to lose that spirit

Carry: Right.

Therapist: Not making the mistake that John made, to make it in some sort of tragedy, forgetting the true essence of your being. That love is eternal.

Carry: Yeah.

Therapist: Now, the spirit world is wide open to you. Is there more we need to explore or discover? How do you feel?

Carry: Really good. We're all high fiving. It's really ridiculous. They're going to be there on the other side.

We're slowly ending the session here.

Case 19: Elizabeth
I am what I am

Elizabeth is a 35-year-old psychiatrist who is searching for a deeper connection to her higher Self, and to free herself from the conditioning of the world.

Therapist: Now, tell me, is it daytime or nighttime?
Elizabeth: Night.
Therapist: Are you inside or outside?
Elizabeth: Light.
Therapist: You're in the light? What are you aware of?
Elizabeth: I feel really good.
Therapist: Yeah. Where are you now? Are you in a body, or are

you not in a body?
Elizabeth: I think so.

She seems to be in a place outside of the body. So, I attempt to connect her again with a past-life experience.

Therapist: Tell me what is the first thing you notice?
Elizabeth: Sad.
Therapist: Look around you. What do you see?
Elizabeth: The sun is bright.
Therapist: When you look down at your feet, what, if anything, are you wearing on your feet?
Elizabeth: Sandals.
Therapist: What else do you wear?
Elizabeth: Like a robe.
Therapist: Is it a one-piece robe or multiple pieces?
Elizabeth: One piece.
Therapist: When you look at your skin, what is the color of your skin?
Elizabeth: Very tan.
Therapist: What is your age now?
Elizabeth: Three.
Therapist: Are you a boy or a girl?
Elizabeth: I'm a boy.
Therapist: What are you doing here in the sand? Is it a desert?
Elizabeth: I think that it may be a desert. I'm not sure.
Therapist: Just look around you, and tell me what you're aware of, other than the sand. Give me a general description of the area where you are.
Elizabeth: There's a town.

Therapist: What does it look like, this town?

Elizabeth: Market. People are selling things.

Therapist: What are the other people dressed like? The same way you are?

Elizabeth: Yeah.

Therapist: What is sold in the market?

Elizabeth: Fruit.

Therapist: Are you in the market right now?

Elizabeth: Yes. I'm walking.

Therapist: How do you feel when you're walking through the market?

Elizabeth: I feel known and comfortable.

Therapist: Do you live in this town?

Elizabeth: I think so.

Therapist: What do the buildings look like?

Elizabeth: Seems to be more put together. They're not put together with equipment, more like by hand, molded.

Therapist: What's the color of these buildings?

Elizabeth: More like huts.

Therapist: Is it a big town or a small town?

Elizabeth: Small.

Therapist: Can you tell me where your house is, and what it looks like?

Elizabeth: I'm not sure.

Therapist: Where are we?

Elizabeth: I feel like it's in the Middle East, like Jerusalem.

Therapist: Israel?

Elizabeth: Yeah.

Therapist: So this is a busy area?

Elizabeth: Yes. It's busy all around. Everyone's a moving group, crowds of people, and they're all doing their things, and following together, walking. Just walking.

Therapist: What are you doing in this place?

Elizabeth: Observing.

Therapist: Is that what you like to do, to observe?

Elizabeth: I like to.

Therapist: What are your thoughts when you're observing this town and all the busyness?

Elizabeth: I feel good.

Therapist: What is it that you do on a day-to-day basis?

Elizabeth: I teach.

Obviously, he is not 3 years old now. He moved forward in time himself.

Therapist: How old are you now?

Elizabeth: 20.

Therapist: What do you teach?

Elizabeth: The way.

Therapist: The way? What kind of tradition do you represent when you teach the way?

Elizabeth: I mean, I feel drawn to biblical-like ideas.

Therapist: What year are we in? What comes to mind? Whatever pops up in your mind is fine.

Elizabeth: BC, like right before Jesus.

Therapist: Beautiful. What is your name?

Elizabeth: Jeb.

I'm moving her forward in time in the life of Jeb.

Therapist: Tell me what is happening now, Jeb?

Elizabeth: I'm sitting on a field, a meadow, looking in front, and being connected to, feeling a connection to this oneness.

Therapist: Beautiful. As you're sitting in this meadow, is it far away from the town where you were earlier?

Elizabeth: It's really calm.

Therapist: How old are you now, Jeb?

Elizabeth: 50.

Therapist: Tell me more about this feeling of being connected.

Elizabeth: I just feel that we're all one together.

Therapist: Do you often feel like this, or is it just a rare moment in your life?

Elizabeth: In the present, I feel like this.

Therapist: What can you tell me, between the ages of 20 and 50, how your life has been? What have you been doing during these last 30 years?

Elizabeth: I learned to be.

Therapist: You dedicated your life to an inner search?

Elizabeth: Yeah.

Therapist: Have you still been teaching while you were developing?

Elizabeth: Yes.

Therapist: Do you also have disciples? How do you teach?

Elizabeth: We have a temple.

Therapist: Do you teach at the temple?

Elizabeth: I teach at the temple.

Therapist: What does the temple look like?

Elizabeth: Stones. The temple is made out of stones.

Therapist: Do you live near the temple, or do you just teach there?

Elizabeth: I live nearby.

Therapist: Is it correct to assume that you dedicated your life to teaching and the spiritual search?

Elizabeth: Yes. Yes. Yeah, it's really good.

Therapist: Just enjoy it for a moment.

Silence.

What made you become a teacher and a searcher for spiritual truth? What led you to this?

Elizabeth: I just knew it was what I was meant to do.

Therapist: You knew it from a young age?

Elizabeth: Yeah, just about.

Therapist: And you feel now at 50 it's coming to a culmination?

Elizabeth: Yeah.

Therapist: Now at this point in your life, at 50, what is the most relevant observation about your life, either within you or around you?

Elizabeth: That peace can be mine to feel at all times, and to bring it to others.

Therapist: Beautiful. What happens within you when you are in this state? How do you experience this peace?

Elizabeth: I feel it on a cellular level, and then transcend up, with deep connection to myself, and to all around me, and that we are all here together.

Therapist: Is the culture in which you live supportive of this pursuit?

Elizabeth: I had to go far from there to here to feel this because they weren't ready. But we are already here, so I feel safe here, away.

Therapist: Who's we? Are you with a group of people?

Elizabeth: Yes.

Therapist: Do you all live together?
Elizabeth: We do. We live together.
Therapist: What does that group life look like?
Elizabeth: Community, understanding, giving.
Therapist: And you all follow the same principles?
Elizabeth: Yeah.
Therapist: Is there a leader in this group?
Elizabeth: We all step up when needed.
Therapist: So it's an enlightened community?
Elizabeth: Yes.
Therapist: Are you far away? You said you had to go far away.
Elizabeth: We did.
Therapist: Where do you live now then? Look around you, look at the area.
Elizabeth: It feels green, with water.
Therapist: Is it still in Israel?
Elizabeth: We got here on foot, so I'm not sure how far, but within walking distance.
Therapist: And you're pretty safe here?
Elizabeth: It's away from the city.

I move her forward in time again.

Therapist: Tell me what is happening now.
Elizabeth: In class.
Therapist: How old are you now, Jeb?
Elizabeth: I'm surrounded by everyone I love. Yeah. I'm going, but I'm excited.
Therapist: Are you on your deathbed?
Elizabeth: I feel complete with this, with self-care, and everybody.

Therapist: What is happening now?

Elizabeth: Everyone is with me, and everyone's hands are on me, and they're all with me, feeling, pinching me.

Therapist: What do you think about this life you just lived as Jeb?

Elizabeth: I feel complete. I feel fulfilled.

Therapist: What did you learn as Jeb?

Elizabeth: I learned to be. I learned community, togetherness, and trust.

Therapist: Where are you now?

Elizabeth: I'm on the bed; I'm in a room, surrounded by... They're with me, and I feel one with everyone, and I feel guided.

Therapist: What is your last thought or awareness as you leave the body?

Elizabeth: Readiness.

Therapist: Where are you now in relation to the body you leave behind? Can you still see it?

Elizabeth: I can. I feel so light, magnetically pulled.

Therapist: How do you feel about your death?

Elizabeth: I feel complete.

Therapist: What are you feeling right now?

Elizabeth: That an aspect of me is still there, and I'm letting it rise up, and comforting that part of me that doesn't feel like this is real, but it's okay because, in time, I will feel the death of me.

Therapist: Just let yourself expand higher and further, connecting to the soul-Self completely. What do you notice?

Elizabeth: Tingling. I feel tingling.

Therapist: When you look at your soul-Self, what do you feel like? Do you feel like a light, or a frequency, or just pure consciousness, or a combination of these?

Elizabeth: Floating. I feel floating.

Therapist: What about the energy in which you exist? How does that feel around you?

Elizabeth: Vast.

Therapist: Do you feel you are moving, or do you feel you've already arrived?

Elizabeth: I'm moving. I'm allowing it to show the feelings of fall.

Therapist: Just keep on moving. You know that the loving power is guiding you home.

Elizabeth: Ah. I'm so cold.

Therapist: The state of oneness and connectedness you felt when you were in the body as Jeb, are you entering that same state right now?

Elizabeth: Slowly.

Therapist: Slowly?

Elizabeth: Slowly.

Therapist: Just share everything, so I can stay with you.

Elizabeth: I see light surrounding me, but I'm not sure where I'm going. I feel pulled.

Therapist: Just allow yourself to be pulled. Is it the light that is pulling you?

Elizabeth: I feel pulled, but also heavy.

Therapist: If you like, you can drop the resistance, and just allow yourself to be pulled. It's just a decision that you're going to make yourself. Just drop it, and let it go. Allow yourself to be pulled. Know that a loving power is guiding you home.

Elizabeth: I hear a voice, saying to trust. Trust this, trust this. Allow it all. Feel.

Therapist: Perfect. Let go.

Elizabeth: You are where you are. It's perfect.

Therapist: Beautiful, so let it go. Trust it.

Elizabeth: Yeah.

Therapist: What happens when you let go?

Elizabeth: A light. I'm free, and I'm going so quickly, so quickly. And I feel this from my heart center.

Therapist: Beautiful. Just keep on going, and tell me what happens when you get there?

Elizabeth: They said I've always been there.

Therapist: What does that mean? Does that mean you belong to this realm?

Elizabeth: I feel very warm.

Therapist: When they said that you've always been here, who is talking to you? Is it a higher consciousness, or is it a guide? Or is it coming from deep within your Self?

Elizabeth: I'm learning to trust what's coming through.

Therapist: What do you notice?

Elizabeth: Well, they comfort my fear that I had been feeling, of not doing a good job.

Therapist: Are they saying you're doing a good job?

Elizabeth: Yeah.

Therapist: What is it that they like you to focus on in your life?

Elizabeth: They're allowing me to feel comfortable right now saying this out loud to even you. Because there are some expectations of myself that I need to let go to fully be in this experience. And so that is happening now for me.

Therapist: Good.

Elizabeth: And I can let go. Of any perceptions, expectations, or notions that I may have, and those are drifting away from me now so that I can feel fully connected to the oneness in me.

Therapist: Excellent. Just let it go. Take your time. Does that feel better?

Elizabeth: Yeah. Letting go of any feelings of wanting to perform in any way and really hone in, that I'm allowed to have my authentic experience at all times in this world, and I can let go of any expectations that I may perceive others have of me, and that I put on myself, and fully be the light that I am, and I always will be.

Therapist: Beautiful. That's so beautiful.

Elizabeth: And knowing that all these answers that I speak are always within me, and always have been. The continual search for something outside of myself is also part of it all, and natural. When I really feel into myself, I will have the inner knowing that I have it all inside of me and that this narrative of needing to seek it externally will then start to dissipate. I then feel the intuition and the oneness of all of them with me and know they've all been with me all the time. And even though at times I feel very disconnected, I'm just resistant to my true Self. But there's always that connection. I just didn't have an awareness of it at that time.

Therapist: Perfect.

Elizabeth: I'm just honing in and allowing for this deep connection and this deep awareness of my authenticity.

Therapist: Isn't that what it's about? To find that light within yourself. It's not external. It is who you are, and it's connected to all things. Like a drop is part of the ocean. Center everywhere, circumference nowhere. This is who you are. Part of everything, yet each point is conscious and aware. Speak your truth. Be that. How does it feel to wake up to that?

Elizabeth: That I felt this longing to be led. That is what I'm here to do, and I'm here to accept my gifts because I have the full feeling of them and possession of them.

Therapist: When you connect with them to guide you, how do they want you to unfold?

Elizabeth: I feel like stepping into the leader that I am and that

I've led many, many times, and always will be.

Therapist: How can Elizabeth shake off this fear that prevents her, and chokes her from speaking?

Elizabeth: There is a perfect way, and that is knowing that every way that's happening is perfect, and what it is exactly meant to be. To break free of the patterns that analyze, and judge, and explain, and need to create this narrative that she was trained to believe when she didn't fully trust herself. And instead of keep doing that, it's okay to release it. That doesn't have to be part of the identity anymore and can be fully released.

Therapist: Doesn't it apply to all ancestral patterns and identifications that she has carried along?

Elizabeth: Yes.

Therapist: How do you feel?

Elizabeth: Euphoric.

Therapist: Beautiful. Now, when we think about life in the Middle East, and the attainments there achieved, how can Elizabeth learn to integrate that achievement into her current incarnation?

Elizabeth: She was shown that to know that she's done this before. That she is here to lead, teach, and also learn. And that anything that feels good is what she should be doing more of, and she can trust that regardless of anything outside of herself saying otherwise.

Therapist: When you look at your soul-Self as separate from Jeb, and Elizabeth, going to that euphoric Self, who or what do you think you really are?

Elizabeth: Love.

Therapist: And how in the different incarnations do you like to express that love?

Elizabeth: By seeing love in everyone else and feeling it just as deeply for everyone as for myself. Feeling the oneness of all, and that we are all that. We're all from that, and we all go back to that.

Therapist: Is that the underlying current of your leadership and your teachings?

Elizabeth: Yes.

Therapist: Beautiful, really.

Elizabeth: It has been shown to Elizabeth when many times she reflects on her present life in different instances. It's learning to trust that initial feeling.

Therapist: Right, to go with it. Not to allow the intellect to take over. That's what Jeb was good at.

Elizabeth: Yes.

Therapist: He was able to step into that. How could Elizabeth learn to trust that?

Elizabeth: To practice being with Self. And even though she has this amazing drive to want to learn more, to sit with what she already knows because she has it already inside, and she's actually already learned it before. So, she can let go of this feeling that someone knows it better than her. We can just sit and allow that to come down without the conventional ways that we've been programmed to believe. Not through memorization or working hard. Accepting that in order to know, she just must be. And that is all there is to do. Letting go of this humanness to want to do and want to be.

Therapist: Beautiful. Otherwise, there is this incessant drive and restlessness to learn more, by always running away from the reality that deep down inside you are. Is there a way you can transfer this feeling into the body and mind of Elizabeth? Let it gently flow through her body and her mind.

Elizabeth: (silence) Ah...

Therapist: That's right. Now by doing this, what really happens is that we are burning a new neural track in the brain of

Elizabeth, and this neural track is an imprint of the power of this moment. And this neural track contains the memory of this change and will serve as a seed and a portal to go back into this state again.

It is now an actual imprint in the brain and body of Elizabeth. And once it exists there as an actual memory, it can be accessed again later. We establish a link between what is in her memory and her higher Self, an open channel. Now, let it calmly settle down and normalize the nervous system. Feel you are adjusting your nervous system, your body, and mind in such a way that you can carry this high current gracefully and gently.

How does it feel?

Elizabeth: It's circulating through the chakra. Really feel into the femininity of this incarnation and let go of any thought that is no longer feeling congruent with my light body.

Therapist: Remember that the divine creative power is also a feminine force and that you are part of that Source energy. Allow that flow within you gracefully, in harmony with the universe.

Is there any advice that your higher Self likes to share with Elizabeth?

Elizabeth: Trust the feeling first. And know that everything is happening for you, and it's also happening through you, that you are everything that is being created. You're always being guided and being led. We are here with you.

Therapist: Beautiful. Is there anything that Elizabeth needs from your higher Self?

Elizabeth: She has felt such a strong connection with Jeb and that community. But rather than compare her life with that, she should realize that she knows this already and that it will naturally flow to her as well. She doesn't have to feel separated from that state or that community. Though at times it may feel overwhelming, it's all happening at the perfect time for her, and exactly when it was meant to happen, and she's not behind in any way. It's also not happening too quickly. She needs to just allow, know, and trust the timing, which is really not real, because it's all happening at the same time. She's living as Jeb and Elizabeth at the same time, so she can feel both experiences, and can share that oneness now. There is no lack, only abundance. Lack is only something the mind has created, so all she has to do is feel this truth right now, into this presence of infinite possibilities, and know that it's all here.

Therapist: Beautiful, yes.

Elizabeth: Ah...

Therapist: It's a powerful realization, isn't it?

Elizabeth: Trust the natural rhythms of life. You don't have to fear and feel you must be in that state now. You can allow that space between. It has its reasonings too, and it has its lessons, and it has its importance. There's no need to judge. No feeling or emotion is greater or lesser than. They're all here to experience what we are, and what we are not. Holding that duality is beautiful, and is okay. You can laugh more and not take everything so seriously. We were showing you the way.

Therapist: Keep it light.

Elizabeth: Releasing this critical voice. It's been there for generations. You feel it strongly, this deep connection to your mammal. This critical voice was passed on to her, and you can let that go, and you're not doing anything wrong. You come from love, so you can feel that flowing through you. Releasing the critic because that is no longer needed, and it has its place, and it's had its time, and it's gone, and it's done. That voice is gone. Ah... You're here for this human experience of Elizabeth, to not have to be anyone else. And that is enough. And that is enough.

Therapist: Self with capital S.

Elizabeth: Self.

Therapist: Beautiful. How liberating is this?

Elizabeth: Very liberating. Ah...

Therapist: How would you summarize this?

Elizabeth: There is nothing that I need to release. There is nothing to be healed because I am. I am love and light. Even let go of the feeling of needing to heal because there is nothing that needs to be healed because it is all perfect and as is supposed to be. This is also an illusion of the mind.

Therapist: It's where you identify, right? When you identify with Self, everything else can be let go of. Now tell me, how do you feel?

Elizabeth: Ah... I feel that any of this longing that I have for anything external is really just a longing to connect to the internal, to the Source.

Therapist: To the Self.

Elizabeth: Connecting to the bliss in me, living in this bliss, being an embodiment of this bliss, and letting go of all expectations. Because there's nothing that I have to do, or am here to do, besides just feel this bliss. And through that, I will overflow and be the embodiment of that for everyone. So I don't have to do, or try to do anything. I just get to be, and I can feel into that. Allow that, feel that. Allow the space for in between that as well. There's no need to judge that either.

Therapist: Yes, that is freedom. Accepting the ebb and flows of the body, the mind, and the environment, not controlling, not holding on, free into the awareness of being.

Elizabeth: I feel an intense vibration of every cell vibrating in me in perfect resonance. Ah...

Therapist: Would you like a few moments?

Elizabeth: Yes, please.

Therapist: Yeah, take your time, and when you're ready, let me know, and we'll take it from there.

Elizabeth: Okay, thank you.

We slowly bring the session to an end.

Case 20: Minnie
The desert healer

Minnie is a 50-year-old scientist, seeking a greater inner unfoldment, and breaking limited paradigms that have been holding her back.

Therapist: Tell me, is it daytime or nighttime?

Minnie: It's daytime.

Therapist: Are you inside or outside?

Minnie: Outside.

Therapist: As you become aware of your environment, when you look straight ahead of yourself, what is the first thing you notice?

Minnie: It's white.

Therapist: It's bright?

Minnie: Very.

Therapist: What if anything do you wear on your feet?

Minnie: I'm barefoot.

Therapist: What else are you wearing?

Minnie: It's really soft, like a really exquisite cotton. It's like a tunic. Long sleeves, loose.

Therapist: Is it a one-piece or made out of multiple pieces?

Minnie: One piece.

Therapist: Do you wear anything on your head?

Minnie: No.

Therapist: What is the color of your skin?

Minnie: Brown.

Therapist: Are you a man or a woman?

Minnie: I'm not sure.

Therapist: That's okay. What's your age approximately, as you're standing here in this exquisite outfit?

Minnie: 17.

Therapist: When you look at your own outfit, does it feel like it's luxurious, wealthy, kind of upper class, or is it just ordinary?

Minnie: Very ordinary.

Therapist: Now, you said it's very bright where you are, look around and give me a general description of the environment.

Minnie: I'm on a dirt path. Smooth dirt, but there are big rocks around. But worn rocks, not jagged rocks.

Therapist: Are they on the path or on the side of the path?

Minnie: On the side of the path and in the hills.

Therapist: Is it hilly where you are?

Minnie: Yes.

Therapist: Are you alone in this place or are there others on this path?

Minnie: I'm alone.

Therapist: As you're walking this path, are you high up or are you still down?

Minnie: I think I'm down.

Therapist: What are you doing on this path and where are you going?

Minnie: It's like I'm on a pilgrimage. It feels really wonderful.

Therapist: Where are you going on a pilgrimage? Which country are we in?

Minnie: I feel like it's the Middle East.

Therapist: Do you feel you've been here before, or is this a new adventure for you?

Minnie: It's new.

Therapist: I guess you must be excited about going on this pilgrimage. How are you feeling?

Minnie: It's hard to put words around.

Therapist: Yeah. I can imagine.

Minnie: Like I'm part of everything around me.

Therapist: It seems you're already in a high state of mind. Beautiful. Now, what year comes to mind as you're traveling along this path?

Minnie: 1400.

Therapist: Being on this path and on the way, in the hills and looking ahead, are you pretty remote, or is there a town nearby?

Minnie: I see it off into the distance, it's stone or mud structures. But well-formed.

Therapist: Well-formed, ok. Is that your destination or is this one of the stops along the way?

Minnie: I think it's my destination.

Therapist: Has it been a long journey?

Minnie: Yes.

Therapist: What made you go on this pilgrimage at 17 years old and on your own?

Minnie: Freedom.

Therapist: Tell me what freedom means to you.

Minnie: That there is something bigger for me to learn to be a part of.

Therapist: It's amazing that at your young age, you're able to understand these things and can travel and explore your freedom. What kind of family do you come from that allows this? Or did you break away on your own?

Minnie: I think I left, but it wasn't negative.

Therapist: Beautiful. At this point in your life, age 17, what is your most significant observation either within you or around you?

Minnie: I feel I'm a boy. I don't feel at all afraid.

Therapist: Beautiful.

Minnie: I feel very trusting.

I move her forward in time as this young man.

Therapist: Tell me, what is happening now?

Minnie: I'm inside a structure.

Therapist: What does the place look like? Can you describe it to me?

Minnie: It's reddish clay walls. It would be dark, but there are openings to the outside.

Therapist: What is the nature of this structure?

Minnie: Sacred.

Therapist: Are there others here?

Minnie: No, not right now.

Therapist: It's just you. How old are you now?

Minnie: 31.

Therapist: What is your relation to this place?

Minnie: I help people.

Therapist: Tell me more. Do you help them from within this place?

Minnie: Yes.

Therapist: Are you the caretaker of the sacred space? Is this your sacred home?

Minnie: Yes.

Therapist: Tell me more about how you help people in this place, what your role is, and what kind of work you do.

Minnie: It's really beautiful.

Therapist: I see.

Minnie: It's really simple.

Therapist: When you say it's beautiful, is it the power and the beauty of this place?

Minnie: It's the spirit that's there. People feel safe when they come.

Therapist: Are you like a priest of some kind, or a healer or caregiver? What is your role in this place?

Minnie: I think a healer.

Therapist: In what way do you help them? In what way do you heal?

Minnie: It's spiritual, but that translates into physical sometimes for some people.

Therapist: Do you do certain rituals, or is it more on a mental or spiritual level? In more practical terms, how do you help them?

Minnie: I see, it's an altar where there's a wooden ball, and it has different dried plant material in it. It's part botanical and part spiritual and mental.

Therapist: How do you know what they need? Is that something you always had as a child, or did you develop or discover these gifts?

Minnie: That's why I left.

Therapist: Tell me a little bit about that.

Minnie: I knew things that nobody had taught me.

Therapist: So you had the insight and intuition from childhood?

Minnie: And that was why I left, to try and learn.

Therapist: Continue.

Minnie: Access beyond me so that I can have access to that. Access more of that information and knowledge.

Therapist: Between the ages of 32 and 17, how did you develop and how did you learn more of these skills and develop your intuition? Was there a teacher?

Minnie: There was a teacher, an older man.

Therapist: Was he part of this temple?

Minnie: Yes.

Therapist: Is he still there?

Minnie: He's not there anymore.

Therapist: How was your relationship with him during these years?

Minnie: It was like so much time compressed because I learned so much. He knew so much, and I was ready to learn. So, I learned quickly and deeply from the time I spent with him.

Therapist: Beautiful. Do you have a name? What do the people call you?

Minnie: The word Sensei popped into my mind.

I move her forward in time again.

Therapist: Tell me what is happening now.

Minnie: I'm on a path. Yeah, I'm 70. I'm up in a mountainous area, but it's still a smooth path I'm walking on, but it's rocks, and boulders around me.

Therapist: Are you alone or is there anybody with you?

Minnie: I'm alone.

Therapist: What are you doing on this path? Where are you going?

Minnie: I'm headed to another place, it's very remote. I'm headed there to be alone.

Therapist: Is it a permanent move or is it just a temporary retreat of some kind?

Minnie: It'll be permanent.

Therapist: Where are you coming from? Is it from the temple?

Minnie: I feel like I've been somewhere else in between.

Therapist: Is it a secluded retirement where you're headed? Is that why you're leaving and going to this remote place?

Minnie: It's for me to take care of myself.

Therapist: Help me understand what you mean by that.

Minnie: I feel very good, but I feel very tired.

Therapist: Move a little bit forward and tell me what this place is about, where you're going, what it looks like, and how you're living your life there.

Minnie: It's greener than where I was. There's kind of a scrubby, low forest. No big trees, but there are smaller scrubby pines, and there's a little bit of grass. And it's like a sheltered area where I am.

Therapist: Is there some sort of dwelling while you're staying?

Minnie: There is, it's really primitive.

Therapist: What does it look like, this dwelling?

Minnie: It's some old, dried wood, like a lean-to. The front of it is open, but there's not a proper doorway. But it's very comfortable.

Therapist: How do you spend your days? You say you are here to take care of and look after yourself spiritually, and mentally. What does that imply? Do you have a natural connection to the divine?

Minnie: It feels like a very natural connection to the divine, but also through the landscape and the animals that are there.

Therapist: How would you describe your mental and spiritual state at this point?

Minnie: Rich. Completely at peace.

Therapist: Beautiful. Now, if you look back over these last 30, 40 years as a healer, how has that life been for you?

Minnie: It's been incredible. It hasn't been lonely, but I've been by myself. But it hasn't been lonely at all.

Therapist: Have people come to you for healing?

Minnie: Yes, yes.

Therapist: But you lived on your own in the sacred places.

Minnie: Yes, but I had a lot of interaction with other people.

Therapist: How did it feel to be this healer? What did it do to you? How was it experienced from your side?

Minnie: So humbling. It's almost like a channel, a conduit.

Therapist: When you say a conduit, was that something happening automatically through you?

Minnie: I think it evolved over time. I think I was open to it. But I think that over time it just became natural for it to flow like that. It wasn't normally an effort to have to consciously choose that.

Therapist: As the transmission happened, were you aware of that power and energy? And the impact it made on others? Or was it just so automatic that you weren't even aware of it?

Minnie: I felt like it's just what it was. I don't think I really thought of it at the moment.

Therapist: It just happened.

Minnie: I could understand the gift that it was to people, but I didn't feel like it was from me, it was just coming through me.

I move her to the last day of her life as the healer.

Therapist: How old are you on this last day of your life?

Minnie: 92.

Therapist: Is there anything going on around you or within you that suggests that your physical death will come this day?

Minnie: No.

Therapist: Where are you? Is the setting familiar?

Minnie: I'm in the same place I was.

Therapist: Looking back over this life, what do you think about this life you just lived as Sensei?

Minnie: I loved it.

Therapist: What was most precious to you when you said, "I loved it"?

Minnie: That I understood that I was connected to everything, that I was part of everything and everything was part of me.

Therapist: What was the most important thing you learned in this life?

Minnie: It's hard to put into words.

Therapist: If you tried, what comes to mind?

Minnie: To not get trapped in my mind.

Therapist: In this life, you were pretty successful in transcending the mind and connecting to all things that are, is that correct?

Minnie: Very. Very.

Therapist: Now, what is your last thought or awareness as you leave the body?

Minnie: Gratitude.

Therapist: What was the cause of your death?

Minnie: Heart.

Therapist: Was it just an instantaneous leaving of the body?

Minnie: Yes.

Therapist: How do you feel about your death?

Minnie: It was perfect.

I move her along.

Therapist: What is the first thing you notice?

Minnie: It's really bright. Like a huge alpine meadow.

Therapist: How does it feel to be here?

Minnie: Light.

Therapist: What is the energy of this place?

Minnie: Unlike anything I've experienced. I feel completely at home at the same time.

Therapist: When you look at your own soul-Self, do you have a shape, or is it more like a light form or an energy form, or frequency, or a combination of these?

Minnie: More light.

Therapist: Does it have colors?

Minnie: It's sparkly, like sunlight on water.

Therapist: Beautiful. As you're here in this meadow, I can only assume there may be wise ones nearby, or a soul group or other beings. Is this a place where you initially come to rest, or is this a place where you're going to meet others?

Minnie: It's more a collective, a blur between wholeness and the potential for there to be individuals.

Therapist: Right, right. Like waves in an ocean, so to speak.

Minnie: Yeah.

Therapist: I assume that is how you feel about yourself right now; on the threshold between?

Minnie: Yes. Yes.

Therapist: If you would want to reach out to others, to another presence, how would you go about doing it? Do you have your own guide or guides?

Minnie: I don't feel like it's individual like that. I feel like it's there for me to access.

Therapist: Like knowledge flowing through you.

Minnie: Yes, yes.

Therapist: I get it. Beautiful. In other words, you're self-luminous and you're able to access and expand consciousness, kind of in the same way healing power flows through you and enlightens your understanding. Is that a good way of putting it?

Minnie: Yes.

Therapist: Beautiful. Now, being here in this place, what is the first thing that comes to your awareness about your journey, about yourself, and why you're here?

Minnie: To recognize the vastness of what's there.

Therapist: What is your relation to this vastness?

Minnie: It's like I'm part of that. I think it's infinite, but there's also this part that's separate.

Therapist: Wonderful.

Minnie: But not disconnected.

Therapist: Center everywhere, circumference nowhere. As if each point in the vastness is its own consciousness, yet it is all part of the same infinite ocean. Is that a good way of putting it?

Minnie: Very.

Therapist: When you look back on your journey as Sensei, now objectively looking at that life, what was that life about?

Minnie: I felt like it was about going beyond myself and trusting. Trusting what I knew was inside and opening up to that.

Therapist: In other words, stepping beyond the boundaries of ego and mind and allowing the infinite universe to flow through? To what degree did you succeed in that life?

Minnie: In that life, I think I did so well with that.

Therapist: To what degree is Minnie able to manifest and transcend that ego?

Minnie: She's growing, but it's very hard sometimes. She gets locked in. She gets locked in her body and in her mind.

Therapist: How is her experience different from Sensei's? What is the cause of her not being able to manifest it as freely as Sensei did? Why that block?

Minnie: I think a lot of it has been her getting trapped in the environment that she's in, and getting lost in what she's always felt like she was supposed to be doing, rather than doing what is natural for her to do.

Therapist: Do you think it is due to the lack of higher consciousness of the culture in which she was born, or is it due to her karma that caused her to be born with these particular parents?

Minnie: I think it's both.

Therapist: Which one do you feel was the predominant force?

Minnie: Culture.

Therapist: Now, what caused her to be born with these parents? When we look at your soul journey and already having achieved such exceptional states of consciousness, what was the main purpose for taking up this life under these circumstances?

Minnie: I think it was for me to understand the imprisonment that we put on ourselves so that I could help other people release themselves from that.

Therapist: What you're saying is very significant because, if I understand this correctly, and correct me if I'm wrong, it wasn't a karmic cause, but it was about learning to develop deeper levels of sympathy and understanding on the human plane. Looking at yourself from this life between life state, to what degree is your soul free?

Minnie: And I'm part of it.

Therapist: You say, "I'm part of it", why are you born? If not governed by karma, what is behind your incarnations?

Minnie: I feel like this birth was primarily to be able to open up as a healer for others.

Therapist: What is it that your soul aspires to become, to expand into? Let me give you an example. Some people don't want any more births, whereas others don't mind being instrumental, even after awakening. They don't mind being there to teach, to share, to love. Whereas others say, "Enough of this, I want to be eternally free."

Minnie: I feel as a soul I'm ready to stop coming back as a human, but to still be experiencing being a part and still helping the whole.

Therapist: So more helping.

Minnie: But from a different place.

Therapist: Would you heal souls who are like you in this in-between state, even if they may have to come back to Earth, or would you help them from here directly on Earth?

Minnie: I think both.

Therapist: Looking at Minnie's life and the way she's unfolding at age 50, is there anything else that she could do or an attitude she can change to help her express herself better?

Minnie: She needs to release the rigid framework that she tries to put on things, and trust what she feels.

Therapist: Like Sensei did.

Minnie: Yes.

Therapist: If you could help her, from your elevated state of awareness, looking at her objectively, how can you help her now to release some of these boundaries and self-imposed walls?

Minnie: Putting energy towards time alone where she can connect. Because she's able to connect. But for her to move beyond where she is, she needs to be more devoted to that.

Therapist: Are you saying it's due to a lack of application that she is alienating herself?

Minnie: Yes.

Therapist: Innately, her problem is not the connection. It's that there is rust on the kettle, and it needs to be polished off.

Minnie: I think that's a good way to say it.

Therapist: In what way would you advise Minnie to protect herself, and put up appropriate boundaries? What is the best way for her to walk that middle path to be on the one hand very open, and on the other hand be protected?

Minnie: She has the knowledge of how to do that. It's a matter of being still and listening to that and trusting and moving forward. But she has an innate ability to protect herself.

Therapist: She mentioned that sometimes even anger could protect her, but that she doubts this is a very healthy attitude. What can you say about that?

Minnie: I think a lot of her anger comes from frustration, from being trapped in her mind and body. When she opens up, a lot of that is going to disappear.

Therapist: Would you agree that if she meditates on Sensei and this amazing life that she already lived, and realizes how beautiful she is when she looks at herself in the spirit world, it is easy for her to just let it all come to her? Because this is who she is.

Minnie: Yes.

Therapist: She has already accomplished all of this, right?

Minnie: Yes.

Therapist: It seems to be that the environment plays a role. Is moving to another place conducive to this unfoldment?

Minnie: Yes, it is. Sometimes it's hard for her to accept it because she doesn't feel like she deserves it.

Therapist: Would you agree that deserving is not an appropriate word?

Minnie: It's a terrible word.

Therapist: How would you help her reframe that? Just teach her right now, from a higher perspective. I want you to go deeper and deeper into that soul-Self for a moment. Step out of Minnie, step out of Sensei. Go deeper and deeper into Self. Feel the beauty of your nature as you are both an individual sparkling soul and part of this infinite ocean, like a wave that is never disconnected.

Feel your power, your oneness, and your unity with this. And from here, look back over this journey of Sensei, and perhaps many other lifetimes of healing and teaching. And then transfer it back into Minnie, that she now flows in accordance with your true soul purpose. No holding back, no apology, just you and infinity. Full integration. Just let the ocean flow through Minnie right now. Take your time to be that. How does that feel?

Minnie: I feel like I'm floating.

Therapist: Just keep floating. Nothing is required, just be that. And without losing that connection, there is one more important thing I would like you to have an objective look at. And that is this notion that as Sensei you lived very much alone, yet you were in service of others. Knowing that there is a need to connect to the divine in order to sustain service as well as transcend it to find rest. And that Minnie has a similar balance to find. Where is that balance to take time for herself to develop, to break boundaries and be that channel, versus grounding herself in the world and having enough to eat and to live?

Minnie: It's time for her to move on from what she's been doing. And it's like Sensei leaving home. Not from a negative place, but going towards something bigger and more important. And that's where she is right now. It's just that she's 50, not 17.

Therapist: It's a trust in your innate capabilities to follow your calling, and everything falls in place once that is being listened to, right? Is that a good way of putting it?

Minnie: Yes. Yes.

Therapist: Beautiful.

Minnie: She doesn't have to be able to see everything. She's always felt like she needed to see everything, but she doesn't.

Therapist: It's more like listening and being in tune with who we really are. Like Sensei did, he trusted it.

Minnie: Yes.

Therapist: Sensei wasn't looking for security. He was living in accordance with his higher nature. True to himself. Because undoubtedly these powers were manifested in him, as they are now in Minnie.

Minnie: Yes.

Therapist: How would you summarize what you have seen?

Minnie: She's doing really well. She feels like she's been slow, but she's been so determined and relentless, and following what she knew was true. But it's time now to open up to that in a very different and fuller way to continue on her path the way that she's meant to and the way that she wants to. And she'll be able to.

Therapist: Is there anything that Minnie needs from your higher Self?

Minnie: Yes, coming back to this regularly and with the intent to remember. To not stay entrapped.

Therapist: Do you think that is the most essential thing that Minnie needs to do and to seek help from the higher Self to keep that connection going?

Minnie: Yes. In this life, she's always pushed that aside.

Therapist: Right.

Minnie: I think she's been afraid.

Therapist: Due to consequences it would have on her external world and the way she lives?

Minnie: And the mental part: "But who am I to be able to live a life like that?" If she does live like that, she'll be free.

Therapist: Realizing that these are just the ramblings of mind and ego versus trusting the universe and your true divine identity. Sensei may help her provide that courage and understanding. How do you feel?

Minnie: I feel incredibly grateful and satisfied. It feels complete.

We slowly bring the session to a close.

Case 21: Devi
Beyond loneliness

Devi is a 30-year-old woman, therapist, and entrepreneur, who recently lost the love of her life. Apart from dealing with grief, she is trying to find a deeper spiritual connection and understanding of herself and her life's purpose.

Therapist: Now tell me, is it daytime or nighttime?

Devi: Daytime.

Therapist: Are you inside or outside?

Devi: Outside.

Therapist: Are you alone or with someone?

Devi: I'm standing alone.

Therapist: Look down at your feet. Tell me what, if anything, you see on your feet.

Devi: Sandals.

Therapist: What else are you wearing?

Devi: It's a flowery dress.

Therapist: What kind?

Devi: It's one piece with a belt.

Therapist: What is the color of your skin?

Devi: It's tan.

Therapist: What is your age approximately?

Devi: 22.

Therapist: What is the color of your hair?

Devi: A light brown.

Therapist: Can you give me a description of the general surroundings where you find yourself right now?

Devi: It's like a street. Like I'm at a market or something.

Therapist: Can you describe the market? What kind of market is it?

Devi: There are people. It's lively.

Therapist: What do the people look like? What do they dress like?

Devi: It's just people selling all kinds of things.

Therapist: Is it a city or is it a town?

Devi: It seems like a small city.

Therapist: What's the weather like?

Devi: It's nice. It's mild.

Therapist: Where in the world are we? What region are we in?

Devi: Somewhere in Europe.

Therapist: What date comes to mind?

Devi: It's early nineteen hundred.

Therapist: How are you feeling as you're standing here in this marketplace?

Devi: It's cheery.

Therapist: Are you shopping as well or are you just standing here looking?

Devi: I'm looking, but I have a basket with me.

Therapist: Tell me more. What is going on within you or around you at this moment?

Devi: There are different smells from foods being prepared. I like going to the market. I walk down. I like seeing people.

Therapist: Do you live nearby?

Devi: Yeah, it's not too far. It's easy to get there.

Therapist: What does the place where you live look like?

Devi: It's a small house.

Therapist: Is there anybody living with you?

Devi: Doesn't seem like it.

Therapist: You live on your own?

Devi: Yeah.

Therapist: How do you feel living on your own?

Devi: Independent.

Therapist: How do you survive? How do you manage to take care of yourself?

Devi: Something about writing and publishing.

Therapist: Do you take care of yourself financially?

Devi: Yeah, I think so.

Therapist: You said independent, so you appreciate that independence that you have?

Devi: Yeah.

Therapist: If you would describe to me the most significant observation, either within you or around you about this moment in your life, what would it be?

Devi: I like my independence and I feel like I can just do what I want.

Therapist: Beautiful. What is your name?

Devi: It's Miriam.

Therapist: I'm going to call you Miriam. Miriam, I'm going to count from 3 down to 1. On the count of 1, we're going to move forward in your life as Miriam to a moment a few years later and a relevant time in your life, going from 3, 2, 1. And you're there. Tell me what is happening now.

Devi: I'm out in nature looking over a beautiful view. I'm writing, just thinking and writing.

Therapist: How do you feel when you're writing?

Devi: Trying to get inspiration.

Therapist: What kind of things do you write about?

Devi: I want to inspire people.

Therapist: In what way? Is it about nature or love or poetry or philosophy? In what way does your heart want to express itself?

Devi: I want to inspire people to find freedom, so I like to go up in nature and look at the broad, open views and just feel it so I can write about it.

Therapist: What does it mean to you personally, freedom?

Devi: Not feeling bound to anything.

Therapist: Beautiful. Do you feel that state of freedom at this moment?

Devi: Yes, but there's still pressure because I have to write about it to support myself.

Therapist: How old are you now, Miriam?

Devi: 30.

Therapist: Are you still living on your own?

Devi: Yes.

Therapist: When you look at the landscape, can you describe this landscape to me?

Devi: I'm sitting on top of a mountain. There are open fields where I'm looking. It's just very open. The air smells really fresh, clean.

Therapist: What's your most significant observation about this moment?

Devi: I'm doing something that I love to do. I feel it in myself. And I also feel pressure to write in a way that people can relate to. It's hard to translate.

Therapist: How would you describe your state of mind at this moment, at 30?

Devi: I'm happy. I'm struggling a little bit with the writing.

I move her a few years forward in her life as Miriam.

Therapist: Tell me what is happening now?

Devi: I'm standing in front of a big house. It's an old house. It's really big. There's something important that I'm there for.

Therapist: Are you going inside?

Devi: I'm hesitating, but I have to go in.

Therapist: Tell me what happens when you go in. And what is going on here in this big house?

Devi: It smells old, dusty, like paper, like old books. Like an old library.

Therapist: What's this place about?

Devi: It seems empty, abandoned.

Therapist: Why are you here? Do you have any plans or meetings in this house? In what way is this house relevant to you?

Devi: I published things here. It's where my writing got published.

Therapist: And it's abandoned now.

Devi: It doesn't seem like much is happening there anymore.

Therapist: Are you just visiting? Why are you here?

Devi: I feel I need closure.

Therapist: Why?

Devi: I'm done writing.

Therapist: How old are you now, Miriam?

Devi: Early 40s.

Therapist: Why are you done writing?

Devi: I couldn't reach people in the way that I wanted to, and it just wasn't working anymore.

Therapist: How do you feel about that?

Devi: I felt sad at first, but I found peace with it.

Therapist: You've come here to find closure in this place where it all began.

Devi: Yes. It was an important thing for me to do.

Therapist: Did you initially have some success with your work?

Devi: Yes. People liked my writing.

Therapist: But you were not satisfied.

Devi: I was at first.

Therapist: What do you do now in your early 40s after you're stopping writing?

Devi: I'm not sure.

Therapist: Are you able to financially survive?

Devi: I don't think I have that house anymore.

Therapist: Where do you live now?

Devi: I think I just want to explore. I don't want to be rooted down anywhere. Just want to explore.

Therapist: Is it the same urge for freedom?

Devi: Yes. Maybe there's more.

Therapist: Explore means that you want to travel and not stay in one place?

Devi: Yes.

Therapist: What do you have in mind?

Devi: I'm independent. I've always been. And I can do this, I can explore.

I move her forward in time again.

Therapist: Tell me what is happening now?

Devi: I'm alone in a dark place. I'm comfortable, but it's not much; just a place for me to sleep.

Therapist: Are you permanently staying here? What is this place about?

Devi: I think I'm just taking it day by day.

Therapist: How old are you now? Miriam?

Devi: Late 40s. 48.

Therapist: Have you been traveling these last few years? What have you been doing?

Devi: Yes, exploring, traveling. And I'm a little bit tired of traveling.

Therapist: How were these last few years traveling?

Devi: I got to see so much. I traveled by train, and I got to meet a lot of people and get new perspectives.

Therapist: What's your state of mind now at 48, after all of these travels and experiences? How do you feel inside?

Devi: I feel content.

Therapist: When you say you're now in this dark place, what

can you tell me about it?

Devi: I need to find another place to settle because I've been on the move for so long and I just need somewhere to be.

Therapist: I want you to move forward in time a little bit, Miriam, to that moment, if and when you find that place, and tell me about that.

Devi: It's in the countryside.

Therapist: Do you have a little house or a little place? Where do you stay?

Devi: It's a small, little cottage. It seems like there are farms around. And these nice people are hosting me there. I'm helping them on the farm.

Therapist: How does that make you feel, being a farmer now?

Devi: I like the openness and I like being in nature. I like helping.

Therapist: Are you happy?

Devi: Yes. And I'm writing some again, but not to publish.

Therapist: Just for yourself?

Devi: Yes.

Therapist: Are you still single, Miriam?

Devi: Yes.

Therapist: Do you like being single?

Devi: Yes.

Therapist: What made you decide to be and stay single?

Devi: I wanted my independence and my freedom. And I didn't want to have to give an account of my life to somebody else.

Therapist: In retrospect, do you feel happy about the decision?

Devi: Yes. I enjoyed my life, but it did feel lonely at times.

I move her forward in time again.

Therapist: Tell me what is happening now?

Devi: I feel weak.

Therapist: How old are you now?

Devi: My 60s.

Therapist: Are you still on the farm or are you somewhere else?

Devi: I'm inside a house and someone is caring for me.

Therapist: How do you feel?

Devi: I feel weak like I'm sick with something.

Therapist: Is it terminal or serious?

Devi: It's my lungs. I have difficulty breathing.

Therapist: I want you to move to the last day of your life as Miriam, and tell me how old you are now, Miriam.

Devi: 64.

Therapist: Is there anything going on around you or within you that suggests your physical death will come this day?

Devi: No.

Therapist: How's your health?

Devi: I'm ill, and there's nothing they can really do to help.

Therapist: Are you in bed?

Devi: Yes.

Therapist: How are you feeling?

Devi: I'm okay with it.

Therapist: What do you think about this life you just lived as Miriam?

Devi: I liked my freedom, but it would've been nice to have company at times.

Therapist: What did you learn from this life?

Devi: I learned that it's okay to have people around. It's important. That it's possible to have freedom, but it's okay to have people care for me.

Therapist: Freedom and people are not necessarily mutually

exclusive.

Devi: Right, they're not.

Therapist: Was that different from you when you were younger when you were more adamant to be alone?

Devi: Yes.

Therapist: You've slightly changed your mind.

Devi: Yes, I have.

Therapist: What is your last thought or awareness as you leave the body?

Devi: I'm resting. I'm at peace.

Therapist: Where are you now in relation to the body you leave behind? Can you still see it?

Devi: Yes. I'm looking at it there. People that were caring for me, they're there at my bedside.

Therapist: How do you feel about your death?

Devi: I feel okay. There's sadness, but mostly for the people that are there next to me.

I move her to the in-between-lives dimension.

Therapist: What is the first thing you notice?

Devi: I feel light, unburdened, expansive.

Therapist: When you look at your own soul-Self, does it have any form or is it light, awareness, consciousness, or a combination of these?

Devi: I don't see any form.

Therapist: It's just an awareness?

Devi: Yes.

Therapist: How do you feel about the energy where you are right now?

Devi: There's like a stillness. It's very calm, it's very peaceful.

Therapist: Just take a moment and enjoy the peace and calm. Do you have a feeling there are other beings nearby or around? Or do you feel you're alone in this expansive reality?

Devi: At the moment, I am alone. I sense that I'm surrounded, though.

Therapist: Just take your time. And when some of those beings present themselves, let me know. No hurries. Does it feel like this is welcome?

Devi: I just feel a lot of peace.

Therapist: Beautiful.

Devi: Like I can just breathe.

Therapist: Just enjoy it. Now, without interrupting this peace, as you're getting more adjusted, perhaps soon one or more of those around you may feel like stepping forward. Is there anybody, any such being that you feel drawn to?

Devi: There are waves and colors. Blue.

Therapist: What or who are those waves and colors?

Devi: Vibration. There's a flow. I'm not sure how to describe them. They're colors, but they're also sound.

Therapist: Is this part of that infinite expanse or are these other beings?

Devi: They're beings.

Therapist: Beautiful.

Devi: But they don't have a definite form, they're just vibrating light.

Therapist: Beautiful. Do you feel there are differences in nature between some of these beings, some of them higher or some of them more communicative? Or are they all expressing themselves in the same way?

Devi: Rafael comes to mind.

Therapist: Tell me about Rafael.

Devi: He's there. He's coming closest.

Therapist: Is he welcoming you first?

Devi: Yes.

Therapist: What is Rafael's energy like?

Devi: Guiding, like he's been there the whole time.

Therapist: I understand that communication at this level of expansive reality could be telepathic and intuitive, so what are you picking up from Rafael?

Devi: It's like he's reaching out to me, guiding me upward.

Therapist: Follow him as he's guiding you upward and tell me what happens.

Devi: It gets brighter. Where I was, it was darker with some lights ebbing in and out, and now it's getting lighter, brighter.

Therapist: What is the nature of this brighter frequency?

Devi: It's bright.

Therapist: How does it feel?

Devi: It's like I'm merging more with it. Things are falling behind as I go upward. It feels really nice.

Therapist: Tell me what happens when you reach.

Devi: There are other beings in a semicircle.

Therapist: Is it like a Council of some kind?

Devi: Yeah, it feels like that.

Therapist: How does it feel to be in their presence?

Devi: Good. They care about me.

Therapist: Who's the first one to start the communication?

Devi: It's one on the left. There are many of them.

Therapist: Do they each have a different type of energy, a different type of purpose?

Devi: It's bright, like light. They're all just light.

Therapist: What do they have to share with you regarding the life of Miriam?

Devi: I had the experience that I wanted to have, and that was good.

Therapist: What was planned before the life of Miriam? What is it that she wanted to experience in that life?

Devi: She wanted a life alone. She wanted the opportunity to just observe the world and just be free.

Therapist: What do they have to share with you about that? Did you do a good job?

Devi: Yes. And it's like they're asking me.

Therapist: What do you say?

Devi: To reflect upon it myself.

Therapist: What is your conclusion?

Devi: I tell them that I would like company next time.

Therapist: What is their answer?

Devi: I realized that freedom does not mean being alone, and that was good.

Therapist: Do they offer positive constructive criticism about Miriam, something that she hadn't thought about, that she could have done differently?

Devi: Friends, more friends. But she didn't really want to be attached to anyone.

Therapist: What plans were made for Devi's life beforehand?

Devi: In this life, in Devi's experience, she makes connections, but also experienced loss as a result of connections.

Therapist: It's an interesting observation that in the last life your soul wanted to experience being alone, and in this life, you're seeking the opposite, the connection, which implies also losing these connections. What does the Council have to add to that?

Devi: They want me to recognize that there's a balance. And

Devi wanted to experience connection and attachments, but with attachment comes the experience of loss. And that's inevitable.

Therapist: And what is the balance that they want you to understand?

Devi: They want me to experience both and then understand how to transcend both.

Therapist: In Miriam's life you were completely detached. In Devi's life, we're attached and experiencing loss. And they want something higher beyond this detachment and this attachment.

Devi: Well, Miriam didn't experience loss because she never allowed herself to form any attachments.

Therapist: She didn't love either.

Devi: No. She just wanted to be independent and free and tell people they can be free too. But she never experienced the depth of connections or the depths of loss.

Therapist: What the Council was hinting at earlier is that they want your soul to take it one step further and transcend both of these extremes.

Devi: Yes.

Therapist: What does that look like for your soul, that next state of transcendence?

Devi: Well, it's seeing that when attachment and loss are transcended, they only exist relative to one another. It's only a perception. It's only because we create attachments that we experience loss. The one doesn't go without the other.

Therapist: Am I correct to understand that what they want for you is a higher, more expanded state of consciousness? One where you can find peace within. And inner peace allows the capability to detach as well as attach. Yet it is transcendent in its expansive sense of awareness, love, and inclusiveness. Is that a good way of putting it?

Devi: Yes. It floats above those seeming opposites.

Therapist: That is so beautiful. Was loving and losing your loved one an important lesson in this regard? Why did this happen?

Devi: Yes, that was important. There was tremendous love, so tremendous loss. Devi needs to find a way to be in a space of all-encompassing pure love. In that space, there's a sense of infinite connection.

Therapist: Beautiful. Taking it from the personal into the infinite. It doesn't exclude the personal, but it includes the impersonal and all other things as well so there's no sense of loss in this all-encompassing divine connection. Is that a good way of putting it?

Devi: Yes.

Therapist: How does it make you feel when you're being presented with such beautiful high thoughts and insight?

Devi: The soul that was my partner is in that space too.

Therapist: Can you feel him now?

Devi: Yes.

Therapist: Can we invite him to this Council meeting as well?

Devi: Yes.

Therapist: What does the Council have to say to both of you?

Devi: The Council wanted us to learn the infinite nature of our being through the layers of our incarnations.

Therapist: Beautiful.

Devi: That we exist, we just exist, and we continue to exist.

Therapist: Beautiful. It's really a transcending of limitations. Transcending the lower life forms and laying bare the infinite nature of our soul. This is where we all connect, where we're all one, which permanently exists. Is that a good description?

Devi: Yes.

Therapist: But to achieve that you first need to understand

what real love is like you have experienced with him. Then only one is qualified to transcend it. Miriam wouldn't qualify yet because she didn't have the capacity to love as Devi did.

Devi: Correct.

Therapist: Miriam learned what pure detachment feels like and that it also is not the answer. And so the next level is universal awareness and connection.

Devi: Yes. Devi still needs to learn to be in that state.

Therapist: Now that we are here with the Council and we look ahead at Devi's life, what will be the best way for her to continue her life in alignment with her divine purpose?

Devi: She needs to focus. She tends to lose focus. She gets distracted.

Therapist: What would be a good way to help her focus?

Devi: She knows this. She needs discipline, daily practice, and focus more on connection with the Soul-being she really is.

Therapist: Does it matter what kind of work she does? What does the Council advise?

Devi: We want her to share her experiences with others. She needs to talk to other people about it. They need to hear her journey through what she's going through.

Therapist: What's the best way for her to do that? Is it some sort of leadership role, is it writing or is it more on a more personal level? What is the Council's advice?

Devi: She needs to speak to people. They need to see her.

Therapist: When you say speak, is it like she needs to speak up or she needs to do that in a more professional setting?

Devi: She doesn't have the confidence right now. She needs to build that confidence to share her experiences as they come so that other people can learn from them.

Therapist: How can she develop that confidence?

Devi: Practice. Small groups first. She needs to let go.

Therapist: That would be very much in alignment with her purpose. As she helps other people understand her journey, she will in turn also be more in alignment with her own purpose, of seeing and connecting to love everywhere. Is that a good way of putting it?

Devi: Yes. She thinks she must wait until she knows everything and figures it all out, but she doesn't.

Therapist: She rather needs to practice and develop, not wait.

Devi: Yes.

Therapist: Because only through practice and starting will she develop to become that.

Devi: Yes. More pieces will come as she takes steps.

Therapist: What other insight is the Council willing to share with your higher Self? Something we have not perhaps thought about today or discussed.

Devi: Things are shifting in the collective, and Devi wants to play a role in that. And she will play a role in that as she takes steps. Many people are awakening to this shift. She has to be brave, not fear. She fears being seen and being heard. She has to be brave.

Therapist: How can you assist her? How can you communicate more powerfully with her while she goes about her life as Devi?

Devi: She needs to set aside time to connect. All the guidance is there, she just needs to set aside time to connect. She knows how to do that.

Therapist: Today we clearly see that she is perfectly capable of making this connection with the Council and with higher consciousness, so there is no reason to assume that when she practices herself that she cannot be reconnected back to all of you here now, right?

Devi: Right. And she knows that she fears. She fears what will emerge from her and the gifts we have given her. She fears using the gifts.

Therapist: What is at the root of this fear? And how can we get rid of it?

Devi: She fears being rejected, not appreciated for what she has to share.

Therapist: How can you help her understand that it's nothing more than an idea in her head?

Devi: It just needs to happen. She needs to set aside those fears because it needs to happen now.

Therapist: That's why you said earlier that she needs to start with small groups and start expressing herself. She'll then discover that rather than being rejected, she will be appreciated, and she will feel good about herself. Is that how she should start?

Devi: Yes, small groups that will hear her voice.

Therapist: What is the role of her friends in her life? How can they help?

Devi: They will be in that group. She needs to start with them. She has surrounded herself with the souls that will support that expansion.

Therapist: What about her daughter and her son? What is their part in her evolution and vice versa?

Devi: They will learn from watching her take these steps. She needs to start taking these steps. And it will help them on their journey.

Therapist: The message you're giving her is pretty clear.

Devi: Yes.

Therapist: Is there anything else you want to share with her, any blessings?

Devi: This experience will be enough.

Therapist: The spirit world is wide open to you. Is there any other place that your soul wants to visit? How do you feel at this moment?

Devi: I will be able to visit those places later. It's not necessary for me to go anywhere now.

Therapist: How do you feel?

Devi: I feel calm.

Therapist: Would you like to stay a few moments in silence with your guides and your partner?

Devi: Yes.

Therapist: All right, just stay here as long as you want. And when you're ready, just let me know, okay?

Devi: Okay, I'm ready.

Therapist: How do you feel?

Devi: I'm glad because I know how to come back. I see other beings around behind the Council.

Therapist: Who are these beings?

Devi: It's like they're just showing themselves to me. They're people I've met throughout my lives, and they're all there.

Therapist: Your other lives and this life as well?

Devi: Yes. They're all there.

Therapist: Is anything being said or is it more like a love connection?

Devi: No, they're happy to see me. They're happy I see them.

Therapist: Beautiful. Just take your time with them.

Devi: It's so great to see everyone. This is our home. We all come back here.

Therapist: Is there anything you want to tell them?

Devi: I will remember. I know I'm equipped with everything I need in this life. And I'll be back.

Therapist: How do you feel?

Devi: I feel they're giving me encouragement, just encouragement to do the things I need to do for the rest of my life here.

Therapist: You see, they believe in you. Are they still talking to you?

Devi: I just don't want to say goodbye.

Therapist: You can stay longer. There's no hurry. You stay as long as you want. And when you're ready to say goodbye, just let me know. Okay?

Devi: Okay, I'm ready.

We slowly bring the session to an end here.

Case 22: Mike
Surfing the waves of infinity

Mike is a 29-year-old technician and profound seeker of truth. Mike suffered a lot in his early childhood but was able to transform his life and place himself on the spiritual path.

Therapist: What is the first thing that comes to mind?
Mike: Suits.
Therapist: What kind of suits?
Mike: 1940s.
Therapist: Are you wearing a suit as well?

Mike: Yes.

Therapist: How old are you, approximately?

Mike: 30s.

Therapist: And there are multiple people with suits around you?

Mike: Yes.

Therapist: What kind of suits?

Mike: Just work suits.

Therapist: Are you walking somewhere or is this your work environment?

Mike: I'm standing. Everyone's walking around me.

Therapist: What kind of place is this?

Mike: A city.

Therapist: Are you outside or are you inside?

Mike: Outside.

Therapist: What's the weather like?

Mike: It's a nice day. It's hot.

Therapist: It is a big city or a small city?

Mike: Like medium size.

Therapist: What kind of buildings do you see around you?

Mike: I see skyrises and buildings that are lower.

Therapist: Does any city come to mind that reminds you of this place?

Mike: Baltimore.

Therapist: So here we are in Baltimore, in the 30s. Are there cars outside or just pedestrians?

Mike: Just noticing pedestrians.

Therapist: How do you feel?

Mike: I feel good.

Therapist: Yeah?
Mike: Relaxed.
Therapist: What do you think you're doing here in the city with your suit, relaxing?
Mike: Observing.
Therapist: Is it something you like to do, observe people?
Mike: Yes.
Therapist: What goes through your mind as you're observing them?
Mike: Wonder what their lives are like.
Therapist: Have you always been a philosopher?
Mike: Yes.
Therapist: What is it that you do in your day-to-day life?
Mike: Wander.
Therapist: You wander from place to place, or you wander more in your mind?
Mike: In my mind.
Therapist: Do you work in the city?
Mike: I think so.
Therapist: If you look at your own body, what kind of body type are you?
Mike: Rather short, skinny.
Therapist: Do you have a hat on or not?
Mike: Yes.
Therapist: What kind of a hat?
Mike: Shirley hat.
Therapist: What's your name?
Mike: Frank.
Therapist: I'm going to call you Frank. So, you like to wander in your mind.

Mike: I daydream.

Therapist: Does it provide you comfort or is it because you're bored with what you're doing? Or are you just thinking?

Mike: I wonder about the experiences of everyone. Wonder where they go at night?

Therapist: Do you do anything with these observations, like write them down or is it just something that you like to do internally?

Mike: Internally.

Therapist: Now tell me, Frank, do you have a family that lives nearby, or do you live on your own?

Mike: I live on my own.

Therapist: Let's go there. Where do you live? Do you live in an apartment or a house?

Mike: I like it here.

Therapist: In the city?

Mike: Yes.

Therapist: What makes it so appealing to you?

Mike: I like the concrete, I like the structures, and I like the people.

Therapist: Have you always lived in the city, Frank?

Mike: No.

Therapist: Where did you come from?

Mike: A poor house. It's falling apart.

Therapist: Was your family poor?

Mike: Yes.

Therapist: What about now? How are you doing now financially?

Mike: I seem comfortable.

Therapist: Are you doing some kind of work that pays well?

Mike: Must be.

Therapist: What it is that you do?

Mike: Office work.

Therapist: If you would describe to me the most significant observation about this moment as you're here in town, watching all these people, what would it be?

Mike: I feel lost. Everyone else knows where to go and I don't.

Therapist: Is it like an existential feeling?

Mike: Yes.

Therapist: What is it that you're looking for?

Mike: Safety.

Therapist: How so?

Mike: A safe place.

Therapist: Do you think the city is not safe?

Mike: Mentally.

Therapist: What does that mental safety for you look like? Do you have any concept of what it could mean to you or is it something that you're searching?

Mike: Searching. I don't know what it should look like.

Therapist: Have you always felt this way or is it something that is starting in your life?

Mike: Always.

I move him forward in his life.

Therapist: Tell me Frank, what is going on in your life now?

Mike: I'm in a park.

Therapist: How old are you now?

Mike: Older. It's hard to say.

Therapist: What are you doing in the park?

Mike: Feeding the ducks, observing the people again.

30 Cases of past-life and life-between-lives regressions

Therapist: Has anything changed since the last time we met?

Mike: I feel more peaceful.

Therapist: What do you attribute this peace to?

Mike: Self-knowledge.

Therapist: You feel you're more in touch with higher ideas and different concepts within yourself? Is that what you're trying to say?

Mike: Yes.

Therapist: In what way do you feel this? What have you learned since the last time?

Mike: I used to just look at the people and wonder where they were going and now I don't concern myself with where they're going and just observe the people and look at the happiness.

Therapist: It's a shift in the way you regard people, and you regard life.

Mike: Yes.

Therapist: How has that positively affected you or what caused that change?

Mike: Careful self-reflection.

Therapist: Do you do a lot of reading, Frank? Or do you philosophize quietly in your head?

Mike: Yes, I read, but I don't read about philosophy.

Therapist: So, the more existential stuff is something you figure out on your own?

Mike: Yes.

Therapist: Do you have any friends or groups that you belong to where you can discuss these things? Or are you more like a loner?

Mike: I go to the bar.

Therapist: You can talk about these things in the bar?

Mike: Sometimes.

453

Therapist: Is it just a regular bar?

Mike: A regular bar. It's quiet during the day.

Therapist: Is it where you meet people to talk about life?

Mike: Yes, sometimes. We don't always talk about life, but that's my favorite thing.

Therapist: Go to the bar or talk about life?

Mike: Talking about life.

Therapist: And once in a while, you may find somebody there to talk about these things.

Mike: Yes. It's completely by chance.

Therapist: There aren't too many people with whom you can talk about these things?

Mike: No.

Therapist: Why do you think that is? People are just not interested? Or is it that people are too busy? What do you think is the reason that nobody seems to be interested?

Mike: Too busy. Too preoccupied with their daily lives.

Therapist: And you are calmer, more collected?

Mike: Yes.

Therapist: Are you still living alone, Frank, or do you have a family?

Mike: Alone.

Therapist: Is that by conscious design?

Mike: Yes.

Therapist: You're not interested in any intimate relationships?

Mike: No.

Therapist: Why do you think that is?

Mike: I want to have unfiltered, independent thought.

Therapist: You're very conscious about your mental and spiritual pursuits, your state of consciousness, and your state of mind, right?

Mike: Yes.

Therapist: You're protective of it?

Mike: Yes.

Therapist: This is how you are naturally.

Mike: It seems to be so.

Therapist: From where you are now, Frank, sitting on the bench in the park and thinking about life, what is it that you're aiming to be or achieve?

Mike: A higher sense of understanding of love. Love for myself.

Therapist: How is your relationship with yourself at this moment, Frank?

Mike: Pretty good.

Therapist: Yeah?

Mike: I'm pretty peaceful.

Therapist: You're in a good place in your life right now?

Mike: It seems to be so.

Therapist: Beautiful. Now, what is the most significant observation about this moment in your life?

Mike: Self-knowledge is extremely important.

Therapist: Can you help me understand why this is so important to you?

Mike: Important to help me. Important to help others.

Therapist: What does it do for you spiritually speaking, that self-knowledge?

Mike: It's hard to attain, what little I have.

Therapist: When you compare yourself to others, who are not in this pursuit of self-knowledge, to what degree is self-knowledge benefiting your internal world?

Mike: Tremendously compared to others. I seem to be able to

protect myself more.

Therapist: You're very much aware of the benefits of what this is doing for you?

Mike: Yes. Yes.

I move him forward in time again.

Therapist: Tell me Frank, what is happening now?

Mike: I'm in bed.

Therapist: What are you doing in bed?

Mike: Reading a newspaper.

Therapist: Are you well?

Mike: No.

Therapist: Are you ill?

Mike: Yes.

Therapist: Is it serious?

Mike: No.

Therapist: It's not terminal?

Mike: No.

Therapist: Okay. How old are you now, Frank?

Mike: 60.

Therapist: Where are you now? Are you at home?

Mike: I think I'm home. It's a day where I don't have to work.

Therapist: You're just kind of chilling out?

Mike: Yes.

Therapist: How has your life been during the last few decades?

Mike: Lonely.

Therapist: How has your pursuit of self-knowledge been going?

Mike: Stalled.

Therapist: How come?

Mike: It's the loneliness.

Therapist: Is that a recent phenomenon or is that something that has been pursuing you for a while, this loneliness?

Mike: It's pursued me. I kept it at bay and now I'm getting older, I don't have contact with my family.

Therapist: And no relationship, no marriage?

Mike: No.

Therapist: You're kind of living on your own?

Mike: Yes, I'm in an apartment, with one bedroom, and a small kitchen.

Therapist: Is it in the city?

Mike: Yes.

Therapist: You said earlier that you love to be alone, which was by design. And now that you're getting older you seem to be regretting this decision.

Mike: No, no regrets.

Therapist: No regrets?

Mike: Just should have added more.

Therapist: What do you mean by more?

Mike: Relationships, less time with myself.

Therapist: Your intention has always been correct, and you don't regret it, but looking back, you think you could have enriched your life by being more interactive with people.

Mike: Yes.

Therapist: Is it people contact that you're missing or is it an intimate relationship that you're missing?

Mike: Both. Love. I miss love. I can only have so much self-love.

Therapist: And now you discover that your spiritual pursuit has kind of stalled a little bit because of this?

Mike: Yes. I'm like the people I used to observe, just going about my every day, wrapped up in everyday things.

Therapist: Was this a gradual loss of purpose or is it just something that you're realizing now?

Mike: Gradual.

Therapist: Where do you think that started to happen?

Mike: At work.

Therapist: Why your work?

Mike: Just the daily routine of it.

Therapist: The grind?

Mike: Yes, earning money.

Therapist: This pursuit of material comfort, the amount of energy that is required for it, started to become detrimental to a carefree life of purpose-seeking and relationships.

Mike: Yes.

Therapist: There was no family money, I assume. You had to fend for yourself, right?

Mike: Yes, but I was never destitute.

Therapist: Looking back, where on the one hand you have the inevitability of needing to make money, and on the other hand your pursuit for internal perfection, is there anything you could have done differently?

Mike: Opened my heart to others, trusting others. I don't trust people.

Therapist: Why do you think that is, Frank?

Mike: It's hard to say, something from my childhood.

Therapist: Did something happen in your childhood?

Mike: It's being part of a big family.

Therapist: How did that big family contribute to this lack of trust?

Mike: Neglect.

Therapist: You're one of too many?

Mike: Yes.

Therapist: Are you saying that you didn't get the personal attention that you craved, and kind of fell between the cracks?

Mike: Yes. Disappointment. I feel unworthy of other people's attention.

Therapist: Do you think this has also contributed to you becoming sort of a philosopher?

Mike: Yes.

Therapist: There is a fine line between being a philosopher that is distrusting of the world and seeking connection and meaningful love.

Mike: It's important to feel uncomfortable sometimes. Put yourself in places you're uncomfortable. Know that not everyone is there to harm you while at the same time looking inward. It's a balance.

Therapist: Do you think that though your intentions were good and you were very sensitive, the balance tipped a little bit too much towards oversensitivity?

Mike: Yes.

I move him forward to the last day of his life.

Therapist: Tell me how old you are now, Frank, on this last day of your life?

Mike: 70s.

Therapist: Is there anything going on around you or within you that suggests that your physical death will come this day?

Mike: The sun. It's shining. I'm alone.

Therapist: Where are you now?

Mike: In the hospital.

Therapist: What is happening?

Mike: Lying in my bed. The sun's shining through the window.

Therapist: How does it make you feel?

Mike: At ease.

Therapist: What do you think about this life you just lived as Frank?

Mike: One has to love, but not without self-knowledge. That was very important for me.

Therapist: What did you learn and achieve as you reflect upon your whole life?

Mike: I learned that helping myself is the best way to attempt to help others. I never fully reached that connection with anyone.

Therapist: Though you dedicated your life consciously to the pursuit of self-knowledge, you couldn't connect to others allowing you to share that love and knowledge?

Mike: That's right.

Therapist: You said earlier that you think it was because of some childhood issues of feeling neglected. Was that still an issue at the end of your life or was it something that you were able to overcome?

Mike: I just lost focus. Got too into my routine. Childhood trauma wasn't as prominent. I just lost track of it.

Therapist: Was it the worldly pursuit that took too much of your energy or was it just a kind of carelessness?

Mike: Both.

Therapist: What do you think you'd want to remember on your journey?

Mike: Balance. Balance. Balance is the key.

Therapist: Balance between what?

Mike: Between introspection and outward action.

Therapist: Maybe we add to that connection? Outward action and connection, or is that what you mean by action?

Mike: Yes. Action, to make a connection.

Therapist: Beautiful. Seeking for a balance between the search for internal perfection, versus...

Mike: The connection with others.

Therapist: There was too much of an emphasis on the mental and too little on the heart.

Mike: That's right.

Therapist: What is your last thought or awareness as you leave the body?

Mike: Exhaustion.

I move him past his death.

Therapist: Where are you now in relation to the body you leave behind?

Mike: Standing over it.

Therapist: Is there anybody near you at the time of your death?

Mike: No.

Therapist: What are you feeling looking at your body?

Mike: Pity.

Therapist: In what way?

Mike: I could have done so much more.

Therapist: Are you aware of what it is you could have done more?

Mike: Yes. A life of connection. It was very profound, which is what exhausted me so much.

Therapist: What, the search for connection?

Mike: The ignorance of it.

Therapist: The ignorance of the lack of connection?

Mike: The ignorance of beginning to search, because I didn't know where to begin.

Therapist: The search itself caused so much exhaustion?

Mike: Yes.

Therapist: You didn't have anything left anymore to seek meaningful connection?

Mike: Yes.

I move him to a higher plane of consciousness.

Therapist: What is the first thing you notice?

Mike: Light.

Therapist: Is it one light or is it light everywhere?

Mike: White light all around.

Therapist: Are you in this light?

Mike: Part of it.

Therapist: You are part of the light?

Mike: Yes.

Therapist: Beautiful. Now, do you see yourself as a form, a light form, or part of an infinite reality?

Mike: Infinite lightness.

Therapist: And you are part of that?

Mike: Yes.

Therapist: Do you feel you have arrived, or do you feel you're still moving further into it?

Mike: Moving.

Therapist: What does it feel like to be in this light?

Mike: I imagine surfing.

Therapist: It's like soul surfing?

Mike: Yes.

Therapist: Do you feel you're going somewhere, or do you feel you're just moving within it for the sake of it?

Mike: Just moving. No worries.

Therapist: Do you have any thoughts or feelings as you're surfing this light?

Mike: Not for long.

Therapist: All right, take your time. Do you want just a moment to quietly enjoy this light?

Mike: Yes.

Therapist: All right, take your time. When you're ready with that, just let me know. Okay?

Mike: This is how it should be.

Therapist: Just free?

Mike: Yes.

Therapist: Is this what you've been looking for?

Mike: Yes.

Therapist: What can you tell me about this?

Mike: I don't have to think. Just ride the wave of complete trust. It's not something you get in a physical body.

Therapist: What does it require?

Mike: Nothing at all. That's the beauty of it.

Therapist: This is what you've been seeking while you were in the body?

Mike: Yes. That's what I always seek.

Therapist: Are you seeking it as Mike as well?

Mike: Yes.

Therapist: When you reflect on Frank's life, knowing what you know now, that you are part of this infinite light, what comes to mind?

Mike: Frank valued self-introspection. Frank did not look in the right areas. This lack of connection with others, this, what I am experiencing now, is that connection. This white flowing wall of love and peace is just like a river. I didn't understand that it is here at all times.

Therapist: Was it something lacking in his awareness?

Mike: Yes. Yes. He had a filter and a veil and could not see through that.

Therapist: What was the nature of that veil that limited him? Was it the times he lived in, the lack of collective awareness? Was it a lack of intellect, or a lack of spiritual awareness? A lack of guidance?

Mike: Guidance. A veil just kept him from understanding fully.

Therapist: Do you think it was just a matter of not being ready, evolutionarily speaking, or was it something he did wrong?

Mike: No, not wrong. Not wrong.

Therapist: He just wasn't there yet?

Mike: Just not there. Yeah. Too concerned with meaningless things.

Therapist: If you compare that with Mike and his current journey…..

Mike: Yes. It's much the same. Much the same.

Therapist: Is Mike having the same tendencies as Frank?

Mike: Yes.

Therapist: Where does he differ and where does he have similarities?

Mike: Mike is not open, not trusting.

Therapist: He carried over distrust from Frank?

Mike: Very much so.

Therapist: The distrust that Mike is experiencing, did it get reinforcements in this life? Or is it something that purely originated in Frank's childhood?

Mike: Both. Something I struggle with a lot.

Therapist: As you are now surfing the waves of infinity, from this place of love and knowledge, what could you tell Mike about this trust issue?

Mike: It's important to remember what's within. It's important to remember this river. Everyone is on it though we may do bad things to each other, deep down, there's the river. You can gather strength and peace from it.

Therapist: He should not look at their humanity, but he should look at their divinity.

Mike: Yes.

Therapist: Would it be fair to say, that in order to do that, it requires Mike to be more connected to divinity?

Mike: Yes. This is what he lacks.

Therapist: What is it that makes him lack that?

Mike: Self-discipline. Self-discipline. He's attempted to do this, but he has no discipline.

Therapist: What constitutes discipline?

Mike: Moving past selfishness. Being selfish is the biggest block. He wants to do the things that he wants to do, but that's just his body and his physical mind telling him that he needs those things.

Therapist: What does he need instead?

Mike: To connect with his higher Self and with others.

Therapist: It's kind of the same theme as Frank had.

Mike: Yes.

Therapist: At this time, he has a much higher awareness though, doesn't he? Is the veil still there in Mike?

Mike: Less so.

Therapist: But there's still a veil?

Mike: Yes.

Therapist: What is the nature of this veil in Mike?

Mike: It's a matter of refocusing. Refocusing energy towards meditation, towards self-introspection, but also caring. Those two are not exclusive.

Therapist: Right.

Mike: Mike, he thinks they are.

Therapist: That's a misunderstanding, right?

Mike: Yes. He doesn't understand that there's a spiritual connection between himself and others.

Therapist: Wouldn't it be correct to say that he cannot truly connect to the highest level and surf the waves unless he's introspective?

Mike: Indeed.

Therapist: They go hand in hand.

Mike: Yes.

Therapist: Selfishness in this context means allowing yourself to be lost in distractions.

Mike: Yes.

Therapist: The whims of the mind and the body?

Mike: Yes.

Therapist: That's what you said earlier. Is that correct?

Mike: Yes.

Therapist: It's very different from what Mike thought. He thought paying attention to himself and being introspective was selfishness.

Mike: Yes. That's the connection.

Therapist: It's not selfish when you are introspective to see the oneness with one and all.

Mike: That's right.

Therapist: That's where Frank kind of went wrong then.

Mike: Yes. Yes.

Therapist: Do you see that now, that nuance, the difference

between Frank and Mike?

Mike: Yes. It's the connection. It's the thing that should always be at the forefront of the mind.

Therapist: But no ordinary connection, understanding what is behind.

Mike: Yes.

Therapist: That Ocean or the river of Infinity.

Mike: Yes.

Therapist: When you're here in this light, surfing these waves of light consciousness, is that what constitutes truth? Or is there something higher or more?

Mike: This is what I look for. This is one small part of the larger truth. It's the truth that we forget.

Therapist: What is that larger picture? Can you go there now?

Mike: I cannot.

Therapist: You cannot?

Mike: I cannot.

Therapist: This is as high as you can go now, surfing this light?

Mike: This light leads somewhere.

Therapist: What do you think it is, and where will it lead?

Mike: I do not know.

Therapist: What if right now you could allow yourself to go into that light, and see where it would lead you? Rather than searching, you just let go and see how far you can get.

Mike: Okay.

Therapist: Just take your time and let me know what you discover.

Mike: There is a beam coming out of the sun, that seems to lead to a ball of light. I can't get there.

Therapist: Just follow your intuition and see if you can figure out what this is. Just experience it from the heart and from the soul.

Mike: It's a synapse of the brain.

Therapist: Like a superconscious?

Mike: Yes.

Therapist: What's your relationship relation with that?

Mike: It seems to be a travel point. Use it to move to other places.

Therapist: Do you have to go into it or connect with it?

Mike: Both.

Therapist: Is that something you can do now?

Mike: Something is happening.

Therapist: Look at it now without forcing anything. See if you can get an overall understanding of what it is that you're witnessing.

Mike: It's beautiful.

Therapist: If you would explain what you're witnessing to a layman, how would you go about it?

Mike: It's energy that's feeling, it's living, it's pure and white.

Therapist: Is it like a hub of consciousness?

Mike: In a way.

Therapist: Like a center point?

Mike: A stream. This is part of a stream. Like the synapsis of the brain connecting.

Therapist: Where do these energies converge?

Mike: Yes. There's energy coming in.

Therapist: What is your relation to it?

Mike: I'm looking at it, floating.

Therapist: Are you able to connect to it?

Mike: I'm observing. I can't connect with it.

Therapist: What would happen if you connected to it? You may not do it now, but what would happen if you would?

Mike: I believe that it takes me somewhere.

Therapist: To another state of being?

Mike: Possibly. To wherever I'm meant to go next. I can't tell if I've already arrived or if I'm yet to go.

Therapist: Would it mean you would leave this behind?

Mike: No. No. The white light always is.

Therapist: You have a feeling that you're not really supposed to go there now, but you're looking ahead at what's waiting for you.

Mike: Yes.

Therapist: When would this take place?

Mike: It may not happen anytime soon.

Therapist: Not within the range of Mike's life?

Mike: No.

Therapist: Beyond that?

Mike: Beyond.

Therapist: So, you're getting a preview of what is to come.

Mike: Yes.

Therapist: Summarizing, what is the most important task ahead?

Mike: The connection. It's always the connection.

Therapist: How can Mike do that differently?

Mike: Discipline.

Therapist: The discipline of awareness.

Mike: Yes. Being able to drop the less important things and refocus energy on the substantive.

Therapist: I like your concept of discipline. It's very different from some orthodox and established religious ideas of discipline, which are very restrictive. But your discipline is one of high consciousness, a discipline to keep the mind clear, focused, and in tune with what matters. That is really the highest form of discipline.

Mike: Yes. Discipline is freedom.

Therapist: Yes. And after a while, it doesn't become discipline anymore. It becomes nature.

Mike: This is correct.

Therapist: Now that we are here and you're surfing in the light, what would you like to tell Mike?

Mike: Be brave. Put yourself in situations to foster connection. Raise yourself and reprioritize yourself towards good and light. Don't worry so much about what other people are doing, what other people are thinking. Just live your life.

Therapist: How do you feel?

Mike: A bit anxious. Not in a bad way.

Therapist: In what way?

Mike: In an anticipatory way.

Therapist: Would you like to surf in this light again and shake off this anxiety?

Mike: Yes.

Does it feel better?

Mike: Yes.

We slowly bring the session to an end.

Case 23: Gloria
Surrendering to love

Gloria is a 36-year-old stay at home mom, with a history of alcoholism, depression, and anxiety. In spite of, or perhaps due to these struggles, she's been on a quest toward greater understanding and genuine inner fulfillment.

Therapist: When you look in front of you, what do you notice?

Gloria: It's grassy everywhere, hilly.

Therapist: Is it hilly, you said?

Gloria: Yes, hilly.

Therapist: Is it everywhere around you or is it more in front of you?

Gloria: Everywhere.

Therapist: When you look down at your feet, what if anything, are you wearing on your feet?

Gloria: Boots.

Therapist: What are these made from?

Gloria: I don't know.

Therapist: What else are you wearing?

Gloria: Just a T-shirt, and pants.

Therapist: Are you a boy or a girl?

Gloria: I think I'm a boy.

Therapist: What age?

Gloria: Old.

Therapist: How old?

Gloria: Late fifties.

Therapist: What is the color of your skin?

Gloria: It's light.

Therapist: What about your hair?

Gloria: It's gray.

Therapist: Look straight ahead of you and tell me what you see there, apart from the grass.

Gloria: There are sheep with animals grazing and some grass.

Therapist: Are these your animals?

Gloria: Yes.

Therapist: Are you looking after them?

Gloria: Yes.

Therapist: What's the weather like?

Gloria: It's beautiful.

Therapist: How do you feel here in the fields with the sheep?

Gloria: Feels so good.

Therapist: Do you like it here?

Gloria: Very much.

Therapist: What does it smell like in this place?

Gloria: It's fresh.

Therapist: Where in the world are we?

Gloria: I don't know. It's just hilly and there's grass. There's a little creek, there are sheep and a little house.

Therapist: What does the house look like?

Gloria: It's just small.

Therapist: Is this your house?

Gloria: I live there.

Therapist: Please go there and tell me what this place looks like.

Gloria: It's just simple.

Therapist: What is it made from?

Gloria: Wood. Just like one room.

Therapist: If you go inside, can you tell me what the inside looks like?

Gloria: It's just simple. There's a fire and a table and a bed.

Therapist: You said there's a fireplace?

Gloria: Yeah, a fireplace.

Therapist: Do you live here alone?

Gloria: Yes, alone.

Therapist: You like that, being alone in this place?

Gloria: It's ok.

Therapist: What is your name?

Gloria: Bill.

Therapist: Now, Bill, what is the most significant observation either within you or around you about this moment in your life in your fifties? Being here with the sheep at your house, in the fields.

Gloria: It's calm.

Therapist: Do you like the calm?

Gloria: I do.

Therapist: What does it do for you, this calmness?

Gloria: I feel content.

Therapist: Are there certain things that you think about when you are here with the animals?

Gloria: I'm just happy.

Therapist: You're just happy?

Gloria: It's busy. There are a lot of people. It's like a city or something. There's like lots of people.

Therapist: What do they look like, the way they are dressed?

Gloria: Simple and drapey. There are lots of carts that are being pulled and lots of people.

Therapist: Is it a town or a city?

Gloria: Like a city.

Therapist: Where are you now? Are you in the middle of the city?

Gloria: Yeah.

I move her back in her life as Bill.

Therapist: How old are you now Bill?

Gloria: 10.

Therapist: Are you alone or is there anybody near you?

Gloria: There are people everywhere.

Therapist: Is anybody connected to you here that takes you around or are you wandering by yourself?

Gloria: Just wandering by myself.

Therapist: How do you feel being in the city?

Gloria: Just feels really dirty and cluttered and busy.
Therapist: Is this where you live or is this where you visit?
Gloria: No, I think I live here.
Therapist: Where is your house? Can you take me there?
Gloria: It's in the middle of it. I don't really have stairs.
Therapist: Is your family here?
Gloria: Lots of people.
Therapist: The family itself consists of a lot of people?
Gloria: Lots of people.
Therapist: How does that make you feel?
Gloria: Unimportant.
Therapist: Nobody's really paying attention to you?
Gloria: Yeah, I just wander around.
Therapist: When you say lots of people, do you mean lots of brothers, sisters, or uncles and nephews?
Gloria: Yeah, lots of kids. Too many people in a small area.
Therapist: Now, what is this most significant observation about this moment in your life Bill?
Gloria: That there's all these people but I could still go and be happy just by myself. I don't need all those people.

I move her forward in time.

Gloria: I'm on a boat.
Therapist: What kind of a boat?
Gloria: Like a sailboat. It's sailing away.
Therapist: Is it a big boat or a small boat?
Gloria: Well, a medium boat.
Therapist: Tell me what this looks like and who's all here if there's anybody else.

When Souls Transition

Gloria: It just seems like there are dry guns on it. I hitched a ride or I'm working on it.
Therapist: Is it a lake or an ocean?
Gloria: It seems all of a sudden I just decided to go.
Therapist: How old are you now?
Gloria: Not even 20.
Therapist: What does the water look like? Is it an ocean or a lake or a river?
Gloria: Like a river or an ocean. Probably looks like an ocean.
Therapist: What do you look like now Bill?
Gloria: Brown hair. But I am able to go off on my own.
Therapist: What motivated you to be on this boat?
Gloria: Wanting to get away from where I was living.
Therapist: Where were you living at this time?
Gloria: With all the people in the city.
Therapist: You want quietness.
Gloria: Change.
Therapist: Change. What is it that you are seeking?
Gloria: All that comes to my head is not that.
Therapist: Just getting away from the noise and the people. What goes on in your mind and your heart on this boat?
Gloria: I'm relaxed.
Therapist: Are you happy you made the decision to go?

In this case, she jumped all over the timeline of Bill, from old age to childhood, to mid-age, and now back to old age.

Gloria: I'm just sitting in the house by myself at the table.
Therapist: How old are you now?
Gloria: I'm old.

Therapist: Are you still alone?
Gloria: Yes, with my sheep.
Therapist: How do you feel now?
Gloria: Fine. I'm happy and content. I'm tired, but content.
Therapist: Why are you tired?
Gloria: It was hard work living by myself.
Therapist: What is the secret of your contentment?
Gloria: No expectations.
Therapist: From the world or for yourself?
Gloria: From the world.
Therapist: Did you spend many years alone with your sheep?
Gloria: A few.
Therapist: And it has been a happy life.
Gloria: Yea.
Therapist: Has anything changed since we last met at 50 or is it still the same?
Gloria: It's the same.
Therapist: And you're okay with that?
Gloria: Yea.

And we're now on the last day of Bill's life.

Therapist: How old are you on this last day of your life as Bill?
Gloria: I'm 72.
Therapist: Is there anything going on around you or within you that suggests that your physical death will come this day?
Gloria: I don't want to get up out of bed.
Therapist: Are you tired?
Gloria: Yeah.
Therapist: Are you ill or are you just really tired?

Gloria: Just really tired.

Therapist: Is there anybody there?

Gloria: No, just me.

Therapist: What is happening at this moment?

Gloria: It's just quiet and still.

Therapist: What do you think about this life you just lived as Bill?

Gloria: It was good.

Therapist: What did you like about it?

Gloria: I feel content like I lived the life that I wanted.

Therapist: Were you pretty successful in doing that?

Gloria: Yeah, it was relaxing.

Therapist: What did you learn from this life?

Gloria: That I could do it. That I didn't have to depend on a whole lot of people. I could go and do it on my own.

Therapist: You became self-reliant?

Gloria: Yeah. I didn't need anybody else to help me. I could do it on my own.

Therapist: Beautiful. Now what is your last thought or awareness as you leave the body?

Gloria: Just contentment.

Therapist: Where are you now in relation to the body you that you leave behind? Can you still see it?

Gloria: I'm above it.

Therapist: What do you think about your death? How do you feel?

Gloria: I don't have a lot of connection to it.

I move her into a higher place after death.

Therapist: What is the first thing you notice?

Gloria: I feel happy. Excited. Overjoyed.

Therapist: When you look at your own soul-Self, what do you feel like or what do you see? Do you have a form or a light or are you a frequency or consciousness or a combination of these?

Gloria: Like a cloud of particles.

Therapist: Do you have any colors?

Gloria: No, I just feel it.

Therapist: Just the vibration of it?

Gloria: Just feel it. Like it's here but it's not here.

Therapist: Beautiful. Just feel yourself expanding in it completely and enjoy it. And tell me how you experience the space around you.

Gloria: Like it's open. Uplifting.

Therapist: Take a moment and discover the beauty of your own Self, tune in even deeper, and expand even further. Do you feel we are in a plane of existence where you're now supposed to be, or do you feel you're just on your way?

Gloria: I'm just on my way.

Therapist: Just keep on going and tell me what happens when you arrive at where you need to be. You can just go there at will and with your thoughts.

Gloria: Nice, clean, and fresh.

Therapist: What are you aware of around you?

Gloria: It's open but there are forms but not really forms.

Therapist: Are these other beings?

Gloria: Yeah, and there are structures.

Therapist: They're energy?

Gloria: Yeah, you can see through them, but they're there.

Therapist: Right. Wonderful. Now that you've arrived in this place, look around you and see if there's anybody coming to greet you. A guide, an elder, anyone. Just take your time. and enjoy this new place. How do you feel?

Gloria: It feels expansive and open.

Therapist: Beautiful. Who do you want to meet?

Gloria: I want to meet my guide.

Therapist: Just call them. It could be one or perhaps even more. Allow them to present themselves to you.

Gloria: I feel like I'm standing outside a big structure. With big pillars and steps, but it's kind of open at the same time.

Therapist: Are you supposed to go inside?

Gloria: I know. I'm standing out front. I want to go inside.

Therapist: Just go ahead and tell me what happens next when you get inside.

Gloria: There is a hall, that's big and tall and open.

Therapist: Is this where the Council is or where your guide is?

Gloria: I don't know what's inside. I don't know.

Therapist: Take your time. Allow yourself to look around. Get adjusted and very soon you will find out who's waiting here for you. Is this just a waiting space or are you supposed to go further?

Gloria: I think we will go further. I don't know. I feel kind of lost.

Therapist: Do you want me to help you call the guide?

Gloria: Yes, please.

Therapist: All right. Calling in the guide now. Is this a male, a female, or an androgynous guide?

Gloria: Male.

Therapist: Does he have facial features or is he more of an energy?

Gloria: More of an energy.

Therapist: What is his energy like?

Gloria: I feel proud of him. I feel proud and excited.

Therapist: What does he say about Bill?

Gloria: That I lived a good, contented life.

Therapist: What is it that you wanted to experience and achieve in that life?

Gloria: Going off on my own.

Therapist: And the guide, what is his idea about it?

Gloria: Yeah, I did a good job. I was successful.

Therapist: Does he also offer some positive criticism? Is there something you could have perhaps done differently or something you didn't think about?

Gloria: He was selfish too. I just realized that all of a sudden.

Therapist: What does he say about that?

Gloria: I had to in order to fulfill my life.

Therapist: He doesn't think it's a problem?

Gloria: No.

Therapist: What were the best characteristics of Bill when you look back at him?

Gloria: He wasn't afraid. He was self-sufficient and calm.

Therapist: What are some of the parallels between Bell and Gloria's incarnation?

Gloria: Gloria doesn't take chances. She likes to have a lot of support. She wouldn't take off like that.

Therapist: What does the guide say about the difference between Gloria and Bill?

Gloria: It's like an opposite lifetime.

Therapist: Why did the guide show you this past life of Bill? What is it that your soul needs to understand that could help Gloria?

Gloria: Being around a lot of people can feel overwhelming. I have to live this lifetime. I get my support from these people. Whereas Bill got strength by himself, Gloria draws her strength from having her people. That feels overwhelming sometimes.

Therapist: What can Gloria learn from Bill?

Gloria: That we already lived a lifetime by ourselves.

Therapist: And?

Gloria: We don't need to do that again.

Therapist: Does Gloria sometimes feel like she wants to live like Bill?

Gloria: Yeah.

Therapist: But it would just be repeating an old pattern. What does the guide want instead for Gloria?

Gloria: To embrace all the people and not try to hide in solitude.

Therapist: Not to run away?

Gloria: Yes.

Therapist: Go back to that moment with your guide before starting Gloria's life. What is it that you and your guide discussed that needed to be experienced and developed in the life of Gloria?

Gloria: Relationships.

Therapist: Tell me more.

Gloria: Bill didn't have relationships. You have to work through different relationships with different people and different situations.

Therapist: How is the guide telling you Gloria is doing so far with relationships?

Gloria: She has a lot of relationships.

Therapist: How is she doing?

Gloria: She needs to have more patience.

Therapist: What needs to be developed before this incarnation is over?

Gloria: To focus more on relationships and less on herself.

Therapist: And why is that important for her soul growth?

Gloria: That's the whole point of this life.

Therapist: What does it help her become?

Gloria: She's already had a lifetime to work on herself.

Therapist: Why is she experiencing anxiety, depression, and insomnia? If you look at this mission of connecting with others, why are these issues happening in Gloria's life? Ask the guide if you want to.

Gloria: She gets too caught up in it and gets too worried about how everything feels instead of just letting it be. You can't control relationships. You can just live in them.

Therapist: Now that you're seeing it from a distance, does it get clearer?

Gloria: No.

Therapist: How can the guide help and offer support?

Gloria: She has to remember that she's here because of relationships. When she focuses on those, it's going to fill up her.

Therapist: Has she been fighting it because of Bill, unconsciously resisting it? Could this depression and anxiety be in some unconscious way connected to this?

Gloria: She pulls away and she tries to find contentment on her own, but she's not going to find it there.

Therapist: That's interesting. Bill's purpose was to be alone. But this time you came with a completely different purpose and if you try to repeat the old purpose in this life, it won't work. You're resisting the new lesson and the lesson is to live these relations. Not to fight them and the emotions, but to accept them and flow with them. Is that a good way of summarizing it?

Gloria: Yeah. To embrace the moments with people.

Therapist: Beautiful. Not to run away, not to resist, but to live with it.

Gloria: Don't look for contentment yourself.

Therapist: That's an important lesson.

Gloria: She has to look for it with her loved ones.

Therapist: That's an important lesson that everybody can learn, right? Gloria feels that there are more talents within her that perhaps she's not utilizing. When you look at it from the soul's perspective, what are some of the other interests or talents that Gloria could manifest if she wanted to?

Gloria: She just has to focus on relationships. Everything's going to fall into place. She needs to put time into people and relationships, and she doesn't have to worry about any of that.

Therapist: Would these be considered diversions?

Gloria: It'll just present itself. It'll be clear.

Therapist: So that it will fit in with other relationships?

Gloria: Yes, exactly.

Therapist: Is there any karma that stands in the way? Anything that you carried over from Bill or perhaps other lifetimes?

Gloria: No.

Therapist: It's pretty clear then?

Gloria: It is.

Therapist: She's always feeling that she is in a hurry. Where does that come from?

Gloria: Of not having time for people.

Therapist: Is that a Bill hangover?

Gloria: Yeah.

Therapist: When you're used to being always alone, being with people feels like an obligation. Is that it?

Gloria: Yeah. Always in a hurry to be by yourself.

Therapist: That's a good point. Looking at that, what does your guide tell you about addressing that? What should you be thinking and feeling instead as a replacement?

Gloria: Don't reach for contentment. Contentment and solitude fight. Be patient and enjoy the moment with your people. Don't be in a rush.

Therapist: You talked about Gloria's tendency to fall into alcoholism and addiction. Looking at it objectively, what is the root cause?

Gloria: I don't know.

Therapist: Just ask your guide. He's here now.

Gloria: She needed that because when she's with people she feels like she has to quiet her mind. She looks for solitude. But then when she's in solitude, it doesn't feel comfortable either.

Therapist: She used the substances instead.

Gloria: But she doesn't need that. She just has to embrace the relationships.

Therapist: And that will fill the gap that she's trying to fill with addiction?

Gloria: Yes.

Therapist: When she tries to run away to fulfill that gap, she uses alcohol and drugs. Whereas instead, if she tried to fill that gap, not with alcohol or drugs, and tried instead to fill it with the satisfaction that comes from surrendering to these relationships she'd find fulfillment there.

Gloria: Yeah. She needs to put her energy into finding fulfillment and love in relationships.

Therapist: Then the heart will be full, and she doesn't need to fill that with anything else.

Gloria: Yeah.

Therapist: The theme of what this life is about is very clear then isn't it? If we look beyond Gloria, beyond Bill, and just look at the beauty of your soul, who are you as a soul? What, as a soul, do you aspire to be and experience?

Gloria: Love.

Therapist: How do you see fulfillment as a soul at the end of all these lives and through all these lives?

Gloria: Not to get caught up in all the little moments.

Therapist: Are you saying that instead what you should be looking for and eventually become is a continuous love consciousness?

Gloria: Yeah.

Therapist: Not divided by little things, but one continuous flow of love.

Gloria: Don't let the little stuff get in my way.

Therapist: Beautiful. What attitude change and awareness could be brought into Gloria's life to start working toward this continuous love flow?

Gloria: Not to be rushing and trying to have solitude but take the time to enjoy the moment with the people around her.

Therapist: Because that is love, isn't it?

Gloria: Yeah, that's love.

Therapist: It's bigger love than being alone, which is a more selfish form of love, which is narrower and more constrained.

Gloria: That's how Bill lived his life.

Therapist: Yes.

Gloria: It feels warm.

Therapist: Can you see and feel the difference between that self-love of Bill and this warm feeling of a much bigger love?

Gloria: Yes, that's what I'm feeling now.

Therapist: Remember this difference deep in your heart. If ever there is a tendency to go back to loneliness and escape, remember the difference in love, where you're running towards something smaller, not bigger. And when you know the difference, then you don't need to do it anymore and see that there's no benefit in it.

Therapist: Looking at some of the other players in Gloria's incarnation, like her parents, what is their role in her overall evolution?

Gloria: Learning to deal with different personalities and be happy in relationships no matter who the person is.

Therapist: This entire list of people that she's noted demands the same answer?

Gloria: Yes. They are who they are, you can't change them.

Therapist: Now, I want you to have a look at your soul-Self, without losing your awareness of the higher Self, look at Gloria objectively and see where her anger is coming from.

Gloria: She can't get away from people.

Therapist: At the root, it is the same cause, is it not?

Gloria: Yeah.

Therapist: You're seeing it so clearly now. Do you see that as clearly as Gloria?

Gloria: She didn't.

Therapist: But now you're seeing it, right?

Gloria: I do.

Therapist: It's interesting because your understanding, that the anger comes from the resistance of not being able to run away and wanting to get self-satisfaction versus finding a higher satisfaction in a larger loving group consciousness is very quick, intelligent, and clear. Is that correct?

Gloria: It's very clear.

Therapist: Is there anything else you want to explore here with or without your guide? How do you feel?

Gloria: I feel good. I feel light.

Therapist: How do you feel about everything you've discovered today?

Gloria: Relief.

Therapist: Does your guide want to share something with you as a summary or as a blessing?

Gloria: Just that Gloria's on the right track. She just has to keep up with her relationships and put her energy into that.

Therapist: Then all her problems will fade away, won't they?

Gloria: It'll just fall into place.

Therapist: How does it make you feel when you see that?

Gloria: It makes sense.

Therapist: Is there anything you want to say or express to the guide?

Gloria: Just appreciation.

Therapist: Are you satisfied?

Gloria: Yeah.

Therapist: Would you like to stay a little moment longer to be in this blissful space?

Gloria: No, I think we're done.

We slowly bring the session to a close.

Case 24: Jake
A short life

Jake a 69-year-old Vedic Astrologer, martial artist, and retired sales manager. As an astrologer, he's very much in his head and tries to understand his path, but it ends up causing him more confusion.

Jake: It seems like daytime.
Therapist: Are you inside or outside?
Jake: Inside.
Therapist: Are you alone, or is there anybody with you?
Jake: There seem to be people around.
Therapist: Looking straight ahead, tell me what the first thing you notice is.

Jake: I can feel the wind.

Therapist: Are the windows open?

Jake: I've walked through a screen door. I'm on a porch.

Therapist: What's on the porch? What does this place look like?

Jake: It's wood.

Therapist: Is it a fancy or a simple house?

Jake: A farmhouse.

Therapist: When you look around at the farm, is it remote or are there neighbors nearby?

Jake: I don't see neighbors. I'm looking out the back, I see a field.

Therapist: Is it flat or is it hilly?

Jake: I don't see hills.

Therapist: Looking down at your feet, tell me what if anything, you see on your feet.

Jake: Brown kind of boots.

Therapist: What are they made from?

Jake: Looks like leather.

Therapist: What else are you wearing?

Jake: Blue. I first thought jeans, maybe it's canvas. With a red shirt.

Therapist: Are you a man or a woman?

Jake: A man.

Therapist: What's your age approximately as you're standing here on the porch?

Jake: 14.

Therapist: What is the color of your skin?

Jake: I guess white. I tanned in the sun.

Therapist: Looking at the landscape as you're standing here at 14 years old, where are we?

Jake: It seems to be in the United States.

Therapist: What time approximately?

Jake: 1800.

Therapist: As you're standing here around 1800, looking out of the porch at the fields, do you have any thoughts or emotions?

Jake: Maybe it's later, 1840.

Therapist: Do you have any thoughts or feelings at this moment?

Jake: I'm standing on the porch. There's something funny, it's a wooden porch, it should be wooden steps, but it's not. I guess its cement or stone.

Therapist: The steps coming down from the ports are made out of stone.

Jake: Seems to be.

Therapist: If you would describe to me the most relevant observation about this moment, either within you or around you, what would it be?

Jake: A calm before the storm.

Therapist: Do you have a feeling something is up, and that something is going to happen?

Jake: Yes. It's Kansas, Missouri, and I'm on the border.

Therapist: You have a feeling that something is about to happen?

Jake: Yes.

Therapist: Do you have any idea what it is, or you're just having this feeling?

Jake: There's going to be an insurrection. I don't think I got much older.

Therapist: Okay, just go to the last event in your life. Take your time describing what happens.

Jake: I've been shot.

Therapist: Tell me what happened.

Jake: I'm unclear.

Therapist: I need you to go back to the events leading up to this death. Not going to the final moment but going back a little bit before.

Jake: There is a lot of blood.

Therapist: Is it your blood or other people's blood?

Jake: It's a lot of blood, and it seems like mine.

Therapist: Where are you now?

Jake: There's a barn, and I'm by the barn.

Therapist: What is happening near the barn?

Jake: There is a barn. Maybe I was in the barn and came out.

Therapist: Who are the people responsible for all this blood?

Jake: They're vigilantes, and they're raiders.

Therapist: What do they want?

Jake: Us.

Therapist: Why?

Jake: We were on the wrong side.

Therapist: The wrong side of what?

Jake: Slavery.

Therapist: Were you in favor or were you against it?

Jake: My family was against it.

Therapist: And these raiders, they're pro-slavery?

Jake: Guerrillas.

Therapist: And they've come here to kill everybody who is against it?

Jake: Yes.

Therapist: Are they coming for your entire family?

Jake: Yes.

Therapist: Go to the last moment of your life and tell me what happens.

Jake: It's peaceful, it's over, I'm floating.

Therapist: Where are you now in relation to the body you are leaving behind?

Jake: It's behind me.

Therapist: Can you still see it?

Jake: Kind of, I see the area.

Therapist: And what are you feeling?

Jake: There's my mother and my family.

Therapist: Are they with you now or are they still in the body?

Jake: They're dead and they seem to be in some way around.

Therapist: You don't see them clearly?

Jake: I'm not in pain. I can feel that I was shot, but I'm not in pain.

Therapist: How do you feel about your death?

Jake: Well, that was the problem, it was needless.

Therapist: Just a stupid death?

Jake: I don't sense that my father was around, or he was killed earlier, maybe in town and then they decided to kill us because we were on the route. I see drunken raiders. We were just against what they were for, and they used it as an excuse to kill and rob. The blood has moved away, there's no one there.

Therapist: Are you ready to leave?

Jake: Maybe a dog that was in the field with my father.

Therapist: Would you like to reach out to the dog? If you do, go ahead, and reach out to the dog.

Jake: I think I have.

Therapist: You already have? All right, good. Are you ready to move on?

Jake: I'm glad to get out.

I move him to a higher frequency.

Therapist: Have you started to move away from the body?

Jake: I'm comfortable again.

Therapist: Where are you now? What are you aware of?

Jake: I'm comfortable, I'm secure. I'm not in a body, but I feel my identity around me, but I'm not 14.

Therapist: Right. When you say your identity, does it feel like a light form, a frequency, or a consciousness? How do you express that identity?

Jake: There feels more consciousness around me than in the past life when I was dying, and people were riding off. And I'm in a safe place.

Therapist: This safe place, does it feel like you have arrived here already, or does it feel like it is a waiting place? How do you experience this place?

Jake: It's spirit, but it's almost like I am in a hospital ward.

Therapist: What do you mean by a hospital ward? Like a reception where you are for a while?

Jake: It's comfortable and I'm being taken care of and healed.

Therapist: Is this healing a particular process?

Jake: There's a whirling green light, it's gone from swirling to subsiding, and the treatments change.

Therapist: This green light, is it a conscious presence, like a being, or is it more like an energy?

Jake: It is more like healing energy, but now there's a presence.

Therapist: Is it like healing energy, or is it something else or somebody else?

Jake: There's green energy on the outside of it.

Therapist: And there is a presence?

Jake: Yeah, like a more solid, substantial color with depth.

Therapist: Does it feel like a male, a female, or a more androgynous kind of energy?

Jake: There are multiple.

Therapist: Okay. These multiple energy points, what are they doing now? Are they still healing you?

Jake: They're healing and probing.

Therapist: How does it make you feel?

Jake: Nobody's really talking.

Therapist: I understand that communication at this level is likely telepathic. Are you receiving any kind of impressions from them?

Jake: Yeah, I think they want to see that I'm okay.

Therapist: Do they have any comments about the life you just lived? Is there anybody stepping forward who is more communicative?

Jake: They're just asking me how I feel, and I feel terrible.

Therapist: About this life?

Jake: Yeah.

Therapist: What do they say about it?

Jake: I feel like I did something wrong, and they're saying no. And I guess I felt responsible for my mother and sister's death, my father not being there.

Therapist: They obviously don't agree with that.

Jake: No, it had to do with time and place.

Therapist: What was the purpose of this young, short life?

Jake: It was to learn values.

Therapist: Help me understand what that means.

Jake: I'm not sure what I learned, except to witness a household, and a family, and the structure.

Therapist: Does the death and the way it went down have anything to do with what it is that you needed to learn?

Jake: It said to learn rules.

Therapist: Did you learn the rules?

Jake: I think so. I was exposed to the rules, which I guess was the point.

Therapist: Do they offer any insights into that?

Jake: Yeah, they're talking to me now.

Therapist: Please share it with me, so I can stay with you.

Jake: It's about rules and rigidity.

Therapist: Do you understand what they're trying to tell you?

Jake: It was to balance out some other notions that I had, and this was about strict boundaries.

Therapist: The lesson has been learned?

Jake: The correct answer is yes, but there were a lot of lessons.

Therapist: Do they offer any sort of positive criticism about what you could have done differently?

Jake: I learned the rules, but I overcompensated, so there's guilt. I assumed too much responsibility.

Therapist: You took it upon yourself too heavily?

Jake: Yes, the responsibility of my mother, and my sister. At 14 I couldn't do enough.

Therapist: Now that you're here in the spirit realm and they're here with you, do they offer any sort of consolation? Do you realize that you were just a boy when all of this went down?

Jake: They want me to realize it.

Therapist: How is that working for you now that you're looking back at it?

Jake: They're saying, "Pretty good."

Therapist: Are they going to keep you here in this place, discussing this life? Or are you perhaps being taken somewhere else? What happens next?

Jake: They want me to go somewhere.

Therapist: All right, describe to me what this new place is like.

Jake: I think I'm going to my next life, I guess that's the life I'm living now.

Therapist: Before you do, tell me what the plan is for this next life.

Jake: I think my mother is the same, maybe my father is the same. Maybe my father was a friend before in another life, and he was remote. The reasons flood in, and I'm codependent on my mother because I'm the responsible type.

Therapist: Jake has carried over the feelings of the little boy in his last life, feeling somehow responsible.

Jake: Jake has the same relationship with his mother in his last life that wasn't resolved. And in this life, mom drinks, so she's there and she's not there. And my father was not there either.

Therapist: Before you choose this birth, I assume that you made a plan.

Jake: My mother couldn't have a child till I came along, so I did her a favor and I agreed to come. My father is a friend, but someone I had a conflict with in a past life. It was about healing these issues and I agreed to be their child.

Therapist: When we talk about the dharma of Jake and the best advice to move forward, is this related to these issues?

Jake: Yeah, just not like how I thought.

Therapist: Is it a different kind of dharma?

Jake: I was to become independent. Not so much in the ways of the world but becoming independent emotionally. That 14-year-old had conventional values, but the values were polarized.

Therapist: In this life, the idea was to develop a more integrated sense of autonomy and become more mentally and spiritually independent.

Jake: To think through it, and to become an independent thinker.

Therapist: Looking at Jake now, are these issues solved?

Jake: It's not solved. There are residuals of codependency. I picked up from the last life this sense of dutifulness. And that duty binds you to conventional thinking.

Therapist: What then is the best way forward for Jake?

Jake: To drop it.

Therapist: We're here in the soul sphere and look at these two lives. Beyond these lives is your true eternal Self. From this perspective, how can you help Jake drop that?

Jake: I will do it slowly living my life, and this is a life where I'm paying off karma to certain people. The other life and death were being in the wrong place at the wrong time. This can happen on Earth. Death is part of life on earth, and I need to let it go in the same way that a person would let go of codependency. And the only way to let it go is independent thinking, with a higher consciousness.

Therapist: Could we add to that the realization that you're neither that little boy nor Jake?

Jake: Up here I know it, and it's for Jake to do it. But Jake's equipped, his head was in the clouds, but he has the ability to do it.

Therapist: Beautiful.

Jake: There was too much emotion wrapped up in the last life. In this life, it's a fear of failure, that somehow, he can't do it or that he won't do it.

Therapist: But Jake is aware of that now?

Jake: In the last life and in this life, he was fulfilling and paying off certain things and learning things the hard way, that were caused in other lives. But as he pays that off, and he learns to think independently and see through the veil, he doesn't have to do this anymore.

Therapist: How is he doing at this point in his life?

Jake: There's one thing to pay off, and he wants to do that. The rest of this life is up to him.

Therapist: He can be as free as he wants to be, to the degree he drops it.

Jake: Yes.

Therapist: What would be the best way to drop it?

Jake: He has to simply drop the mental constructs and feel it.

Therapist: Beautiful. For the remaining phase of his life, what would that life purpose look like based on everything you've said so far, to help Jake navigate the last years of his life, and be in tune with that purpose?

Jake: It's up to him. The fears that he had from that previous life are needless. He feels pressed to do too many things now.

Therapist: He shouldn't put so much pressure on himself?

Jake: Exactly. He can pay his obligations and do what he wants to do. The idea is to stop striving on the one hand and to stop being afraid on the other.

Therapist: It's wise and beautiful what you say. Because it considers the eternity of the soul. There are many opportunities to work things out under so many different scenarios. It doesn't have to be all done in Jake's life. It can be done casually.

Jake: By rushing things, they won't be done perfectly, and he gets stuck in a hole because the perfect is getting in the way of the good.

Therapist: Right. He must loosen up and look at the big picture.

Jake: If you're afraid of dying then you can't feel in this life. Some of what he thinks are debts to pay were just experiments to get in touch with his feelings.

Therapist: Right, he took it too literally.

Jake: He did not want to be a writer till he had experiences. He's had experiences.

Therapist: What are the best practices for him though? Using that new frame of mind for the remainder of Jake's life.

Jake: By living his life he is learning to feel and have a healthy relationship. Trying to understand what he thinks are wasted days. If you're only thinking, then you're going to overthink it and make it complicated.

Therapist: He must live, and enjoy being in the flow of things, is that a good way of saying it?

Jake: And to do what he did earlier in the coffee shop, smell the coffee.

Therapist: Right, beautifully said. The theme is very clear, the incapacity to trust and to flow is a result of his previous life's early death.

Jake: His higher Self is taking him away from other things, away from his intelligence to learn how to feel, away from the idea of control. It's about stepping away from reasoning into another brainwave. Once he lets go things will come to him. His previous fear of his early death made him hang on to his life too rigidly and prevented him from letting go.

Therapist: As we can see today, you easily get into this brainwave of higher consciousness, allowing you to transcend and look at this objectively. He knows that it was a trauma of his past life, and now that he knows it changes everything. Because when you understand why, you can forgive that little boy for being so afraid.

Jake: Astrologically, if you're under the grasp of certain planets, there's an earthly struggle sometimes. There's confusion and fog. But that's done for him, he may go for it, and there's nothing stopping him. Even if he dies, he'll take everything he learned to the next life.

Therapist: There's no fear and no loss.

Jake: No loss. The more mental constructs he makes, the thicker the veil, and the more the struggle will be to get past it.

If he could turn that off, this world would become his.

Therapist: Not to be in that mental place, but to be in that spiritual frequency. And from here you can allow that attunement to take place.

Jake: That is the only thing that is holding him back, and once he does, he will stay out of fear, and out of a regimented sense of duty.

Therapist: That basically summarizes everything you said today.

Jake: When you are stuck at that mental level like he was on the farm in the past life, you feel you must follow the rules and accordingly become subject to a sense of toil and drudgery. He has learned that his consciousness is separate and that he can be in touch with that all the time.

Therapist: If you boil it down, the only practice that is required is one where he steps out of practice and lets it go.

Jake: There's a certain guilt in this life that really comes from the last life. All he must do is say, "The past life is over." He paid off that karma, and it's done. He's neither terrific nor a failure, the soul is neither.

Therapist: They're just mental blocks, right?

Jake: Yes, and just hurdles to get over. But he has the key in his imagination.

Therapist: And the imagination can be used to connect to this higher frequency, to step out of it all, and get out of the mind and get into the frequency.

Jake: All of the time, he has channeled before.

Therapist: Yes, he should trust that from now on. It's a talent as well.

Jake: It is. But that person who died in that life is holding onto the fear that he could feel in his chest, it's inhibited his breathing in this life. Though that death didn't hurt long, and it was over quickly.

Therapist: Isn't it amazing how these thought patterns, though unreal from an absolute standpoint, can have this tremendous impact on the physiology of Jake? Now that you can see that correlation, it also gives you the key to drop it all.

Jake: Yes. All the toil and the constructs are in his mind. He found the key and it's his way out.

Therapist: But at this moment you're not subject to these constructs, are you?

Jake: No.

Therapist: What does it tell us about the state of mind Jake can live in if he allows this to manifest within him all the time?

Jake: Yes, and he wants to come back here, not in death, but in life. And there's nothing holding him back.

Therapist: He can integrate this consciousness into his day-to-day life.

Jake: Yes.

Therapist: To the extent he allows that, to that extent his past is gone, and these frameworks do not have a hold over him.

Jake: He has more ability to do it than most.

Therapist: Jake has a question about where he thinks he lived a life as a Vedic Buddhist hybrid in the 15th century. He wants to understand this better.

Jake: He's sensing that he's spent time in those places. He is learning that he is not the first person to have a conflict in paths between Vedic and Buddhist, Vedanta and Buddhist thought. But according to the rules in that past life, the black-and-white nature of it makes him in this life have to pick one or the other.

Therapist: That's another mental construct.

Jake: Yes, and it doesn't matter, even if that life was a mistake or there were confusions, which there were. Everything doesn't have to be perfect; he just has to keep practicing.

Therapist: The purpose behind it all is to come to a transcendental awareness.

Jake: Yes.

Therapist: In and by themselves they have no other purpose.

Jake: As with any practice, you learn as you go. Even if you don't do it perfectly, it allows you to have realizations.

Therapist: Right, that's what matters.

Jake: That life helped him, it didn't hurt him. And the confusions are just another way of saying that it's the perfect getting in the way of the good. He gets over it by getting out of beta, going to alpha, and going to theta.

Therapist: How would you put it all together, if you would summarize all of what you have seen here today?

Jake: If he stood there and did nothing but felt his feelings and got outside of himself, the inner world would be his.

Therapist: I love it. Isn't that incredible?

Jake: It's so simple from this perspective.

Therapist: What would you like to tell Jake?

Jake: Just the basics. His breathing was inhibited from birth because of that murder. He just has to get back to watching his breathing, to simply let it go, to simply stand in the morning and do postures, or whatever he thinks makes him get in touch with his feelings and his higher Self.

Therapist: Beautiful. You have boiled this down to an elegant simplicity. Is there any other question that Jake has for your higher Self?

Jake: He will grow past these constructs.

Therapist: What you just said is the secret to everybody's liberation.

Jake: It should be easy for everyone. But what he sees around him now is people who are polarized. People can't let go of the hatred or the constructs, and they're all paralyzed.

Therapist: It's a good analogy. It's our responsibility to transcend because there is no escape from this duality.

Jake: He is close enough, he's chipping away.

Therapist: Now that you've answered that question for Jake, is there a final word that you have for Jake?

Jake: Relax, enjoy. The internal path will eliminate the constructs and then what happens here won't matter.

Therapist: Beautiful, that's it. Now, is there anything else or do you feel we've seen what we needed to see today?

Jake: Yes, he knows that karma travels with you. So whether he took a life in India in the 1500s, or he took a life in Kansas in 1800, it doesn't matter. His lessons are the lessons till you get tired of the lessons and you get past the lessons. So I would only suggest to him that if he's getting tired of it, he has the path out. And he may not take the direct route, but time is on his side. He's far closer than he thinks.

Therapist: To the degree he's able to transcend his consciousness, to that degree he's free.

Jake: True. And that of course gives him more choice in the matter.

Therapist: Karma still matters, because it either helps or obstructs the freedom of the mind, which is needed for transcending consciousness. If you create fires, you'll be so distracted putting out fires that you cannot get the mind into transcendental consciousness. Whereas if you clear up karma, there'll be more freedom and peace to connect.

Jake: He is on his way. He is freeing himself up of karma in this life. He has the chance now to make bigger gains, and the more he frees himself, the more the karma eases, it all begins to work for him rather than against him.

Therapist: You've come to this crucial point in your evolution where you are not passively subject to karma, but where you have the awareness to distance yourself from karmic bondages and place your mind into the highest state of consciousness.

Jake: As he understands it and has a get-out-of-jail-free card.

Therapist: Yes, beautiful.

Jake: He just must use it.

Therapist: You see, it took all these lifetimes to come to this understanding. It's not so easy to come to this point. And that's what all this time has done for your evolution, so you have understanding and power. And once you are here, and have this feeling of, "I have a choice now," that's where freedom begins.

Jake: Once he's there I think he would like to come back and help others. The most help he can give to everyone else is to help himself.

We slowly bring the session to a close here.

Case 25: Jake
Rising above duality

We continue the journey of Jake, a 69-year-old martial artist and Vedic astrologer, whose story started in our previous chapter. In his second session, we see his inner being unfolding, taking his previous experience to a whole new level.

Jake: I'm outside. But the building is open.
Therapist: What kind of building is this?
Jake: Stone.
Therapist: Tel me more.
Jake: It's nice.
Therapist: OK.

Jake: There are grapes.

Therapist: I see.

Jake: And nice furnishings.

Therapist: You say the building is open. Is this some kind of patio? What does it look like?

Jake: Maybe it's a courtyard.

Therapist: OK.

Jake: There are steps.

Therapist: When you look around you, the general environment, what does the place look like?

Jake: It's a courtyard, a walled enclosure.

Therapist: Is it a garden?

Jake: Not with flowers, but with vines.

Therapist: Looking down, what do you wear on your feet?

Jake: Sandals.

Therapist: What else do you wear?

Jake: A robe.

Therapist: What kind of robe?

Jake: A single piece but draped.

Therapist: What is the color of your skin?

Jake: White but tanned.

Therapist: What's the color of your hair?

Jake: Maybe blonde that's turning light brown.

Therapist: What's your age right now?

Jake: I'm aging through life.

Therapist: Let's start first here on this patio.

Jake: I'm blonde as a child.

Therapist: Are you a boy or a girl?

Jake: A boy.

Therapist: Where in the world are we now?

Jake: Crete.

Therapist: What date comes to mind?

Jake: A 1000, but maybe, BC.

Therapist: Are you doing anything on this patio?

Jake: Standing.

Therapist: Do you like it here?

Jake: I do.

Therapist: Looking at this patio and this walled enclosure, does it strike you as affluent, more normal, or perhaps even simpler than that?

Jake: Affluent.

Therapist: How do you feel?

Jake: I was brought up in this house. This house becomes mine. I'm driven.

Therapist: You're driven in what way?

Jake: To be important.

Therapist: You already feel that at a young age, you want to be important?

Jake: I'm molded in the household to be important.

Therapist: Okay, so it's your upbringing that asks of you to become important.

Jake: Yes. It's the culture. It's the aristocracy.

Therapist: Now if you look around this place, is there anybody else at home?

Jake: My father.

Therapist: Is he at home?

Jake: No. I can see his face.

Therapist: What about him? What does he look like?

Jake: He is a leader.

Therapist: He's important?

Jake: Yes.

Therapist: I see.

Jake: Not a king, but of military importance, which is also of political importance. He's always gone by ship but has darker hair than mine and darker skin.

Therapist: So, he's highly ranked in the military.

Jake: Now he seems to be more political.

Therapist: OK.

Jake: But he was in the military.

Therapist: I see.

Jake: He moved up. But he's always gone.

Therapist: How do you feel about your father?

Jake: He may now be in trade.

Therapist: How do you feel about him? I know he's gone a lot. But, when he's there, how do you feel about him?

Jake: I don't seem to know him well. He seems kind, always calm.

Therapist: Distant.

Jake: Yes.

Therapist: What's your name?

Jake: It starts with a D.

Therapist: Can you spell it out for me?

Jake: D-O-N-T-A-R-I-N-O

Therapist: Dontarino. Does that sound right?

Jake: Dontarino.

Therapist: Dontarino. Okay. I'm just going to call you a Dontarino. Okay?

I move him forward in his life as Dontarino.

Therapist: What is going on right now?

Jake: My parents are both gone.

Therapist: I see.

Jake: I inherited the house.

Therapist: OK.

Jake: I have a family. I seem to be like my father. I'm gone.

Therapist: What kind of work do you do right now, Dontarino?

Jake: Sailing. Trading.

Therapist: Are you doing well for yourself?

Jake: Diplomacy. I was not, and then I am.

Therapist: Initially, you were not, and now you are successful?

Jake: Yes.

Therapist: Did you have to learn it, is that why?

Jake: There seems to have been a war that didn't go well.

Therapist: And that affected your business?

Jake: Yes.

Therapist: When you say diplomacy and trading, are you doing that on behalf of the state or is this more for your personal affairs?

Jake: Both. But my personal affairs seem to be doing better than the country's affairs.

Therapist: Is something going on in the country that is not going well?

Jake: We seem to be ruled.

Therapist: Is there an aggressive force?

Jake: It seems that I have left the country.

Therapist: Where are you now then, Dontarino?

Jake: In Greece.

Therapist: You have left the island of Crete?

Jake: Yes.

Therapist: What happened to the house that you inherited?

Jake: It seems it's there.

Therapist: But you're not going back to it.

Jake: Not now.

Therapist: You say that like your father, you're always gone. What about your family? What are your feelings about them?

Jake: They're there. I'm here.

Therapist: You don't have any attachment to your wife and children?

Jake: It's not that I don't love them. I don't see them.

Therapist: How do you feel about that?

Jake: I wanted the life my father had. Now I have it.

Therapist: You mentioned earlier that trying to be important moves you and drives you.

Jake: Yes.

Therapist: Are you important and successful right now?

Jake: Not as important as I want to be.

Therapist: What is it that you want to do, Dontarino?

Jake: I was pushed into this life.

Therapist: By whom? By your upbringing, and your aristocracy?

Jake: I'm confused when I look back. The culture pushed me into this life. I thought my mother molded me into this life. But she was pushed into this life, no less or no more than I was, I suppose.

Therapist: When you say confused, on the one hand, you're saying you want to become more important, but on the other hand you say you're pushed into it, which is the predominant feeling?

Jake: They are one and the same. It wasn't really a choice.

Therapist: And you're okay with that?

Jake: Something happened in Crete.

Therapist: What was it?

Jake: There was certainly a takeover by another group. The life that I had is available now. But it can be available in another place.

Therapist: Was your life plan disrupted, causing further confusion?

Jake: The world is full of frailty, and I had security for most of my life.

Therapist: And then this happened?

Jake: I'm in maritime trade. I was not in the military. Crete has not fared well. But I am faring well. I'm having a drink.

Therapist: Where are you now, Dontarino?

Jake: I've come from a function. I'm home.

Therapist: Where is home?

Jake: Greece.

Therapist: Tell me more about you. How old are you now, Dontarino?

Jake: 40.

Therapist: Is your family still in Crete or are they here with you in Greece?

Jake: My family seems to have been killed. And I seem to have a different wife and young children.

Therapist: What is your emotional state right now at 40 years old?

Jake: Wondering how things might have been different had circumstances been different.

Therapist: That nobody invaded your island.

Jake: That life is gone. I make money and am fortunate. But

I'm part of the new culture, where I don't have power. I had political aspirations. I had my father's trade. I was successful. I was probably better at it than he was. But they're not my people.

Therapist: You cannot get involved in local politics?

Jake: I'm an outsider.

Therapist: Your political aspirations for more power are thwarted.

Jake: Just not possible.

Therapist: How do you spend your time Dontarino? Are you retired? Are you still working?

Jake: I'm still working. But people work for me.

Therapist: Are you more at home now?

Jake: I'm home. But it's not home.

Therapist: Right. You're in this place. How do you feel about your new wife and the children?

Jake: I don't like her as much.

Therapist: How does that make you feel?

Jake: Better than the alternative of not having anything.

Therapist: So, you make do?

Jake: This marriage was arranged for business, to do business.

Therapist: Her family is well-connected. Is that it?

Jake: Not politically.

Therapist: Financially?

Jake: With the port, with commerce.

Therapist: I see.

Jake: But I miss where I lived, the home and life I had.

Therapist: Right.

Jake: And the culture and the people that pushed me are gone. This is just, in a way, survival.

Therapist: Right. Now, Dontarino, if you would describe to me the most significant observation, either within you or around you at this moment in your life around 40 years old, what would it be?

Jake: There's not the joy of standing on that patio or that courtyard, where times are secure.

Therapist: Right.

Jake: The memories of the past are enjoyable. I feel that there is no real home except on a ship.

I move him forward in time. He jumps to the end of his life.

Therapist: How old are you now?

Jake: I'm about 60. A few years from 60. And I've just died. I'm glad it's over.

Therapist: Let us go back to the last day of your life. Just before you die. And tell me what is the cause of your death?

Jake: It seems to be sudden.

Therapist: What do you think about this life you lived as Dontarino?

Jake: In Crete, with my family, we were all one big womb. I long for security, I miss the security.

Therapist: Was it a big loss in your life?

Jake: Yes. The people I was successful for, and what I wanted out of life no longer existed.

Therapist: At the end, you felt you were not working for anything worthwhile?

Jake: I was working for security. And that, to make a joke, kept me afloat.

Therapist: I see.

Jake: My father liked life on a ship. I was better at the business portion and the trade portion.

Therapist: OK.

Jake: I grew tired of ships and sailing and being gone. I don't think he ever did.

Therapist: What did you learn from this life?

Jake: Security is in being smart because things change, people change.

Therapist: What does it mean to be smart?

Jake: Being smart allows you to adapt.

Therapist: How did you deal with this balance of finding security, being smart, and being able to adapt?

Jake: Mentally?

Therapist: Yes.

Jake: I was prepared by my mother and educated. And the people that I lived with, as an adult, weren't as smart or as cultured.

Therapist: What about your new wife?

Jake: She was. They were driven, and seafarers.

Therapist: So they had a great capability to adapt?

Jake: My father would have liked that kind of life and would have fit fine with these people, me less so.

Therapist: What is your last thought or awareness as you leave the body?

Jake: I miss my mother. I miss my wife.

Therapist: Which wife?

Jake: The first one.

Therapist: You've just died, and you're moving away from the physical body. Are you floating above your body or are you already gone from it far away?

Jake: I'm gone from it far away. My body was set fire to.

Therapist: How do you feel about your death?

Jake: I'm glad to be gone.

Therapist: What is the first thing you notice?

Jake: Everything is a gold color.

Therapist: How do you feel about this gold color? Is it an expanse of gold color?

Jake: Yes.

Therapist: What about you? When you look at your own soul-Self, does it have a color as well, or is it pure consciousness?

Jake: Consciousness. I'm looking down.

Therapist: What is your observation as you're looking down at this gold expanse?

Jake: I was looking down at a volcano.

Therapist: Does that volcano exist in a different realm?

Jake: I don't know. It's turned to mud and water.

Therapist: Is it a place that we need to get in touch with? Or is it just something that you're just observing from above?

Jake: I'm looking from above. I died in that volcano.

Therapist: I see. So, you're looking back at what happened at your death?

Jake: Yes.

Therapist: Was it sudden, like a lava burst, or a cloud or something that swept your body away? Is that why it was burnt?

Jake: Maybe I was one of the dead, maybe the lava flew over. Now I see floods, but this may be after the lava cools, and the rain comes, and it's just the passage of time.

Therapist: How do you feel seeing that?

Jake: I'm really just looking.

Therapist: You're just seeing the historical events unfold.

Jake: Yes.

Therapist: When you are ready to move away from that, let me know. You can go higher, connecting to the highest consciousness of your mind. And instead of looking down, see if you can connect to a higher frequency.

Jake: I realized my life changed and that world changed because the volcano took it away.

Therapist: Now that you're here in a disembodied state and you look back upon that life, how would you look at it from a more detached Soul perspective?

Jake: That trauma didn't go away nor did the longing to have that cultured kind of life.

Therapist: Do you feel that longing is still there with you?

Jake: Well……

Therapist: What is it that you had set out to achieve in that life? What is it that you wanted to satisfy, to learn, to understand, to develop in that life?

Jake: The nature of change. But more, the trauma of having everything removed brings everything that you hold on to into question.

Therapist: And you wanted to experience that in that life?

Jake: If you're molded in that life to be successful and to be important, it doesn't go away. But if everything else goes away, it doesn't mean anything.

Therapist: Help me understand.

Jake: In Greece, people weren't cultured. What I knew I wanted didn't matter. I couldn't find it. And so, the money meant nothing. What I had meant nothing to me. And whether I was a pirate, a military man, honorable, or less honorable, it was just about survival.

Therapist: Because the culture and the quality to sustain that experience wasn't there.

Jake: It wasn't anything that I wanted.

Therapist: All right, I understand that. But my question is from a higher perspective, now that you're looking at this as a disembodied spirit, knowing this was just one life. When I asked you, what is it that you wanted to experience in that life, you told me, "I wanted to experience what it's like to be in a situation where everything changes." To what end? What does your soul want from that experience? Not just as Dontarino, but from your Soul's evolutionary perspective?

Jake: How not to be angry.

Therapist: When situations change?

Jake: Yes.

Therapist: To what degree did you succeed?

Jake: It didn't.

Therapist: When we look at Jake's situation, when we look at Dontarino, we look at the life in Kansas, are some of these issues still at play that originated in that life?

Jake: Yes.

Therapist: Which one in particular?

Jake: In the second one, the world was taken away, and I was left. And I was unhappy because I didn't get what I wanted. In the first one, my life was interrupted. So, I don't know what it would've been like.

Therapist: Is that sense of dissatisfaction and sense of incompletion still at play in Jake's life?

Jake: Yes. I'm struggling with him.

Therapist: Why did your soul take up the circumstances of Jake? What is it that your soul wanted to fulfill or further develop through the circumstances of Jake's birth?

Jake: Part of the mission was to be a child to my parents and do a favor to my mother.

Therapist: I see.

Jake: To get to know a father. But he was still absent in his own way. But that began a second mission in this life, to work on the idea that when things get taken away or when things change, not be angry.

Therapist: And how is Jake doing in that regard right now, compared to Dontarino and to life in Kansas? Is he doing better now?

Jake: Better. But there's a self-centeredness that holds him back. One needs to get passed all of this. It's really to not be concerned about whether the world literally blows up.

Therapist: What is it instead then that your soul should be experiencing That one should be in a state of being that is not affected by the ways of the world?

Jake: At a soul level, I have everything that I need to be happy. And, as long as I'm caught up in attachments to the world, to people, to whatever, it's not enough just to be smart. That has nothing to do with being happy.

Therapist: Right. Let us take this very moment in this soul state to accentuate the experience of what it is like to be this soul, the one that is detached, the one that is divine consciousness, the one that is aware of its freedom. Can you get into that state right now a little deeper and feel what it's like to be in this blissful free, elevated state of consciousness? Find your mind expanding into that state further and deeper, away from all these births, just to remind yourself that this is who you really are. Do you feel that?

Jake: Yes.

Therapist: What if you could take this state back into Jake's life, how would it change things?

Jake: Compared to those other lives, this is heaven on Earth.

Therapist: If Jake could sustain such a state of well-being and spiritual enlightenment in his day-to-day life, how would it change his mental and spiritual state of being?

Jake: I think this is the umbilical cord I was looking for.

Therapist: Let's make that connection then that umbilical cord. So Jake will always be able to connect to this state, knowing that circumstances will change, that his wife will progressively get more ill, that he's going to have to be a caregiver, and that his own body will eventually get older. But that there is this umbilical cord that leads his awareness into this higher state of consciousness, that this is his true home, an ever-unchanging reality, which supersedes all these worldly ever-changing circumstances. Establish this strong connection now. How does it feel?

Jake: It feels wonderful.

Therapist: Let's have a look at Jake's interest in the East. Looking at it from this transcendent perspective, what are your thoughts about that?

Jake: Given my trauma in the past, there was always the idea that the world would evaporate, and that I couldn't find a better state to exist, that it didn't exist. And obviously, through meditation, one can know this does exist. If I get into the trauma and look at it in this detached way, it's a good lesson. There's nothing in the world that's going to get me back to the courtyard in Crete. There's nothing that could have kept me from getting shot. But martial arts made me feel better. It helped create a path where I could get back to inner knowing, of both body and mind. It has been a vehicle to get back to that spot, is, just like meditation has been.

Therapist: Right.

Jake: Vedic astrology too. A different method, but with the same results.

Therapist: It seems like in all these other lives you tried to achieve things in the world, only to realize that finding happiness in the world is a slippery path because things are always changing, and eventually all things will be destroyed.

But then you went full circle, started to retract, and said, "Well, if the world cannot supply me this stability, peace, and transcendent consciousness, I need to find it somewhere else."

And so, you looked at the Orient to find those techniques, an umbilical cord back into the state of calm, transcendent consciousness. Is that a good way of summarizing it?

Jake: Yes. I had a good mind in this life. When I used my mind, the lesson was that it would take me back into the world, where I would find pain. If I got past my mind, I was back on the path of light. In the same way that if you had a brain injury, you would create a workaround, I was using my mind as a workaround.

Therapist: And that is true spiritual intelligence, right? Not to apply it to things of the world, only to get more bound, but to use that mind to transcend itself and the world into a spiritual state of being.

Jake: Yes.

Therapist: Do you feel you've come to this point right now?

Jake: Yes. I've also come to the point where I have been around a lot of people who have had trauma. And, to see its lasting effects. To see the trap.

Therapist: I see.

Jake: I recognize it. Otherwise, I have to come back again and again and get immersed until I do. It's the equivalent of a bad relationship.

Therapist: You're breaking through the never-ending cycle of samsara. How would you advise Jake in these last years of his life and what would you tell him?

Jake: It doesn't matter if our body goes first, or if the world goes first, or whatever happens. What you have control of is to get out of duality.

Therapist: Beautiful.

521

Jake: Well, it's just the way.

Therapist: It is.

Jake: All of these paths that I found are essentially the same path. It can only lead me so far. If you're smart, it saves you from some pain. The next part of the journey, for me, would be to get out of the self-centered approach to remove myself from duality.

Therapist: How would you do that? Is it more of an attitude? Or is there anything practical that you would be doing?

Jake: To let go of me, myself, and I, and to transcend that I consciousness into service. And, whether it's astrology, meditation, or martial arts, it's just a method into alpha. That gets you to the next stop to get into where I am now.

Therapist: Yes, that is a beautiful summary. Is there anything else that comes to your awareness right now?

Jake: I'm fine.

We slowly end the session here.

Case 26: Sue
The executioner

Sue is a 45-year-old Southern woman, who stepped away from her Baptist strict upbringing. She is plagued by an incomprehensible sense of guilt and wants to understand why.

Therapist: What is the first thing that comes to mind?
Sue: A crowd.
Therapist: What can you tell me about this crowd?
Sue: They're angry and happy.
Therapist: Are they angry and happy?
Sue: They're screaming and happy and angry at the same time.

Therapist: Are you in the middle of it or are you watching from a distance?

Sue: I'm above it.

Therapist: You're above it? How are you above it?

Sue: I'm on a platform.

Therapist: You're looking down on it, from a platform above it?

Sue: I'm on the platform looking at the crowd.

Therapist: What can you tell me about this platform? Don't be afraid, you can just tell me.

Sue: Death.

Therapist: Is this an execution?

Sue: Yes.

Therapist: What kind of execution?

Sue: Women.

Therapist: Are you one of the victims? Or one of the executioners. Are you a man or are you a woman?

Sue: I'm a man.

Therapist: How old are you approximately?

Sue: Forties.

Therapist: What is your mood when you're standing here and witnessing this?

Sue: Powerful.

Therapist: Are you the one giving you orders or are you the one executing?

Sue: No.

Therapist: What is your role in this?

Sue: I bring them here.

Therapist: Is this your job?

Sue: Yes.

Therapist: Look down at your feet and tell me what, if anything,

you see on your feet.
Sue: Shoes.
Therapist: What else do you wear?
Sue: Pants.
Therapist: What do you wear above the pants?
Sue: A long shirt.
Therapist: Do you wear anything on your head?
Sue: Yes.
Therapist: What?
Sue: I can't see it.
Therapist: A hat of some kind?
Sue: Yes.
Therapist: What era or year comes to mind?
Sue: 15, 16.
Therapist: 15th, 16th century?
Sue: Yes.
Therapist: Where are we?
Sue: It's like a castle.
Therapist: Are you inside the castle?
Sue: It's a big yard inside the castle.
Therapist: What are your emotions when you're bringing these people here? You say you're feeling powerful. What can you tell me about it?
Sue: I'm scared.
Therapist: Yet you're feeling powerful at the same time. Is it because you have the power to bring these people here?
Sue: I am strong.
Therapist: Is it a huge crowd that is here?
Sue: Yes.

Therapist: Some are angry, and some are happy.
Sue: Yes.
Therapist: Who's giving the order for this execution?
Sue: It's a man.
Therapist: Who is this man? What is his role?
Sue: I don't know, but I'm afraid of him.
Therapist: Does he have anything to do with this castle?
Sue: Yes.
Therapist: Is he a king or a landlord of some kind?
Sue: Yes.
Therapist: Do you work for him?
Sue: Yes.
Therapist: I see.

I move her forward in the life of this man.

Therapist: Tell me what is happening now.
Sue: I'm alone.
Therapist: Where are you?
Sue: In a small room.
Therapist: Can you describe the room for me?
Sue: Stone. The floor is stone, but dirty with hay.
Therapist: What are you doing in this room?
Sue: Sitting.
Therapist: Are you locked up or are you able to go in and out?
Sue: I don't.
Therapist: How do you feel?
Sue: Not good.
Therapist: What's going on now? How old are you now?

Sue: My forties.

Therapist: How did you get to be in this room?

Sue: I think I was made to go here.

Therapist: How so?

Sue: I was made to go here.

Therapist: You were made to go. Is it some sort of cell block?

Sue: Maybe.

Therapist: Is it in the same castle where you were before or is it a completely different place?

Sue: I don't know.

Therapist: You don't know how you got here or even know who is responsible for this?

Sue: That man.

Therapist: How come? Did you displease him in some way?

Sue: I think he's crazy.

Therapist: He just locked you up for no particular reason? You're not aware of anything you did?

I try to move her forward in time in the life of this man.

Sue: I'm on a stage.

Therapist: What kind of stage?

Sue: There are lights.

Therapist: Describe the scene for me. Just walk around and tell me what is going on there.

Sue: There are people and they're watching me.

Therapist: Is it a performance of some kind?

Sue: I'm singing.

Therapist: Are you a good singer?

Sue: Wonderful.

Therapist: How old are you now?
Sue: 30.
Therapist: Is the same life that we're talking about?
Sue: No.
Therapist: I want you to go back to the life of this man who was locked up but to a time later and a different period in that life. What is happening now?
Sue: I don't see anything.
Therapist: Did you die?
Sue: I think so.
Therapist: Where did you die?
Sue: In that cell.
Therapist: I want you to go to the last moment of your life in that cell. How long have you been here in the cell?
Sue: Not long.
Therapist: Why are you dying in the cell?
Sue: I'm sad.
Therapist: Are you dying because of sadness or is something else going on?
Sue: I think I'm sick.
Therapist: What do you think about this life you just lived?
Sue: I don't like this life.
Therapist: Have you been able to learn something from this life?
Sue: I learned what fear looks like.
Therapist: What is your last thought as you leave the body?
Sue: I'm sorry.
Therapist: Are you still floating above it? Do you still see it?
Sue: I only see black.
Therapist: What are you feeling?

Sue: Cold.
Therapist: How do you feel about your death?
Sue: I'm not sad and I'm not happy.
Therapist: You're neutral about everything?
Sue: I am.
Therapist: What is the first thing you notice?
Sue: Warmth. Bright light. Bright, but warm.
Therapist: Is the light everywhere or is it just in front of you?
Sue: Everywhere. Everywhere.
Therapist: Does it feel like you have come home, or do you feel you're still traveling?
Sue: This doesn't feel like home.
Therapist: What does it feel like?
Sue: It's just a space.
Therapist: How do you feel within this space?
Sue: Warm and light.
Therapist: Do you have a form or are you also a light form?
Sue: I don't see a form.
Therapist: Stay here for a moment and enjoy this warm white space. Expand yourself in the best way you possibly can. What kind of place is this?
Sue: I'm healing.
Therapist: Be here and allow the healing to unfold.
Sue: Someone is waving to me to come to them.
Therapist: Go ahead and go there and tell me who's waving.
Sue: Michael.
Therapist: Is Michael a guide?
Sue: I don't know.
Therapist: His name is Michael?

Sue: I just know that name.

Therapist: What does he look like? Does he have a form or is he more like an energy form?

Sue: I just sense him.

Therapist: All right, just go to him. What is it like to come near his presence?

Sue: Powerful.

Therapist: Go on.

Sue: I feel like I'm becoming him.

Therapist: Tell me what happens.

Sue: It feels very good.

Therapist: What is his energy like?

Sue: Perfect.

Therapist: What does perfection mean to you?

Sue: Good. Love. Calm. Gentle.

Therapist: Allow it to integrate. Embrace it. Are you going somewhere or is this the place where you dwell?

Sue: I just am.

Therapist: Beautiful. Are you alone here or are there other beings here?

Sue: I don't see anyone else, but I'm not alone. I think I'm still with Michael. I think we're one.

Therapist: Now that we're with Michael, is this a good place to talk about a few things?

Sue: Yes.

Therapist: What can you tell me about this last life? You can look at it objectively without getting emotionally involved. This is all about learning and understanding your growth and your patterns. What needed to be learned?

Sue: I needed to make choices for myself.

Therapist: Help me understand. What does that mean?

Sue: I hurt a lot of people.

Therapist: How is making your own choices related to hurting people?

Sue: I obeyed.

Therapist: Your obedience led to hurting many people because you didn't stand up for yourself.

Sue: Yes. I was afraid. I was afraid.

Therapist: And as a result, you did what he wanted, and you hurt others.

Sue: And I hurt others.

Therapist: Before you started that birth, what was the plan?

Sue: I had the chance to make a difference.

Therapist: Go on.

Sue: But I was too afraid I didn't do it.

Therapist: In what way could you have made a difference?

Sue: I see a protector. I could have been a protector.

Therapist: And instead, you became a servant?

Sue: Yes.

Therapist: What does Michael say you should have done instead?

Sue: I needed that life.

Therapist: Help me understand why you needed that.

Sue: I needed to learn what fear looks like.

Therapist: What does it look like?

Sue: It's ugly. And I didn't like it, but I needed to understand it.

Therapist: What have you learned from that understanding?

Sue: That it has no place in my life. That it doesn't belong here.

Therapist: Could we also add that fear leads to a subservient nature, and subservient tendencies, rather than expressing the good qualities of the Self?

Sue: Yes.

Therapist: You needed to understand what not standing up felt like, and allow the fear to dominate and witness evil come out of that.

Sue: I caused fear. I brought fear to so many people.

Therapist: How?

Sue: As I was walking them to their death.

Therapist: What made you do that?

Sue: I want so badly to have another answer, but it was my pride.

Therapist: You're just being honest. Honesty heals once you understand.

Sue: I was proud. I thought I was doing the right thing.

Therapist: It gave you a sense of power?

Sue: Yes.

Therapist: A sense of identity?

Sue: Yes.

Therapist: From where you are now, from the Soul perspective, what are your objective observations about it now?

Sue: I don't ever want someone to fear me.

Therapist: Sue has this feeling and awareness that there is unwanted residue from a past life. Do you think this is where it originated?

Sue: Yes.

Therapist: The guilt?

Sue: Yes.

Therapist: But now that you look at yourself in the spirit world, how do you see yourself?

Sue: Pure, beautiful.

Therapist: This was just a lesson?

Sue: This was a lesson.

Therapist: If you look back upon this and turn this into a positive, how has this transformed you?

Sue: I choose love.

Therapist: Can we say that this terrible experience made you aware that what you choose is not fear, nor obedience, but love?

Sue: Love.

Therapist: So from that perspective, it has been a successful life.

Sue: Yes.

Therapist: Now that we understand this, does Sue still need to carry this guilt?

Sue: No.

Therapist: Looking down at Sue, do you see that residual guilt and fear in her?

Sue: It doesn't belong to her.

Therapist: But she was feeling it, correct?

Sue: She carries it.

Therapist: How can we release that now?

Sue: Choose love.

Therapist: Go ahead and do that for her, and I want you to tell me how you go about doing it with Michael.

Sue: Just breathing.

Therapist: OK, breathe love through, like flushing it out.

Sue: Flushing it all out.

Therapist: Good.

Sue: We're only filling it with love.

Therapist: Beautiful. Keep going until there's not one trace left.

Sue: I don't know if this ever stops.

Therapist: Well, let it go on in the background because love is infinite, right? Can we talk about Sue for a bit? What is the purpose of Sue's life?

Sue: Love.

Therapist: How is she doing in the manifestation of love?

Sue: She gets it.

Therapist: Is there anything that she needs to avoid that works against this love? Are there tendencies from the past that work against it?

Sue: I think she needs to be careful with what she eats.

Therapist: Where does that need to eat come from?

Sue: Trying to feel better or trying to find a reason to feel worse. I think she eats to feel guilty.

Therapist: Is it because of the guilt of the past?

Sue: Either she doesn't know how to release it, or she is comfortable with the feeling.

Therapist: How can we look upon this body from your real divine nature in the spirit world? Tell me what this body feels like in the divine realm.

Sue: It's strong. It's powerful.

Therapist: How does it feel? Does it feel heavy or light?

Sue: It feels powerful.

Therapist: What does power represent to you in the spirit world?

Sue: Perfection, completion. Strength.

Therapist: Can you transfer that to the mind and body of Sue? Let Sue's mind and body feel it. Can you feel it in the body?

Sue: I can.

Therapist: And in the mind?

Sue: I can.

Therapist: Realize that this is who you are. What do you want for this body?

Sue: I want it to feel pure.

Therapist: Isn't that the nature of your true Self? Is there any reason why this body and this mind couldn't feel this way as well? It's your choice, right?

Sue: I get it.

Therapist: What kind of work would be best for Sue?

Sue: Does she have to work?

Therapist: What is her purpose?

Sue: To hold space. To hold space for love.

Therapist: Isn't that the highest work? Purpose is a much more beautiful word. Does Sue understand what that means?

Sue: Yes.

Therapist: When we talk about self-love, has Sue been loving herself?

Sue: She does. She loves herself.

Therapist: Yet she's been wondering how she can love herself more.

Sue: I think I have released the guilt.

Therapist: OK.

Sue: It's hard to hold space for self-love when there's guilt.

Therapist: We're turning a new page. Now that you're releasing the residual guilt, what remains?

Sue: Pure love.

Therapist: That's all she needs. How can others connect to the true gift of who you are?

Sue: I think I need to touch people.

Therapist: How?

Sue: I need to share love.

Therapist: What is a good way for Sue to do that?

Sue: Physically. She needs to hug, hold and touch.

Therapist: Wonderful.

Sue: But there's something more, and I don't know if I'm afraid of it.

Therapist: Go on.

Sue: She may need to touch. She may need to heal.

Therapist: Work with her healing capabilities.

Sue: I don't know why that scares me.

Therapist: It may scare Sue but go back to your higher Self. During this process today, we can go back and forth. In and out of Sue. Whatever we need to do, we work both ways. Go back now into your higher Self with Michael. Now deep within yourself, listen to that call of the heart, the call of the divine deep within your essence. You said that more than holding space is required.

Sue: She just needs to be. She just needs to be love.

Therapist: She doesn't have to complicate it any further than that. Beautiful.

Sue: It's so real.

Therapist: To be a channel of love, basically?

Sue: Yes, love.

Therapist: So there's no need to teach, heal, or do anything complicated?

Sue: No.

Therapist: I want you to go back for just a moment and look at this other life where you're dancing and singing on stage. Let's just have a quick peek there. What can you tell me? Describe the scene to me.

Sue: Here is that crowd, but this time I am giving them

something beautiful. I am singing.

Therapist: You said earlier that you have a beautiful voice, correct?

Sue: I do.

Therapist: Tell me more.

Sue: I'm in a costume. Fancy, it's fancy. Everyone else is dressed up too.

Therapist: Are you inside or outside?

Sue: Inside.

Therapist: What does the place look like?

Sue: Beautiful. Ornate.

Therapist: Like an opera setting?

Sue: Gold. Yes.

Therapist: What time period?

Sue: There are wigs.

Therapist: Like Mozart's time?

Sue: I'm not sure timewise, but yes.

Therapist: You are an accomplished singer?

Sue: Yes.

Therapist: How does it feel to be on stage and sing like this?

Sue: It's beautiful.

Therapist: How do you feel when you're singing?

Sue: I feel like I felt when I saw Michael. It feels warm and bright and white, and I feel like every breath is love.

Therapist: Is this a life after the dark life or before?

Sue: It's after.

Therapist: I want you to go back to Michael again and place this in context with the dark life.

Sue: She was a performer in both lives. She was on stage, and she was sharing something with many people. In the first life, she chose something other than love. Maybe safety, maybe she was afraid. It provided her with safety. In the second life, she chose love. She chose to perform with love.

Therapist: Was that in reaction to this dark life?

Sue: Maybe.

Therapist: Get into it a bit deeper. There must have been a correlation between the two lives.

Sue: I think she hurt a lot of people. So she needed to heal people.

Therapist: To what degree was she successful after that life as a singer? Did it neutralize things?

Sue: No.

Therapist: There was still some residual left in Sue, right?

Sue: In all of her lives and his lives.

Therapist: What do you mean? All these lives in between?

Sue: I think all these lives carried a great deal of guilt.

Therapist: Until now?

Sue: Until right now.

Therapist: Are you finally ready to let it go, after all these years?

Sue: It's not mine.

Therapist: It was just an experience, right? Flush through some more of that love and let all that go now. Understand the big picture and see that along with love there needs to be an understanding of what happened. Through understanding comes forgiveness, and then you can let it go. You've carried your guilt long enough, don't you think? You've paid your dues. But also realize what beauty has come out of that. The awareness to choose love, pure love.

Sue: Yeah.

Therapist: Now, after everything we've seen today, looking at

Sue, who is now 45 years old, and knowing where we want her to go in the future, what else would you advise Sue?

Sue: I just want her to breathe.

Therapist: Breathe love.

Sue: Always love.

Therapist: I want you to go back to Sue for a moment and feel how Sue feels after everything we've gone through today, flushed, cleansed, understanding, full of love. Is there anything you want from Michael? What is it you need from him?

Sue: That feeling I had when I first saw him.

Therapist: Which is?

Sue: The feeling of becoming him.

Therapist: When Sue ever forgets and she feels small, she goes back to Michael and says, this is my identity. This is who I am. There's no reason to think that Sue in this life cannot manifest that. True?

Sue: True.

Therapist: Is that the goal?

Sue: Yes.

Therapist: Are there any questions for Michael?

Sue: No.

Therapist: How are you feeling?

Sue: I feel good. I would like to stay another minute with Michael.

Therapist: Stay as long as you want.

We slowly bring the session to an end.

Case 27: Tiffany
The fur trader

Tiffany is 25 year old Army lieutenant, as well as a therapist, who experienced a very difficult childhood with her mother. She also suffers from nerve issues in her shoulder. She's experiencing a lot of dreams and moments of déjà vu, that push her on a journey inward.

Tiffany: It's daytime.
Therapist: Are you inside or outside?
Tiffany: Outside.
Therapist: Are you alone or with someone?

Tiffany: I'm alone.

Therapist: Looking down at your feet, tell me what if anything you see or sense on your feet.

Tiffany: I'm on stone.

Therapist: Are you barefoot or are you wearing any footwear?

Tiffany: Barefoot.

Therapist: What else do you wear?

Tiffany: I don't know.

Therapist: Look straight ahead of you and tell me what you see in front of you.

Tiffany: Trees. I'm up high.

Therapist: Can you give me a general description of where you are?

Tiffany: I'm on top of something. I can see trees and mountain peaks in the distance.

Therapist: Is there snow in the mountains?

Tiffany: Clouds.

Therapist: What's the weather like?

Tiffany: Overcast. There are clouds, but it's bright.

Therapist: Is it cold, moderate, or warm weather?

Tiffany: It feels like fall.

Therapist: What are you doing here?

Tiffany: I came to look for something.

Therapist: Did you lose something, or you are trying to find something?

Tiffany: A person.

Therapist: You're looking for a person?

Tiffany: Yes.

Therapist: Why are you looking for this person?

Tiffany: They're important.

Therapist: They're important to you?
Tiffany: Yes.
Therapist: Did you lose them?
Tiffany: I didn't lose them.
Therapist: You didn't?
Tiffany: I didn't.
Therapist: What happened?
Tiffany: They got lost.
Therapist: Is it one person or multiple persons?
Tiffany: One person.
Therapist: This person got lost on the mountain?
Tiffany: They left. I think they meant to come back, and they didn't.
Therapist: Who is this person?
Tiffany: Close. There's a cabin. It is all made of wood and with a clearing.
Therapist: Is this your cabin?
Tiffany: It's my family's cabin.
Therapist: What does it look like? Can you describe it to me?
Tiffany: It's not big. From chopped down trees.
Therapist: How old are you now?
Tiffany: 16.
Therapist: Have you a better idea if you were a boy or a girl?
Tiffany: A boy.
Therapist: What's the color of your skin?
Tiffany: White.
Therapist: How many are in this cabin?
Tiffany: There's three of us children.
Therapist: What about your parents? Are they there too?

Tiffany: I don't see them.
Therapist: Do you think it's any of them who is missing?
Tiffany: No.
Therapist: It's somebody else that's missing?
Tiffany: Yes.
Therapist: Any idea who it is?
Tiffany: My sister.
Therapist: Why do you think she left on her own?
Tiffany: She's curious.
Therapist: She likes to go out on her own?
Tiffany: She likes to try.
Therapist: When you say try, does it mean she does it kind of secretly?
Tiffany: It's dangerous in the woods.
Therapist: Why is it dangerous?
Tiffany: There's something out there.
Therapist: Is it people or animals?
Tiffany: I don't know.
Therapist: How do you feel now that she's gone?
Tiffany: I didn't protect her.
Therapist: Is she older than you or is she younger than you?
Tiffany: Younger.
Therapist: So you feel bad about it?
Tiffany: Yes.
Therapist: Tell me about life in the forest. Do you live alone in the forest with your family?
Tiffany: Yes.
Therapist: There are no other families nearby.
Tiffany: They're miles away.

Therapist: Where are we? In which part of the world?

Tiffany: I don't know.

Therapist: What do you feel is the most relevant observation about this moment, either within you or around you as you're here in the forest?

Tiffany: It's getting darker outside. I still can't find her.

Therapist: How long has she been gone?

Tiffany: A day.

Therapist: What is your name?

Tiffany: I don't know.

I move her forward in this life as a boy in the mountains.

Therapist: Tell me what is happening now.

Tiffany: It's lightning outside, a lightning storm.

Therapist: Where are you?

Tiffany: I'm walking through a village.

Therapist: How old are you now?

Tiffany: I'm 19.

Therapist: Can you describe to me what this village looks like?

Tiffany: There's cobblestone. All the shops are made of wood.

Therapist: Is this village in the mountains or in a flatter area? Where are we?

Tiffany: It's in the mountains.

Therapist: So it's kind of a mountain town?

Tiffany: It's at the base of the mountain.

Therapist: Is it a big village or a small one?

Tiffany: It's average.

Therapist: What are you doing in the village?

Tiffany: I came to trade something. I have a pack on my bag.

Therapist: Is it stuff that you got from the forest?
Tiffany: It's stuff for my family.
Therapist: What is it that you're trading?
Tiffany: Fur.
Therapist: Did your family make those furs?
Tiffany: I did.
Therapist: Are you a good hunter?
Tiffany: I had to be.
Therapist: What do you trade the furs for in town?
Tiffany: Food. Not meat.
Therapist: No meat?
Tiffany: We eat the meat.
Therapist: Where do you go to get your food?
Tiffany: There's a woman who sells other food. She has treats for my sisters.
Therapist: Did your sister ever come back?
Tiffany: No.
Therapist: How do you feel now in your life at 19 years old?
Tiffany: My parents died. I have to take care of my family.
Therapist: Are you taking care of your sisters?
Tiffany: Yes.
Therapist: So it's the three of you?
Tiffany: Yes.
Therapist: How do you feel that you have to do this for your sisters?
Tiffany: That's what I'm supposed to do.
Therapist: You're okay with it?
Tiffany: Yes.
Therapist: Are you managing okay?

Tiffany: For right now.

Therapist: What do you mean by right now?

Tiffany: Winter was hard.

Therapist: Was it very cold?

Tiffany: It was.

Therapist: Is it harder to trap when it's winter? Or is it more the cold that is difficult?

Tiffany: It's the cold.

Therapist: Are you high up in the mountains?

Tiffany: Yes.

Therapist: How far from town are you where you live?

Tiffany: Three or four miles.

Therapist: Are you still living in the cabin with your sisters?

Tiffany: Yes.

Therapist: Are they younger than you?

Tiffany: Yes.

Therapist: What do you hope to do with your life?

Tiffany: Get into fur trading.

Therapist: Make it a bigger business?

Tiffany: Yes.

Therapist: Do you have any plans for that?

Tiffany: Talk with the French.

Therapist: With the French?

Tiffany: Yes.

Therapist: Why the French?

Tiffany: They need the fur.

Therapist: You're not French?

Tiffany: I'm not from France.

Therapist: Where are you from?

Tiffany: Just one of the colonies at Cayton.
Therapist: You're in America?
Tiffany: I'm in America. But it's not America.
Therapist: It's not America yet. The French are occupying.
Tiffany: Yes.
Therapist: Do you think of trading with them?
Tiffany: Yeah. I'm working with the natives. I've been away from home for a long time. I have to go send money back to my sisters.
Therapist: What have you been doing with the natives?
Tiffany: Trading.
Therapist: What have you been trading with them?
Tiffany: Fur and tools.
Therapist: How has business been?
Tiffany: It's been hard.
Therapist: How come?
Tiffany: There's a conflict.
Therapist: What kind of conflict?
Tiffany: I don't know.
Therapist: Is it between the natives and the other people?
Tiffany: Some. It affects a lot of people.
Therapist: Are you involved in it in some way or other?
Tiffany: They want me.
Therapist: Who wants you?
Tiffany: The French.
Therapist: Are you still trading with them?
Tiffany: Not as much.
Therapist: Mostly with the natives?
Tiffany: Yes.

Therapist: And the French want you on their side? Why do they want you?

Tiffany: I'm strong.

Therapist: Do you have any choice in the matter or are they just trying to convince you?

Tiffany: They're threatening my sister's engagement.

Therapist: So the French are politically involved in this area?

Tiffany: Yes.

Therapist: They can stop this engagement?

Tiffany: Yes.

Therapist: What are you going to do about it?

Tiffany: I feel torn.

Therapist: How so?

Tiffany: I have a good relationship with the natives.

Therapist: So the French are working against the natives?

Tiffany: Yes.

Therapist: What is it that they want from the natives?

Tiffany: Land.

Therapist: When you join the French, you would be fighting against your own friends the natives?

Tiffany: Yes.

Therapist: What do you end up doing?

Tiffany: I don't know.

I move her forward as this young man in time again.

Therapist: How old are you now?

Tiffany: I'm 25.

Therapist: You have been gone a while to collect money. Are you going back to your sisters now?

Tiffany: Yes.
Therapist: Are you far away from home as you're trading?
Tiffany: Yes.
Therapist: How do you go back to your sisters?
Tiffany: I need to get a horse.
Therapist: Do you buy it or borrow it? How does it work?
Tiffany: We had a good season. I was given a horse in payment.
Therapist: All right. How is the meeting when you see them again?
Tiffany: It's sad.
Therapist: How so?
Tiffany: One sister, she's sick.
Therapist: What happened?
Tiffany: I don't know.
Therapist: Is it serious?
Tiffany: We don't know yet.
Therapist: Which one is sick?
Tiffany: The next oldest.

I move her forward in time again.

Therapist: What is happening right now?
Tiffany: There's fighting. It's very cold.
Therapist: Who fighting?
Tiffany: They're hiding in the trees.
Therapist: Who is hiding?
Tiffany: The natives.
Therapist: What about you? Are you involved?
Tiffany: Yeah, near a stream.
Therapist: Did you join any party?

Tiffany: I had to join the French.
Therapist: And now you're fighting the natives?
Tiffany: I'm trying not to.
Therapist: How old are you now?
Tiffany: 32.
Therapist: What's your name?
Tiffany: Benjamin.
Therapist: What happened to your sister? Did she recover?
Tiffany: She got married and then she died in childbirth.
Therapist: What about the other sister?
Tiffany: She never came back.
Therapist: Is there anybody left of your family now?
Tiffany: No.
Therapist: Why are you still fighting for the French then?
Tiffany: I gave them my word.
Therapist: What is it like to be fighting this war?
Tiffany: It's cold.
Therapist: Are you in the mountains?
Tiffany: I'm not at the top. There's a lot of trees.
Therapist: Do you have any weapons with you?
Tiffany: Yeah. I had a musket, but I lost it in the water.
Therapist: What do you do now without a musket?
Tiffany: I have a knife.
Therapist: Are you with your platoon or are you separate?
Tiffany: I'm separate.
Therapist: Are you hiding out on your own?
Tiffany: I'm not hiding.
Therapist: You're not hiding?
Tiffany: No.

Therapist: You're fighting.
Tiffany: We have to separate.
Therapist: Everybody's kind of forming a line?
Tiffany: Yes.
Therapist: What is your state of mind as you go through this fighting?
Tiffany: I don't want to do it.
Therapist: How long have you been fighting?
Tiffany: A couple of years.
Therapist: What is the most relevant observation about this moment in your life?
Tiffany: I'm stuck.
Therapist: In what way?
Tiffany: I gave my word.
Therapist: So you have to stay with them?
Tiffany: But I don't make it easy.
Therapist: What do you mean?
Tiffany: There are women and children in the villages. I don't touch them.
Therapist: You don't harm them.
Tiffany: No.
Therapist: How do the French react to that?
Tiffany: They don't know.
Therapist: You're secretly trying to protect them?
Tiffany: Yeah. It doesn't work all the time.
Therapist: I bet it must be hard.
Tiffany: Yes.

I move him forward in time again.

Therapist: What is happening now?

Tiffany: I'm standing in the forest. There's no more fighting. My house is burnt.

Therapist: Are you there now near your old house?

Tiffany: Yes.

Therapist: Did you just come back from the war?

Tiffany: No, it's been over for a little while.

Therapist: What are you doing now that the house is gone?

Tiffany: I have to salvage. It's going to be winter soon.

Therapist: And you're going to make a new building?

Tiffany: Yes.

Therapist: How did it end up with you and the war? How did you manage to get out?

Tiffany: I was shot in the shoulder.

Therapist: Which shoulder?

Tiffany: The right one.

Therapist: What happened to your body after that?

Tiffany: I couldn't use the musket anymore.

Therapist: Are you still able to use your arm now?

Tiffany: Yes, but it hurts. I have to swing an axe with the other arm.

Therapist: You can't use much force anymore?

Tiffany: No.

Therapist: How old are you now, Benjamin?

Tiffany: 37.

Therapist: What do you now plan on doing in this phase of your life?

Tiffany: Rebuild.

Therapist: And what is it that you want to rebuild?

Tiffany: I want a family.

Therapist: I want you to move forward a little bit in time and tell me what happens next. Do you have a family?

Tiffany: A small one.

Therapist: Tell me about them.

Tiffany: Yeah. I have a wife. I have a daughter.

Therapist: How do you feel being a father and a husband?

Tiffany: Scared.

Therapist: How come?

Tiffany: I couldn't protect my sisters.

Therapist: Are you afraid the same thing will happen to them?

Tiffany: I'm afraid I won't be able to protect them.

Therapist: Where are you now?

Tiffany: We're in a house further down the mountain.

Therapist: Did you make this yourself or did you move into this house?

Tiffany: I made it.

Therapist: What do you do for a living now, Benjamin?

Tiffany: I'm trying to farm for trade.

Therapist: You don't do any anymore fur trading?

Tiffany: Not as much.

Therapist: How come?

Tiffany: Relationships broke.

Therapist: With the natives?

Tiffany: With everyone.

Therapist: Is that because of the war?

Tiffany: Yes.

Therapist: Is it just you that broke relations or is everybody else kind of in a panic mode?

Tiffany: There's no panic. They just died.

Therapist: All your contacts died?

Tiffany: Some contacts died.

Therapist: So you had to adjust?

Tiffany: Yes.

Therapist: Apart from being scared for your wife and your daughter, what is the state of your mind in this phase in your life?

Tiffany: I need to keep building.

Therapist: Are you motivated?

Tiffany: I'm ready to get started.

Therapist: Right.

Tiffany: I had broken my leg.

Therapist: What happened after you broke your leg?

Tiffany: It didn't heal right.

Therapist: And then what happens next? Is it some infection of some kind?

Tiffany: I think so.

Therapist: Where are you now?

Tiffany: I'm in the cabin.

It seems he's seriously ill.

Therapist: Go to the last day of your life. Is there anybody with you?

Tiffany: My wife.

Therapist: How are you feeling as you're here on this last day of your life?

Tiffany: Faint.

Therapist: How has your life been during these last few years?

Tiffany: Peaceful.

Therapist: Have you been able to manage?
Tiffany: I managed.
Therapist: Have you been able to rebuild?
Tiffany: Enough.
Therapist: Is your daughter still there?
Tiffany: Yes.
Therapist: When you look back on your life, how do you feel about it, Benjamin?
Tiffany: Testing.
Therapist: In what ways?
Tiffany: Obligation over morality.
Therapist: How do you think you did?
Tiffany: I think I could have done better.
Therapist: In what way?
Tiffany: Not helping the French. I would've found my sister.
Therapist: Have you been able to learn certain lessons during this life?
Tiffany: You make the most of what's given to you. But it's hard.
Therapist: What is your last thought or awareness as you leave the body?
Tiffany: I'll do better.
Therapist: Is there anybody near you at the time of your death?
Tiffany: My wife.
Therapist: What are you feeling as you leave the body?
Tiffany: Relief.
Therapist: How do you feel about your death?
Tiffany: It was time. I'll stay a minute.
Therapist: What do you want to do while you stay for a minute?
Tiffany: Say goodbye to my sister.

Therapist: How do you reach out to her?

Tiffany: I feel for her.

Therapist: Is she able to pick up on it?

Tiffany: I think she can somehow.

Therapist: How does it make you feel as you reach out to her?

Tiffany: Hopeful.

Therapist: Do you wish to reach out to someone else or are you ready to go?

Tiffany: I'm ready to go. It's beautiful.

I move her to a higher level of awareness.

Therapist: What do you notice? What do you see?

Tiffany: Shades of color, purple.

Therapist: Is it everywhere around you or is it near you?

Tiffany: It's around me.

Therapist: Beautiful. Do you have a feeling that you have arrived in this place? Or do you have a feeling you're still moving?

Tiffany: I feel like I've arrived.

Therapist: Beautiful. Now, what about your own Self? What do you feel like?

Tiffany: Energy.

Therapist: Beautiful. Does the energy have colors or is it more like an awareness?

Tiffany: It's a soft glow.

Therapist: What does this color feel like?

Tiffany: Home.

Therapist: Take a moment and connect to it. And while you do that, sense around you and see if there are perhaps any other beings here. Just take your time and sense around you. Tell me what you become aware of.

Tiffany: There are small glows in the distance.

Therapist: Are there many or are there just a few?

Tiffany: Just a few.

Therapist: Are they to your left, to your right, or in the middle?

Tiffany: In the middle.

Therapist: All right. Just move towards them while they move towards you. And when you reach, tell me who's here to connect with you.

Tiffany: Someone I've known.

Therapist: Is it somebody you've known at the astral level or somebody you've known on Earth?

Tiffany: On Earth.

Therapist: Is that soul welcoming you?

Tiffany: Yes.

Therapist: What happens during this welcoming?

Tiffany: They welcome me back.

Therapist: Multiple beings?

Tiffany: There are two.

Therapist: What is your relationship with them? Do they belong to your group or are they like a welcome party?

Tiffany: They feel like my group, but they're the ones who welcome me back.

Therapist: And they are also part of the group?

Tiffany: Yes.

Therapist: Your soul group?

Tiffany: Yes.

Therapist: Are they also nearby?

Tiffany: I can sense them.

Therapist: Tell me what happens as you approach the group and you're being welcomed by these two.

Tiffany: What I learned.
Therapist: You're discussing with the group what you learned.
Tiffany: Yes.
Therapist: Is there anybody taking the lead or is it everybody involved?
Tiffany: One of the two that welcomed me.
Therapist: Is that kind of an elder of the group or a guide?
Tiffany: A guide.
Therapist: Do you recognize this guide? Is that somebody who's been with you before?
Tiffany: At the astral level.
Therapist: Is it a male, a female, or an androgynous kind of energy?
Tiffany: Androgynous.
Therapist: Tell me about this conversation with the guide. What does it say about how you did in the life of Benjamin?
Tiffany: It was about moral obligation, not a physical one.
Therapist: Help me understand.
Tiffany: I had strong emotions, but I didn't always listen to them.
Therapist: What does that mean in regard to moral obligations?
Tiffany: I was in the war for a reason, but I fought against my emotions.
Therapist: Was that your love for the natives?
Tiffany: Yes.
Therapist: What does the guide say about that?
Tiffany: I tried to make both sides happy. It didn't work.
Therapist: What does the guide suggest you could have done instead?
Tiffany: Follow my instincts.

Therapist: In this case, what would've been those instincts?

Tiffany: The natives.

Therapist: You should have followed your heart instead.

Tiffany: Yes.

Therapist: Was that the tussle between the obligation that you thought you had towards your sisters versus following your heart?

Tiffany: Yes.

Therapist: The guide says that you should have followed your heart instead of these moral obligations?

Tiffany: You could find a moral explanation for following your instincts.

Therapist: So you could have thought it through a little bit deeper. Is that it?

Tiffany: Yes.

Therapist: Why did you make that choice then? Was it made out of fear?

Tiffany: The unknown.

Therapist: The fear of the unknown?

Tiffany: Yes.

Therapist: You surrendered your instinct to the fear of the unknown?

Tiffany: Yes.

Therapist: What else does the guide say about your life as Benjamin?

Tiffany: My sister was supposed to be lost.

Therapist: She was?

Tiffany: Yes.

Therapist: So it wasn't your fault?

Tiffany: It was a test.

Therapist: What kind of test?

Tiffany: It needed to happen to put the pieces in play for when the war came.

Therapist: Can you help me understand what that means?

Tiffany: The emotions I went through when she got lost were necessary. I had to get stronger with my emotions.

Therapist: So it helped you get in touch with your inner feelings?

Tiffany: Yes. I was supposed to face them then.

Therapist: But you didn't?

Tiffany: I did not.

Therapist: What plan was made before starting Benjamin's life? What needed to be accomplished or worked on?

Tiffany: To listen to instinct and to trust.

Therapist: How well did you do in the grand scheme of things?

Tiffany: I didn't do as well this time.

Therapist: Let's look at Tiffany's life. What is the theme of Tiffany's life? What is she here to learn?

Tiffany: To embrace instincts.

Therapist: So it's a continuation of Benjamin's theme?

Tiffany: Yes.

Therapist: How is she doing in that regard now?

Tiffany: Better.

Therapist: She's picking up from where she left off, and she's doing much better this time around.

Tiffany: We had different tests.

Therapist: You mean Benjamin and Tiffany had different tests?

Tiffany: Yes.

Therapist: What are some of the big tests that have been taking place in Tiffany's life?

Tiffany: She had a rough childhood, emotionally. She lost

her siblings, but she can get them back. She should trust her instincts and her emotions.

Therapist: This time, she should follow her instincts and her emotions.

Tiffany: Yes.

Therapist: Are those siblings in any way related to the life of Benjamin? Or are they different souls altogether?

Tiffany: Related.

Therapist: In what way?

Tiffany: I'm not sure.

Therapist: What role should Tiffany play in this lifetime? What can the guide tell us about that? She feels drawn to be in the field of service and helping others.

Tiffany: Somewhere where she can touch people.

Therapist: What would it be?

Tiffany: Healthcare. She needs to build something.

Therapist: For herself?

Tiffany: And others.

Therapist: What do you mean by building something? Help me understand.

Tiffany: Create something. An instrument.

Therapist: Help me understand what you mean by that.

Tiffany: A tool that she can help create.

Therapist: In a literal sense?

Tiffany: Yes.

Therapist: As a technique or an actual physical tool?

Tiffany: A physical tool.

Therapist: Can you give her an indication as to what that could be, to help her on her way?

Tiffany: It has to do with neurons and connections.

Therapist: She needs to develop a tool that will help with the neurology of connections in human beings.

Tiffany: Yes.

Therapist: How will she do that? What path does she need to take to set that in motion?

Tiffany: She needs to learn how the mind works.

Therapist: From a neurological standpoint?

Tiffany: Yes.

Therapist: Does she need to go back to school for that or what does she need to do?

Tiffany: She needs to go back to school.

Therapist: What kind of school?

Tiffany: Where they teach psychology and anatomy.

Therapist: Is that something she can do while she's in the army or do it after she leaves the army?

Tiffany: She can do it during.

Therapist: She can start right now?

Tiffany: Yes.

Therapist: Some kind of University program.

Tiffany: Yes.

Therapist: Like neuroplasticity or something like that?

Tiffany: That's the field.

Therapist: What kind of role does karma play in her current life? Are there any karmic forces at play in her life or is it more about lessons?

Tiffany: Lessons.

Therapist: So there's nothing standing in the way?

Tiffany: She needs to learn to let go.

Therapist: Let go of what?

Tiffany: The fear of the unknown.

Therapist: Is that something that had its origin in Benjamin's life?

Tiffany: It started before Benjamin.

Therapist: Is she still holding on to this fear of the unknown?

Tiffany: A little.

Therapist: Has this fear of the unknown influenced her decisions?

Tiffany: In her childhood, she got tired of being afraid.

Therapist: So she was aware of this fear when she was younger?

Tiffany: Yes.

Therapist: And so she has been able to redirect that?

Tiffany: Yes.

Therapist: Is she doing better?

Tiffany: She's not done yet.

Therapist: How can she overcome that?

Tiffany: She needs to follow her instincts.

Therapist: It's interesting. Fear becomes more prominent when there's less trust in her instincts just like it happened in Benjamin's life, correct?

Tiffany: Yes.

Therapist: As she listens more to her instincts, this fear is slowly disappearing. Is that a good way of saying it?

Tiffany: Yes.

Therapist: Excellent. Is Tiffany's mom part of the soul group?

Tiffany: Yes.

Therapist: Tiffany believes that her mom deliberately played a difficult role in order to help her.

Tiffany: Yes.

Therapist: Can you have a look at her true nature now and see who she really is?

Tiffany: She's a teacher.
Therapist: Look at her colors and her energy.
Tiffany: She's a soft yellow.
Therapist: How do you feel seeing her real nature now?
Tiffany: Strange but familiar. Acceptance.
Therapist: Why did she take up this difficult role?
Tiffany: The last test didn't work.
Therapist: What was the last test?
Tiffany: The sister.
Therapist: She was the sister?
Tiffany: No, she was part of the idea.
Therapist: The sister ran away and it evoked an emotional state in Benjamin, but it wasn't strong enough and didn't produce the correct result.
Tiffany: No.
Therapist: So this time something more intense was needed?
Tiffany: Yes.
Therapist: Did it work this time?
Tiffany: Yes.
Therapist: That's pretty incredible, is it not?
Tiffany: Yes.
Therapist: How does it make you feel realizing that now?
Tiffany: I feel like I've learned something, but I can't put it into words.
Therapist: How would you express it emotionally?
Tiffany: It rounds things out and smoothes it.
Therapist: Wonderful. When we look at your soul group as a whole, what is its character?
Tiffany: Calm, but eager.

Therapist: Eager for what?

Tiffany: Expansion.

Therapist: They're all into expansion?

Tiffany: Growth.

Therapist: Growth towards what? What is your end goal as a group?

Tiffany: To go higher.

Therapist: What does that look like?

Tiffany: The lights come together. As one continuous glow.

Therapist: A oneness?

Tiffany: Yes.

Therapist: Beautiful. Is it just the group that becomes one or does the group itself become as if one with everything?

Tiffany: It starts with the group. It's like a branch.

Therapist: Like a unified consciousness that then branches out into something bigger?

Tiffany: Yes.

Therapist: What does that look like?

Tiffany: It's calm and there's peace. It's a feeling of a purpose being fulfilled.

Therapist: When you mention a branch, do you mean to say that other groups also become part of the tree and unify?

Tiffany: Yes.

Therapist: Together as One.

Tiffany: Yes. There are different groups that form different branches.

Therapist: Beautiful.

Tiffany: But they all lead into the same trunk.

Therapist: At the end of the day, the goal is to become one.

Tiffany: Yes.

Therapist: Tiffany feels that though her mind is strong, her body is struggling. What can the guide tell us about this?

Tiffany: She has to trust the emotion. She's been given a more fragile body than Benjamin.

Therapist: Are you saying that if she had a stronger body she would not be forced to be aware of her emotions?

Tiffany: She would not be as aware.

Therapist: Is there anything that she can do to strengthen it?

Tiffany: She should fuel her body.

Therapist: With what?

Tiffany: She needs to care for it. It seems more like a nuisance to her right now.

Therapist: She should embrace it more and not see it as an enemy.

Tiffany: Yes.

Therapist: And to fuel it, to take care of it, to nurture it?

Tiffany: Yes.

Therapist: Do you think that that gunshot wound in Benjamin's life is still emotionally carried over affecting Tiffany's shoulder?

Tiffany: It wasn't a gunshot wound. It was an arrow.

Therapist: I see. Is it still affecting her today?

Tiffany: Yes.

Therapist: Is there a way the guide perhaps can help with this?

Tiffany: With energy.

Therapist: How could you go about starting that process?

Tiffany: I'll just be here for a moment.

Therapist: Do you want to be quiet for a moment?

Tiffany: Yes.

Therapist: All right. Just stay there for a moment and go through it. And let me know when you're done, okay?

Tiffany: Yes….. I am good now.

Therapist: Tell me what happened.

Tiffany: It was nurturing.

Therapist: Has the guide been able to help you with it?

Tiffany: My group was.

Therapist: OK. Do you feel that the energy has changed in your shoulder?

Tiffany: Enough of it.

Therapist: Good. Excellent. This will help definitely with the healing process, right?

Tiffany: Yeah.

Therapist: How would you summarize the most important theme of your soul journey?

Tiffany: You must trust yourself to fail. But trust yourself to grow. That's the only way.

Therapist: To not be afraid?

Tiffany: Yes.

Therapist: Is there any issue that we haven't discussed?

Tiffany: There was an emotional moment when Tiffany saw a large wave the size of a mountain. She wants to know why that affected her.

Therapist: What does the group say?

Tiffany: That was one of her first deaths.

Therapist: Some sort of tsunami in another lifetime?

Tiffany: Bigger than a tsunami.

Therapist: A massive flood?

Tiffany: Yes.

Therapist: You're just now remember that trauma?

Tiffany: She remembers the fear.

Therapist: Is that fear still an issue today?

Tiffany: Yes.

Therapist: Is there anything we can do with the guide and the group present?

Tiffany: They give me the reassurance that it was a different life.

Therapist: Do you think that is enough of a help?

Tiffany: Yes.

Therapist: This was not a premonition, but a memory, correct?

Tiffany: Yes.

Therapist: And therefore, it has no relevance in this life?

Tiffany: Yes.

Therapist: How are you feeling? Are you satisfied?

Tiffany: Satiated.

Therapist: Excellent.

We slowly bring the session to an end.

Case 28: Lynn
The little girl in the forest

Lynn is a 73-year-old College Professor who came to the session at the request of her husband Derick, whose case we've seen in chapter 5. Had it not been for his encouragement, the case of this very shy and most wonderful soul would have been lost to us.

Therapist: Tell me, is it daytime or nighttime?
Lynn: Daytime.
Therapist: Are you inside or outside?
Lynn: Outside.
Therapist: When you look straight ahead of you what do you see?

Lynn: A forest.
Therapist: Is it a dense forest or an open forest?
Lynn: It's rather dense. With a waterfall.
Therapist: Are you close to the waterfall?
Lynn: I can see it.
Therapist: What do you wear on your feet?
Lynn: I'm barefoot.
Therapist: What else do you wear?
Lynn: Just a very simple gown. Very simple.
Therapist: Is it made out of one piece or multiple pieces?
Lynn: One piece. With a belt.
Therapist: What's the material?
Lynn: It's woven. I don't know what it's made of. It's comfortable.
Therapist: What is the color of the skin?
Lynn: Like flesh.
Therapist: Does it have a color?
Lynn: Tan.
Therapist: Are you a boy or a girl?
Lynn: A girl.
Therapist: How old approximately?
Lynn: 12.
Therapist: What does your hair look like?
Lynn: It's long.
Therapist: What color?
Lynn: Dark. Almost black, not black. But almost black.
Therapist: How do you feel near this waterfall?
Lynn: Very peaceful.
Therapist: Is there anything in particular you are doing here?
Lynn: I'm just listening.

Therapist: What do you feel when you are listening to the forest?

Lynn: I'm just happy. I feel really close to God.

Therapist: Where do you live? Do you live nearby?

Lynn: I guess I live in the forest.

Therapist: Are your parents or your people nearby?

Lynn: Not very close.

Therapist: Why don't you go there and tell me what the place where you live looks like?

Lynn: I live by myself. I've made it kind of a safe place. I'm using branches.

Therapist: Like a hut of some kind?

Lynn: Oh..It's not really a house. It's just a shelter.

Therapist: And you live alone in this shelter?

Lynn: Yes.

Therapist: How come you're living alone at such a young age? Where are your parents?

Lynn: I don't know.

Therapist: Have you always lived alone?

Lynn: Yes.

Therapist: How do you feed yourself?

Lynn: From the forest. I find food.

Therapist: Interesting. You never feel lonely?

Lynn: Oh, I can go and see people and talk to them.

Therapist: Where are these other people that you can meet?

Lynn: In the village.

Therapist: What does the village look like? What kind of village is it?

Lynn: Rural. With simple houses.

Therapist: What kind of girl are you?

Lynn: Oh.. Well, the people like me.

Therapist: Where in the world are we right now? Any idea?

Lynn: Well, I guess, North America.

Therapist: What year comes to mind?

Lynn: I don't know when I'm here.

Therapist: How do you feel?

Lynn: I'm happy. People like me. They like to listen to me talk.

Therapist: What are the things you talk about when you are with these people?

Lynn: About loving and helping people. About seeing.

Therapist: So you're quite the mystic.

Lynn: I guess so. Yeah.

Therapist: What does their little settlement look like?

Lynn: Out in the country. They farm.

Therapist: What do their houses look like?

Lynn: They're adobe.

Therapist: And the people themselves if you describe them, just pick one person, what does that person look like?

Lynn: It's simple. They make what they wear.

Therapist: They are close to nature and the earth.

Lynn: Well, yes. They farm.

Therapist: They don't think it's strange that a girl so young is living by herself.

Lynn: No. I've been there so long. They are just glad I'm there. They're glad to see me.

Therapist: Beautiful. If you described to me the most significant observation about this moment in your life, either within you or around you, what would it be?

Lynn: The light that I live in, it's peaceful. And the joy!

Therapist: The light of your consciousness?

Lynn: Yes, yes.

Therapist: What can you tell me about that light?

Lynn: Oh, oh it's God. It's God. It's all around us. It's what we are. And it's fun to experience the world.

Therapist: Beautiful. Beautiful.

I move her forward in her life as this girl.

Therapist: What is happening now?

Lynn: I'm a young woman now. There's a young man who likes me. And I like him. But we're still in the same place.

Therapist: Is he from the village?

Lynn: Yes.

Therapist: What happens next?

Lynn: Well, I've become a teacher.

Therapist: Are you teaching?

Lynn: Yes.

Therapist: In the village?

Lynn: Yes.

Therapist: What do you talk about? What do you teach?

Lynn: We are talking about what we have, who we are. And they bring me their questions. I answer them. They're very happy.

Therapist: How do you know the answers to all these questions?

Lynn: I don't know.

Therapist: You just know?

Lynn: I just know. I know. It seems so obvious to me. Most of the time, at the beginning, they don't understand. So, I've learned to make a connection between what they do know and understand to what I am saying. And thinking about and exposing them to the world we live in. And that makes them happy.

Therapist: Has your life changed in any way from when you were a little girl?

Lynn: Well, I've become a woman.

Therapist: Your internal world, did it change in any way?

Lynn: I suppose my capacity to see and understand. I mean, I talk to God all the time. That's where I am, and I guess as I age, I'm more aware of that.

Therapist: Do you still live alone?

Lynn: Well, the young man stays with me sometimes.

Therapist: But you're still in the forest?

Lynn: I like it there.

Therapist: What makes you live there instead of in the town?

Lynn: I like the forest better.

Therapist: Beautiful. What is the most significant observation about your life at this point as a young woman?

Lynn: Well, it's troubling, in a way. That I'm able to bear a child now. And I am not quite comfortable with that knowledge.

Therapist: You don't want that?

Lynn: Well, I am. No, it's not that I don't like it. I don't understand it. It's so incredible. That I could bear a life. That another life would be created inside me. And it's just amazing.

Therapist: Is that what is happening now? Are you with child?

Lynn: No, I'm not.

I move her forward in her life.

Therapist: Tell me, what is happening now.

Lynn: I had a child. It's growing. It's a delight to me to see it grow and become aware. I still live in the forest. But people still come, from far away sometimes. Just to visit. And I teach. I teach my child, how to be human. A happy time.

Therapist: Is that young man still living with you?

Lynn: Yes.

Therapist: You are a family unit now?

Lynn: Yes.

Therapist: Did anything change in your internal world after bearing this child?

Lynn: Well, I think the dimensions of life. The possibilities of life are greater. Because of, not just me, but this little person.

Therapist: Are you still going to the villages to teach? Or are they coming to you now?

Lynn: They come to me more. But, if I'm asked to go somewhere else if I can, then I'll go.

Therapist: Is it just knowledge you're sharing or is it also medicine?

Lynn: What I know of medicine. The natural arts. The plants.

Therapist: So some healing of the body is involved?

Lynn: Yes.

Therapist: Beautiful. Now let us jump forward to mid-age. On the count of 3. 3,2,1, you are there and tell me what is going on now.

Lynn: I'm becoming older. My hair is gray. The child is grown and gone.

Therapist: How do you feel?

Lynn: Sad.

Therapist: Because it's gone?

Lynn: Yes.

Therapist: What happened to the light in your mind?

Lynn: The light?

Therapist: The light, talking to God?

Lynn: That's the same. And that's my comfort.

Therapist: OK.

Lynn: It's a whole new dimension of life. But the light holds on to it in the same way.

Therapist: When you commune with the light and with God, what happens to you during that state?

Lynn: I have a cocoon that I see inside me. It's made from light that is spun, like silk. And it shines. It's kind of golden but it's not. It's light. And when I'm sad, that's where I go. In my mind, I go there. And then everything's better.

Therapist: Does God go into that cocoon as well?

Lynn: It is. He is.

Therapist: He is the cocoon.

Lynn: Yes. Yes.

Therapist: Is that where you get your knowledge from? You commune directly with God?

Lynn: I think so. It's just so natural. It has always been part of me and I guess I don't always understand why I'm this way. People don't realize that it could be the same for them.

Therapist: The knowledge just kind of flows through you effortlessly.

Lynn: It's just there.

Therapist: You were always like this; from the day you were born?

Lynn: Well, I think so. I've always known it. When I was growing up and I would see things like the winter and the snowflakes, I always felt like laughing. I always felt like laughing because that was God, and it was obvious. It was so obvious to me.

I move her to the last day of her life.

Therapist: How old are you on this last day of your life?

Lynn: 87

Therapist: Is there anything going on around you or within you that would suggest that your physical death will come this day?

Lynn: I know that I'm going away and I'm going to go to sleep. And it's good.

Therapist: Is anything going on with the body?

Lynn: Oh, I'm tired. The body's tired.

Therapist: Where are you now?

Lynn: In the forest.

Therapist: Is there anybody with you?

Lynn: No.

Therapist: What do you think about this life you just lived?

Lynn: Very happy. It's been hard sometimes.

Therapist: In what way?

Lynn: Oh, seeing the child go away. That was hard. But I understand that there's more to God than I know. And that it was okay.

Therapist: What did you learn from this life?

Lynn: That God is everything. Everything that is. And that all we have to do is be able to see it. Once you see it and you know it, it changes the way we experience things.

Therapist: What have you been able to learn and develop in your relationship with God and nature?

Lynn: That, sometimes, even pain is part of God.

Therapist: In what way?

Lynn: Seeing things that hurt someone, cruelty, doesn't make sense to me. But I know that it's part of what is. I have to think about wrapping that in my mind. And putting it in a box and carrying it to another part of my mind. And leaving it there.

Therapist: So you are accepting it as part of the oneness of God's existence.

Lynn: Yeah, think I have to. How can it not be?

Therapist: Right.

Lynn: But I don't have to understand it. I don't have to make it part of me.

Therapist: It is what it is.

Lynn: Yeah, and so I just tuck it away in that little room.

Therapist: What are your last thoughts, awareness, or feeling as you leave this body?

Lynn: Oh, I'm glad to be finished with my work.

I move her past her death.

Therapist: What do you feel as you leave that body behind? How do you feel about your death?

Lynn: I don't feel much of anything. It's just another day.

I move her further.

Therapist: What is the first thing you notice?

Lynn: The music. It's all around. Pervasive. It's part of who I am and I'm part of the music.

Therapist: When you think of yourself as spirit, do you have a form, a light form, or is it just pure awareness, pure consciousness? How do you experience your divine self?

Lynn: Well, I am uniquely who I am. But I am also part of the light. Words don't work very well with this.

Therapist: Like each point is conscious, yet, I am infinity itself.

Lynn: It's just joy. There are other entities there, all around. But, you don't need a body to recognize another.

Therapist: Each point is conscious in and by itself. Is that what it is?

Lynn: It seems to be.

Therapist: Is there any sort of communion?

Lynn: Words are too little. I'm no longer alone. The last time I had a body I recognized God when I was just a child. And that never left me. But now, I don't need the body, and I am glad.

Therapist: Without the body, is that communion even stronger and better?

Lynn: Oh yes. There are no distractions. None at all.

Therapist: Only God consciousness exists?

Lynn: I mean, that's all there is. Consciousness of God. And my consciousness is God. Just like I am now.

Therapist: Like a drop in the ocean.

Lynn: I guess. It's like Life. More than water.

Therapist: Beautiful. What made you choose the life of this girl in the forest?

Lynn: I wanted to know the beauty of the earth. I wanted to sing my song.

Therapist: Beautiful. You don't incarnate all that often?

Lynn: Not anymore.

Therapist: So you're free?

Lynn: It just doesn't even come up. It doesn't.

Therapist: There's no need. No point?

Lynn: Yeah. I'm done.

Therapist: Why did you take birth as Lynn if there was no more need?

Lynn: It seemed to best express who I am. I was able to be who I am, better.

Therapist: Was there any particular plan for this life of Lynn? Was there anything you wanted to accomplish or express in this life?

Lynn: I just wanted to express and show people how beautiful God is. And how easy it is to be part of Him. To recognize that

I am part of Him. And these other people are part of Him. They don't see it sometimes. And so they are sad.

Therapist: Is that what you do? You live these lives to share the light of God?

Lynn: I try to get rid of the things that interfere with that.

Therapist: But you're not bound by karma, and you are already free in that way?

Lynn: I don't think of those things.

Therapist: You don't feel bondage in that way?

Lynn: No. Not anymore.

Therapist: Beautiful.

Lynn: I'm just happy that I have this body.

Therapist: What do you like about it?

Lynn: The experiences. I never know what I am going to experience in the next body.

Therapist: What is it that your soul wants to do or to be after this body is left behind?

Lynn: I just want to be with God. It's safe.

Therapist: No more births?

Lynn: No more pain.

Therapist: What do you feel right now?

Lynn: I feel like this is exactly where I am supposed to be.

Therapist: Accepting reality for what it is?

Lynn: It's good.

Therapist: What do you think were the similarities between your life in the forest and the life of Lynn?

Lynn: Well, teaching. There's an opportunity for teaching all the time. And there are opportunities for words to heal people.

Therapist: Beautiful. What are the main differences between these two births?

Lynn: I don't think I live in the forest.

Therapist: Yeah, that's true.

Lynn: I mean, where I am now is a good place.

Therapist: What about your internal world?

Lynn: I'm in a safe place now. It's quiet. There's laughter and there's music and there are opportunities to see reality here. And then, to see that God has upped that reality. It's very satisfying. And I see it.

Therapist: Do you think that Lynn can see God as easily as that girl in the forest did?

Lynn: Sometimes. Very much so, yeah.

Therapist: Beautiful. So she's never lost that connection?

Lynn: Well, whenever Lynn was in a situation where she was forgetting, something would happen. It reminded her. So she always knew.

Therapist: Never too far away from it.

Lynn: No, never. And it wasn't something that I did. It was just something that happened.

Therapist: Beautiful. Is there anything that Lynn still wants to do, experience, or achieve in the remaining years of her life on earth?

Lynn: I guess I've learned not to project. Because whatever comes is part of God too. I just need to be able to see it and understand it to find peace.

Therapist: Beautiful. Now, the spirit world is wide open to you. Is there anything else that we need to explore in this world?

Lynn: Not really. I don't want to choose it. I think that God knows exactly what I need to explore. And those things will come. And it really doesn't matter what it is. Because I think that I've learned to see it all as coming from God.

Therapist: Beautiful. The same feelings the girl in the forest had when she accepted everything as part of God.

Lynn: Yes. Oh yes.

Therapist: Beautiful. That is so beautiful.

Lynn: I wish I'd learned it sooner.

Therapist: But you do. In a past life, you had learned it already.

Lynn: I think that's why we encase ourselves with flesh so it's a vehicle to experience God in a unique way.

Therapist: Beautiful.

Lynn: And the joy of it comes when we wake up in a situation that was hurting us and we recognize what it really is. And then the hurt goes away.

Therapist: Yes, because we have a higher perspective of reality.

Lynn: Well, it's certainly different. It's bigger.

Therapist: How do you feel right now?

Lynn: Peaceful, happy.

Therapist: Is there anything else we need to experience?

Lynn: I'm very happy that I'm here.

Therapist: Would you like to stay a little bit longer in that peace, quietly? Are you ok?

Lynn: No. I'm fine. I'm good.

We slowly bring the session to a close.

Case 29: Jaimy
The golden bowl rom the temple of healing

Jaimy is a 35-year-old Southern woman who is seeking healing and a deeper understanding of life.

Therapist: Are you inside or outside?

Jaimy: Outside.

Therapist: Are you alone or with someone?

Jaimy: Alone.

Therapist: Look down at your feet tell me what if anything you see on your feet.

Jaimy: Shoes.

Therapist: What kind of shoes?
Jaimy: Boots.
Therapist: What kind of clothing are you wearing?
Jaimy: A dress.
Therapist: What is the color or the material of this dress?
Jaimy: Linnen.
Therapist: Is it a nice or fancy dress?
Jaimy: It's simple.
Therapist: If you look down at your arms and hands what is the color of your skin?
Jaimy: I'm white.
Therapist: What's your age approximately?
Jaimy: I'm young.
Therapist: When you look straight ahead of you, can you give me a description of your surroundings?
Jaimy: Beautiful, the sky is beautiful.
Therapist: What else do you see or notice around you?
Jaimy: An iron railing. It's rustic.
Therapist: What else do you notice? Take your time to observe this place.
Jaimy: I'm standing on a wooden floor.
Therapist: Is this in a city or a town?
Jaimy: Looks like homes.
Therapist: If you look around at these homes what style of homes are they? What era do you think this is?
Jaimy: Spanish.
Therapist: Do you notice any of the detailing on these homes?
Jaimy: The rooftops.
Therapist: And are there any other buildings like churches that

you notice?

Jaimy: The mountains.

Therapist: Take a moment and explore a little bit more. You can move around.

Jaimy: I'm standing in a dark room, like a shed.

Therapist: Where is this shed?

Jaimy: On a farm.

Therapist: Is this your shed?

Jaimy: I don't think so.

Therapist: What are you doing in the shed right now?

Jaimy: I'm just looking at the view.

Therapist: Describe that view for me.

Jaimy: There are red-orange-looking houses and a clear blue sky.

Therapist: How do you feel right now?

Jaimy: I'm just feeling calm.

Therapist: Have you noticed anyone else around you?

Jaimy: A male presence. I feel like I'm in a workshop

Therapist: Keep going.

Jaimy: I'm helping.

Therapist: OK, you're helping and who is this male presence?

Jaimy: It's family but I don't know.

Therapist: Can you go over to this man?

Jaimy: I walk over. He's working with steel. Looks like he's making a knife.

Therapist: Is he a blacksmith?

Jaimy: Yeah.

Therapist: Can you look a little closer at him?

Jaimy: His hair is dirty.

Therapist: What age do you think he is?

Jaimy: Close to mine.

Therapist: Could this be a significant other?

Jaimy: I don't think so.

Therapist: Is this perhaps a family member; a brother or a cousin?

Jaimy: I think he's my brother. He just keeps working away.

Therapist: Do you think you could ask him his name?

Jaimy: It's Samuel.

Therapist: Samuel. And what does he call you?

Jaimy: Patrice.

Therapist: What are you doing here in this shop with your brother Samuel?

Jaimy: Community.

Therapist: It's a community?

Jaimy: It's family work.

Therapist: So it's a family business.

Jaimy: Yes.

Therapist: Patrice, are you married or are you single?

Jaimy: I'm single.

Therapist: About how old are you now?

Jaimy: I'm in my 20s.

Therapist: And how are you feeling working in this family business?

Jaimy: I'm okay. I like to help.

Therapist: And who do you help or what do you help with?

Jaimy: The community fixing things.

Therapist: Are there any other folks in the community that you're close with or friends with?

Jaimy: I'm helping neighbors, yeah.

Therapist: Before we move on to another significant moment, later in this life as Patrice, is there anything else you'd like to share in this place or about this moment?

Jaimy: No.

I move her forward in time.

Therapist: Tell me, what is happening now.
Jaimy: I'm writing something, a letter.
Therapist: Do you know what this letter is about?
Jaimy: It's urgent, an urgency.
Therapist: And what's so urgent? What's happening?
Jaimy: Someone's sick.
Therapist: Do you know who's sick?
Jaimy: It's Samuel.
Therapist: It sounds like you and Samuel are close. Are you the one caring for him?
Jaimy: Yes.
Therapist: And who are you writing a letter to?
Jaimy: A doctor, a healer.
Therapist: You're trying to get some help for Samuel.
Jaimy: Yes, desperately.
Therapist: How are you feeling at this moment?
Jaimy: Desperate.

I move her forward in time.

Jaimy: He's dying.
Therapist: Tell me what else is going on? Are you alone with him? Or is there anyone else in the room?

Jaimy: No, I'm there now.
Therapist: Are you're married?
Jaimy: Yes.
Therapist: And is your husband there with you?
Jaimy: Yes.
Therapist: What's your husband's name?
Jaimy: John.
Therapist: What's happening now?
Jaimy: I can't do anything for Samual.
Therapist: Samuel is dying right now. Is that what's happening?
Jaimy: Yes, slowly.
Therapist: Is there anyone else there besides you and John?
Jaimy: No.
Therapist: Is there anything you say to Samuel as your last words before he leaves Earth?
Jaimy: I love him.
Therapist: Move forward in time a little to a time when things are peaceful.
Jaimy: I'm just cooking.
Therapist: Are you in your house?
Jaimy: John's house. My house.
Therapist: What's the energy like of your husband John, his character? Are you happy in your marriage with him?
Jaimy: I'm lonely.
Therapist: Is John not providing you with everything you need?
Jaimy: Yes, it's just different.
Therapist: Where are you now?
Jaimy: In front of the fire and I'm tired.
Therapist: What else is going on?

Jaimy: John's tired.
Therapist: How come you both are so tired?
Jaimy: We're just getting older.
Therapist: How old do you think you are here?
Jaimy: We're in our 50s.
Therapist: Are there any children around in the household?
Jaimy: We have a daughter.
Therapist: What happened to her?
Jaimy: She's grown.
Therapist: And what's her name?
Jaimy: Melinda.
Therapist: How is your relationship with Melinda?
Jaimy: Good.
Therapist: What are her characteristics?
Jaimy: She's always happy.
Therapist: What else do you notice?
Jaimy: She's excited about her life. She's just so happy.
Therapist: Take a moment and just enjoy the happiness of your daughter Melinda.

I move her to the last day of her life.

Therapist: Is there anything going on or around you or within you that suggests that your physical death will come on this day?
Jaimy: I'm in bed.
Therapist: Is this your own home?
Jaimy: My own home.
Therapist: What's happening now?
Jaimy: I'm coughing a lot. I'm sick.

Therapist: Is there anyone else around you?

Jaimy: John's there. Melinda and her husband too.

Therapist: How are you feeling right now, knowing that your physical life is coming to a close

Jaimy: Sad but ready.

Therapist: Are you sad because you have to leave your family behind?

Jaimy: Yeah, especially Melinda.

Therapist: Ah your daughter. What do you think about this life you just lived as Patrice?

Jaimy: It was hard.

Therapist: What did you learn?

Jaimy: It's about communities and community.

Therapist: How so?

Jaimy: How to help your fellow man.

Therapist: What's your last thought before you leave your body?

Jaimy: I'll miss them.

I move her just passed her death.

Therapist: Where are you now in relation to the body you just left behind?

Jaimy: I'm moving away.

Therapist: What do you notice about those who you left behind?

Jaimy: They are really sad.

Therapist: What do you see around you right now?

Jaimy: The sky.

Therapist: How do you feel about your death?

Jaimy: It's okay, but it was hard.
Therapist: What was so hard about it?
Jaimy: Because we were poor.
Therapist: What did you learn from that?
Jaimy: To keep trying.

I move her on to a higher consciousness.

Therapist: What is the first thing you notice? Describe everything that's happening so I can stay with you.
Jaimy. It's like a cloud that just hugs you. It's nice here.
Therapist: What does the space feel like?
Jaimy: Vast. Very large.
Therapist: What are you in relation to this vast, large cloud-like space? Do you have a form?
Jaimy: I'm just here, just existing.
Therapist: Do you feel that you're moving or are you staying here?
Jaimy: I'm staying for a minute. Sam is here.
Therapist: Would you like to connect to Samuel while you're here?
Jaimy: Yeah.
Therapist: Let's take a moment and connect.
Jaimy: His energy is good.
Therapist: What's Samuel doing now?
Jaimy: Just talking, he's just proud of me.
Therapist: Are you still talking to him?
Jaimy: No, now we're moving; onwards.
Therapist: Where are you being moved to?
Jaimy: I guess home.

Therapist: What do you feel?

Jaimy: Calm.

Therapist: Is Samuel also moving with you?

Jaimy: Yeah, we're together.

Therapist: So he's been waiting for you?

Jaimy: Yeah.

Therapist: Just keep on moving, allowing yourself to be drawn to your spiritual home. Know that a loving power is bringing you home to a safe place. Tell me when you can see beyond your immediate surroundings.

Jaimy: There are a lot of lights. It's like a Christmas tree.

Therapist: So there are multiple lights?

Jaimy: Yeah.

Therapist: Are you moving closer to it?

Jaimy: Yeah.

Therapist: If you could count the lights, how many lights do you see?

Jaimy: Four.

Therapist: Are they bunched together or spread out?

Jaimy: They are spread out.

Therapist: Are they moving?

Jaimy: Yeah.

Therapist: Does one seem any larger than the rest?

Jaimy: Yeah.

Therapist: And do you need to move to the right or continue straight ahead or move to the left to intersect or connect with the lights?

Jaimy: No, just moving ahead.

Therapist: Just float towards the light while the light floats towards you. And as the light comes closer to you and you move closer to it, I want you to notice if it's bright or dim, or perhaps even has a color.

Jaimy: It's blue.

Therapist: And is this just the one light that has come to you or are there multiple lights?

Jaimy: One is blue the other one is yellow.

Therapist: Can you describe the shape or appearance of these blue and yellow lights that have come to meet you?

Jaimy: The yellow one is circular, sphere-like. She's really happy to see me.

Therapist: So it's a female energy?

Jaimy: Yes. She's overjoyed.

Therapist: Who is this yellow spherical light that is so happy to see you?

Jaimy: I'm not sure. The blue light is happy too. It's more masculine.

Therapist: Is it possible for you to ask them who they are, and why they've come to meet you?

Jaimy: It's Gwen.

Therapist: And the other one?

Jaimy: Otis.

Therapist: Why have they come to meet you?

Jaimy: They're part of my group.

Therapist: They're part of your soul group?

Jaimy: Yes. And Sam is still here.

Therapist: Notice and sense this light of them enveloping you or around you. What's happening now?

Jaimy: Gwen grabs my hands and cubs them, telling me I did a good job.

Therapist: Do you know what she's referring to?

Jaimy: My life I just lived.

Therapist: The life of Patrice.

Jamy: Yes.

Therapist: Describe what you see and feel.

Jaimy: Her energy, she's overjoyed and happy that I'm here with them.

Therapist: What's their role? What do Gwen and Otis do in the spirit realm?

Jaimy: They both guide us.

Therapist: They are spiritual guides?

Jaimy: Yes. Leaders of my group. Otis is kind but he stands up. A masculin energy. He's authoritative. Gwen is loving and kind.

Therapist: Are there more details you notice about them?

Jaimy: They are usually together.

Therapist: They work together?

Jaimy: Yes.

Therapist: I realize no earthly speech sounds exist in this place, but are you receiving telepathic communication?

Jaimy: It's just feeling.

Therapist: You're feeling them.

Jaimy: Yeah.

Therapist: How do Gwen and Otis call you in this spirit realm?

Jaimy: Mell.

Therapist: Is it OK if call you Mell for now?

Jaimy: Yeah.

Therapist: Notice a few more characteristics about your guides so that you can add in your conscious mind all of the features and characteristics of your spirit guides so that these mental images will always remain with you. Are there any special messages that they'd like you to receive today?

Jaimy: There's an agreement to come here.
Therapist: To come to Earth?
Jaimy: Yes.
Therapist: What was the agreement for?
Jaimy: To learn.
Therapist: To learn what?
Jaimy: Kindness, helping others. That was agreed upon.
Therapist: How do you feel about it looking at it now?
Jaimy: Good. Just not what I thought it would be.
Therapist: Can you help me understand? What do you think it would be?
Jaimy: Things are not so evolved.
Therapist: What is not so evolved?
Jaimy: Humanity.
Therapist: What's your role in all of this?
Jaimy: I need to be kind. To give love.
Therapist: Do you review any goals you established in advance with your guides?
Jaimy: They say they need me.
Therapist: Who are they?
Jaimy: Family.
Therapist: What family?
Jaimy: The one I'm in.
Therapist: Mell's family or Jaimy's family?
Jaimy: Both.
Therapist: How would you compare the last life of Patrice with the life of Jaimy in terms of continued development?
Jaimy: There is more love now.
Therapist: And how does that help?

Jaimy: I can give more, help more.

Therapist: Tell me about how your guides are helping you during and after your lives.

Jaimy: They are seeing how well I can grow on my own.

Therapist: So they're kind of watching how you're developing on your own?

Jaimy: Yes.

Therapist: Okay.

Jaimy: They help.

Therapist: In what way do they help you sometimes?

Jaimy: They make sure I'm being kind when I need to be.

Therapist: Do they remind you somehow?

Jaimy: Yeah, at a low point.

Therapist: How do they remind you when you're at a low point? Is there a sign or something?

Jaimy: They help me stay calm. In stressful situations.

Therapist: What advice are you being given at this stage of your journey?

Jaimy: It'll come to you.

Therapist: Anything else?

Jaimy: Don't worry so much.

Therapist: Is that something that Jaimy tends to do?

Jaimy: She stresses a lot.

Therapist: How do Gwen and Otis help Jaimy when she is feeling stressed?

Jaimy: She runs, she has a lot of energy.

Therapist: Are you saying that energy has to go somewhere?

Jaimy: Yes. And running is the easiest way.

Therapist: Is there any other way she can positively channel her energy?

Jaimy: Volunteering.

Therapist: What would be a good way to volunteer?

Jaimy: A food bank.

Therapist: How would Jaimy feel doing that volunteer work in a food bank?

Jaimy: It will make her grow. She needs to get out.

Therapist: Anything else? What can Mell suggest to Jaimy?

Jaimy: Any kind of ocean activity is good for her.

Therapist: Are you saying to connect with the ocean?

Jaimy: Yeah.

Therapist: What about the ocean is helpful?

Jaimy: It cleanses.

Therapist: She can cleanse herself by going into the ocean?

Jaimy: Yeah.

Therapist: This is all very helpful information. Thank you Mell for sharing this. Is this a good time to move to your next stop?

Jaimy: Yeah.

Therapist: Is there any particular place in the spirit realm where you want us to move to right now that would be a great benefit to you?

Jaimy: I need to go to a temple.

Therapist: Are you ready to travel now to this temple?

Jaimy: Yeah.

Therapist: OK let us go there now and tell me what this temple looks like.

Jaimy: It is a marble temple.

Therapist: What else do you notice about this temple?

Jaimy: The sun.

Therapist: Is there a sun inside? Or is it a symbol?

Jaimy: There is a sun symbol.

Therapist: What kind of Temple is this? What happens here?

Jaimy: It's for recharging.

Therapist: Is it like a recharging station?

Jaimy: Yeah.

Therapist: Like a healing temple?

Jaimy: Yeah.

Therapist: Are you suggesting that your soul needs some time for healing and recharging in this sun temple?

Jaimy: Yes.

Therapist: Finding yourself moving to the space within this temple that most feels comfortable and where you can receive this divine healing light to recharge the energy for your soul. Allow it to wash over you. And as you're experiencing this healing process, be aware and notice what's happening. How are you feeling now?

Jaimy: Renewed.

Therapist: Do you know what just happened in this healing temple?

Jaimy: Yes.

Therapist: Is there anything else you want to share while you're here?

Jaimy: No.

Therapist: Take a look around before we move on and notice if there's any kind of element or symbol that's there, that you could perhaps take with you that could be of help to Jaimy later on.

Jaimy: There's a golden bowl.

Therapist: Is this a gift to you from the Sun Temple?

Jaimy: Yeah.

Therapist: Take that golden bowl with you as an appreciation of love and gratitude, knowing that whenever you need to recharge, this bowl is here as a reminder that you can connect to this sacred healing temple. Is there anything else you wish to explore in this temple?

Jaimy: No.

Therapist: Is it time to rejoin your soul group and your friends?

Jaimy: Yes.

Therapist: Where do you all meet or gather?

Jaimy: We gather in a group.

Therapist: Let's move there now. And tell me as we get closer, how do they come to greet you?

Jaimy: Calmly and lovingly.

Therapist: Tell me what you see them doing.

Jaimy: They study.

Therapist: What are they studying?

Jaimy: Books.

Therapist: What kind of books?

Jaimy: They are writing in them too.

Therapist: If you look a little more closely, what kind of books are they writing and reading?

Jaimy: They note down experiences.

Therapist: Are these some kind of like records that they are keeping?

Jaimy: Yes.

Therapist: Ah, so is this some kind of like library you find yourself in with your group?

Jaimy: It's a library.

Therapist: Take a moment and explore this space a little bit more. Do you notice any books standing out to you?

Jaimy: Yeah.

Therapist: Go over to this book and see if you can take it out and take a look at it. What do you find?

Jaimy: It's orange, with golden pages.

Therapist: Let's look at some of the pages. Does it have any kind of writing or symbols in it?

Jaimy: It's simple writing. It's a big book. Very big.

Therapist: By holding this book or looking at it, are you able to understand or figure out its contents?

Jaimy: It's golden, heavy and I've been trying to figure out the symbols and translate them.

Therapist: So it's in a different language?

Jaimy: Yes.

Therapist: What language do you think this is? Is it some kind of spiritual language? Help me understand.

Jaimy: It's from another realm.

Therapist: Why did you pick up this particular book? What was it you're supposed to know or learn or remember?

Jaimy: It is supposed to help Jaimy.

Therapist: So this book is for Jaimy?

Jaimy: Yes.

Therapist: And what does it say? How can it help Jaimy?

Jaimy: It can help her deal with her family.

Therapist: Is it kind of a guide to dealing with family?

Jaimy: Yes.

Therapist: Take a moment and tune into that book and let it download into the memory of Mell so that it can be passed along to Jaimy. Whenever you're done downloading just nod your head. Good. Now that you've come to this special sacred library and you picked up the book for Jaimy and downloaded all that wisdom and information to help her, when ready you can put that book back. Begin to reconnect with your soul group, finding them once again. Of all the souls you see here, who's in the life of Jaimy?

Jaimy: Gwen came back with me.

Therapist: Who else?

Jaimy: Samual was there before, but not now.

Therapist: What about Otis?

Jaimy: No.

Therapist: Otis remains in the spirit realm?

Jaimy: Yeah.

Therapist: Have one last look around and see if you notice anybody else. Is there a soul mate?

Jaimy: Not particularly.

Therapist: If I was a visitor to your soul group, what impression would I take away about all of you? Do you share any common characteristics?

Jaimy: We're all giving.

Therapist: Do you engage in any activities in the spirit world?

Jaimy: Yes.

Therapist: And what's that?

Jaimy: We do group activities.

Therapist: What kind of group activities?

Jaimy: Study and prayer.

Therapist: You all like prayer and study?

Jaimy: Yeah.

Therapist: What kinds of prayers do you do? Are you praying for others?

Jaimy: Yes.

Therapist: Beautiful.

Jaimy: We're making connections.

Therapist: While you're here in this beautiful spiritual state, there are some questions that Jaimy has in her life that she was hoping to get some clarity on. Is it a good time to ask you now?

Jaimy: Yes.

Therapist: One of the questions that Jaimy would like to ask is what am I doing here on Earth?

Jaimy: To be kind.

Therapist: What's holding her back?

Jaimy: Herself.

Therapist: In what way?

Jaimy: She needs spiritual guidance. She needs to focus more on the spiritual.

Therapist: How can she ask for and receive help?

Jaimy: make time. Just making more time.

Therapist: Does she mostly come back as a female on planet Earth?

Jaimy: Usually, but not always.

Therapist: How often has she had to come back to Earth, and how much more does she have to come back?

Jaimy: It depends on how much she grows.

Therapist: She has a question about her karma. How can some of these issues be resolved?

Jaimy: She needs to seek more spiritual growth.

Therapist: Is there anything specific that you could point her to?

Jaimy: She needs more forgiveness.

Therapist: Is there anything in particular she needs to forgive to help her move on?

Jaimy: Herself.

Therapist: Is this a good time for her to forgive herself?

Jaimy: Yes.

Therapist: Can you tell Jaimy it's time to forgive yourself?

Jaimy: She can. She knows. She's hard on herself.

Therapist: How might she remember to be a little bit softer on herself?

Jaimy: Take it day by day.

Therapist: Jaimy had a question about her career, what would be a good direction for her to go in for continued spiritual growth and evolution?

Jaimy: Anything where she can take the time to grow spiritually. Then things will come. Kindness and love are the keys.

Therapist: Is there anything else you'd like to share with Jaimy while in this state?

Jaimy: Don't worry. Live in the moment.

Therapist: How do you feel about what you've experienced here today? How would you summarize what you've learned and discovered that you can take back with you into the life of Jaimy?

Jaimy: Profound and helpful.

We slowly bring the session to an end.

Case 30: Eric
The alchemist

Eric is a 39-year-old Professor and Ballet Company Director. As an intuitive, he spontaneously remembers some of his past lives and had many other intuitive and meditative experiences during his life.

Eric: It's daytime.

Therapist: Are you inside or outside?

Eric: I'm inside.

Therapist: What are you aware of inside?

Eric: I'm in a tower in maybe a castle. There are lots of beakers, glass bottles, and vials everywhere. I'm some sort of scientist, alchemist. I'm an alchemist.

Therapist: Are you alone here?

Eric: I'm alone.

Therapist: How high up in the tower are you?

Eric: I'm high. I can see out in the countryside.

Therapist: Is there glass in these windows?

Eric: Yes, there is glass.

Therapist: Are you a man or are you a woman?

Eric: I'm a man.

Therapist: What are you wearing?

Eric: I'm wearing a robe, like a grayish robe. Very simple. It goes all the way down to the floor and yeah, it's gray and I have a purple sort of rope tied around my waist.

Therapist: If you lift this robe a little bit, and you look at your feet, what if anything are you wearing on your feet?

Eric: There are sort of simple black boots that go up to the knee and I have pants on under that as well.

Therapist: What is the color of your skin?

Eric: Sort of olive-colored.

Therapist: What about your hair?

Eric: It's long but curly. It's black, dark brown and there's some silver in it, but mostly dark brown.

Therapist: How old are you now?

Eric: 45.

Therapist: Looking around this room with these beakers and vials, what's the general energy of this place

Eric: This is a laboratory and there are lots of books, tomes, codex, and ancient texts around.

Therapist: How do you feel in this place?

Eric: I feel happy and at peace in this place and nobody bothers me.

Therapist: Is this your creation, this room with all this stuff in here?

Eric: Yes, I acquired all of these things to do my work.

Therapist: What is that work?

Eric: I am an alchemist and also a scholar, researcher, and soothsayer, I guess.

Therapist: When you say alchemist, what is it that you're trying to accomplish?

Eric: I mostly try to create, I do a lot of healing potions and elixirs for people in the court.

Therapist: Are you at a court right now?

Eric: Yes, I'm in a royal court castle.

Therapist: How is your relationship with everybody there?

Eric: I am revered. Some people are scared of me.

Therapist: Tell me a little bit about your alchemy and how you managed to create these potions. Is it based on trial and error or is it based on intuitive revelation?

Eric: A lot of it is intuitive. I have a sort of council of other alchemists that meet secretly. We share secrets. Right now I seem to be working on trying to increase the vibrational frequency of water in some way. So I have metals, stones, and different crystals and things around. I'm trying to infuse the water for the purposes of healing.

Therapist: How do you feel about yourself and your current state of being?

Eric: I feel powerful on the one hand, but I'm also a little scared, and suspicious. I feel like the work that I do is not understood by a lot of people and I sort of walk this tightrope between being respected and being feared.

Therapist: When you say being feared and being cautious, are there consequences to being feared?

Eric: Yes, I feel like I'm being followed, watched. I can tell people sometimes, despite me locking the room, somehow get in and look around and try and find things.

Therapist: Are you protected by the king or is he the one who is suspicious?

Eric: I'm protected by the queen actually and the king is dead, so yeah, she's the only one that has the most confidence in me, so I do feel protected by her, but she can't be everywhere all the time.

Therapist: Where in the world are we right now?

Eric: A Scandinavian country.

Therapist: What year approximately?

Eric: 1322.

Therapist: What is your name?

Eric: Artemis is one thing I'm called, but that's more of a title, but it's Artemis.

Therapist: I'll call you Artemis.

I move him forward in time.

Eric: I'm in a cell. I've been imprisoned and it's just me in a cell. There's some hay or something on the ground underneath the castle that I've lived in.

Therapist: How did you end up in this cell, Artemis?

Eric: I was accused of witchcraft.

Therapist: By whom?

Eric: Some young men in the court had political ambitions. They felt like I had the ear of the queen and they'd wanted me out of the way, so they accused me of consorting with the devil.

Therapist: The queen couldn't do anything to protect you?

Eric: They convinced her to turn on me.

Therapist: How do you feel right now, Artemis?

Eric: I feel defeated, but I'm trying to find a way. I meditate a lot and I'm trying to find a way to reach someone that was in my counsel to come and convince her to let me out, but I'm having trouble making contact.

Therapist: When you talk about a counsel, is it a physical counsel or in a metaphysical world?

Eric: This is the physical council that I would meet with this lifetime.

Therapist: So you're trying to telepathically connect?

Eric: Yes.

Therapist: How long have you been locked up Artemis?

Eric: Two years.

Therapist: Is there any sign of hope or is this supposed to be lifelong?

Eric: I'm afraid I will die in the cell.

Therapist: How's your health right now?

Eric: Not good. I have a cough. Difficulty breathing sometimes and they don't feed me very much, so lost a lot of weight.

Therapist: How old are you now?

Eric: 53.

Therapist: What is the most significant observation about this moment?

Eric: I'm using this opportunity to strengthen my spiritual connection and there's a spider in the corner of the cell that is almost like a golden color, which is weird and I talk to it and I get wisdom from it. I don't know if this is a hallucination or what, but I get insights from it. Sort of starting to break a little bit from the physical form because of the suffering.

Therapist: How do you see your own mental and spiritual state?

Eric: I'm beginning to see visions of light. I think that lack of food is actually helping my spiritual vision, but I do want to get out because the queen is in danger. There's a coup attempt at work and I would like to warn her, but she isn't receptive to my telepathic messages.

Therapist: Have you been able to telepathically connect to the council?

Eric: Yes, I can connect with them sometimes.

Therapist: How do you know about this coup?

Eric: That's also intuitive. Sometimes late at night, I can hear other people talking in the castle, even though they're not physically near me. So I've overheard whispers.

Therapist: Do you feel that despite these hardships you're able to elevate your mind and your consciousness?

Eric: Yes, at this point most of the time I'm not fully in my body, so I'm able to observe things, but I leave enough of my energy in my body so that I can stay alive for the time being.

I move him ahead in time.

Therapist: Tell me what is happening now.

Eric: I'm on trial. I'm on trial and I'm kneeling. There's a sort of court above me. The queen is in the center and there's the man that I have always known who has been out to get me, questioning me about my abilities and where they come from and accusing them of not being of the light.

Therapist: How do you feel going through this?

Eric: There's a lot of sorrow and I'm explaining that there's nothing evil about what I'm doing, but I'm being accused of consorting with demons and evil spirits. In particular, a negative forest spirit entity that my people believe in that they believe has possessed me. I'm trying to reason with them but they won't listen to me.

Therapist: Is there no sympathy on your behalf?

Eric: Yes, the queen won't look at me. I think she feels bad, but I think she's afraid that if she saves me people will think she is weak and that she also has been possessed by some evil spirits.

Therapist: So this is a foregone conclusion?

Eric: Yes.

Therapist: What happens next?

Eric: I am sentenced. They're going to tie me to a boat, a canoe-like thing, and set me out at sea to die.

Therapist: Is that how you die?

Eric: Yes.

Therapist: Now before we actually leave this body and look back on the life of Artemis, what are your thoughts about it?

Eric: I did a lot of good, I healed a lot of people, but I was seen as a heretic and people just didn't understand. And despite all of my efforts to hide and keep my work secret, people are fearful of what they don't understand.

Therapist: What did you learn from this life and these situations?

Eric: I learned that ignorance can always usurp wisdom, and a big takeaway was to keep myself more secret if I'm doing metaphysical or energetic work because of misinformation and distrust. But it strengthened my spiritual connection a great deal, and I developed a lot of really useful spiritual skills. Psychic and energetic healing abilities. I gained a lot of ancient wisdom from ancient texts that I retained in various lifetimes.

Therapist: What is your last thought, feeling, or awareness as you leave the body?

Eric: I'm glad to be free of that lifetime. It was a lot of darkness and ignorance and I've always felt I was ahead of my time so as soon as I am set out to sea, and it's cold, I knew I wouldn't last long. I leave the body pretty quickly.

Therapist: How did death occur? Is it because of hypothermia?

Eric: It's very cold. It was hypothermia and I was already weak so I just let go. Dying's easy.

I move him past his death.

Therapist: What are you aware of? Can you still see the body?

Eric: Yes, I can still see it. I'm pretty far above it now, but I sort of shift my awareness away from it and leave. So now it's dark.

Therapist: How do you feel about this death?

Eric: I'm good with it. I'm ready to move on from that body and lifetime. It was a tough life. Before I leave, I share 18 sparks of energy with various people in that lifetime, some to my earthly council, the queen, and some others, and give them a dream of me so that they can share their dreams.

Therapist: What kind of dream do they receive from you?

Eric: It's basically me. It's a parting image I give them of me sitting in my laboratory just telling them that I love them and thanking them for the moments we shared in that lifetime so that they can remember me. I send the sparks and then I'm off.

Therapist: Do they receive it?

Eric: Yes.

Therapist: How does that make you feel when they receive those?

Eric: Good. I want all of them to remember that this physical life is not all there is, which I often taught in my teachings in that life. So I want them to not doubt that their consciousness will survive and I forgive the queen for her choice and I can specifically tell her that in her dream.

Therapist: Beautiful. Now are you ready to move on from here?

Eric: Yes. Well, I'm met immediately by a guide to start to unpack the last lifetime. It's sort of common when I enter to get to work immediately., She's a female energy, and she's asking if I need any healing and I always seem to say no, but she sends it to me anyway.

Therapist: Is she the one sending healing to you?

Eric: Yeah, she sends me golden spirals of energy that start from what would be the crown even though I don't have a body, down to what would be the feet and just sort of undulates this golden energy and it's very efficient. It removes all the debris, especially the emotional debris from that lifetime, and just erases it.

Therapist: You say the guide is a female energy?

Eric: Yeah, she usually presents herself as female, but it can shift. But yes, at this time it's a feminine energy.

Therapist: Does she have a form or some shape or is she more energetic?

Eric: It shifts. She usually presents herself in a very refined female form, with elvish-like features, but then shifts into a crystalline form, like a clear quartz crystal with purple and blue light, and gold flecks. It's the way our soul group tends to present itself.

Therapist: Is she part of that soul group or is she the one mentoring you and the soul group?

Eric: We're all part of the same soul group. She is more like a colleague, but she no longer needs to come to earth as she's chosen to guide from the inner planes.

Therapist: During this review of Artemis' life, what's discussed? For example, what is it that you wanted to accomplish?

Eric: The goal was to bring through as much metaphysical and spiritual wisdom as I could. Writing it down, and teaching it, without being able to communicate in the language of the day, and do it with courage. I did that, but I underestimated the effect of the fear that was pervasive at the time. I was trying to refine people's senses so that they could perceive these things, but oftentimes they couldn't.

Therapist: When you say "I underestimated it," help me understand how this impacted your plans.

Eric: In the planning of that life, I knew that it was a darker time in terms of human knowledge and their capacity to understand certain concepts and I thought that people would be more open than they were. There were other alchemists, wizards if you will, that understood these things and we would meet and talk, but outside of that people had a lot of fear and superstition and I underestimated how they turned on me. And even though I was savvy with people, I sometimes would divulge things to people who didn't understand. So I overestimated people's ability to handle what I was telling them.

Therapist: Had there been less fear, what would you have liked to achieve?

Eric: I was trying to awaken people, and show them different ways of viewing themselves. With the kind of frequency of callousness and cruelty that existed at that time, there was no understanding of the energetic and spiritual effects of that kind of behavior on humans. Many of the bodies that were incarnated were wired up in a way that was brute-like. And so it was difficult to get through.

Therapist: Is that what you do as a soul or as a group to come down and awaken people?

Eric: Yes.

Therapist: What can you tell me about your guide and your group and who you are as a collective?

Eric: There are 12 that would be considered a sort of primary counsel. They're like creator beings who were responsible in large part for the creation of the physical human form, particularly the psychological and mental wiring, like architects. We volunteer at various points to come down and enter the human incarnation game to awaken and enlighten others.

Therapist: Are you one of those 12?

Eric: I'm not one of the 12, but I'm from the same space that the 12 come from. Those 12 came before us, but we're a small group.

Therapist: What is your relationship with those 12?

Eric: I am in training if you will, to become what is called an elderling. It's a small group of us, but I elected with a few others, two or 300 others, to come down and start human incarnation so that we could try to communicate some of the things that we need humans to learn to evolve.

Therapist: You don't have to reincarnate as a result of karmic bondage, you choose to incarnate.

Eric: Yes, but once we choose, we have to commit to thousands or millions of lifetimes. So not everybody chooses to do it.

Therapist: So once you get into that cycle, you're going to be subject to its karmic repercussions?

Eric: Yes. And some have gotten lost and all of us have in various incarnations, working through the different planes of consciousness and the forces of those planes.

Therapist: What happens in between these lives? Do you refresh your sense of spiritual Selfhood or are you temporarily blocked from this knowledge and access?

Eric: Yes. We go back to the group. It's interesting that the group advances as a whole, but once you choose to take human incarnations, you have to move through the planes as any other soul would. And so we progress through the planes like any other soul, but we reside in a different dimension that holds a wisdom frequency that allows us to start with a little bit more knowledge.

Therapist: Okay. Help me understand. Even though you are basically free from the beginning, when you choose to incarnate you become subject to karmic repercussions. What is the purpose of going through these births when you lose that connection to the divine that you intended to teach with?

Eric: It's to develop empathy as a human soul for the ignorance of human beings who can get lost. So to understand that fully, we have to experience it fully.

Therapist: Are these training programs for you as a group so that later on you have these experiences at your disposal to help other souls?

Eric: Yes. Correct.

Therapist: Looking back on this life of Artemis, how did you do?

Eric: This was one of my more perfect lifetimes in a spiritual sense, because I didn't ever let my connection wane. I always stayed connected to the spiritual and my truth and despite being punished, which I have in other lives for speaking that truth, I maintained my connection.

Therapist: What are some of the parallels between Artemis's life and then Eric's life?

Eric: Eric has at times also been punished for speaking his truth, but the difference is that there was more doubt in Eric's mind of what came true was true and accurate. Whereas in Artemis's lifetime there was no doubt that what was coming through was truth.

Therapist: Where does that doubt in Eric's mind come from?

Eric: It's the way that the left and right hemispheres of the brain are balanced. Though Artemis was very intelligent, he was more intuitively focused. And while Eric gets a lot of direct guidance almost all the time, that's the way our soul group works, he doubts what's coming through and sometimes gets stuck in analysis rather than letting it flow. And then when it doesn't flow, it sometimes stops.

Therapist: What's the purpose of this birth of Eric?

Eric: It was specifically to work. As I've incarnated over and over again, I've sort of refined the specialization and in this lifetime I'm specifically trying to energetically restructure aspects of the human mind to work with empathy. Specifically what we call the disease of narcissism and attempting to pinpoint and understand all the nuances of the human ego, so the DNA no longer has to experience lack of empathy or narcissism. So that as a race, human beings can stop harming each other in the ways that they do.

Therapist: So there is a very specific purpose in this life, and that's why he needs more of his left brain to accomplish this.

Eric: Yes, he needs to be able to understand on an intellectual level what's happening psychologically, so that he can help to heal it.

Therapist: It is almost unavoidable, that the intellectual purpose for which he came would block some of his spiritual and psychic powers, because he's less intuitively engaged.

Eric: Yes. There's still great access to the intuitive, where his knowledge comes from, and he now needs to simply trust the intuition. He needs to trust that when he describes or explains something without having read or known what it was, that's the way it's supposed to come.

Therapist: What is the best way for him to serve humanity with the knowledge that he has?

Eric: There's a healing modality that he knows at some point he's supposed to bring, that seems on the surface to be merely a psychological tool but is deeply spiritual and energetically virulent. It will begin to eliminate the gaps in the DNA where empathy is missing in some people and humanity as a whole. This is in conjunction with the 12 on the inter planes who are doing this on a larger planetary level by sending energy.

Therapist: Will he be able through this modality to affect physiology as well?

Eric: Yes. It will re-encode parts of the DNA for those who are entirely missing empathetic strands.

Therapist: Is that a part of epigenetics?

Eric: In a way yes. It's a form of epigenetics and it's also part of the new. In two to 300 years, if humans can make it that long, there will be this new DNA structure that will be the norm rather than the exception.

Therapist: Beautiful. So this is his main work in this lifetime?

Eric: Yes.

Therapist: Beautiful. Now, how many are in your group?

Eric: There are 212, so there are the 12 eldering, the first 12, and they have never incarnated, and then the 200 who have incarnated at various times and there are nine who have completed their physical incarnations, one of which is my guide. I will not necessarily have to incarnate again unless I choose to come down as a teacher. This if I choose to be, could be my last physical incarnation.

Therapist: What are your thoughts about that?

Eric: I've already committed to coming back as a teacher, but it needs to be at a time when I won't have to filter the information. So humanity needs to be a little further along.

Therapist: There are nine that have completed their incarnations. What do they do?

Eric: They work specifically as guides, ascended masters, or teachers.

Therapist: Within the 200 group or beyond that as well?

Eric: Within the 200 there are various souls at different levels of their incarnation. Some are still on the third plane and above. There are few that are still young that have just decided to start their incarnations and the nine are guiding them.

Therapist: Okay. Beautiful. Now about Eric and his incarnation, how come that at this point in his life at 39, he has not been able to find meaningful a relationship with someone?

Eric: Well, he's met one of his soulmates in this lifetime who is part of his soul group. Because of the way that this body is wired up, too much emotional energy, especially love or infatuation, even though he craves it, can overwhelm his system and take him off track. As he experiences the emotions of love and infatuation very strongly, he can always choose to invoke karma with someone else. As of three years ago, his personal karma was eliminated. So he has to borrow karma to stay in physical form. To have a relationship, he would have to initiate a timeline with someone, which if he plugs into any frequency or timeline and is not careful, can take him off course.

Therapist: Which would tie him down to another cycle of karma with someone.

Eric: Yes. And it would be amplified because of where he is.

Therapist: Would it would change anything if that somebody could be of the same elevation as he is belonging to the same group.?

Eric: Yes, that would increase his spiritual power. But it's hard to find them. He's found one.

Therapist: Though not impossible, it needs to be one of the same caliber.

Eric: Yes. It would be counterproductive for his mission if he became too deeply intertwined with someone not at the same frequency.

Therapist: Okay. What about some of the depression he has been experiencing from time to time? Where is that coming from?

Eric: Some of it is a carryover from various lifetimes, sort of karmic or astral imprints. Some of it is genetics. He chose a body and an ancestral line that struggles with depression and the personality that he chose is inclined towards melancholy. So while at times he can dip into depression it is also what fuels his creative endeavors.

Therapist: Tell me more.

Eric: It is important to move his body, to move the energy through, which is why he dances. And writing is a big part of his expression and helps him move energy through. Not only creative writing, but also channeling, which he used to do some writing. It's a good way to connect with the higher Self and the 12. A lot of what he experiences as depression is just energy that's stuck or stagnant.

Therapist: So when he moves energy through the depression will be flushed out as well. What about some of his other ailments?

Eric: Much of the physical ailments are karmic. So even though he has now been released of the need to incarnate again, he still has a body, and the body still has karma in terms of the physical human form and the things that are experienced in this life. The body is a mechanism and we all have to live by the rules of human life.

Therapist: Would Western medicine, Eastern medicine or energetic healing be better for him?

Eric: A mixture of both, but he responds very well to energetic healing, massage, and also self-healing, Like tapping into the correct places, also sound baths and crystal healing. Those modalities will be very amenable to him as it sort of mimics what happens on the inner planes with healing, which he will recognize and respond to on a spiritual level.

Therapist: Is there any other place or any other frequency you would like to connect with?

Eric: I would like to connect with the records, the Akashic field as there's a piece of that that is relevant to this life in terms of accessing the full range of my ability.

Therapist: Well, let us go there now then. Maybe your guide can help us show the way and when you get there. Tell me what this is like and what is happening.

Eric: Well, I'm there. At first, it appears like books, but the books will sort of alternate between being a book and then being a silhouette of a person or a building or animal. So there are sort of holograms that are shifting and my guide is inviting me to approach any of these shifting holograms and tells me to "just plug in."

Therapist: Is there anything specific you're seeking?

Eric: Well, they don't seem to be people that I necessarily know, it's just people's records. I think she's showing me how to access the record of each person or myself for that matter. But it's actually quite easy. It does come in a download and I would recognize the download by tingling physical sensations in the body. I've done this my whole life, which I now recognize, but I always thought I was just making things up about people.

Therapist: What do you get from people's records?

Eric: Specifically their mental, emotional, and psychological experiences.

Therapist: Of individuals or of the collective?

Eric: Of individuals. I could plug into the collective. It takes a little more concentration and meditation. Now I'm seeing something I used to see in meditations. It's like a grid where I can plug into an event, say a political event or a natural disaster, and get information about what's happening. And also ask for energetic intervention in some things, which doesn't come from me of course. It's like a 3D chess board, but with people. It's the individual life, and their past lives, and what might be influencing their current problem or issue they would have. And it's on a need-to-know basis of course.

Therapist: What do you hope to attain by tapping into the Akashic records of these individuals?

Eric: It's finding, when you tap into the feeling intuitively, where the imbalances are.

Therapist: Is it for healing purposes or for you to understand them?

Eric: Yes, both.

Therapist: What if you tap into your own? What it is that you are discovering?

Eric: The same thing, it's to create balance and to remove chaos in the energetic system in both the astral and etheric template. And then restructure the cells in order to create harmony or symmetry so that more light can come through. This is a way that I can do self-healing

Therapist: Can you do that now for the sake of Eric? Is there an adjustment that you can make right now? If you want a minute or so to do it quietly. Go ahead.

Eric: Yes.

Therapist: Just let me know when you're ready.

Eric: Okay. Yes. I've smoothed out some rough edges and there were some symbols that represent thought forms stuck in various parts of my aura. They've been removed and I've filled them in with a blue and indigo light that, once put in that place, turns into gold and then eventually white. So that's done.

Therapist: Beautiful. How do you feel?

Eric: Good. I feel peaceful and comforted.

Therapist: What are your thoughts about your own journey in this incarnation and beyond?

Eric: I feel more self-assured that the things that I perceive and know are real and from beyond my limited self. And I feel more in my own power so that I can tap into this whenever I need to and when doubt arises because I don't have any of that now.

Therapist: What is it that you would like to share with Eric?

Eric: Be courageous and bold with your love and know that as long as you are open and in line with your purpose, everything will always be just perfect, even if it doesn't seem like it is on a human level. And that working from 100% intuition is the highest level of intelligence and that it can be supported by the intellect and of course the physical senses. But all you need is intuition. It is the highest level of guidance that you can have, and paired with common sense, which you have due to the many, many, many incarnations, the only way to get it wrong is to turn that off and not listen to yourself.

Therapist: Do you think, after what he has seen here today, he can override a little bit that tendency to get stuck in the analytical?

Eric: Yes, it will give him the confidence to trust and that's all he needs. He has plenty of analytical abilities and there's a time and a place for that.

Therapist: That is an important insight. If I may say, as an external observer, that though there is a great capacity for analysis, it doesn't mean that there isn't an even more powerful intuitive capacity and that these are just different tools to be used on different occasions. It's not either or.

Eric: Yes, that's correct. It's vital to his happiness and success in this lifetime.

After a few more summarizing conclusions, we slowly bring the session to an end.

About the authors

Pieter and Jenna are a husband and wife team of professional past-life and life-between-lives regression therapists. They are the founders of the Path of Light Center in Montvale Virginia (Roanoke), a healing and wellness center in the Appalachian mountains.

Pieter, a former monk in an Eastern tradition, has lived in 5 different countries and on 3 different continents. Born and educated in The Netherlands, Pieter studied for 5 years at the renowned Design Academy in Eindhoven, specializing in Industrial Design. Though he graduated with honors, Pieter felt there was more to life and had a deep spiritual yearning for truth and set out on a long journey of self-discovery that brought him to France, India, England, and finally the United States. After coming to the United States, he channeled his experience as a gifted motivational speaker as a Vedic minister, and background in philosophy and international cultural diversity, into the field of Clinical Hypnotherapy and regression. He is the author of, among several books: 'When souls awaken, real-life accounts of past-life and life-between-lives regressions.'

Jenna Iantorno Elsen is an author, Newton past-life and life-between-lives regression therapist as well as a gifted spiritual counselor and an intuitive life coach. Jenna combines her extensive knowledge as a Certified Yoga Therapist, Massage and Bodywork Therapist, and energy healer into all of her work. Jenna has helped countless clients find purpose, meaning, and value in their lives.

FOR MORE INFORMATION:

www.pathoflightcenter.com
or email:
elsenhypnotherapy@gmail.com

Here are some of our other books. Check it out Amazon:

- When Souls Awaken - Real-Life Accounts of Past-Life and Life-Between-Lives Regressions
- When Souls Transition - 30 Cases of Past-Life and Life-Between-Lives Regressions
- Brother Sun - Guided by Grace. Memoirs of a Western Yogi
- How to do your own guided past-life regression - A self-hypnosis regression guide
- Hypnosis to help yourself and others: A quick guide to learn hypnotherapy
- Introduction to Guided Imagery: Fundamental Concepts
- The Mind Book 100 Mindful Questions: From SUB-conscious to SUPER-power
- CUANDO LAS ALMAS DESPIERTAN: Narraciones reales de regresiones a vidas pasadas y a la vida entre vidas
- Karma Yoga: Het geheim van Werk (Dutch Edition)

For those interested in becoming a Past-Life Regression fasciliator, please visit us here:

https://pathoflightcenter.com/certification-training/